THE
BUSINESS
STUDENT'S
HANDBOOK

THE BUSINESS STUDENT'S HANDBOOK

Skills for study and employment

Sixth Edition

SHEILA CAMERON
The Open Universtiy Business School

Harlow, England • London • New York • Boston • San Francisco • Toronto • Sydney • Auckland • Singapore • Hong Kong
Tokyo • Seoul • Taipei • New Delhi • Cape Town • São Paulo • Mexico City • Madrid • Amsterdam • Munich • Paris • Milan

PEARSON EDUCATION LIMITED
Edinburgh Gate
Harlow CM20 2JE
United Kingdom
Tel: +44 (0)1279 623623
Web: www.pearson.com/uk

First published 1999 (print)
Second edition 2002 (print)
Third edition 2005 (print)
Fourth edition 2008 (print)
Fifth edition 2009 (print and electronic)
Sixth edition published 2016 (print and electronic)

ISBN: 978-1-292-08864-8 (print)
         978-1-292-08867-9 (PDF)
         978-1-292-08865-5 (ePub)

British Library Cataloguing-in-Publication Data
A catalogue record for the print edition is available from the British Library

Library of Congress Cataloging-in-Publication Data
Names: Cameron, Sheila, author.
Title: The business student's handbook: skills for study and employment /
    Sheila Cameron.
Description: Sixth edition. | Harlow, England; New York: Pearson, [2016] |
    Includes bibliographical references and index.
Identifiers: LCCN 2016007264 (print) | LCCN 2016009075 (ebook) | ISBN
    9781292088648 | ISBN 9781292088679 ()
Subjects: LCSH: Business—Vocational guidance—Handbooks, manuals, etc. |
    Business students—Employment—Handbooks, manuals, etc. |
Classification: LCC HF5381 .C25353 2016 (print) | LCC HF5381 (ebook) | DDC
    650.1—dc23
LC record available at http://lccn.loc.gov/2016007264

10 9 8 7 6 5 4 3 2 1
20 19 18 17 16

Print edition typeset in 9/13 Stone Serif ITC Pro by Lumina Datamatics
Printed and bound in Malaysia (CTP-PJB)

NOTE THAT ANY PAGE CROSS REFERENCES REFER TO THE PRINT EDITION

BRIEF CONTENTS

PART 1 EMPLOYABILITY AND HOW BEST TO MANAGE YOUR LEARNING

PART 2 ESSENTIAL LEARNING SKILLS

PART 3 WORKING WITH OTHERS

PART 4 CONCEPTUAL SKILLS

CONTENTS

PART 2 ESSENTIAL LEARNING SKILLS

PART 3 WORKING WITH OTHERS

PART 4 CONCEPTUAL SKILLS

PART 5 INTEGRATING YOUR SKILLS

LIST OF FIGURES

PREFACE

This book was written because so many students, often despite considerable effort on their part and that of their lecturers, fail to gain much benefit from their degree studies. Even if they pass, probably with lower marks than they hoped, they find it hard to get jobs, and progress slowly once they find employment. At the same time, graduate recruiters complain that it is hard to find graduates with the key skills they are looking for. This is true of graduates in most subjects, including business studies.

You probably chose business studies in the expectation that it would prepare you for a successful career. This book is intended to help you develop the skills that recruiters seek, thus increasing your employability. Fortunately, these same skills will help you to enjoy your course, to learn more, and to gain better marks. This will greatly increase the return on your investment of time, effort and money in study.

The book applies basic management concepts – many of which may already be familiar to you – to the process of learning. (All concepts are clearly described, in case your course has yet to cover them.) It addresses basic study skills – reading, note-taking, using numbers, finding information, report and essay writing. Managing your learning is also covered. All these skills will also be useful in the work situation. More obviously transferable skills such as team work and personal management (including time and stress management) are also covered. Finally, the book looks at skills you will need when moving from study into employment, including writing a good CV and job application, responding to various selection tests and how to perform well in an interview.

This edition has increased emphasis on employability, and includes updated material on virtual learning environments, presentation software and virtual team work. I hope that international students will find it easier to use than earlier editions. Some of the

Neill Cameron, www.neillcameron.com

chapter titles have been altered to reflect shifts in emphasis in content. (I apologise to lecturers who may have to alter lecture notes because of this, but I hope you will find the new structure is more logical, and the updated content more relevant to today's business context. It should be relatively easy to map the new onto the old.)

To develop the skills covered you need to use this book rather differently from most text books. It offers few 'facts' and 'theories' to learn. Instead, it provides a range of activities, supported by text, which you can use to help you do better on your course for less effort, and to become more employable than you otherwise would. The reading is easy, and I hope interesting. The activities are more challenging, but the thinking and practice they demand will develop the transferable skills that will prove invaluable to you throughout your career. Engaging with the activities will lead to more effective learning, better grades, and a more successful and stimulating working life. Simply reading the book will be much less effective!

ACKNOWLEDGEMENTS

Among the many people I should like to thank are Penelope Woolf for persuading me to write this book in the first place, and Natalia Jaszczuk for support throughout the present edition; the Open University as an institution, and close colleagues in particular for giving me the space to write, and my students for being an endless source of challenge, stimulus and ideas. Last, but definitely not least, I should like to thank Hester, Neill and James for their research, comments, suggestions and general support throughout, and in particular Neill for the superb artwork in this edition.

Shelia Cameron

Publisher's Acknowledgements

We are grateful to the following for permission to reproduce copyright material:

Cartoons
Cartoons on page xiv, page 14, page 27, page 122, page 155, page 230, page 271, page 309, page 361, page 401 from Cartoon by Neill Cameron, www.planetdumbass.co.uk.

Text
Exhibits on pages 280–1, pages 479–80 from Natalia Jaszczuk.

PART 1
EMPLOYABILITY AND HOW BEST TO MANAGE YOUR LEARNING

Introduction to Part 1

This book aims to make you a better manager while at the same time helping you get a better degree. Studying for a degree represents a major investment in your future – an investment by taxpayers, by educational institutions, perhaps by your parents, but most of all by you. You are spending three or more years studying when you could be travelling, or making your first million. Because so many people now get degrees, the letters after your name are not a passport to success. You need to use your time at university to get a *good* degree and, perhaps even more importantly, to learn those skills that will help you to get a good job on graduation, and to ensure that you go on to achieve all that you would wish for from the career that follows.

This book is designed to help you to take control of and *manage* your learning so that you maximise the return on investment for yourself and for the other stakeholders in the process. It is designed to help you to develop the skills that you need for learning, both as a student and in your working life. The good news is that many of the skills addressed are common to all these areas.

The first part of this book looks at management learning and its context – why are you learning, and how, given this, can you learn most effectively. Chapter 1 assumes that you are studying Business and Management with a view to a career in, or related to, management so looks at what potential employers are likely to be seeking in a graduate. If you understand this, you can start to develop into the person they are looking for. One key skill will be the ability to continue learning throughout your career, so learning skills are explored. Another is the ability to work across cultural boundaries, so gaining value from diversity is also discussed. The overall aim of the first chapter is to help you use your studies to make yourself highly employable in a global and multicultural environment. Features of the book which will help you achieve this are outlined.

Personal management skills are high on the list of things employers look for, and essential for study success. The second chapter aims to develop such skills, including your ability to plan your work, and monitor and manage your achievements, time usage and stress levels. Your whole career, as well as success in your degree studies, will depend on these skills.

The third chapter explores the issue of professional development and the reflective learning that most professional institutions see as an essential part of this. If you join such an institution you will be expected to demonstrate a level of competence as a requirement for joining, and to show evidence of continuing professional development in order to renew your membership. The chapter considers how best to reflect, including collaborative reflection online, the use of different senses in learning, and the many software tools available to help you keep a learning diary and manage other evidence of developing competence.

As you work through the book you will find that topics are often interrelated. As a result, they may be dealt with in more than one place. An idea or technique may be introduced in one context, and developed in a later chapter. In such cases a marginal symbol is used to point you to the chapter where you can find more on the subject.

An important part of skill development is to practise skills and gain feedback on your performance – from yourself, fellow students and teaching staff. This part of the book aims to establish a habit of active and reflective learning through frequent exercises, pauses for reflection and filing of the results of activities within a file, or ePortfolio. You can draw on this during your study, and it will be an invaluable resource when you want to demonstrate your skills to potential employers or assessors for professional qualifications.

Most of the activities which form an important component of the book will contribute to this file, but when they are particularly important, there will be a file icon in the margin (see the example here). To help with this there will often be templates available as web resources. As with other web resources, these will be indicated by another icon, as shown.

Some activities will serve more than one purpose. It is really important, if you are to get full value from the book and your studies, that you *do* the activities as suggested, rather than merely read them. If at all possible, work through the exercises with one or two other people. Confucius said, over 2000 years ago:

> When three of us are walking together I am sure to have a teacher. Having noted his competences, I imitate them: his incompetences I avoid.

A rather more interactive way of working as a group, giving each other feedback on perceived competence and incompetence, can be even more effective. Working in this way will require more time and effort than merely reading the book passively. But this effort is essential if you want to develop the skills covered and to reap the many potential benefits for study and/or for employment.

1
BECOMING A HIGHLY DESIRABLE GRADUATE

Learning outcomes

By the end of this chapter you should:

- understand what is meant by 'transferable skills' and 'employability'

- know which skills are likely to be important, both to recruiters and as your career develops

- have started to plan how you can develop these skills during your studies

- have started to consider what you might want from a job.

Introduction

In deciding to study, you have taken a major investment decision – to invest in developing yourself, probably with a view to a successful career once you graduate. This chapter explores aspects of the job market for graduates and suggests how you might use your time as a student to maximise your employability as a graduate. Fortunately, many of the skills recruiters look for, and which will accelerate your promotion thereafter, will also help you get a good degree: they transfer easily from the academic to the work context.

Employment prospects for recent UK graduates were promising in 2014. Using data from over 250000 recent UK-based graduates, the Higher Education Support Unit (HECSU, 2014) found that

- 12.6% had continued with further study or training
- 5.6% were working and studying at the same time
- 70% were in employment (earning on average £19k to £23k depending on their occupation)
- only 7% were unemployed.

However, not all employed graduates are in 'graduate' jobs. HECU (2014) quotes data suggesting that 66% of all graduates in the UK for whom employment information was available were working in professional or managerial jobs. That leaves ⅓ of graduates in other employment. Even in 'good times' the better jobs are highly contested, and having a degree does not guarantee a good job. (Although 81.3% of graduate recruiters surveyed in 2013 said they still intended to use degree classification as their main benchmark when recruiting graduates – Association of Graduate Recruiters, AGR, 2013).

UK higher education has expanded greatly in recent years, and in some places (such as central London) graduates are now in the majority (Office for National Statistics, 2014). To get a good job in the UK you need to be more attractive to prospective employers than other graduates. (If you plan to work in a country with a lower proportion of graduates your degree may be more of an advantage.)

In 'bad times' the situation can be far worse. The market for recent graduates fluctuates considerably depending on the state of the economy. In a recession it is much cheaper for an organisation to pause graduate recruitment than to cut existing staff. In addition to gaining a good degree, you can make yourself attractive to potential employers by seizing every opportunity to build a portfolio of employment related skills, capabilities and experience. This will give you a substantial competitive advantage over other graduates with a similar degree, and should you graduate in a time of economic downturn, such a portfolio may gain you a job where others fail.

One key skill is the ability to learn. Hill (2014) argues that 'developing a growth mindset' is important, and suggests five steps that will make you valuable to an employer: A study resource on 'Developing a Growth Mindset' is provided at the end of the chapter.

Even if you are only at the start of a degree programme, it is not too soon to be looking at employment skills. This chapter explores the nature of these skills, and suggests that you start now to think about the sort of career you would like, and the skills that would be relevant. It also explains how best to *use* this book to become a successful learner.

As you may already be discovering, learning at university (like learning at work) is very different from learning at school. A large part of the responsibility for your learning rests with *you*. You need to be able to plan and *manage* your own learning. Planning and time management skills are essential for this, and are also key skills for employment. You will need to learn with and from others. Team working and communication skills are equally important for study and for work. You will need to locate and use a wide range of information sources, which will require knowledge management skills – again highly transferable. But above all, you need to understand what learning *means* at this level, why it is so important and how to do it well.

Employability

Definitions of 'employable' vary. Strictly, it should mean capable of being employed – in some capacity or other. Because the job market is highly competitive, it is important to take steps *now* that will increase your chances of a successful career. This chapter will help you work out what is important to you, and help you clarify your employment goals. The final section of the book will complete the process.

The introduction to Part 1 alerted you to the fact that you will need to *respond* at intervals, rather than merely sit back and read. The process starts *now*, with capturing your starting position. You can return to this at intervals, and note how your thinking is developing. You can also check that you have not inadvertently ignored something important.

Activity 1.1

If you have access to anyone who employs graduates, ask them what they seek in recruits. Look in the recruitments sections of a few newspapers, and/or visit the websites of companies you might like to work for. From this, build a list of the qualities mentioned as essential or desirable for graduate recruits.

_____

_____

_____

Were you more impressed by the similarities between employers, or by the differences? Employers are far from agreed on what a graduate can bring to a job. Variation is not surprising; recruiters will be seeking to fill widely disparate jobs, and there are likely to be as many different views of what constitutes an 'ideal graduate recruit' as there are an 'ideal husband or wife'. Employers may be looking for people to interact with customers, to solve technical problems, to work with pre-existing teams of various kinds, to 'fit in' and be effective as quickly as possible, or to act as a force for change.

Organisations vary in many ways, including size, flexibility and concern with innovation. What they seek from recruits depends on where they sit on these different dimensions. As a graduate this variability may be an asset. Someone, somewhere, is going to see your set of skills as just what they want. Your task while a student is to ensure that the skill set you develop is attractive to the sort of employer for whom you really want to work. This means deciding on the sort of job you want and the type of organisation you want to work for, identifying those skills, and then making sure that you develop them.

My own trawl of adverts (2015) came up with phrases like

- 'passion, creativity and the drive to bring innovations and projects to life' (major oil company
- 'the ability to live by our values of integrity, responsibility and collaboration. Building networks and relationships . . . ambitious and motivated to succeed, keen to take ownership of your work' (academic publisher)
- 'strong communication skills with the ability to make your clients feel loved . . . ambition' (travel consultant)
- 'A talent for leadership with drive and determination to succeed, . . . real passion to learn, with the drive to tackle new experiences head-on . . . excellent communication skills . . . genuine enjoyment of fast-paced, varied environments' (major supermarket chain).

You may a have been struck by similarities in requirements. Almost every advert I found sought good communication skills, and many mentioned other interpersonal skills, planning skills and motivation. The Association of Graduate Recruiters survey of summer 2006 suggested that team working, oral communication, flexibility and adaptability, customer focus and problem solving were the qualities most frequently sought by graduate recruiters. A more recent study in the US (Forbes, 2014) put team work first, followed by decision-making and problem-solving skills, then communication, then planning and organising, then finding and processing information, quantitative analysis, relevant technical knowledge, using software, report writing and editing, and selling and influencing others. You will probably find similar requirements commonly referred to in your own investigations, and may find it interesting to make international comparisons. It is the common, widely relevant, transferable skills that you need to develop, and which this book seeks to address.

Key Skills and Applications for Learning and Employment

Higher education's Quality Assurance Agency (QAA) has specified a set of core skills which it feels all graduates should have, and be able to apply at European and international levels. It has developed a set of benchmark standards for these. You can obtain the full set of benchmarking standards from the QAA website at **www.qaa.ac.uk**. They include:

- **Cognitive skills** – critical thinking, analysis and synthesis. You need, for example, to be able to identify assumptions, evaluate statements in terms of evidence, check the logic of an argument, define terms and make appropriate generalisations
- **Problem-solving and decision-making skills** – quantitative and qualitative. You need to be able to identify, formulate and solve business problems, and generate and evaluate options, applying ideas and knowledge to a range of situations

- **Research and investigative skills** – resolve business and management issues, both individually then as part of a team. You need to be able to identify relevant business data and research sources and research methodologies, and for your research to inform your learning

- **Information and communications technology skills** – you need to be able to use a range of business applications in any job

- **Numeracy and quantitative skills** – data analysis, interpretation and extrapolation You need to be able to use models of business problems and to draw conclusions from the information you obtain

- **Communication skills** – both oral and written and using a range of media. You need, for example, to be able to write business reports

- **Interpersonal skills** – talking and listening, presentation, persuasion and negotiation. You need to be able to interact effectively with a range of people, including colleagues and customers

- **Team-working skills** – leadership, team building and influencing. You need to be able to manage or contribute to team projects

- **Personal management skills** – time planning, motivation and initiative – the need for these skills is obvious

- **Learning skills** – reflective, adaptive and collaborative. You need to be motivated to learn and able to do so effectively in a range of contexts

- **Self-awareness** – sensitivity and openness to others. You need to be alert to how others will react to situations – the significance of 'emotional intelligence' is now becoming recognised.

Activity 1.2

For each of the above categories, think about your current skill level (use any available evidence, including feedback from friends, teachers, past employers and your own feelings). Give yourself a rating on a scale of 1 to 10, where 1 is very low, and 10 is as high as you can imagine needing. File your responses for future reference; you will need them for subsequent work. (An electronic template is available to make this easy.)

In relation to work, the relevance of these sets of skills is fairly obvious; however, whenever the skills are addressed in the book, they will be highlighted. What may be less immediately apparent is the extent to which these 'employment skills' will help you to learn more effectively at university, and to get better marks. Communication is obviously crucial to working with others; for example, in group projects. Good communication skills will help you to present information face to face, and to write better assignments. Self-management skills are valuable for improving your own learning and performance and performing your own part of a group's task. Addressing problems involves using information. You can see not only that the skills are relevant in both contexts – they are highly *transferable* – but that they are closely interrelated. Finding a simple classification of something as complex as higher-level human skills is difficult.

There have been many other attempts at providing lists of sets of skills. For example, Harvey *et al.* (1997), drawing on information from a wide range of graduate employers, suggested the importance of looking at skills involved in:

- **fitting in** – blending into a team and becoming effective quickly
- **persuading** – whether within the team or in relation to the wider organisation or customers beyond it
- **developing ideas** – analysing situations rather than merely responding to them, often best done in a team
- **transforming** – which adds to all the above the ability to apply intellectual skills and leadership skills in order to steer change.

If you are seeking to develop an 'employability mindset' you may like to use the online resource adapted from Hill (2014), who argues that a mindset is more important than a skillset.

Finally, you might like to look at the results of a study carried out in the US (Luthans *et al.*, 1988) into what a wide range of managers actually did. They found that managerial activities could be categorised into the following four sets:

- **communication** – paperwork and exchanging information
➤ Ch 2
- **'traditional management'** – planning, decision making and controlling (more on this in the next chapter)
- **networking** – interacting with outsiders, socialising and politicking
- **human resource management** – motivating, disciplining, managing conflict, staffing and training.

Activity 1.3

Look back at your assessment of your own strengths and weaknesses in the light of what you have subsequently read. Amend your earlier list if improvements suggest themselves at this point. Add in any areas where you now feel that your study, as well as your employability, might benefit from development.

As you will now realise, many of the activities scattered throughout the book will be cumulative, and you need a file (paper or electronic) in which to store your responses for easy reference. You will probably find it useful to file your answers and notes by chapter to start with. Once you have accumulated enough material, there will be suggestions as to how
➤ Ch 3
you can organise your notes into a more structured *personal development file or ePortfolio.*

Careers within Today's Organisations

Earlier I suggested that careers are becoming far more fluid: this means that at regular intervals you will need to think about what you want from work. This will allow you to decide which jobs are most likely to meet your needs, and then to concentrate on the most relevant skills for development.

Activity 1.4

Log your initial thoughts about working life, both good and bad. Don't agonise about your answer, just write down the first thing that comes into your head. Aim to write down between 10 and 20 words in response to the following prompts:

The things I am afraid a job might be:

_____

_____

Characteristics of my ideal job would be:

_____

_____

If possible, discuss your answers with four or five other people, to see where their views differ from yours and where they are similar. How many of you are afraid a job will be boring? How many of you want it to offer variety or the chance to meet interesting people? Do you want the chance to learn more, or to travel, or to help other people? Is status important? Were the responses from those who already have jobs different from those who have not? If the discussion made you aware of things that are important to you but which you had omitted from your list, then construct a revised version and file this as well.

Career – a series of jobs seen in retrospect?

If your 'fears' included boredom, predictability, lack of freedom (the sort of thing that I was worried about most as a student), you were possibly thinking of the traditional 'graduate career' within a large, multi-layered organisation, where good behaviour and following the rules would lead to steady progression. Large employers do still recruit graduates, but massive organisational restructuring in recent years has reduced the volume – though at the same time many of these jobs are, if anything, more interesting.

The 'career' as an organised succession of increasingly senior jobs has probably always been less common in reality than people believed. I can still remember being struck in 1971 by the 'definition' of career as 'a series of jobs seen in retrospect' by Ruth Lancashire, then one of the main researchers in the area, speaking at a conference on careers. Charles

Handy (1989) describes how, when starting his first job in the 1950s, he was given an outline of his future career. This was to culminate in a job as chief executive of a particular company in a particular country. He left long before he was in sight of this pinnacle, and both the projected company and even the country had ceased to exist.

Certainly my own subsequent 'career' could not have been planned and seemed at the time to have been driven primarily by external forces. Yet the different jobs I have done have prepared me remarkably well for my present role, one which is more rewarding than any job I could have dreamed of as a student. And careers are becoming ever more 'unplanned' because of the ways in which organisations are changing.

Competitive pressures have driven major restructuring. Organisations have sought to cut costs and increase the speed with which they can respond to competitors and to changes in markets. Developments in information and communications technology have meant that many of the things which managers traditionally did – to do with filtering and funnelling and transmitting information – no longer need so much human intervention.

Organisations are changing

Most large organisations responded to competitive pressures by taking a hard look at their hierarchies and 'delayering', cutting out whole layers of middle management, just the sort of jobs which many graduates have filled in the past. While this decimation of management in itself cut employment costs, many organisations 'downsized' or 'rightsized' (euphemisms in this area abound) more generally, reducing the number of employees at other levels too. They also identified their 'core' business and concentrated on this, looking at ways of contracting out more peripheral activities such as cleaning, catering, warehousing, IT and even graduate recruitment.

The aim was to avoid using full-time permanent staff for non-core work. Such staff is expensive, and it may be slow and expensive to reduce staffing when business is poor. Increasingly, organisations have 'outsourced' non-core activities to specialist suppliers. Flexibility in staffing was also increased by using part-time employees or those on short-term contracts. Also, many large, specialist departments at 'head office' have been reduced by devolving a lot of their responsibilities to line managers.

Neill Cameron, www.neillcameron.com

Implications for Graduate Employment

Graduate recruitment prospects at the time of writing are extremely favourable, and the organisational changes outlined above make it clear why the 'thinking' skills developed by means of a degree are so important.

Statistics from the Higher Education Statistics Agency's Destinations of Leavers from Higher Education survey show that graduate employment prospects in the UK have been recovering in recent years, and in 2015 were 'better than ever before' (HECSU, 2015), with unemployment finally dropping below pre-recession levels, and more graduates in professional-level jobs than before. However, graduate recruitment is highly susceptible to economic conditions, and you will need to check the current situation when you are nearer to graduating.

Even in a favourable recruitment situation, there will be fierce competition for the more attractive jobs. Jobs will vary in both starting salary and subsequent prospects. The survey above found that the average full-time graduate salary in the UK was £20 637. Another survey by High Fliers (2015) found that some graduate recruits (notably those joining banks or law firms) earned much more than this, with The European Commission and Aldi offering the highest starting salaries for graduates (over £41 000).

Recruiters noted that they received more and better applications in 2014 than in previous years, reinforcing the message throughout the book that you need to pay attention to developing transferable skills throughout your degree. In particular, the High Fliers survey noted the importance of prior work experience. Nearly half the recruiters who took part said applicants with no previous work experience were unlikely to be offered a job. However, over 80% of the UK's leading graduate employers now offer paid work experience for students and recent graduates, either as vacation internships or longer work placements as part of a degree programme. You would be well advised to seek such experience, whether through an internship or other route. Alternatively, you may change because you are seeking to develop additional skills or to broaden your experience. This is an important consideration: the wider your skills and experience, the greater your chances of obtaining a higher-level job, or of finding another role or job if you are made redundant. It is vital in the current situation to take responsibility for your own development, always considering yourself through the eyes of potential employers. This will maximise your chances of continued satisfying employment, come what may.

Seeing yourself as a product

You need to regard yourself as a *product*, one which you are continually developing with an eye on the *market* for this product, now and in the future. Those responsible for marketing a product find that SWOT analysis is a useful framework for thinking about their strategy. If you have not yet come across this, it is very easy to understand and use. SWOT is short for:

- **Strengths** – which you already have, and might build on.
- **Weaknesses** – which you have but could possibly reduce or otherwise work around.

- **Opportunities** – which the market offers and you might be able to exploit better than other people.
- **Threats** – from outside, which you need to be aware of and take action against.

Figure 1.1 shows this framework diagrammatically. To carry out a SWOT analysis on yourself, fill in each of the boxes. Note that you need to be continually alert to likely developments in the employment market, aware of the types of skill and experience that are assuming importance and have a sound assessment of your own skills and experience. You also need to think about how you can *continually* develop these in ways that will open up future employment opportunities; otherwise you may find you face an ever more restricted range of possible jobs.

Such an approach means taking a much more active, and proactive, approach to your own 'career', seeing it as *your* responsibility rather than that of your employers. Seeking continuous learning and development will be a part of this. You will probably need to make absolutely sure you take advantage of all the training and job moves available in your company. If your employer does not encourage training, you may need to pursue a further qualification in your own time and at your own expense while working. The prospect of taking responsibility for your own development can be somewhat frightening. However, if 'boredom' and 'security' were listed as fears rather than as desiderata in the activity above, the excitement and risk associated with owning your own future should appeal to you.

Being highly employable means:

- seeing yourself as a product
- watching the market
- developing yourself continuously
- being prepared for change.

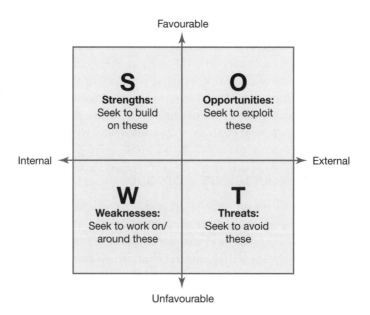

Figure 1.1 Framework for a SWOT analysis

The level of competition in the job market means that you need to start *now* to think about the skills that employers need and look for (not always the same thing) and about how to develop these and to *demonstrate* that you have developed them.

Activity 1.5

Use the SWOT framework, and the work you have already done during this chapter to organise your thinking about your strengths and weaknesses as they might be viewed by future employers. Supplement your research into current employer requirements by thinking about likely trends in the job market that may have altered the situation by the time you graduate. If possible, compare your analysis with those of two or three other people, and modify it if this comparison prompts new ideas. File the final version for future reference. Pay particular attention to your strengths – the developing area of strengths-based coaching suggests that building on your strengths is likely to be far more important in developing your potential for success than trying to bring areas of weakness up to the same level as your strengths. You need to address any weaknesses that would stop you from being effective. But once you have achieved an acceptable level of competence in your weaker areas, your focus could usefully move to developing those areas where you are already strong.

What working feels like

If you have not yet had a job, the world of work may seem singularly opaque. Your 'hopes and fears' listed earlier may have been fairly one-dimensional in consequence. And the discussion of structural changes above may have been interesting but not hugely helpful in terms of giving you a clearer picture of what working will really be like. Indeed, given the variety of possible work experiences, it is hard to do this. But the importance of work to your whole future life cannot be overemphasised.

Hating your job is grim. It can even make you physically ill. A significant amount of absence from work is attributed to stress. An experienced and, until recently, successful manager told me that he had been to see his doctor because he could no longer eat, sleep or think straight. Whenever he heard his manager's voice he felt physically sick. Indeed, when telling his doctor about all this he burst into tears. A stressful job with an over-controlling boss had reduced him to total misery and an inability to function. (Some ➤ Ch 2 techniques for managing stress are suggested in Chapter 2, but the best way of managing it is to avoid such situations.)

In contrast, a challenging and worthwhile job can leave you exhilarated and longing to get back to work the next day. The difference between these two extremes is so important that it is worth making every effort to take the challenge posed by this book seriously and do everything you can *now* to ensure that your working experience is positive. This starts with exploring your own views about work, a process that you will need to repeat at intervals throughout the book, and indeed throughout your working life.

Activity 1.6

List as many words as you can that describe your experience of work. Ask as many other people as you can to provide up to 10 words which describe their own experience of current, or previous, work.

_____

_____

You may have been surprised at the emotional level of some of the responses. Work forms a major part of most people's lives. For some, it is boring, or so routine and dehumanising that it is highly stressful and each day becomes something to be endured with difficulty. For others, work is so exciting that they would far rather be working than doing anything else. For some, it is a source of self-esteem; for others, the treatment they receive totally destroys any self-esteem they may have had. Many marriage breakdowns are blamed on the stresses and demands of work. Some jobs have specific health or physical risks associated with them. More generally, sickness rates correlate to different types of work. Studies show that to be without a job at all is highly stressful, destructive of self-esteem and associated with ill health and relationship difficulties.

In evolutionary terms, the centrality of work is perhaps not surprising. Survival has almost always been dependent on wresting food and physical safety from a competitive, if not hostile, environment, normally as part of a social group. And reproductive success, as with other primates, will have depended on status within that group. Without work (whether hunting and gathering or farming or manufacture of some kind), the life expectancy of a person and of any dependants would have been short. Indeed, family members would have been involved in work from a very early age. Survival without work is, in evolutionary terms, very recent.

If you feel it would be helpful to know more about what different types of work offer, there are a number of steps that you can usefully take. The first is to pursue any opportunities for work placements during your course (the learning opportunities offered by such placements are important in a number of different ways). The second is to extend the previous activity and to ask as many people as possible to describe their work experience to you in more detail. Try asking relatives and friends already in employment, fellow students who worked before the course started or who have already been on work placements. The third is to read about the experience of others, and suggested reading is given at the end of this chapter.

If you are asking people about their work experience, which may be extensive, it can help to have a framework of questions. If you are working in a group, discuss possible questions, and agree a common list. The following are merely suggestions to get you started:

- What most surprised you on starting work with your present employer?
- What are the most common difficulties you encounter at work?
- What are the most common frustrations?

- What has given you most satisfaction in the past week (or month or year)?
- If you could choose a new job, how would it be different from your present one?
- How would it resemble your present job?
- How much freedom do you have at work?
- How much impact do you feel you have on the way the organisation operates?
- What advice would you give to someone starting out in your organisation?
- What characteristics would the ideal employee have in your organisation?

The answers to such questions will reflect the person answering as much as the job they are doing. The same job could be very satisfactory to one person and hardly bearable to another. Nevertheless, if you can question a number of different people of graduate or equivalent ability about their experience, you should be better informed about the characteristics of jobs and possible reactions to them. This should help you become more aware of the nature of the type of job you would like.

Activity 1.7

Devise a set of questions for asking about work experience, preferably with a group of others, and use this to question a range of people. If working in a group, discuss the results, comparing what those you asked seem to want from work with what *you* think you might want, and using what they say about their work experience to extend your own expectations and awareness. Add any additional 'wants' to your 'ideal job' file entry. You can find a starter questionnaire, based on the questions above, on the website.

Structure of the Book

Use the brief overview which follows to help you see how to make best use of the rest of the book. Try to get a feel for how you can use it to develop those skills which you will need, both to succeed as a student, and to be highly desirable to potential employers when you start to apply for jobs.

The **first part** of the book maps out 'the territory' of employment, management skills and learning. Once you are more familiar with this context, and the more general learning skills that you will need, you will be better able to use the **second part** of the book, which addresses the specific skills that you will need in order to do well academically: reading critically, and taking effective notes; writing – and arguing – clearly; working with numbers; using computers and the Internet and doing well in assessment (including exams). You may already be more than expert in some of these areas. If so, it will be good time management to identify and concentrate on those where you are weaker. Although the main aim of this part is to help you do well in your course, most of the skills covered will be also be useful long after you have graduated.

The **third part** reverses this emphasis. It addresses communication and other aspects of working with other people, either one to one or as a member of a team. Although you will need these skills while a student and will have many opportunities to develop them, you have already seen that they are crucial to success at work.

The **fourth part** addresses skills of equal relevance to study and work: the 'trained mind' that graduates were traditionally deemed to possess. More specifically, it looks at the skills needed to react creatively and appropriately to complicated situations, to investigate them, gather and make sense of relevant information and decide on a way forward. Your course will be addressing problem-solving skills within a specific academic area, but much of the teaching may be implicit. This part of the book aims to make aspects of these skills more explicit and to increase your awareness of them. This should shift slightly your approach to study, so that you are better prepared to tackle problem situations at work.

In the **last part**, the different areas are brought together in looking at project management, both in general and in the context of any project that is part of your course. Finally, the 'project' of finding a good job is addressed. In this way the circle is completed and you will come back to the issues raised in this chapter, refining your work objectives and developing the skills needed for making a successful job application and doing well in interviews.

The structure of the book in terms of the skills covered can be charted, as shown in Figure 1.2. Inevitably, there are many interconnections between the skills covered in different chapters. In particular, the end of the book is designed to draw on almost all that has gone before. You can see that when you are ready to organise your file you will face a considerable challenge. But by then you should have a clearer idea of the skills that are important to you for more effective study, as well as those which are likely to be important to your chosen prospective employers. This will make it easier to design a system well suited to your particular situation.

This chapter has looked mainly at the world of work, arguing that there is a substantial overlap in the skills needed for study and those for employment, and that given the competitive nature of employment you need to start *now* to think about what you want from a job, and what skills you will need to develop it. You will find as you work through the book that each skill addressed will have the added benefit of helping you gain higher grades. This will help you further in your search for a better job. The transferability of most of the skills covered has its roots in two factors. One, obviously, is that if you are studying a course designed to prepare you for employment, then you are likely to be asked to develop those skills that employers' value. The second, and less obvious, factor is that the most successful managers are those who continually develop themselves. The ability to learn is vital in a world where organisational contexts are fluid and constantly presenting new challenges. Becoming an effective learner is thus crucial to both contexts. And it is effective learning along with the equally important ability to display your learning ability that this book primarily addresses, as the next two chapters make clear.

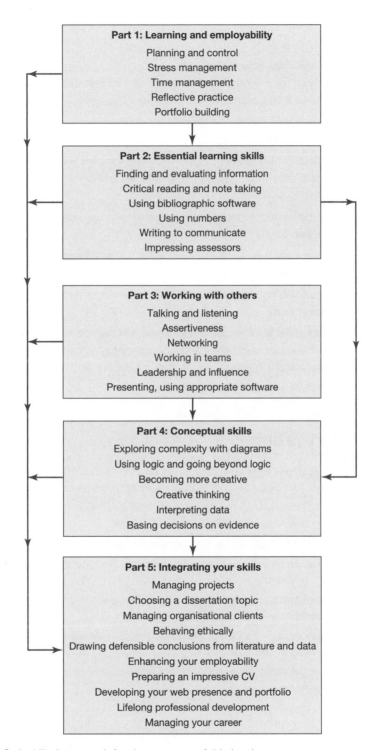

Figure 1.2 A skills framework for the purpose of this book

SUMMARY

This chapter has argued that:

- Studying for a degree represents a major investment: there are opportunity costs as well as direct financial costs.

- To get good grades and become an attractive employee you need to take responsibility for your own learning.

- Graduate opportunities have improved in the past few years but the situation is still highly competitive. Organisational restructuring has broadened the range of interesting jobs available.

- You can expect to work in several different organisations during your lifetime: managing your own career is important.

- To make yourself attractive to prospective employers you need to develop and demonstrate the skills they seek.

- The transferable skills which this book seeks to develop are relevant to both study and employment.

- These skills are interpersonal as well as intellectual, and include the skill to learn from experience as well as reading, the ability to manage yourself, basic skills in numeracy, literacy and IT, interpersonal, group-working and communication skills, and skills in analysing and solving problems.

Further information

Fineman, S. and Gabriel, Y. (1996) *Experiencing Organisations*, Sage. An easy-to-read set of stories told by students after their six-month work placements.

Frost, P.J., Mitchell, V.F. and Nord, W.R. (eds) (1997) *Organisational Reality: Reports from the Firing Line*, 4th edn, Addison Wesley Longman.

Reed, J and Stolz, P. (2013). *Put Your Mindset to Work*. London: Penguin

www.agr.org.uk – the Association of Graduate Recruiters – for information from the perspective of the employer.

www.prospects.ac.uk – 'the UK's official graduate careers website' for a range of information on graduate employment.

www.qaa.ac.uk – the Quality Assurance Agency – where you can find information on benchmarking and academic standards.

https://targetjobs.co.uk/search/all/focus/ad_vacancy (accessed 14/7/15) for a wide selection of graduate vacancies.

Study resources

Study resource: Developing a growth mindset

1   Think about your current feelings about your own growth. Do you actively seek learning experiences, or would you rather take a more passive role, hoping to learn mainly by listening to your lecturers? If your answer was 'passive', revisit this question at the end of the chapter – I hope your answer may have changed!

2   If your answer to question 1 was 'actively seeking learning experiences', note down all the work-related learning experiences you have already had, perhaps through volunteering or taking a leadership role in a club or society.

3   Find out more about what employers seek. Look at job adverts in the paper or online. Take advantage of any careers talks or open events held by employers.

4   Start to look for further opportunities to develop important work-related skills and experience. Think, too, about how you could collect evidence of your strengths that might impress a future employer. Take advantage of any available guidance from your careers service.

5   Even if it is a long time until you graduate, start to watch the job market, looking for areas that interest you, and checking that your growth activities are in line with what is being sought in these areas.

Source: adapted from Hill, G. (2014) 'Developing an employment mindset'; available at http://www.hecsu .ac.uk/assets/assets/documents/wdgd_september_2014.pdf

2
MANAGING YOURSELF AND YOUR LEARNING

Learning outcomes

By the end of this chapter you should:

- understand basic management principles, including those of planning and control, and how to apply them to managing your learning

- appreciate the importance of motivation and see how management theory can help you to motivate yourself

- be starting to improve your time management

- be setting yourself objectives and starting to meet them

- understand how stress can arise and how to reduce it.

Introduction

The last chapter pointed out that self-management is a key graduate skill for employability. According to Drucker (1999), history's great achievers have all been good self-managers. Most books on leadership similarly stress aspects of self-awareness, self-control and/or 'personal mastery'. Indeed, self-management forms the basis for all other achievements, including learning. If you develop your skills in planning, managing your time, managing your stress levels and motivating yourself, you will be far more successful in both your studies and your career.

By the end of this chapter you should have assessed your own development needs in this area, and be planning to meet them. The main focus is on clarifying your objectives, and planning and acting, to achieve them (adjusting plans where necessary). To do this, you need to understand the idea of 'control'.

Managing time, managing stress, and sustaining motivation are essential for both academic and career success. This chapter introduces models to help you develop relevant skills, drawing on a range of conceptual frameworks. This will also give you practice in
➤ Ch 8, 12   applying such frameworks to make sense of situations – a further key transferable skill.

Self-Management Skills

Actively managing yourself and your learning will enable you to achieve considerably more with the same or less effort. 'Management', is often defined as 'a process of achieving objectives through the effective use of resources'. As a student, your resources include time, brain power, books and university facilities. These resources are finite and need

---

Activity 2.1

Use this quiz to assess how good you are at managing your course or other work. Score 4 if your answer is 'never', 3 for 'rarely', 2 for 'sometimes', 1 for 'quite often'. File your answers so that you can retest yourself later and assess progress.

Quiz
How often have you:
Spent time wondering what exactly you are being asked to do for an assignment? _____
Put off working on an assignment because you weren't sure how to start? _____
Done less well than you might have because of procrastination? _____
Left yourself too little time to secure resources? _____
Left yourself with no time to redraft work before handing it in? _____
Fallen victim to clashing deadlines and had to rush one piece of work? _____
Asked if you could hand in work late? _____
Stayed up all night to finish something? Failed to complete work in time? _____
Total _____

Cartoon by Neill Cameron, neillcameron.com

to be actively *managed*. You also need to manage the processes, including the learning process, in which these resources are deployed.

Many students (and not a few middle managers) are woefully unskilled in this area. Use the following activity to assess your own starting point (honesty is essential here!).

Of course, there will be some unforeseen circumstances so don't expect a perfect score of 36; many students have skill levels that would score in the low 20s. I receive an endless series of requests to hand in work late. Reasons include things like:

- 'I've had to work a lot of overtime because I've reached my overdraft limit.'
- 'I had another assignment due yesterday and I have only just finished that.'
- 'I have had flu.'
- 'I couldn't get hold of the data I needed.'
- 'The library didn't have the books I wanted.'
- 'It took longer than I thought.'
- 'I had it almost finished, but then my computer crashed.'

Other students submit work more or less on time, but it is clearly rushed, and their marks suffer as a result. 'I couldn't get into it, so I haven't done as much as I should' or 'I'm not sure if this is quite what was wanted.' Or 'I had my marketing exam today, so I've mainly been revising for that.'

Students are not the only ones finding self-management difficult: many managers are unsuccessful for the same reason. Such managers create major problems for themselves and colleagues because of faulty planning for totally predictable events or failure to build in slack for the unpredictable. They miss deadlines because of conflicts between different tasks, which could have been foreseen, or because of poor prioritisation. Projects are held up because key materials were not ordered in advance and cannot be delivered for weeks, or because information is not available at the time it is needed. A new recruit to my own team had to work her full three months' notice, yet when she left her employers had still taken no steps to start recruiting her (very necessary) successor.

It is not surprising, then, that employers see things like self-management and self-motivation as important. Indeed, personal competences such as 'planning to achieve results' and 'managing oneself' feature in many vocational competence frameworks too.

➤ **Ch 3**

Improving your self-management skills will make you much more attractive to potential employers, and far more effective in whichever job you accept.

You will need to go on learning throughout your working life to remain employable. Managing your learning is not just important for your degree studies – it is another key factor for continuing employability. You will find that you learn far more effectively, enjoy the process more and get much better results once you start to actively *manage* your learning. Basic management principles can help you become better at managing both yourself and your learning

The Classic View of Management

It is hard to think of management without thinking, at least in part, of control. Luthans *et al.* (1988) observed a large number of US managers and found planning, decision making and controlling, together with human resource management, including motivation, to be a major part of their jobs. However, long before this, the first management guru, in the modern sense, and still the most quoted writer on management, Henri Fayol, (1916) suggested that management had five main elements:

- *forecasting*, then *planning* for the anticipated future
- *organising* physical and human resources
- *commanding*, or setting in action and continuing, the activities needed to implement plans
- *coordinating* activities to meet goals
- *controlling* this activity to ensure that it is done properly.

Interestingly, almost exactly the same points were outlined as essential elements in successful leadership at a recent seminar.

Forecasting and planning

Planning is essential. You may have heard the motto: 'to fail to plan is to plan to fail'. Imagine you have two essays, each requiring substantial library research, one due in 10 days, one in 11 days. If you work for 10 days entirely on the first, this would be an example of poor planning as you would have no chance of completing the other in 24 hours. It would be better to schedule your work to allow adequate time for each, either by bringing forward the deadline for the first, or alternating work on each. Similarly, it is poor 'planning' to try to borrow the single library copy of a necessary book the night before the assignment is due – you can be sure someone will have borrowed it already. You need to work out ahead of time (the forecasting element) what you need to acquire and to do, and then schedule your activities accordingly.

As well as planning for the predictable, you need to make contingency plans for the unpredictable. For winter exams it makes sense to allow some slack in your revision timetable: then if you catch a cold or flu you can spend a few days in bed. (Even in summer it is possible to get ill.) Most people are incorrigible optimists assuming that everything that can go wrong will go right. A better planning assumption is that at least some of the things that might go wrong will indeed do so.

The surprising thing about forecasting and planning is how often they are neglected, whether at work or in other contexts. Indeed, the more pressure you are under, the stronger the temptation to act like an ostrich and refuse to look ahead. But forecasting and planning are as important for getting a good degree as they will be in your first job, and when you become a director of a multinational company. The sections on planning techniques and time management in this chapter should help you to start improving your forecasting and planning *now*.

Organising

Fayol (1916) was talking more at the level of putting together factories and work teams, but you too need to assemble the resources needed to implement your plan. If you are going home during a study break and have an assignment due on your return, you need to ensure that you take *all* the materials that you will need to complete the work. If you are applying for a work placement, you need to check that your named referees are willing to vouch for you and will be available at the time the request for a reference is likely to be sent. If you are working on a group assignment, you need to make sure that the group has the right mix of skills and that the tasks are distributed to make use of people's strengths where possible.

Commanding

The term is somewhat archaic in this context, but the idea of 'setting action in motion' is still important. My grandmother's (irritatingly) favourite comment was, 'Procrastination is the thief of time.' perhaps you can relate to this cliché. It is no good having the plans and organising the resources if things don't then start to happen. This can be just as much a problem in managing yourself as in trying to get a group to actually do what they have spent a long time agreeing on. Whether you are trying to motivate a whole factory, to ensure that everyone in your group project team does their bit or to just stop procrastinating and write that essay, getting things moving can be a real challenge. An understanding of motivation is important for achieving this.

Coordinating

The need for coordination is more obvious in the case of group projects. Frequent progress checks and rebalancing of workloads where necessary can help in these circumstances. If you are working alone, the distinction between organising and coordinating may be hard to see, but if you depend on input from others, perhaps during dissertation research, it *will* become significant.

➤ Ch 16

Control

Control has authoritarian overtones, but it is absolutely essential to any form of management. There are few situations where you can set things in motion, and then sit back and wait for everything to work out as planned. Instead, you need to make adjustments as you go along either because your forecasts were wrong, your plans were unrealistic, or something totally unexpected has happened.

For example, you might discover a few days into your revision schedule that at your present rate of progress you are going to cover less than half the syllabus, and need to 'adjust'. This might be by spending more hours a day on revision or changing the way in which you are revising. Another 'control' action might be telling a friend that you cannot go to the cinema as planned because you have fallen behind schedule on an essay. Plans often need such adjustments to ensure that you achieve your objectives. In making these adjustments, you are exercising control.

The idea of a control loop, drawn from engineering, is a very simple framework which can help in analysing management situations. The ability to use such frameworks constructively will be an important part of the problem-solving skills addressed in Part 4, and the frameworks or models themselves are likely to form the substance of much that you learn at university. The next section, which explores the basic control loop idea in more detail, is therefore important on a number of levels. The part of your file based on exercises related to control is one to which you may need to.

Basic Ideas of Control

If you have a physics or engineering background, you may already be familiar with a version of the very basic control loop diagram shown in Figure 2.1. In engineering contexts the way such a loop operates is fairly obvious. Take a central heating system, for instance, which is made up of physical parts. Gas and air (say) and water will go into the boiler and the water will emerge at a different temperature to warm the radiators. Other outputs are waste gases. There is a target, which from your perspective is likely to be the air temperature of the house rather than the water temperature. You decide on the setting for this by adjusting the thermostat. The thermostat will continuously sense the air temperature and, when the temperature falls sufficiently below the setting, will send a message to the boiler to switch on and start heating the water for the radiators again.

The same basic control loop can also be used as a framework for thinking about control in more complex management situations. The key feature of the model is that it shows control as a process of checking what is happening against what should be happening, and making adjustments to bring things nearer to what is desired.

For example, you might check to see if spaghetti is cooked by throwing it at the wall (or, less dramatically, tasting a bit) and cook it a bit longer if needed. You might weigh yourself once a week if you are trying to lose weight and adjust your calorie intake in the light of this. Exams can be regarded as the 'measuring output' part of a control loop by which a university seeks to maintain academic standards.

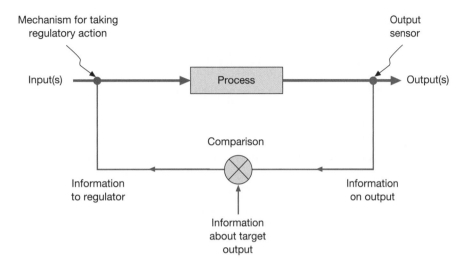

Figure 2.1 The basic control loop

Controlling yourself

So how do you 'use' the model to improve your self-management? The value of the model is that it makes explicit the different parts of the loop that need to exist for control to operate. It directs your attention to these different parts allowing you to consider whether, and how well, these processes are taking place. Are you failing to lose weight because despite the evidence of the scales you are not cutting your calorie intake (or increasing exercise levels)? The model helps you ask questions about the situation that will help you to realise why something is 'out of control', in that objectives are not being achieved. The answers will suggest what might be changed to improve the situation.

Looking at the model, you can see that the essential parts of the loop are:

- a goal or target – 'What am I *trying* to do?' – without this the whole idea of control makes no sense

- a way of sensing or measuring what is happening – 'What am I *actually* doing?'

- a means of comparing this with the target – '*How* am I doing?'

- a way of taking action if a discrepancy is found – 'What *should* I be doing to improve?'

The loop needs to be complete, or closed, for ongoing control to be exercised. Absence of any of these components will mean that there is no control: shortcomings in any one of them will mean that control is seriously weakened.

Activity 2.2

Think of at least one recent occasion when you, or someone you know, failed to achieve something as intended. Try to show what was going on by drawing a control loop, identifying each of the elements in the situation.

What were the inputs? What were the goals or targets? How explicit were they? How was progress monitored? What measures were used, and how were measures compared with the target? What action was taken when a discrepancy was found? Were inputs modified or was it necessary to change the process? Or was the target unrealistic?

If possible, compare your diagram with those drawn by several other people and try to see which parts of the loop seem most susceptible to failure. If you can, repeat the exercise with situations involving different objectives – longer or shorter term, more or less complex than the one you first chose.

- 'Easy to apply' models can provide useful checklists.
- 'Difficult' ones can change the way you think.

This exercise should have shown you three things:

1. It can be surprisingly difficult to apply a simple framework to a complex situation

2. It may be far from straightforward to express goals in a way that progress towards them can be measured – this will be discussed in more detail shortly.

3. It may be surprisingly difficult to *do* anything, even though you are fairly sure that something needs to be done. The reasons are many, but motivation is a crucial component and again there will be more on this later.

Difficulties in using models in this way do not mean that such models are useless. On the contrary, much of their benefit comes from the *effort* of bending a complicated situation to a simple model. This exercise forces you to think differently about a situation, to 'try on' different ways of looking at it and to come up with new insights and creative suggestions.

'Easy' models can provide useful checklists, but not much more. It is the effort of using a model to describe a reality which it does not obviously fit that can help you cope with ➤ Ch 12, 15 complexity and become more creative. You may curse the difficulty because mental effort is something we tend to avoid. But 'no pain' usually means 'no gain', in thinking at least. More on this later in the book.

Setting Objectives

Specifying goals in such a way that progress towards them can be *measured* may be difficult, particularly for ongoing and complex aspects of work. Most organisations appraise employees at least annually, discussing performance over the past year, evaluating it and setting new targets. There is a saying that 'what gets measured gets done' and this is why targets and measures are crucial. Setting the wrong ones – perhaps because they are easier to measure than other, more appropriate aspects of performance – can have a *negative* effect on the goals you really want to achieve. Yet, frequently this is what happens.

A major bank once set new, very high, lending goals to its branches, thereby hoping to increase business. Only one branch in the region met the targets. Because all other branches found it impossible, they asked the 'successful' branch how they had achieved their results. It turned out that what got measured was the paperwork on loan applications. Normally, if a loan was clearly out of the question, the branch would simply tell the applicant so and that would be that: no paperwork was necessary. What the 'successful' branch had realised was that it could start to prepare the initial paperwork for *all* applications, even those which had no hope of being accepted. Of course, this took a lot of (wasted) time and the number of ultimately successful applications which could be dealt with was therefore reduced. The 'successful' branch was actually lending *less* money. But it was meeting the targets it had been set in terms of what was measured.

SMART objectives

Because setting appropriate targets is difficult, various guidelines have been developed. The most memorable is that objectives should be SMART (some say CSMART), that is:

- Challenging
- Specific
- Measurable
- Achievable
- Relevant
- Time defined.

This is a common expansion of the acronym. There are others, but the message is the same. Vague objectives make it difficult to plan and even more difficult to monitor and therefore manage progress, hence the need for the S and M. There is little point in setting out to fail, so why set unachievable objectives? Yet, organisations often do, and it is surprisingly common to set oneself impossible goals – optimism is rife. The bank example shows why objectives need to be relevant and it will be difficult to monitor progress if no timescales are set.

The discussion of motivation which follows explains why unachievable objectives are a bad idea, but suggests why objectives do need to be challenging.

The time dimension is important and worth a little more thought. The aim of control is to ensure that you *meet* objectives, rather than find out afterwards that you have failed to do so. It is therefore essential that you know there is a problem in time to do some-

Activity 2.3

Revisit your examples of non-achievement in Activity 2.2 and think about whether the objectives in question were SMART. If not, rewrite them more clearly below, using these criteria. (For the purpose of control, they need only be SMART; if you want to find out why you were not *motivated* to achieve them you may need to look at the C as well.)

C _____

S _____

M _____

A _____

R _____

T _____

thing about it. The more frequently you measure progress, the more likely you are to detect the need for action while there is still time for such action to be effective. For a fairly major and long-term goal – for example, to submit a 10 000 word project in six months' time, or to sign up 40 new major customers over a similar period – you need to be able to check your progress at regular intervals. It is no good realising four months into the period that you have done about one-tenth of the required work. The following steps are useful here:

- break down objectives into hierarchies of sub-objectives
- identify critical paths through these hierarchies
- identify 'milestones', that is, points on these paths at which you will check your progress
- check as per this schedule.

Hierarchies of objectives

In order to achieve your main goal you may need to achieve several earlier objectives. To travel by bus to another city you need to find out where the bus goes from and when it leaves. You may need to buy a ticket in advance. You need to get yourself to the bus station in time. Figure 2.2 shows how sub-objectives might be organised in a hierarchy.

To construct such a hierarchy you start with the top goal and ask: 'For this to happen, what must I first achieve?' And then for each of the sub-objectives identified you ask the same question. Move down the tree until your objectives are simple actions which cannot sensibly be broken down further. Constructing such a tree can be extremely useful in high-

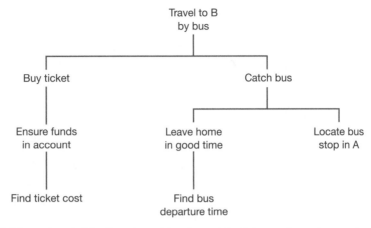

Figure 2.2 Hierarchy of objectives for getting from A to B (assuming prior purchase of ticket needed)

> In an objectives tree each 'rootlet' is something that needs to be achieved in order to achieve the objective above it.

lighting sub-objectives for which you might otherwise neglect to plan. It also gives you a series of much more specific objectives than the overall goal. You can start to think about scheduling the achievement of these objectives, with specific deadlines against which you can measure progress.

Note that you start with the last thing you will achieve, not the first thing you need to do. Having clarified your ultimate objective, you then identify things that need to be done before this can be achieved, moving down the page. This is the logic of an objectives tree, or hierarchy of objectives. Once you get the hang of this slightly counter-intuitive way of proceeding it becomes easy.

Activity 2.4

Think about something you would really like to achieve in the medium term. Examples might include finding a relevant vacation job, writing an article for a periodical, learning a new skill, making an expedition or gaining a qualification in something outside your course. Try to draw a hierarchy of sub-objectives by asking of each objective, 'To achieve this, what do I first need to achieve?' in order to tease out the objectives beneath it. When writing each objective, try to make it SMART.

If possible, get someone to check the logic of the tree when it is finished. It is all too easy for parts of it to come out upside down, with the objectives served being under the sub-objectives rather than on top. Try to arrange your various sub-objectives into a sensible schedule, with time targets attached to each. File this schedule and check progress against it at intervals.

Again, a seemingly simple exercise can turn out to be surprisingly difficult, but if anything this enhances rather than detracts from its value. Try to get into the habit of drawing an objectives tree for each of your goals. It will significantly increase your success in achieving them.

Action Planning

What you were doing in Activity 2.4 was to start to produce an action plan. Action planning is invaluable when you want to make sure that something actually happens rather than stays at the level of good intentions. There are several possible formats for such a plan, but any format should include a list of actions with target dates, and leave room to show completion. More complex plans may list resources needed, specify standards to be achieved, and allow room for ongoing commentary on progress. An example of an extract from a very simple plan is shown in Table 2.1.

The action plans you draw up while working through the book will give you practice in action planning, as well as help you plan and carry out activities which will help your personal development. Many organisations require staff to draw up formal 'personal development plans' as part of the performance appraisal system. Professional institutes may do the same, as one feature of professionalism is to take responsibility for ensuring that your professional skiils are continuously updated. You will find more on personal development planning in the next chapter.

➤ Ch 3

For any project with a number of sub-projects (and your learning could be seen in this light) it helps to have an overall view of progress. A simple summary sheet listing each main objective and key target dates allows you to check on those dates to see if you are on track. The key is to work out a format that suits you and use it at appropriate points during a project.

When action planning, check that each objective is CSMART. You will find this technique can be amazingly powerful in helping you to achieve your objectives because it forces you to think logically about what you need to do, and when, and provides you with a set of targets against which you can monitor progress. This will show you when you need to take corrective action. It will also provide visible signs of progress, thus sustaining your motivation.

Table 2.1 Example of a simple action plan

Goal: Organise next meeting		
Actions	**Target date**	**Completed**
Book room	27/3	26/3
Notify members	31/3	30/3
Arrange catering	4/4	4/4
Inform security staff	7/4	7/4

Activity 2.5

Revisit the plans you started to form in Chapter 1 for developing your skills and seeking relevant work experience. If they are not in a form similar to the example shown in Table 2.1, see whether it would be helpful to put them in a format closer to this.

Planning charts and critical paths

For complex projects you may need a more refined way of thinking about scheduling of sub-objectives and the tasks needed to achieve them. A common approach uses the idea of critical paths. Some tasks will have to be completed before others can be started. For example, when planning a walk between Melrose and Lindisfarne we first needed to decide when we were setting out. Lindisfarne is accessible only at low tide, and this is at a different time each day. It turned out that because of our limited 'window' for the holiday, and the tide times, we had to start at Lindisfarne rather than finish there as we had intended.

Figure 2.3 shows part of a planning chart for a course development project. (Charts of this form are called Gantt charts. You can use computer software to help you generate them. Chapter 15 discusses how to draw more complex charts, based on networks, for managing complex projects.)

➤ Ch 15

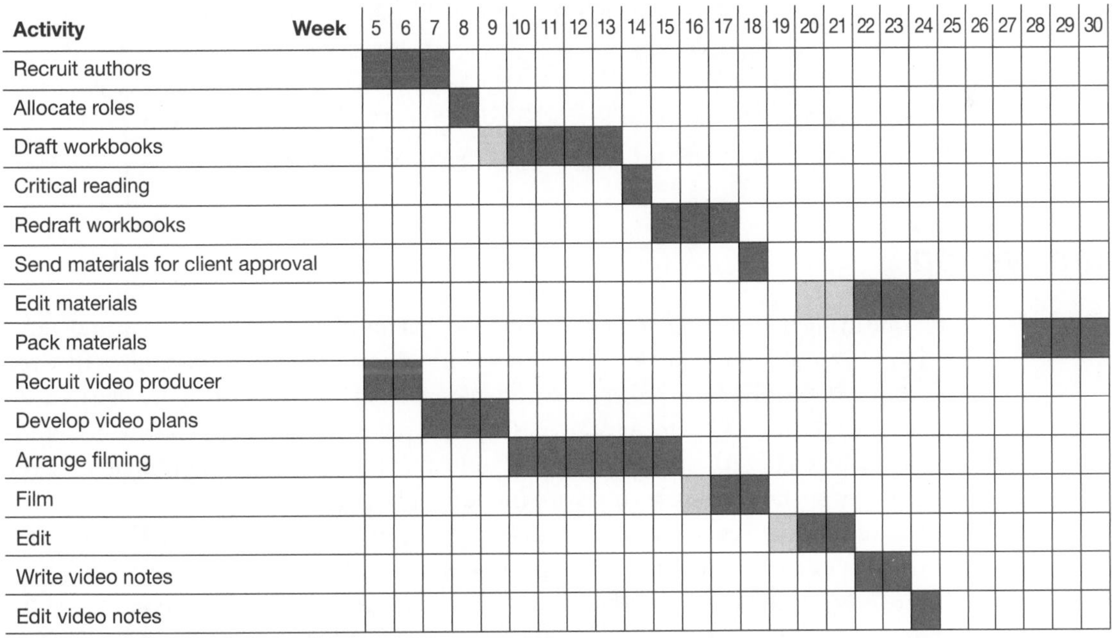

Activity / Week	5	6	7	8	9	10	11	12	13	14	15	16	17	18	19	20	21	22	23	24	25	26	27	28	29	30
Recruit authors	■	■	■																							
Allocate roles				■																						
Draft workbooks					░	■	■	■																		
Critical reading									■	■																
Redraft workbooks											■	■	■													
Send materials for client approval														■												
Edit materials																░	■	■	■							
Pack materials																								■	■	■
Recruit video producer	■																									
Develop video plans		■	■																							
Arrange filming					■	■	■	■	■	■																
Film												■	■													
Edit														░	■	■										
Write video notes																	■	■								
Edit video notes																			■							

Figure 2.3 Planning chart for course preparation

Some of the activities could not start until something else was completed. Workbook drafting could not start before authors were appointed. For others activities there were firm deadlines. On the chart, the solid part of the bar ends at a deadline and starts at the latest point that would allow completion by that deadline. If an activity can be started before this point, the time between the earliest and latest points at which it can be started is called 'slack'. This may be denoted by a broken bar or lighter shading (see Figure 2.3).

You will often need to plan to use slack in order to make best use of available time or avoid overload during a period. For example, the first book I wrote had a publisher's deadline that coincided with a deadline for completing 100 pages of distance learning material. Clearly, the last stages of each project were going to be heavily time consuming. Trying to do both at once would have been a recipe for disaster – and probably a nervous breakdown. Because I was writing the book alone, whereas others were producing some of the course material for me, I brought forward the work on the book, completing it a month ahead of schedule. It would have been difficult to persuade colleagues to bring their deadlines forward for my convenience, but there was nothing to stop me rescheduling my own work. You may need to make similar 'personal schedules' with earlier deadlines than the official ones if you have several pieces of work with coinciding handover dates.

Activity 2.6

Scan the chapter headings for this book. Think about how they relate to your particular course needs. When will you need to be able to work effectively in groups? When will you use numbers or information technology? When will you need to be able to manage a project? When do you want to get a job?

Once you have worked out your own needs in relation to the topics covered, try to draw a planning chart for your work on the remainder of the book. Show any slack time as well as latest possible start dates. From this, work out a schedule for your study. File it and check your progress (or revise the plan if necessary) at intervals.

Motivation

It is one thing to decide what needs to be done, but another to *do* it. You may know that it is only a month until your exam and that you really ought to start revising, or that you need to start writing your project report now if you are to have time to do it justice. Yet somehow it is impossible to get started. Or perhaps you have noticed you are becoming unfit, and need to take up a sport or start going regularly to the gym. But somehow you continue to spend your spare time with friends or playing computer games.

Success as a manager (or leader) depends on ensuring that all the members of your team are motivated to put effort into achieving the team's objectives. Organisational success or failure may depend on the motivation levels of employees. An equally important feature of self-management is making sure that you sustain your own motivation levels. You may have found 'self-motivation' cited in job adverts.

If you are motivated you will enjoy what you are doing and will find considerable satisfaction in succeeding. And your success will motivate you to further effort. This 'virtuous circle' is significantly different from the control loop. There, the emphasis was on achieving a steady output in line with target values. Where these deviated from the target, action was taken to bring them back into line. With *self*-control you can set higher targets in response to success. This increases both achievement and satisfaction. There is a 'higher-order' loop within which the basic loop is nested.

The expectancy model of motivation

Again, conceptual models can help you think about conditions which are likely to increase or decrease motivation. One such model is called the expectancy theory of motivation (Vroom, 1964; Lawler and Porter, 1967). It can be viewed as a 'control of effort' loop. As with the more general control loop, this model helps you to think of the components which must be included if motivation, and therefore effort, is to be present. Figure 2.4 shows a version of this model in diagrammatic form.

Reading this diagram, you immediately notice differences from the basic control loop. While it would be possible to draw the central part of the model as a 'performance' box with 'effort' going in and 'outcomes' coming out, this would leave out some of the most interesting parts of the model. These are the parts that highlight frequent sources of motivational problems, value placed on outcomes, and the assessed probability of these outcomes following on the exertion of effort. The *outcomes*, to be sensed (and evaluated against what is deemed fair or appropriate), are the rewards and punishments or benefits and costs which the effort may produce. Because both of the links – between effort and performance, and between performance and outcomes – are important, the model needs to show three separate boxes. The decision to exert effort reflects motivation: the unmotivated will not bother; the motivated will exert considerable effort. It is the remainder of the loop that determines which is the case.

The next important thing to notice is that the arrows joining effort to performance and performance to outcomes are dotted rather than solid. This is to make the point that it is a *subjective* link, a connection that a person believes to exist rather than any objective

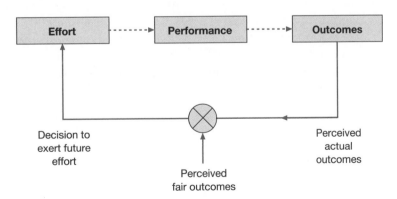

Figure 2.4 The expectancy model of motivation

reality, which affects motivation. The decision to exert effort depends on a belief that the effort will result in performance and that performance will be rewarded.

If you believe that you will fail no matter how hard you try, you will not make the effort to succeed. (Remember the 'A' in SMART. Objectives which are not achievable will not be motivating, so effort will not be 'wasted' in trying to achieve them.) How many times have you not even tried something because you didn't think you'd be able to do it? Similarly, if you feel that no matter how well you perform there will be no reward for performing – or worse, that performance will be punished – you will regard effort directed towards that performance as wasted.

Many managers have a far more simplistic view of motivation than expectancy theory suggests. Using the expectancy framework can direct your attention to important aspects of a situation, and increase your understanding of motivational issues. Is motivation low because people do not believe that they can achieve the required performance? If so, *why* do they think this? Do they feel that 'rewards' are not dependent on performance? If not, are the intended 'rewards' of little or no value to the person rewarded? The model does not provide answers. But it can prompt useful questions.

Some outcomes intended as 'rewards' are seen as punishments. For example, when my son was nine years old the local authority decided to discourage absence from school by 'rewarding' all children who had not missed a day of school in the year. They were invited to a special ceremony in the town hall, received a certificate and their names were read out in assembly. Ever after, my son (and I suspect many others in the '100% club') was 'ill' for a day fairly soon after the school year started so that he could be sure to avoid this 'reward' in future. Adults may similarly differ in what they perceive as rewarding and punishing. Some of the early human relations research in the 1950s suggested that in a coherent and 'negative' workgroup being singled out for managerial praise was not welcomed and people would do much to avoid attracting praise.

Maslow's hierarchy of needs

Another still-popular model helps with understanding what is likely be rewarding, and hence motivating. The first principle here is that something is satisfying if it meets a need, and therefore motivation stems from needs. The psychologist Abraham Maslow (1943) suggested a categorisation of needs that, despite academic criticisms is still widely quoted. There are many other such lists of motives, but Maslow's has the virtues of simplicity and a fair degree of logic. It will be familiar to almost anyone who has studied management. Maslow suggested that human needs could be classified into:

- self-actualisation needs
- esteem needs
- love needs
- safety needs
- physiological needs.

Maslow observed that needs became active only when those beneath them were satisfied. This makes excellent evolutionary sense. If you are starving (a physiological need), your first priority is to find food, and you will take risks you would not take if better fed. Reproductive success is linked to status, so you would worry about personal growth only when you felt you had secured the respect of those around you.

It is probably not worth paying too much attention to this idea of hierarchy – for most people, physiological and safety needs are likely to be met. But if you run out of money you may find your motivation to put in overtime on a part-time job is higher than your motivation to polish an essay (esteem/self-actualisation?). And if you are exhausted you may care more about sleep than the quality of the essay you are writing.

Intrinsic and extrinsic motivation

Expectancy theory suggests two categories of outcome, *intrinsic* and *extrinsic*. Extrinsic outcomes are those separate from the performance itself. They might be pay, praise, promotion or whatever. If you reward yourself with a Mars bar when you finish writing an essay, this is an extrinsic reward. Intrinsic outcomes are those which stem from the performance itself and the sense of achievement it gives. Simply knowing that what you have written 'hangs together' and contains some telling arguments can in itself be powerfully rewarding.

How, then, can you arrange for work – whether paid employment or study – to offer possibilities of intrinsic motivation? The first point is to ensure a strong perceived effort –performance link. Objectives need to be clear, and believed to be achievable, but additional conditions must also be met. Any necessary resources (time, tools, information) must be available and you must have the required skills. (This is where some of the other chapters in this book may help – they will address areas where you may feel your skills need to be improved to increase your chances of successful performance.)

The second step is to ensure performance will lead to intrinsic outcomes. One set of conditions suggested (Hackman and Lawler, 1971) is that jobs should feature four core dimensions if they are to have scope for satisfying those motivated by higher-order needs. These dimensions are:

- task identity – this is the extent to which tasks have a clear beginning, middle and end. It helps if you can see the difference you have made
- variety
- feedback on performance
- autonomy – or the freedom to take decisions about work

It has subsequently been suggested that it is important that the job also has some sort of social value and significance.

Activity 2.7

Stop and think for a minute about what you are likely to be working on during the next week of your course. How strongly motivated do you feel about the various tasks facing you? How can you explain this in terms of the conditions necessary for motivation as described above? What can you do to strengthen your motivation in the light of your analysis?

Task identity

You may have realised that by breaking things down into sub-tasks with their own targets, as you did in Activity 2.4 on hierarchies of objectives, you can greatly increase task identity. Thinking of sub-tasks in the context of the wider objective can increase their significance. Writing a book is a clearly defined task, but the timescale is so long that there would be few satisfactions along the road if I did not set myself shorter-term tasks such as completing single chapters. As each is completed and coloured in on a paper chart I have for the whole book I feel a sense of achievement in the chapter, and in the proportion of the book that is now complete, and am motivated to keep working. You may like to experiment with drawing simple progress charts for aspects of your coursework.

Variety

Variety avoids boredom and I vary the work by mixing writing fairly straightforward chapters with reading material relevant to other chapters which are harder to plan and write, or talking to other people to check their views on a topic. I also alternate between writing the first draft of some chapters and redrafting others written earlier. In the work context, if you are designing jobs for others, variety is an important factor to consider. If possible, the *variety* should come from doing different parts of a whole task. This increases task identity as well. If it is variety for variety's sake – lots of different, unrelated things – it can be of limited usefulness in increasing the motivating potential of a job. Did your suggestions for improvements include any increase in variety? If not, think now whether this might be possible.

Feedback

Reading my own work also gives me some feedback – provided I can leave a decent interval between writing and re-reading. Some parts may make little sense a few days later, others may read better than I expected. Try this with your own writing, but remember to build the 'decent interval' into your schedule. Of course, feedback from others is even better, as long as it is constructive (see Chapter 9 on how to receive – and give – feedback constructively).

➤ Ch 9

What other ways of increasing feedback did you think of in planning your week's work? They might have included making a checklist of sub-objectives and ticking them off when completed (visual feedback on progress), reporting to a supervisor on how you were progressing with something and getting their response, or setting yourself tests to check how well you have learned something that you are revising. Placing completed activities from this book in a growing portfolio, and revisiting them at intervals, will give you further feedback.

Autonomy

Autonomy is not a problem in the case of writing this book: I have been given a fairly free hand by the publisher, although not over the timescale! Your assignments may be more constrained, but there will almost certainly be scope for you to decide how best to approach them. Longer pieces of work such as dissertations allow considerable autonomy.

Social value

Social value is a harder dimension to exploit. In the work context: employees often do not see where their particular task fits into the bigger picture. If this is the case, finding some way of making it clear to them can increase motivation considerably. In your own case it may help to think about your wider life objectives from time to time and relate your particular activities to these. Consider, too, whether you are using skills that are far from universal – this too contributes to a sense of value.

If you are working with a group on a shared project, you can help everyone's motivation by making sure that they each clearly understand the overall purpose and relate every task completed to progress towards this. Praising and celebrating achievements (a drink when the first stage is completed, perhaps) can also be highly motivating. You will also find that looking back on your progress as recorded in your personal development file
➤ Ch 3, 10   (described further in the next chapter) can motivate you to continue.

In fact, your work as a student, provided that you *do* regard it as part of a wider learning enterprise, has the potential to be far more rewarding than many jobs. It is more under your control, you do get feedback and there is a degree of task identity. Furthermore, you are 'self-actualising' and developing your potential more than may be possible at work.

Activity 2.8

If you are still not finding your study motivating, think very carefully about why this is. It may be that the reasons go beyond the issues covered so far. If you do have a persistent problem in this area, seek your tutor's help in addressing it as soon as possible.

Time Management

Time management is an essential skill for employment, and equally important in gaining a good degree. Organisations pay large sums of money for two- or three-day courses designed to teach time management. And yet the principles involved are amazingly simple. They are really only a specific case of the general principles of management discussed above. Working through them should reinforce much of what has already been said in this chapter; you will also be developing an eminently transferable skill.

The difficulty lies in the discipline needed to put these principles into action. Changing habits is difficult, particularly to begin with. Once established, good time-management habits will become second nature and life will become much better. A course can help by making you more motivated. Alternatively, you can work on your time management with a group of others so that you can support each other through the first stages.

Basic time-management principles

The basic principles are simple:

- You should direct your effort *appropriately*, that is, towards the things that are most important.
- You should direct your effort *efficiently*, that is, maximise what is achieved by the expenditure of time and energy.
- You should reduce *time wastage*.

To do this you need to *manage* your time along the basic principles identified by Fayol (1916): plan your use of time and be clear about your objectives, organise other resources needed, motivate yourself to exert the necessary energy and control the process, monitoring your progress to ensure that you are not slipping back into old and bad habits.

Activity 2.9

Reflect on your last week and your achievements during this period. This exercise can be applied equally to a week of paid employment or to a week working on your course. Jot down the answers to the following questions:

- How clear were you about your various objectives?
- To what extent did you achieve them?
- How many hours did you work?
- How many of these hours were spent directly on work aimed at achieving your objectives?
- If you would have liked to work more hours, what prevented you?

➤

- For how many of these hours do you think your work was fully effective?
- What prevented you from being more effective during the hours you did work?
- Did you spend time working on something less important, leaving a more important task undone?

Save your answers in your working file. You can repeat the exercise at intervals (say every two months) to see how well you are progressing. A version is available on the website.

If this activity suggested that you could indeed be using your time to achieve more, you need to think carefully about each of the principles and how you can put it into practice in your particular context.

Directing your effort appropriately

The main dangers if you are studying tend to be:

- *Poor prioritisation*, perhaps working on something interesting and neglecting something more boring or more difficult. The neglected work may be a particular assignment, or even a whole course which you find tedious. The temptation may be strong, but your grades will suffer if you do not resist it. *Aiming for unnecessary perfection.* This may apply to essays or projects, for example, and lead you to endlessly polish a piece of work rather than handing it in and getting on with the next task.
- *Failing to clarify requirements* for an assignment and putting effort into something that is not what your lecturer or tutor wanted.
- *Failing to apportion time fairly* between different assignments set within the same time frame, working exclusively on the first one tackled for much of the time available for all of them – this is very close to the first problem.
- *Underestimating the time a task will need*. This is such a common phenomenon that it is called the 'planning fallacy' in the psychological literature.

All of these hazards arise in employment too. Additionally, managers may misdirect their effort failing to delegate or over-committing themselves. You may encounter some of these hazards in group projects, and are even more likely to meet them at work.

Achieving better direction

The secret of avoiding misdirection is planning. Review your progress towards objectives *daily*, and think about how to make further progress. Some find this review is best done at the start of the working day, others prefer to do it just before they finish work for the day. Whichever you choose, aim to make it a regular habit. Habits save energy!

If you are overcommitted, and with the best plan in the world cannot achieve what you want, think about why the situation has arisen. Talk to a tutor or supervisor and work out an emergency remedial plan as soon as you possibly can. Until the problem is resolved, most of your time and energy will go into worrying about the situation, and you will feel unmotivated to do *anything* since you know you cannot do everything. Think, too, about how to avoid a repeat of the situation in future – this may require you to practise assertiveness skills (see Chapter 9) in order to be firm in avoiding agreeing to what is more than realistic.

➤ Ch 9

If your review showed that you are too much of a perfectionist, do something about this. Modern definitions of quality refer to fitness for purpose, not to absolute perfection. If you bear this in mind you may find it easier to persuade yourself to settle for quality rather than perfection. When thinking about objectives, and planning how to achieve them, think very hard about how good/detailed you need something to be in order to meet learning or assessment requirements. Unless you have spare time, do not devote more time to the task than necessary.

If your review shows that you are spending time on things that are not really necessary, then think hard about whether you can afford this time. One of the joys of being a student should be the freedom to read things and pursue ideas out of pure interest, and it would be a huge shame if you could not continue to do this. But your priority has to be meeting course requirements.

Most jobs have considerable scope for doing unnecessary things in the guise of work. Many people fill in unnecessary forms, file unnecessary papers and attend unnecessary meetings. If you get into the habit of questioning the necessity of work now, you may find it easier to avoid such misdirected efforts when you are in employment.

Sources of ineffectiveness

Once you are directing your effort appropriately, you need to think about how to make it more effective in terms of what you achieve. Procrastination causes many to waste effort on worrying about what they should be doing rather than getting on and doing it. Another source of ineffectiveness is lack of organisation. This might cause you to waste time hunting for misfiled notes, or to forget to prepare for an important meeting with a project supervisor. In employment the scope for being ineffective through disorganisation will be even greater.

Most of us have daily rhythms and will be far more clearheaded and more energetic at some times of day than at others. It is ineffective to waste your 'best' times of day on unimportant or undemanding work. These times are precious. Try to reserve them for your most difficult work. Similarly, it is a waste of time to struggle on when you are so tired that you are getting nowhere. It may be far better to stop work for an hour, or even a day, using the time to make yourself feel better. Indeed, you may be able to increase your 'good' times significantly by simple changes, such as going to the pub less often, resisting late nights during busy periods and getting more exercise. If you are seriously worried that you are achieving less than you need to, drastic measures may have to be considered.

The other common problem is 'flitting'. Instead of working on a task long enough to make substantial progress, you switch between tasks or between task and non-task. (It is now believed that 'multi-tasking' is an extreme form of flitting.) Getting into a task takes energy and if you are switching repeatedly then you are wasting this 'start-up' energy. Allowing other people to interrupt you whenever *they* want, wastes energy in this way. Some variety is needed for motivation but try not to switch tasks too often.

Making effort more effective

The first requirement is obviously to be better organised. Aim to keep your desk (and floor) fairly clear – you will find that you can concentrate far better if you are not surrounded with clutter. Work out a system for keeping things needed for particular tasks together in one place. This is important whether you are working on paper or on your computer. Keep your notes, drafts and any data somewhere safe, and organised in a way that will ensure that you know *what* you have and *where*. It is important to be disciplined about keeping back-up copies of all electronic files. I have known students lose months of work because their computer was stolen or the hard drive failed. Fortunately, cloud storage makes backing up your work easy, and allows you to access files from anywhere. Once you *are* organised, you may be surprised at how much easier it is to work, and therefore how much more you enjoy it, as well as how much more time you have.

> **For more effective use of time avoid:**
>
> - procrastination
> - 'flitting'
> - displacement activity
> - perfection
> - poor prioritisation.

Stop devoting energy to *not* doing things. That is, find a cure for procrastination! This is easier said than done, but well worth the effort. Procrastination is the thief not just of time, but of huge amounts of energy as well. This is expended on thinking of excuses for not starting – all the displacement activities (making coffee, going to the library to look for something you don't really need, moaning to people about how impossible it is to get started) which you will indulge in to put off the evil day – and coping with the feeling of impending doom that comes from having a large and unstarted piece of work hanging over you.

There may be some factor which means that you *cannot* start something. Or you may have deliberately *chosen* to postpone an activity – a key time-management technique. In either case, 'book the work' for some *specific* time in the future. Write it down in your diary and/or on your plan. Consciously deciding when to do it allows you to prioritise sensibly. More importantly, it 'unclutters' your brain. Deciding in advance to do something at a specific time means that you can forget it until that time and concentrate upon what you are doing *now*. You will also find that when the scheduled time arrives, it is much easier to get started as the decision has already been made. Until that time comes, you need not waste energy worrying about the task.

You can extend this technique to make sure that you get full value from the time when you are genuinely not working. No one can work all the time. Remember Maslow. We need exercise, sleep, food, and time with our friends, time pursuing non-work interests. Scheduling your non-working time reinforces its importance as a valid part of your time-management strategy. Time off is essential for you to maintain full effectiveness. So schedule such time and enjoy it. Don't spoil it by thinking, 'I should really be working.' Enjoying *some* time off will help you achieve your objectives.

Some tasks are so large they are scary and fear of their magnitude causes procrastination. If this is the case, try to 'divide and conquer'. This is a variant of the 'hierarchy of objectives' approach suggested earlier. If the task can be broken down into sub-tasks, each with its own objectives, then it will be much more manageable and less likely to be postponed. Completion of each sub-task will be rewarding, motivating you to continue. Even if you cannot break a job down into discrete tasks, it is still worth setting yourself the target of doing some work on the job each day. This is because during the time you are not working on something, resistance to starting actually increases, making it more and more difficult. Even a small amount of work each day or two will prevent the build-up of this negative anticipation.

Make sure that your planning includes sensible deadlines for each task, arranged so that all deadlines can be met. Remember the need for objectives to be 'T' – time defined. And remember, too, that often you will need to set your own deadlines ahead of official ones and stick to these. Use planning charts to help keep these in mind and to aid your motivation – colour in the relevant bar each time you complete a task.

Stress Management

You will almost certainly be subjected to stress at various points in your life. You may feel that now is one of them! Many stressors arise from life circumstances, key among these being relationship problems, shortage of money, house moves and illness of those close to you. Some physiological factors – tiredness, illness or fluctuating hormones – may reduce your ability to handle stress.

Although Health and Safety Executive (2015) data suggest the incidence of stress at work has been broadly static over the last decade in Great Britain (there were an estimated 234 000 *new* cases of stress, depression or anxiety in 2014/15, 440 000 cases overall) it continues to be a major issue for organisations. These cases caused the loss of 9.9 million working days to stress, depression or anxiety in 2014/15, 43% of all working days lost to ill health. Workplace stress may be caused by overload, by the lack of resources or skills or information to do what is required, or even lack of understanding of what *is* required (think back to expectancy theory and the effort–performance link). It may be caused by lack of autonomy, by work that involves a fast pace, by the need to resolve conflicting priorities, by lack of recognition, understanding and support from their managers or colleagues, sometimes even by bullying. Sometimes underload may be stressful.

Learn techniques for coping with stress now, and the pressures of your course will become challenges rather than something negative. You will *feel* better and *do* better. You will also be better equipped to face the pressures of employment when you graduate.

(Stress levels at work are typically highest during the early stages of a new job, whether in a new organisation or after a promotion.)

Many of the techniques already described in this chapter will serve to reduce stress. Being clear about your objectives and exercising time-management skills will go a long way to making any work situation less stressful. Interpersonal skills, particularly assertiveness (covered in Chapter 8), will help too. If work is less stressful, you will be better able to handle pressures arising outside work. If you manage stress outside work better, you will be better able to handle the job. There are some things, however, which are specific to managing stress and which you need to know.

➤ Ch 8

Recognising stress

Stress tends to creep up on us gradually. As it increases we become less capable of rational thought about our situation. Others may therefore be far more aware of the fact that we are stressed than we are ourselves. However, there are a number of signs to watch out for. Almost all of these could have other causes, but if you show many of them, you may need to reduce your stress levels. Symptoms include:

- difficulty sleeping, lying awake worrying about things
- frequent minor ailments such as headaches or digestive problems

---

Activity 2.10

Think about how stressed you are at present. (Note: you should repeat this exercise at intervals, particularly shortly after any change in circumstances, such as starting a new job.)

How did you feel this morning about the day to come? Full of eager anticipation, or with a dull sense of dread and of things to be endured?

_____

How many of the symptoms listed above do you have?

_____

As a result of thinking about these questions, rate your stress level on the following scale:

1	2	3	4	5
(low)		*(medium)*		*(very high)*

Without telling them your score and using the same scale, ask friends how stressed they would say you were.

How do the scores compare? Think about what the two sets of scores suggest (a questionnaire is available on the website).

- asthma and/or eczema
- drinking more than is good for you
- eating problems, either eating too much or not enough
- irritability and poor judgement
- forgetting things (particularly things you should have done)
- general feeling of tenseness.

If you feel splendidly stress-free at present, and your friends agree, leave this chapter until later. But repeat the exercise above roughly every two months and resume work on the chapter if you become aware of stress levels rising. If you already feel somewhat stressed, work on.

Reducing stress

There are two strands to any approach to managing stress: reducing those stressors which you can do something about and learning how to cope better with those that are inevitable. The first step, of course, is to know which is which.

Activity 2.11

List all the pressures or other factors in your life which are contributing to your feelings of stress. Remember to consider things to do with your life in general, with your work in particular and physical factors such as ill health. Divide them into those things which might be capable of being changed and those which you can do nothing whatsoever about. (This may not always be easy. For example, you may be able to do nothing about having insufficient money – unless there is the possibility of earning some more – but may be able to do something about what you are spending it on and therefore how much is available for essentials.)

Things you can do something about

Once you have identified stressors which might be reduced, think about possible ways of doing something about them. You might find it helpful to work with one or two friends on this, to come up with a wider range of ideas and increase your motivation to take some

➤ Ch 15   action. The creativity ideas in Chapter 15 will be useful.

Coping with the inevitable

Many features on your list may be things you can do nothing about. But this does not mean that you can't become better at dealing with them. The three main approaches to coping with the inevitable are:

Activity 2.12

Work out an action plan similar to the format used in Table 2.1, with deadlines, for reducing your stress levels. You may find it beneficial to develop a hierarchy of objectives as a first step.

File your plan and monitor progress towards your objective(s). Revise plans where necessary to achieve your overall objective of stress reduction. A description of this 'campaign', if not too personal, would be an excellent item to include in a portfolio of evidence of transferable skills. It would show planning and control skills and might also, depending on your chosen actions, show effective time-management and interpersonal skills, as well as an understanding of, and ability to practise, one important aspect of stress management.

- changing your attitude
- learning to relax
- becoming physically better able to cope.

Attitude change is not easy to achieve but is important. The old prayer asks for the strength to change what can be changed, the patience to endure what must be endured and the wit to know the difference. I hope you are now more aware of the difference, and no longer wasting energy on trying to change what cannot be changed. Wishing things were different or trying to achieve the impossible can also waste energy. Are you setting yourself unrealistic targets? If so, realise that you don't have to be superman/woman. Being you, with your own ability levels is actually worthwhile: the world needs very few 'superhumans'.

Similarly, don't rail against fate or regret past decisions: accept where you are and do the best with that. If a decision *can* be retaken, consider the cost of doing so and whether you are prepared to pay it. Perhaps you chose a wrong programme of study.

> **Cope with unavoidable stress by:**
> - acceptance
> - relaxation
> - exercise
> - good food
> - sleep.

Can you change that choice, perhaps by repeating a year? If so, do you want this enough actually to do it? If not, what can you do to maximise the benefits of your original choice? Above all, do not expend precious energy on what might have been but cannot be. A close friend of mine lost her daughter in a road accident. She said that the hardest thing was to stop thinking 'if only'. If only she had said something to prevent her going out, if only her own car had been repaired and she had not needed to accept a lift. I hope your regrets will be about lesser things. But if you stop thinking 'if only' you will further reduce your stress levels.

Relaxation techniques can be enormously helpful, but need to be learned. You cannot relax on demand if you have not developed the skill. There are good self-help tapes available. You may be able to find a short course which teaches relaxation.

Meditation and yoga also help. If you feel stressed by things which you cannot change, it would be well worth learning some form of relaxation technique.

Finding a relaxation course is best, but if no suitable course is on offer, the following, extremely basic, approach may help. Find a quiet room with low levels of lighting where you can be alone, or with others wishing to practise relaxation. Sit comfortably or lie down. Think about your breathing, trying to keep it fairly slow and regular. You may wish to focus your thoughts on your diaphragm. Gently discard any thoughts that float into your mind. Return your thoughts each time to your breathing. If you prefer a visual image, instead of your breathing (though keep this slow and regular) focus on a picture in your mind. A lily, rippling water, a cliff top, anything which you can 'see' clearly in your mind and which means peace to you. If you are not a visual person, then repeating a short 'peaceful' phrase over and over in time with your breathing may help. Again, whether using an image or phrase, gently put aside other thoughts which surface, returning each time to the focus of your concentration.

When you have finished your relaxation, 'surface' gently. Get up slowly, move around slowly, letting your thoughts gently come back, rather than instantly rushing around. Practise this concentration for five minutes at first. Eventually, build up to 15 to 20 minutes per day.

Simpler forms of relaxation include a long hot bath, perhaps with a few drops of pure lavender or other relaxing essential oil added. Listen to music, or read poetry or a novel for pleasure. It is an excellent idea to programme some 'unwinding' time between finishing work and going to bed. This is not wasting a study opportunity: you are probably too tired to achieve much. Using the time to relax will ensure a far better night's sleep, and means that you achieve more the next day. If, despite your relaxation time, you still feel under too much pressure to find sleep coming easily, a few drops of lavender oil (if you buy only one oil, this is the one to get) on a tissue by your pillow can help a lot.

Keeping in good physical shape is essential if you are to cope with pressure without feeling stressed. Eating a healthy diet (as fresh as possible and with the emphasis on fruit and vegetables, with animal proteins and fats as accompaniments rather than the focus of a meal) is important. All too often we eat unsuitably (chocolate bars, crisps, biscuits) or drink unsuitably (more than the recommended alcohol unit intake per week) *because* we feel stressed, and yet this makes us less able to cope with stress. Indeed, worrying about food or alcohol may itself become a source of stress, another example of a vicious circle.

Physical exercise is excellent for reducing stress; counteracting depression and making you better able to use your brain effectively. Any exercise that raises a sweat for half an hour or so will work. But choose something you like doing, as you really need to exercise two or three times a week as a minimum. If you spend this walking briskly or cycling to lectures, then any further exercise will be a bonus. If you take no exercise as part of your routine, then experiment with swimming, jogging, a ball game or longer walks at week-ends – or, of course, a mixture of these things. Exercising with friends is more fun and you are more likely to do it even if you do not feel like it as you will not want to let your friends down. Once you get there, you will almost certainly enjoy it, so the initial effort will have been worthwhile.

If you have not exercised recently, start gently. If you overdo it, you will build up a subconscious resistance to further exercise that will be almost impossible to overcome. So deliberately start by doing less than you feel you could manage. And avoid being competitive while you are building up to full fitness. There is always a temptation to 'prove' something, by running further or faster than is comfortable, or trying to beat someone at squash, who is far fitter than you are. As well as creating psychological resistance you will beat serious risk of injury, which will set back your plans considerably.

Sleep is important for good health too. You will probably find that if you exercise more you will sleep better. However, if exercising in the evening, allow time afterwards for relaxation before bed.

Activity 2.13

If you did not use stress management as the basis of an 'exhibit' for your file, and are not taking enough exercise, then consider using this as an example of target setting and self-management. Work out an exercise plan, set yourself interim targets and monitor progress towards them. Adjust targets if experience shows them to have been too hard or too easy, and comment on these adjustments. (Do this with one or two friends if at all possible, to increase your chance of success.) Keep your original plans, revised plans and achievements, together with comments, in your portfolio.

If you are exercising, but are aware of not eating or drinking for optimal health, then set targets for this and document progress towards your targets. (If this is more of a threat to your well-being than low exercise levels, you might like to start with this exercise anyway.)

SUMMARY

This chapter has argued the following:

- Management is about effective use of resources to achieve objectives.
- You need to manage your own time, energy and other resources to be successful as a student and in employment.
- The principles of self-management in either case are broadly similar to those of

management as more generally understood – the management of other people.

- Applying basic conceptual models (the control loop, the expectancy theory and the idea of a hierarchy of needs) can help you understand how to improve your motivation and self-management as well as giving practice in using models to aid analysis.

- The first essential is to be clear about objectives. Ideally, targets will be specific, will be measurable and will have a time specified for their attainment.

- There also needs to be a way of measuring ongoing progress. This will enable you to monitor the extent to which you are on track and to take corrective action if you find things are not going to plan.

- Ongoing monitoring and achievable but challenging objectives will help you keep your motivation high. Our time is a finite and usually scarce resource. Successful self-management will therefore involve good time management: clear and appropriate objectives and an appropriate and efficient direction are important.

- It can be surprisingly difficult to change habits, and developing good time management usually requires sustained and conscious effort until new habits are established.

- Stress is a common feature of both university and working life. Causes include relationship difficulties, health problems, money worries and time pressures, and work itself. Symptoms may be physical (for example, sleep or health problems), behavioural (for example, drinking or eating problems), mental (for example, difficulty concentrating) or emotional (for example, irritability).

- Remedies for stress involve reducing sources of stress where possible and increasing your ability to cope with unavoidable stress through, for example, exercise, relaxation and attitude change.

Further information

Adair, J. and Allen, M. (2003) *The Concise Time Management and Personal Development*, Thorogood.

Allen, D. (2015) *Getting Things Done,* (Revised edn), Penguin.

Caunt, J. (2000) *Organise Yourself*, Kogan Page.

Forster, M. (2006) *Do it Tomorrow: And Other Secrets of Time Management*, Hodder & Stoughton.

Lifeskills International (1999) *Staying Healthy at Work (Life Skills Management)*. This addresses stress, physical health, interpersonal relations and lifestyle planning.

Thompson, G. (2005) *Stress Buster*, Summersdale. http://www.cipd.co.uk/hr-resources /factsheets/stress-mental-health-at-work.aspx for a good overview of stress in the workplace (the CIPD also has a range of other resources relevant to this chapter.)

For a questionnaire designed to assess student stress from life events go to http://www .monmouth.edu/campus_life/counseling/questionnaires/stress.asp (accessed 2/7/15).

For useful resources on stress reduction try http://www.nhs.uk/conditions/stress-anxiety
-depression/pages/ways-relieve-stress.aspx

For a 12-minute guided relaxation based on tensing then relaxing try http://www.dummies.com
/how-to/content/reduce-stress-and-anxiety-a-guided-relaxation-exercise.html
http://yourskillfulmeans.com/ for a wide range of resources and suggestions related to
mindfulness, meditation and stress reduction.

2

MANAGING YOURSELF AND YOUR LEARNING

3

LEARNING, REFLECTIVE PRACTICE AND PROFESSIONAL DEVELOPMENT

Learning outcomes

By the end of this chapter you should:

- have a better idea of what 'learning' means

- appreciate the difference between knowledge, concepts, skills and competence

- understand what is meant by learning style and recognise your own preferred style

- have started to develop less preferred styles

- be starting to develop your reflective learning skills, both individually and collaboratively

- understand the role of feedback in the development of both practical and conceptual skills

- have explored the learning opportunities offered by your degree programme, identified any gaps and be starting to plan to fill these

- be developing a systematic approach to evidencing skills relevant to employment.

Introduction

Good grades – and a good career – come from knowing what and how to learn. In today's rapidly changing business world, employers are often looking for evidence of the ability to learn fast. This ability will contribute to success in interviews and rapid progress thereafter. Membership of a professional institution will depend on the ability to demonstrate ongoing professional development. This chapter will help you to understand the learning process, recognise your own preferred learning style and develop your learning skills, particularly your ability to use reflection as a means of learning. It will help you to start a learning diary as an aid to reflection, and to organise a portfolio of evidence of learning, particularly from experience. A better understanding of the learning process, and of the role of reflection within this will help you gain better grades and maximise the learning potential of any situation you meet at work.

We all learn from the moment we are born, but are often not aware of the process. As you work through this chapter you will become more aware of how you learn, and can start to apply your developing self-management skills to improve your learning both on your course and outside it. Managers or leaders who know how they learn, and who go on learning, are far more effective than those who lack this awareness.

Learning Theory

Children are voracious learners, eager to master walking and talking and countless other skills, including how to influence people, and get their own way. Outside of school, children are seldom aware that they are learning, and indeed you still may not have thought much about what helps and hinders your own learning. Indeed, what exactly *is* learning?

Activity 3.1

Write a brief definition of learning as you understand it. Discuss this with some other people if possible. Unless you have all just done a course on 'learning', which included an approved definition, you may be surprised at the range of possible ways of understanding the term.

_____

_____

_____

Traditionally, learning was seen as acquiring knowledge. There are still countries where 'education', even at university level, consists of giving students information and then testing that they can repeat it. The underlying metaphor is of 'jug and mug', with the 'knowledge' being poured from the jug (lecturer) to the mug (you). Yet, in many situations academic knowledge is not enough. You may *know* that to ride a bicycle you sit on the saddle and use your feet to turn the pedals and your hands to steer via the handlebars. But this knowledge would not stop you falling off the first time you tried to ride. Being able to *do* things is also important. Beyond both, there is the ability to *understand* and interpret situations and respond effectively, even if the situation is different from any you have yet encountered.

It is this learning of *conceptual* skills that is most exciting. And for this, the passive mug metaphor is singularly inappropriate. Learning conceptual skills is necessarily an *active* and continuous process, not a one-off operation performed on a passive recipient. Some years ago, Krishnamurti expressed this convincingly when arguing for a form of psychological learning which goes beyond the accumulation of knowledge or the acquisition of skills. For example, he says:

> Learning is one thing and acquiring knowledge is another. Learning is a continuous process, not a process of addition. Most of us gather knowledge as memory, as idea, store it up as experience ... we act from knowledge, technological knowledge, knowledge as experience, knowledge as tradition, knowledge that one has derived through one's particular idiosyncratic tendencies. In that process there is no learning. Learning is never accumulative; it is a constant movement. You learn as you are going along.

(Krishnamurti, 1995, meditation for 12 January)

Refer to your definition of learning above. Did it include *skills* as well as *knowledge*? Was there any reference to understanding, or to a conceptual dimension? Did it refer to accumulating knowledge or skills? One workable definition of the sort of learning that this book addresses, though it has an accumulative dimension that could be seen to conflict with the view quoted above, is:

> Learning is a purposeful activity aimed at acquisition of skills, knowledge and changed ways of thinking intended to improve effectiveness in future situations.

This begs many questions about what constitutes effectiveness and which situations are relevant, but it teases out a number of dimensions that it will be useful to explore. It covers the three aspects of knowledge, skills and thinking. It also highlights the need to *use* what is learned and implies that others will only know that you *have* learned by observing your more effective behaviour. (You might, subjectively, know that you have learned

Activity 3.2

Rewrite your definition taking the above ideas into account. There is no need to use exactly the words above. Try to find a way of defining learning that feels right to you, as a reflection of what you now think learning is. Then think of three recent instances when you have felt you learned something of significance and check that each would be learning according to your definition. Note your thoughts below:

_____

_____

_____

something because you are aware of increased understanding, but others will need you to translate this into something – words or action – that they can observe.)

Competence and vocational qualifications

In the UK, and some other countries, the early 1980s there was a move towards emphasising the importance, in a work context, of what you can *do*, rather than merely what you *know*. This led to a profound change in the approach to vocational and professional training and qualifications, and the construction of a set of National Vocational Qualifications (NVQs, or SVQs in Scotland) each based on a set of occupational standards against which to assess competence. This prompted the specification of observable learning outcomes for educational and training modules (and book chapters). Organisations frequently develop their own standards, or competence frameworks for use in recruitment and development of staff. Professional institutes usually base their assessment of candidates for membership on a set of standards.

➤ **Ch 2**

Assessment against such sets of standards often requires candidates to present a portfolio of evidence demonstrating their competence against each standard. The use of portfolios has now spread far beyond the NVQ realm. Universities are highly likely to expect you to compile such a portfolio, and will probably offer a centralised system for storing its contents. It is also now fairly common for people further in their careers to develop a portfolio to 'showcase' their work or experience online for potential clients and employers. Throughout this book you will be asked to file the results of activities directed towards developing (and demonstrating) your skills. This will result in part of a portfolio you can draw upon whether to seek a competence-based qualification, to impress potential employers or professional institute, or as a requirement of your university and key part of your learning process. Understanding the portfolio-building process, and developing the skills involved, will contribute to both your learning and your employability. There will be more on developing a portfolio at the end of this chapter.

What are you learning now?

It is worth exploring ideas about learning in more depth. Consider your own current learning. What more do you need to learn than the 'facts' about your chosen subject? How are you becoming potentially more *effective*? The first chapter suggested some things that the government and employers think you should be learning – key skills to do with communication, working with others, using numbers, using IT, problem solving and, of course, 'learning to learn' in the applied sense of improving your own learning and performance in any situation. If you have never thought about the wider learning that your student experience offers, it is worth taking time for a brief audit of this. By the end of the book you should have a clearer understanding of the range of possible transferable skills and be able to update and expand your audit. Do not, therefore, spend too long on the following exercise. Regard it as a rough first draft.

➤ **Ch 1**

If you are not used to thinking of such a wide range of learning and have not reflected on your own learning before, you will almost certainly have found this difficult. Don't worry – it will have raised questions in your mind that you will be able to answer later and highlighted areas that you need to think more about.

Activity 3.3

Think about the modules you are studying this year. What broad areas of specialist knowledge do they address? What skills specific to your subject will you also be developing? Which of the above key skills can you develop within your studies? (For example, you can practise communication skills in class discussions – face to face or online, in negotiating extensions to deadlines with your tutor and in writing assignments. You can practise team skills when working with others on activities from this book, or on group projects.)

List the things that you think you are currently learning. Leave space beneath each to write other things, and file this for future use. If there are key skills which you are *not* earning; for example, if you have managed to avoid touching a computer, or if there is no group work, log these on a separate list. Log also anything which you think you are *supposed* to be learning but for some reason are not.

Kolb's theory

Even for specialist knowledge, an employer would probably be interested in your ability to *use*, rather than merely recite, what you know. Application – that is, using the knowledge to do something *better* – is crucial but often difficult. Using conceptual frameworks to *understand* a situation better is hardest of all. Yet, it is crucial to the sort of learning you need from your studies.

Employers expect graduates to be able to understand problematic situations in order to respond appropriately. What used to work may no longer work when things change. To adapt to a new situation you need to understand what you were doing in the old one, and why it worked there.

Organisational life is complex, and conceptual frameworks, that is, mental models, help you to make sense of it. Some of these frameworks or sets of assumptions you will already be using, probably without being aware of them. Kolb recognised the importance of these unconscious 'theories' and of the role of conscious reflection in their development or change (Kolb *et al.*, 1984). He suggested a model of how ideas and experience are integrated. In this, learning is seen as circular rather than a one-off. You do something, reflect on your experience, try to conceptualise it and then test these concepts through action, which generates more experience. Figure 3.1 shows a simplified version of this process.

Behind the model is the assumption that assumptions, beliefs and often unconscious theories drive our action. Key points to note from this simple model are first that learning is shown as an *active* process. Action generates 'experience' of the results of action, which provides food for reflection. This reflection involves trying to make sense of the experience in the light of existing ideas and understanding. 'Theorising' involves changing your beliefs/ideas/assumptions/unconscious theories in order to make better sense of the experience. You then test your new theories through action, applying them in another

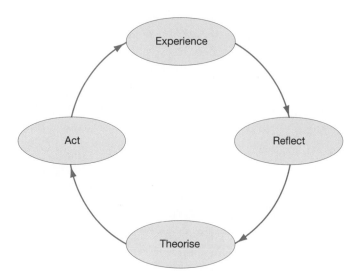

Figure 3.1 Learning as a continuous process (adapted from Kolb)

context and seeing whether experience of the results of your action is as expected. By going round the loop again and again as you have new experiences, you can continue to develop your understanding.

If parts of the process are missing, learning will not take place. You could do something ineffectively for years if you never stop to think about how you might do it better. Experience without reflection will teach you nothing. A friend works for an appallingly bad manager. For decades the manager has never questioned the ways in which he operates. Indeed, he is completely unaware of the 'theories' or assumptions on which his behaviour is based. As far as he is concerned, the way he thinks is the only possible way: anyone who disagrees with him has to be stupid or perverse.

One belief is that a subordinate should account to his manager for every moment. Yet, the job is one which requires thinking, networking and other 'invisible' activities for success. The 'control is all' assumption of this boss is making it impossible for my friend to perform. He and the rest of the team are currently actively seeking other jobs, purely because of this ineffective boss and his faulty assumptions.

Theory unlinked to past experience and untested in new contexts is equally unlikely to contribute to competence development. (In the 1980s most of those on MBA programmes were recent graduates. They tended to be avoided like the plague by most employers.) This is why work experience is a crucial part of an undergraduate business studies degree.

Learning Styles

If learning is to be effective – and it is vital for your studies and for your subsequent career that it is – then feedback and reflection on experience are essential. You need to work to ensure that you get feedback on what you do, and on how you think, and to constantly reflect on your practice and the experience that results. But although this much is true for everyone, people vary in the way they learn, and it is essential to understand your own learning style. There are many different approaches to classifying learning styles. For example, Drucker (1999) suggested that some people learn best by listening, some by reading, some by writing and some by doing.

Another suggestion is that people vary in their dominant sense (see, for example, Andreas and Faulkner's 1996 book on neuro-linguistic programming, or NLP). Some will talk in terms of 'I hear what you are saying,' 'Tell me what ...,' 'That sounds as if ...' For these people, the auditory sense is strongest, and they will presumably learn by listening. Others say things like 'Show me ...,' 'I see what you mean ...,' or 'It looks as if ...' For them, vision is strongest, so they presumably would learn best by watching, or perhaps reading. Yet others will say, 'It feels as if ...,' 'I can't quite grasp ...,' or 'You need to touch on ...' For them, the kinaesthetic sense is important, and presumably they would be the ones who would learn in a 'hands on', or 'doing' fashion.

Educators often talk of VARK (visual, auditory, read/write and kinaesthetic) learning preferences although there seems little evidence that designing learning for particular preferences (even if practicable) is effective. However, considering your own preferences and adapting your approach to learning may help. The idea is certainly interesting, and you can assess your style online.

Activity 3.4

Observe one or two friends talking for a while, noting whether they use 'seeing', 'hearing' or 'doing' words most. Once you have identified their dominant sense, ask them how they feel they learn best. If possible, then ask them to observe you and identify your own sense dominance. If not, observe yourself – it will be easier once you have sensitised yourself by watching them. Think about the implications of this for your own learning and note them in your file.

Kolb devised a complex set of learning styles based on his model, but again there is little evidence that this is helpful. Honey and Mumford (1986), faced by managers who found Kolb's styles model difficult, suggested a simpler way of classifying people in terms of the stages in the Kolb cycle. Although all of the stages are necessary for learning, they suggest that people tend to be happier with some stages of the loop than others. They identified four different *learning styles* which reflect these preferences and developed an inventory to help people to identify their own. There are strengths and weaknesses associated with each style. You can get a 'quick and dirty' approximation of your own preferred style from the following. If you are really interested in your own style you should obtain the full inventory. (Your institution may have rights to use this.)

Activists

If you chose statement 1 in Activity 3.5 you may tend towards activism. If so, you are probably open-minded and love new experiences, get bored easily, are highly sociable,

Activity 3.5

Think about each of the following statements. Check the one that is most characteristic of your own reaction to a learning situation.

1. I'm game to try it – let's get started.
2. I need some time to think about this.
3. What are the basic assumptions?
4. What is the use of this?

love group decisions and bring welcome energy to a task. You are probably not very good at things which require consolidation, or indeed anything which requires sustained effort – even sitting through a lecture may be difficult. Producing a dissertation or other sustained piece of work will be extremely hard for you. You will scorn caution and tend to jump into things without enough thought. Other group members may feel you don't give them a chance in discussions and you may miss opportunities to learn from other people's experience.

Reflectors

If you chose statement 2 you may be a reflector, preferring to think about all possible angles before reaching a decision, taking a low profile in discussions, cautious and unwilling to leap to premature conclusions. You will thrive on dissertations, provided you do not spend far too long on planning, leaving no time for data collection and writing. You will be a great asset as an observer of others and provide useful feedback, but may not take opportunities to get feedback yourself.

Theorists

If you chose statement 3 you may be a theorist, approaching problems logically, step by step, analysing and synthesising, establishing basic assumptions, insisting on a rational approach. You probably hate uncertainty and will have trouble with the chapter on creativity, while loving complex problems which have a clear structure. You will hate having to work with problems where you do not have all the information you need, or where some of the factors can be assessed only subjectively. You may find it infuriating to work with people with a strongly activist style. You will love the more theoretical aspects of your courses, but when you come to apply them in a real situation you may be somewhat at a loss.

Pragmatists

If you chose statement 4 you will love new ideas *provided* you can put them into practice. You will hate open-ended discussion and love problems and the search for a better way of doing things. Theoretical aspects of your courses may leave you cold, but you will really enjoy any skills development as long as there is adequate feedback on performance. You will prefer learning from case study discussions to sitting through lectures and, if you are a part-time student, will benefit greatly from the chance to apply what you are learning to your job. You may tend to leap to practical solutions to problems without thinking about either the conceptual underpinning of what you are doing or whether a more creative approach might be possible.

Any simple classification of something as complex as learning will be an over-simplification. And the self-assessment questions above are crude. If you want a more accurate picture you need to work through the full inventory. But the strengths and weaknesses identified above suggest that if you have a strong tendency to one learning style then you need to be aware of its associated risks and plan ways of coping with these. Furthermore, it is worth seeing whether you can become a more effective learner by developing some of the strengths of your non-preferred styles so that you can go through the whole cycle. Your years as a student offer you an ideal opportunity to do this. The following exercise is designed to help. You will need to do the suggested activities over a period of time, in parallel with other work.

Activity 3.6

Decide which styles you need to develop. Choose at least six of the following activities and make an action plan for carrying them out. Monitor your progress at regular intervals. Describe your experience of each in your file. This could constitute a useful demonstration of your ability to learn.

To develop activism
- Do something completely out of character at least once a week (for example, talk to strangers, wear something outrageous, go to a new place).
- Force yourself to fragment your day, switching deliberately from one activity to another.
- Force yourself to take a more prominent role in discussions. Determine to say something in the first ten minutes. Volunteer to take the chair or make the next presentation.
- Practise thinking aloud. Next time you are thinking about a problem, bounce ideas off a friend, trying to get into the habit of speaking without thinking first.

To develop reflection
- In discussions, practise observing what other people are saying and doing and thinking about why they might be saying, doing or thinking this. (This will be useful in Chapter 10.)
- Spend some time each evening reflecting on what you have done during the day and what you have learned from it. These notes could be kept in your file.
- Aim to submit a perfect essay/assignment next time. Do several drafts, and think carefully about their relative strengths and weaknesses.

● Select a topic you have covered in your course that really interests you. Try to find out as much as possible about it and write a short paper summarising this. (If you have the opportunity to speak about your findings, this will link to work on presentation in Chapter 11.)

● Before taking any decision, force yourself to draw up as wide as possible a list of pros and cons.

To become more of a theorist

● Spend at least 30 minutes a day reading something really difficult about one of your subjects, trying to analyse and evaluate the arguments involved.

● If you hit a problem, whether in your studies or elsewhere, try to identify all the causal factors involved, and work out how they were related and what might have averted the problem.

● Before taking any action, ensure that you are absolutely clear about what you are trying to achieve. Having clarified your objectives, see what you can do to increase your chances of success.

● Listen to what people are saying in discussions, trying to identify any dubious assumptions or faulty links in their arguments.

● Practise asking a series of probing questions, persisting until you get an answer that is clear and logical.

To become more of a pragmatist

● When you discuss a problem, make sure that, before stopping, you have agreed what needs to be done, and who will do it, in order to make things better.

● Do the practical exercises in this book!

● Ensure that you get feedback on the skills you are practising in the exercises.

● Tackle some practical problem (for example, mending clothes or appliances, choosing and booking a holiday, cooking a meal for friends).

● You will find that working through this book will help you to develop all four styles to some extent, provided you do all the activities suggested.

The Role of Reflection in Learning

The activities you have done in this chapter should have introduced you to a range of reflective activities, and started you on the road to developing a reflective learning style as part of a 'full-circle' approach to learning. Reflection is now seen as crucial to professional development, and is receiving increasing emphasis in undergraduate studies in professionally relevant subjects. It is therefore worth looking in more detail at what reflection actually is, and the role it plays in learning. This will help you to use the process to full effect both for your own development and to meet course requirements for evidence of reflection as part of your assessment. This section looks at how reflection 'works' to strengthen learning, and at why it is important to develop a lifelong habit of reflection. It also covers some of the main reflective tools.

Deep or surface learning?

Much of the argument for reflection rests upon the idea of 'levels' or 'depths' of learning. You might, for example, learn five key theories of motivation, their authors and the text-book diagrams in order to regurgitate them for an examination. This is the surface level of learning – it is unlikely that you would then be able to go into a situation where staff seems to be demotivated, find out why and do something to improve the situation in the light of this analysis. Being able simply to reproduce material from the textbook seldom helps you sort out real-life problems. To do this you would require rather more understanding than is implied by mere reproduction, and a deeper level of learning.

Suppose that you get really excited about the idea of motivation. You search for, and read, a range of relevant articles, comparing what different authors said. You assess the relative merits of the different theories you encounter, and their weaknesses, perhaps with a view to writing a new paper. You achieve a much deeper level of learning than the simple ability to reproduce material.

In an educational context, Entwistle (1996) suggests that a *surface approach* is directed merely towards meeting course requirements, often when there is a feeling of being under pressure and/or worried about the work. Study is done without regard to its purpose, beyond that of passing the course. The material is approached as a series of unrelated 'bits'; there is an emphasis on routine *memorisation*, without making sense of the ideas presented.

A *deep learning approach* is driven by the desire to *understand* the ideas, and is associated with an active interest in the subject matter. Thus you try to relate each new idea you come across to your previous knowledge and to any relevant experience. You look for patterns and any underlying metaphors. You look carefully and critically at the author's evidence and logic. Material approached like this is far more likely to be remembered. And if ideas are related not just to other ideas but to relevant experience, they are far more likely to lead to improved practice. A deep learning approach is thus particularly important for any study of vocational relevance. Trying to apply ideas in a work context without fully understanding them often leads to expensive misapplication, and worsens problems rather than improving the situation as intended.

You might think that if you adopt a deep approach you will inevitably get better marks than by taking a surface approach. Usually you will. And you are more likely to be able to remember what you have learned after the course and be able to incorporate it into your practice as a manager. But it is possible to get so carried away by passion for a subject that you forget the course requirements altogether and actually do worse. It is therefore suggested that a third type of approach, the *strategic approach* is important. This is directed at doing as well as possible on a course, always alert to course requirements and the need to use time and effort to best effect in meeting them, balancing deep and surface learning in order to achieve this. Much of this book is devoted to enabling you to do just that.

Ideally, assignments will be designed so that the best marks will be gained by the sort of learning most likely to help your future career.

Rather than making a simple 'surface–deep' distinction, Moon (1999, p. 128) suggests a series of levels of learning with increasing changes to the way you perceive and think about the world. The division between surface and deep would occur around level 3. Moon indicates how your tutor or lecturer would detect this in your work. Note the presence of 'reflective' at the two deepest levels (4 and 5).

1. Noticing – represented as 'Memorised representation'.

2. Making sense – represented as 'Reproduction of ideas, ideas not well linked'.

3. Making meaning – represented as 'Meaningful, well integrated, ideas linked'.

4. Working with meaning – represented as 'Meaningful, reflective, well-structured'.

5. Transformative learning – represented as 'Meaningful, reflective, restructured by learner, idiosyncratic or creative '.

Although this book is trying to improve your ability to be an effective strategic learner, and to get the best grades possible, I firmly believe that it is deep learning which is of importance for your career after you graduate. The emphasis in many of the activities will therefore be to deepen your course learning towards the 'working with meaning' level. This is where you are really engaging with ideas and questioning – and perhaps improving – the mental models with which you make sense of the world. Moon describes this as 'a process of "cognitive house-keeping", thinking over things until they make a better meaning, or exploring or organising the understanding towards a particular purpose or in order that it can be represented in a particular manner'.

Both Entwistle and Moon were considering education in general, rather than vocationally relevant education, and so did not particularly concern themselves with application of ideas to work contexts. While the deeper levels of understanding they identify are important, you need to go beyond making sense of the ideas themselves, and into the area of using the ideas to make sense of work situations. Your course will give you practice in using the ideas to analyse case studies. You can gain further invaluable experience by reflecting on your own work experience and that of others willing to talk to you about their jobs and organisations and issues they have faced.

➤ Ch 11

Consider the difference between being able to recite five different motivation theories (including Maslow's hierarchy of needs, and expectancy theory) and being able to improve the motivation of a disgruntled team in the light of this knowledge. To do the latter you might need to find out what rewards were important to team members, to check their understanding of objectives and their beliefs about their ability to achieve objectives and the likely rewards if they did. You might also, if you had developed a habit of reflective learning, ask yourself what you were doing or not doing as their manager that was contributing to the lack of motivation, and what thinking (beliefs, assumptions, unconscious theories) was driving unhelpful aspects of your behaviour, and therefore might need to change.

Deeper, more reflective learning is far more exciting than surface learning. And if you can make the connection between ideas and real situations it will have an even more profound impact upon your ability to go on learning from your experiences throughout your life. Many professional organisations now require evidence of such ongoing reflective learning and practice as a condition for continued membership. If you already have a habit of 'reflective practice' you will need no convincing of its worth. But you may be relatively new to such learning, or yet to experience it. (There is a suggestion that the ability to learn in this way does not develop until around the age of 20.) If so, it is worth paying attention to developing the necessary skills through reflective practice.

The reflective process

You will remember that Kolb *et al.* (1984) suggested that for learning to take place experience needs to be followed by reflection, and then conceptualising, or theory building. Thus you move from action in the real world, to a process of detached observation taking place somewhere inside your head. Clearly, this is not surface learning. But the nature of this process was relatively unspecified, and there are still differences of opinion as to how best to reflect. It is something many students struggle with. If you are finding the Kolb cycle a bit too abstract, you may prefer to use a simpler cycle. This was shown to me by one of the best management teachers I have ever met, Dr Reg Butterfield. It has three stages in the cycle: Wot? So Wot? Wot next? This is as 'simple' as can be, and with the misspellings and cartoon faces, totally memorable. At its centre is the essence of the whole process, the 'So wot?' 'So what' is the key question in almost any analysis, followed by the equally important issue of what to do in light of your analysis?

What follows works for me and for many of my own students. It is offered for those of you who do not quite know where to start. If your own course has already given you tools, ignore what follows.

> **The basic elements for successful reflection include:**
> - time to reflect
> - something to reflect upon
> - medium for capturing reflection
> - skills in reflection
> - honesty
> - feedback.

Successful reflection depends first and foremost on making time to reflect. Time management will be dealt with shortly, and once you are convinced of the value of reflection, making time for it will become a priority.

So what to reflect upon? Kolb suggests 'experience'. Dewey (1910), the source of many of Kolb's ideas, suggests reflecting whenever something surprises or perplexes you. Perhaps you cannot understand why someone is upset at something you said, or why a team is falling apart or an assignment gets a lower score than expected. Perhaps a theory you are taught does not seem to fit your view of the world at all. The perplexity is a signal that some of your assumptions or theories about some aspect of the situation need re-examining. Reflection on practice is also useful if things went as expected, but you would like them to go better.

For example, you might be working on a group project. After a meeting you might ask yourself what went well, and why, to make sure that it goes at least as well next time. You might also ask if there was anything that might have gone better. How did you feel during the meeting? Was this how you expected to feel? Why? How did your own behaviour influence others in the group and contribute to the progress you made? Were there ways in which you might have been a more effective team member? What might you do differently next time? Any of these questions might prompt useful learning.

You might reflect, individually or better still as a group, upon how well the team as a whole is progressing and ask whether there are ways in which this might be improved. Your reflections on your own and others' behaviour in the light of theory – perhaps motivation theory or what you have learned about effective group working – might also help you to realise the significance of parts of that theory that you had not appreciated before. It might make you aware of shortcomings in a particular theory in terms of its ability to cast light on your experience. You might reflect on the content of the project work in the light of theory you have been taught which is potentially relevant to the project itself, and whether you might make fuller use of that theory or seek other theories.

Some of your reflection might be prompted by reading or lectures. After the event you can usefully deepen your learning (and make it far more likely that you will remember the material) by thinking about how what you have read or heard relates to what you already know. Does it contradict other theories or support them? Does it suggest different interpretations of data on which they are based? Does it relate to your own experience, or to things you have read about business in the newspaper? What light does it shine upon things that you didn't fully understand before? Does it make you realise the importance of something that you had previously disregarded? Does it make you doubt something that you had previously assumed might be true?

Much of this more abstract reflection on the relation between different ideas and on the extent to which they are based on firm evidence relates to the *critical thinking* that you will see listed as a key learning outcome of most university-level study. This will be discussed further in the context of critical reading and writing answers to assignments, which demonstrate critical thinking skills.

➤ Ch 4, 5

Perhaps most important of all, since your primary objective during your course is to *learn*, is to reflect upon the learning process itself. For any experience, whether reading, lecture, other course work or work experience, ask yourself questions such as:

- How did that go?
- How did I feel about the experience?
- What did I learn from it? What did I fail to learn?
- How might I have learned more effectively?
- What will I do differently in future to help me learn better?

Thus reflection is about asking yourself (or yourselves if doing this in a group) a whole lot of different questions and thinking hard about the answers. It is about being prepared to think about how your own thinking is affecting your actions. It is about realising how your thinking is affecting what you are observing in a situation. You are more likely to be able to 'think about your own thinking' if you are working with other people: this way you can find out that others see things differently from you, and then start exploring both the reasons for, and the implications of, these differences.

The role of feelings in reflection

You may have been surprised to see the 'How did I feel' question above, but exploring your feelings is an important part of reflection. Often, your feelings will highlight areas of concern that you have yet to put into words and signal profitable areas for reflection. Suppose, after a job interview, you ask yourself 'How did I feel?' and get the answer, 'Somewhat uncomfortable from the very beginning.' Identifying the source of this discomfort may help you learn a lot. Ask yourself questions like: When did it start? Was it before I even walked into the room? Such reflection might show that you felt unprepared for the interview, with obvious implications for future action. Or perhaps you weren't sure about whether this was a company you wanted to work for – maybe you have concerns about the ethics of their product or way of working. This might affect your choice of companies to apply to in future. Perhaps you felt 'unworthy' of the job? If so, and assuming you were honest on your application and they decided to interview you, does this suggest that perhaps you undervalue yourself? Or did the discomfort start with a particular question that you were asked early on? If so, what was the question and why did it make you feel uncomfortable? I could continue, but you should see by now where exploring feelings can lead you.

Feelings can also be important when you are thinking about things you have read or which someone has said. They tend to be driven by your non-conscious, non-rational brain, which has far more processing capacity than the conscious part. Discomfort here may mean that there is a mismatch that you have yet to access consciously. It may be that assumptions which form a central part of your way of looking at the world are being challenged. It is very easy, and feels comfortable, to dismiss such challenges as rubbish. Our very identity stems from the set of assumptions, values and beliefs about ourselves which act as a filter through which we see and interpret what happens to us. We tend to be very protective of our identities. It can be unsettling, even painful, to have them challenged. But it is through such challenges that 'cognitive housekeeping' – or even an extension to our cognitive house – is achieved.

One of my most profoundly disturbing experiences as a very young trainer in the civil service occurred during an interviewing course I ran for people working in the equivalent of HR. I went through some of the relevant theory and guidelines for effective interviewing, and then had the course members roleplay interviews. Nothing very innovative, but a large number of the participants, most of whom had been interviewing for decades, burst into tears. I had not said anything about their performance; however, reflecting on the roleplays in the light of the material we had covered had made them realise that for years they had been really bad at interviewing. Part of their identity was 'expert interviewer', and this identity was now threatened.

There are three morals to this story. First, the interviewers needed to change their way of thinking not only about what they did but also about themselves, as a step on the way to doing it better. Second, it took honesty with themselves to bring about this change. In order to protect themselves they could have decided that the material I was teaching was wrong or that any feedback they received was useless. Honesty in answering reflective questions is an essential component in learning from reflecting – it is all too easy to rationalise away any need to change. The third message is that such change can be seriously painful, and support may be needed. I was totally unprepared and unqualified to give such support, and failed the group quite badly. You are probably much younger than they were, but you still need to tread carefully when exploring your own assumptions, particularly about yourself, or when working as part of a group which is reflecting.

Activity 3.7

Think about something you have read or experienced, or perhaps received feedback on, which occasioned some discomfort. Think about your feelings in more depth and try to explore why you felt like that. Note any learning points from this exercise.

The value of group reflection

There have been several references to reflecting in a group. For group reflection to be effective, group members need to trust each other, all need to understand the principles of reflective dialogue, and the group needs to agree to abide by these. (You may find it helpful to read the chapter on group working before attempting collaborative reflection.)

Effective group reflection has many advantages over reflecting individually. The aim of reflection is to question not only what happened and how your behaviour affected this, but also to consider the extent to which the thinking which prompted the behaviour needs to change. Since much of the time we behave in a way that seems 'obvious', rather than consciously thinking about what to do, it may be hard to find out what your underlying thinking was. Discussing what happened, or your views on what should happen, with other people provides you with a starting point. By identifying differences of views, and digging into the thinking that generates such differences, you can become more aware of your own 'invisible' theories about how the world works, or what is important. You may find others have noticed different aspects of the situation because of their different unconscious theories or values.

Collaborative reflection need not be carried out face to face. It is possible to work together online, whether synchronously or asynchronously. However, this requires even more attention to showing respect for others and their views. When working online, your body language and tone of voice cannot convey your intent, and people may therefore not feel as valued and respected as you intended. If you are new to online dialogue of this kind, you may find TECHSkills 3.1 helpful.

Collaborative reflection works only if you observe the following rules for effective reflective dialogue:

- Agree that the purpose of your dialogue is to compare and contrast your different ways of perceiving and of conceptualising the situation
- Value each other's views as much as you value your own
- Seek to identify reasons for differences rather than debate which is 'correct'
- Use these differences to become more aware of your own invisible 'thinking tools'
- Be willing, once these are uncovered, to change them if you can see ways in which they may now be unhelpful.

TECHSkills 3.1 Netiquette for virtual collaborative reflection

When working online the same factors apply as when reflecting together face to face: you may find it helpful to read Chapters 9 and 10 on talking and listening, and group work, alongside this file note.

Virtual collaborative reflection offers obvious practical advantages. If you are working asynchronously you avoid the need to find a time when all involved are free. If working synchronously you still avoid difficulties of location. But the cost is the reduced informational capacity of all save the most sophisticated teleconferencing systems.

When you are working face to face, your words carry only part of your 'message'. Body language and tone of voice carry far more. Without these additional channels, your choice of words becomes far, far more important. While you can use 'emoticons' such as smiley faces they do not have the same impact as a real smile.

'Netiquette' (internet etiquette) refers to a set of rules for online interaction that is designed to help with the challenges of working online. Check whether your university has such a set of rules, and if so, study and observe them. If not, start from first principles and remember that reflective dialogue can feel potentially threatening. It is therefore essential to check that anything you post is (very) carefully considered. It helps to:

- Take part! You may want to hold back because you feel your views are less valuable than others, or because your upbringing has suggested that it is wrong to put your views forward, or because of laziness. Whatever the reason, your learning and the learning of others in the group, will suffer if you do not take part

- Greet people at the start of your message, whether as a group ('Hi, everyone') or individuals

- Offer your view as a view, nothing more ('I saw this as....')

- Appreciate others' views before adding your perspective ('That's really interesting, Shen, I hadn't seen it at all like this – I'd assumed that … You've made me wonder whether…')

- Never say anything that suggests someone's view is worthless. They may never dare venture an opinion again!

- Limit your contributions. Too much can be as bad as too little. When you post a message you are asking people to devote time to reading it. Make sure that you have thought enough about your message to be reasonably confident that is worth their time. Note: this point only applies to those who are posting much more than the average. If you are culturally or congenitally reluctant to post any messages at all, ignore it – you probably seriously underestimate the value of your potential contribution!

- Check you have understood a point before disagreeing – it is very easy to assume someone intends something just because they have used a word that provokes a strong reaction, or you assume, from your knowledge of them that they 'would say that, wouldn't they?' Such assumptions are often wrong!

- Read – and re-read – anything you write before sending. Ask yourself: What am I assuming about the people who read this? Are my assumptions justified? Will they know/understand what I mean? Is there any way at all in which they could take offence to this?

In addition to observing any rules, you need to be constantly aware of your choice of words, and their potential impact on others.

Tools for Reflection

You should by now be clear that the main item in your toolkit is a good list of questions. A number of such questions are given in the box above. A slightly longer set is available online, but this is still far from comprehensive. You need to select those questions that work for you, in the contexts in which you are reflecting, adding any which are missing from the list and which you feel are important.

Reflection is essentially a dialogue based around these questions – and honest answers to them – so you need a medium within which this dialogue can take place. I have referred already to the need to create a personal development file as an aid to capturing, evidencing and managing your learning. You should by now have a number of responses to activities that are worthy of filing, so it is time to think about how best to organise this file.

Before doing so, it is worth exploring some of the terms that are used to refer to another important category of tools for reflection, namely, different forms and formats that may be helpful. Key among these are learning logs, learning diaries and journals, development records and plans, audio diaries and blogs.

As is often the case, definitions for many of the terms used vary and are not universally agreed. However, some distinctions are worth noting. The first is between a simple record and writing with more reflective content. The second concerns the extent to which you move on from your reflection to planning further learning.

Simple recording

A learning log might be a simple record of what you learned and when. You could, for example, note key learning points from each lecture and each occasion when you did some course-related reading. A simple format would suffice. The following is one example.

Event and date	Reason for doing	What I learned
2.11 Read first part of course introduction	Required reading	Key management roles, current management challenges (ICTs, globalisation etc.), Kolb's learning cycle
14.11 Attended first tutorial	Get better idea of course (and tutor) requirements	Need to make explicit reference to key concepts in assignments, need to submit on time, word-limit penalties, importance of avoiding plagiarism, value of online discussion

Such a factual record can be useful both to sustain motivation and for quick reference after. Professional institutes may require a similarly basic record of continuing professional development. Thus the Chartered Institute of Personnel and Development (CIPD) requires members to keep a record of their development and suggests the following continuing professional development (CPD) recording format – though it allows any reasonable format to be used. (I've included an extract from my own record to show how this might reasonably be used.)

Key dates:	What did you do?	Why?	What did you learn from this?
5th May	Attended London seminar run by BIOSS on their consultancy model	Wanted to see whether this model would be appropriate for inclusion in new course 'The HR Professional'	How Jaques' ideas on levels have been developed into a full consultancy model – this would be a useful example of theory-driven consultancy

Such records are normally stored on your computer and/or shared storage area. This makes it easy to update records, and to submit them electronically when required. Cloud storage, or use of space on your university server, allows you to access them from anywhere, and to allow access to tutors or others who might need to see them.

Learning journals – a reflective record

Learning logs and development records have their uses but are directed towards demonstrating that learning has taken place (or at least, towards claiming that it has). They do little to encourage more in-depth reflection.

If you want to create a forum for a reflective dialogue – with yourself or with others –then less structure may be helpful. This is where the idea of a learning journal comes in. Reflection on an event or experience is usually best carried out as soon as is convenient afterwards. You are more likely to do this if you use something you always have with you and are comfortable with. Phone, tablet or a small notebook are popular options. Some like to make an audio record, others like to include diagrams with words. If you do use a notebook then you will usually want to transfer notes to your main file. While this can seem extra work, it can also be an opportunity for further reflection. You may also sometimes find that a little distance allows you to be a little more honest with yourself about things that went badly or are challenging your identity. In my own example, above, on the train on the way home I noted in my little book (I was still a paper person at the time):

> This felt really weird – why? Think it was mainly time travel element. Last time I was in this room was 30 years ago – when I worked for the DE just around the corner and was doing my MPhil research on Jaques and his levels. Comforting that some ideas endure, though they seem to have developed it quite a lot. The 'flow' idea from Csikszentmihaly really resonates with my own experience of being over- and under-stretched. Someone mentioned this the other day as relevant to some other research. Wonder if/how it relates to coaching. Need to get his book and read more about it. If we want to demonstrate some HR consultancy underpinned by sound theory this would be a really good example to pursue. Need to contact BIOSS to see if they would be willing to provide a case study.

Part of the 'reflective conversation' needs to take place over a period of time, as your thoughts develop and also as you are able to distance yourself from the original event and your reactions to it, so revisit your reflections from time to time and see if there are additional thoughts you would like to add. (If resolutely paper-based, leave blank spaces in your notebook for such additions.)

Your reflections on learning form what is normally referred to as a learning journal. In contrast to a daily diary entry, a journal is driven by events – you record anything significant fairly soon after it happens, but significant things might not happen every day. Crucially, your learning journal incorporates a strong element of reflection, and captures this in a way that is easy to revisit and extend. Many students find it easiest to keep their learning journal in the form of a blog, and indeed many universities will offer space for personal blogs for staff and students. Such a blog can be private, or a vehicle for collaborative reflective dialogue.

Activity 3.8

Construct a journal entry on your learning from this chapter thus far. Choose your medium. Label your entry 'work on Chapter 3', date it, and write a fairly free-form entry. Possible questions to address, if you are unsure how to start, are:

- What is the most interesting thing I have read in this chapter and why was it interesting?

- What are the three main things I have learned from it?

- What, if anything, that I previously thought was true now seems as if it may be wrong?
- What was new or surprising in the chapter?
- Was there anything missing that I expected to find? Can I find this some other way?
- What am I still unsure about?
- What did I dislike about this chapter and why?
- Was there anything that particularly interested me? Can I find out more about this?
- What do I intend doing differently as a result of reading this chapter?
- What do I need to do to make it more likely that I will carry out this intention?

The questions in Activity 3.8 suggest a journal based purely on words. However, reflection is likely to be far richer if you extend your recording to include diagrams such as mind maps or rich pictures (see Chapters 4 and 12). One of the key elements in reflection is looking at relationships between things, and diagrams are normally far better for this than are words. If you are doing comparisons between different ideas say, you may also find it useful to use a table. The golden rule is to use what works for you and what works for the particular sort of thinking which the learning event requires.

➤ Ch 4
➤ Ch 12

Managing Your Learning

Understanding your own learning preferences and seeking to expand the range of learning styles which you can use will improve your ability to learn. Making time for reflection even – or perhaps especially – if your preferred style is more active will also help you learn in a way that will increase your employability. But perhaps most importantly, you need to *manage* your learning, using the self-management skills and the classic control model introduced in the previous chapter. It is this approach, with its emphasis on identifying learning needs, setting targets and monitoring progress which is likely to do most to improve your ability to learn – as well as practice your management skills. Key steps in managing anything, including your learning are:

➤ Ch 2

- identify objectives
- develop an action plan to achieve objectives
- implement the plan
- monitor progress and make any changes necessary to keep on target.

Targets need to be CSMART objectives (challenging, as well as the other criteria) which are fairly short term (achievable within three months), but which contribute to your achieving longer-term personal or career objectives. They should be based on an accurate assessment of strengths and weaknesses (and adequate evidence), should be agreed with your tutor, supervisor or other appropriate person, and regularly reviewed. These agreed targets need to be the starting point for an action plan which includes target dates for achieving each objective. Interim review dates will help you monitor progress, and you may need to revise the plan if progress slips. If you do, it is worth noting the reasons for any changes.

Formats for planning

Figure 2.3 in Chapter 2 is a simple planning chart which can be used to manage your studies as a whole. But your learning journal may throw up things which are more complex than 'read X', or 'complete assignment Y', which such a chart easily accommodates. A slightly more complex format which sought to capture the 'wot next' in the Butterfield version of a learning cycle would add a 'what next' column for further action.

A separate action plan might then be required for items in this column. Once you have tried a very basic format you might develop your own framework, in the light of course requirements and suggestions and your reflections from experience with the basic model.

The following example uses a format derived from that suggested by the Chartered Institute of Personnel and Development for demonstrating continuing professional development – a condition for remaining a member. It has four columns:

What do I want to learn?	What will I do to achieve this?	What resources and support will I need?	What will be my success criteria?
How to reflect more effectively	Experiment with the formats provided in this chapter to see what works for me. Discuss with tutor whether I could get some feedback	Notebook. Time. Input from others in my learning set. Feedback	To have actually kept journal for a month and submitted it for feedback. To feel I'm learning more effectively. To have used output from reflection to drive further learning via plan. Feedback from tutor to say this approach is acceptable as evidence

If using your plan as part of a portfolio exhibit giving evidence of your ability to manage your learning, you would need to include a commentary describing and justifying all the aspects outlined above; for example, your chosen priorities and learning activities, and the support you sought and obtained.

Learning Opportunities and How to Exploit Them

This chapter has considered learning as a continuous process of changing your thinking and ways of making sense of situations, rather than a series of one-off additions to a stock of relatively static knowledge. Whether you think in terms of the control loop or the Kolb cycle, learning from experience involves a process of sensing results of actions and modifying thinking and/or behaviour as a result. Feedback is thus a crucial component. Almost any situation will offer the scope for such feedback, and therefore the potential for learning, provided you want to learn. This means accepting that you are not yet perfect and all-knowing! While this may sound obvious, it can be quite difficult in practice as Chapter 8 makes clear. It is much more comfortable to see yourself as competent and doing an excellent job, and to blame other people or outside factors if things go wrong, than to accept the responsibility yourself.

➤ Ch 8

People who are protecting their view of themselves in this way will see any feedback which suggests scope for improvement as a slur on their competence, rather than a valuable piece of information. They are likely to reject the feedback with a 'Yes, but ...' reply instead of thanks. Just stop for a minute to check whether you have not already decided that while this may be true of others, you would never act in this way yourself. Learning from experience, from reflection or from feedback takes a degree of self-confidence, together with the belief that you do not have to be perfect to be a valuable person. Many of the books currently available on leadership stress the importance of self-awareness to effective leadership, and an honest self-appraisal as a route to this. (Justified) self-confidence is another key element in leadership.

If lack of confidence is making you avoid reflection, self-appraisal, and unfamiliar situations, your learning opportunities will be limited – new challenges normally offer far greater learning opportunities than the steady state. Welcoming the new is an important aspect of creativity and of leadership. More prosaically, if you actively seek new situations, you are likely to progress faster in any job than the person who stays with the safe, familiar, 'official' role. This is because taking on a challenge is likely to develop new skills, understanding and confidence. Of course, you need to understand your strengths and weaknesses. You will lose respect if you push to be allowed to do something way beyond your capacities. Instead, offer to do small extra jobs when someone senior to you is busy, or to cover for a colleague who is sick. Take on a challenging, but realistic, project. Such things will be noticed by those who can influence your progress, as well as provide material for your CV.

➤ Ch 16

If you have always 'played safe' you can usefully work at improving both your confidence and your motivation to learn. As a student you are in a relatively safe and supportive learning environment. You can take 'risks' very safely. So use the opportunity to experiment with non-preferred learning styles and to practise things you feel unsure about. If you are shy, force yourself to make contributions to group discussions and to make as many presentations as possible. If you hate IT, try to use as many of the bells and whistles on your computer as you can. Sign up for an optional course that you think you will find really difficult. Your confidence will be boosted by trying – and succeeding at – a challenging task. Your desire to learn will also grow.

Work experience

Explore the opportunities for gaining work experience as soon as possible if your experience is limited. Practising your transferable skills in a range of different contexts will help you develop them to a higher level. Potential employers will also be impressed. If your course offers the option of a placement year, start thinking about it *now*. If you are already committed to such a year, start thinking about the sort of placement that would offer the greatest learning opportunities. Think about how you can increase your chances of gaining such a position. If your course does not offer this kind of year, think instead about how to put your vacations to best use.

By the end of this book you should have a clearer idea of what skills areas are most relevant to you, and be much better at finding learning opportunities. But there is no need to wait until then. Each chapter offers you the chance to reflect on your learning needs and suggests approaches to meeting these. Indeed, the activities you have already done should have started this process.

Activity 3.9

Revisit the work you did in Activity 3.1 and the list of transferable skills outlined in Chapter 1. See whether you can add to your file note any learning opportunities that you missed – any situation where you can exercise a relevant skill, either practical or conceptual, and obtain feedback. (You should by now be more aware of possible opportunities.) Now think about whether there are things you are not currently learning but could be, if you sought the opportunity. The learning style exercises should have provided a starting point for thought.

Learning opportunities might come from adding a feedback and/or reflection dimension to things that you are currently doing, from taking a course that you had perhaps rejected as 'too difficult', or from taking advantage of opportunities outside your course during both term and vacations. Link this to the previous activity, to see whether you can progress your plans at all by taking a broader view of learning opportunities. You should be starting to get into a mindset of continually asking: 'What can I learn and how best can I learn it?'

Activity 3.10

Think about the past two weeks. What feedback did you receive on things you did? Did you consider it all carefully? Did you reflect on its implications? How might you have gained more feedback? What things did you fail to do that might have allowed you to learn? Did you take any decisions that would stop you from taking advantage of future potential learning opportunities?

If possible, discuss your thoughts with two or three other people, and plan to do three things differently in the next two weeks to make learning more effective. Review progress and note down your reflections at the end of that period.

Organising Your File

I have talked a lot now about the need to capture your plans, your reflections and your learning file. Indeed, you may be starting to feel that the activities directed at developing a file are just too time consuming. Relax – it doesn't take as long as you might think. And the potential benefits are enormous, even if you are not required to submit your file for assessment. Remember, you are trying to change some of the ways you think and some of the ways you do things so as to contribute substantially to your future success as a manager and leader.

Any change takes time and energy until it is embedded in your normal way of working. In the previous chapter you needed considerable energy to improve your time management. It takes similar energy levels to develop the habits of reflective practice, to seek learning opportunities and to plan actions that will maximise your learning. But as with time management, the benefits far outweigh the 'cost' in terms of effort.

Think back to what you learned about motivation, and apply this to motivating yourself.

- You need a clear goal, and one that will be rewarding to achieve. Remember, you are aiming to manage your learning in order to get a better degree than you otherwise would, and to prepare yourself for a really rewarding career – what you do now will affect much of the rest of your life.

- You need to believe that you *can* do it. It is fairly easy to get started if you use one of the suggested formats for planning and recording your learning. Although the initial time may be a scarce resource, the process is designed to make your learning more effective in future, so should save time overall. You will also be accumulating potential 'exhibits' for use in job applications or for an online showcase.

- You need to set yourself manageable milestones and to reward their attainment. Social rewards are powerful – you might like to work with someone on this. (Providing such rewards is the business of a whole industry of life coaches, but working with a fellow student who is trying to do the same thing allows you to practise 'co-coaching', and give feedback and mutual support.)

You also need to continually reassess your strengths, weaknesses and development needs. It is particularly important to appreciate and value your strengths – from these come both your confidence and your 'competitive advantage' in a group or organisation. As you learn, you will probably become far more realistic in your assessments. To quote Drucker (1999), again:

 Most people think they know what they are good at. They are usually wrong. More often, people know what they are not good at – and even then more people are wrong than right. The only way to discover your strengths is through feedback analysis.

Drucker goes on to explain that this involves writing down expected outcomes of all key actions and decisions and revisiting them a year or so later, comparing what really happened with the expectation and learning from the discrepancies. You could usefully revisit your SWOT at shorter intervals. It is worth making diary notes to ensure that you do revisit these aspects.

What is important is that you work out a file structure that works for you, and that you use it, and develop it further so as to maximise your learning, and create a history of your personal and professional growth during (and after) your time as a student that will showcase your talents and your work to potential employers or clients. Once you are motivated to plan and monitor your actions, and reflect and capture your reflections and learning, you can start to think about how you can usefully organise your file. Remember, the possible purposes for your file include:

- Helping you capture your learning to date so that you can see your progress
- Helping you manage your ongoing learning
- Keeping your reflections in one place, thus helping you to reflect more effectively
- Acting as a source of materials that showcase your learning and experience to tutors and potential employers and clients.

To achieve this you need at very least a clear contents list, sections relating to each of these purposes, and a means of cross referencing items as many may fit within more than one section.

Paper may be great for immediate reflections and notes, but a paper file is not easy to manage once it gets to bigger. Modifying, updating and sharing documents is not easy, nor is including photos, or audio or video recordings. Working electronically has obvious advantages. It is perfectly possible to keep your development file on your computer (with a good system for backing up, as it will become an extremely valuable set of documents). But most find that keeping your file somewhere that you – and others – can access wherever you are has many advantages. Free cloud storage is (currently) available from providers such as Google and Dropbox, or you can use your university's facilities,

---

TECHSkills 3.2 Virtual learning environments and ePortfolios

Universities use virtual learning environments (VLEs), sometimes called learning management systems. Such systems allow the university to communicate easily with students. Administrative information, timetables, assignment briefs, lecture notes, library links and other resources can be provided via the VLE. Staff can monitor student activities like assignment submissions and course registrations. VLEs also allow communication between students through chat rooms, wikis and blogs. Most also offer students an area to store their own learning materials, such as marked assignments, project outputs, reflective learning journals and other evidence of learning. When such materials are organised along the lines suggested for your learning file, they are often referred to as an ePortfolio.

➤

Different levels of access can be granted: some areas of the VLE can be private while some allow access to tutors, some to study group or module members, others may be open to everyone in the university. For students, a VLE makes it easy to share work and ideas with other students because of common formats and frameworks. You will be able to include not only text, but photos, video and audio files. It is easy to link to documents from different 'areas'. Backing up becomes the university's responsibility. Storage is free.

On the potential down side, access will normally be limited to university members, so sharing with friends on similar courses elsewhere will need some other system. More importantly, while you will probably be able to use your area for a year or three after graduating, you will need to remember to export your portfolio to some other system before your access is withdrawn.

Providers of ePortfolios outside of university

There are also new players in the market that offer ePortfolios independently of the VLEs. As they are stored outside of the university systems and access is usually more flexible – i.e. you are able to restrict access to particular documents only to yourself, to your peers, to your lecturer, to the whole institution, but crucially, also to the wider world.

This could allow you to share your portfolio with a potential employer, and even build a website that you could link to, for example, from LinkedIn. Importantly, they may also allow you to keep the portfolio live after you graduate – this way, the work comes with you, wherever you go.

An important caution, though, is that in making a portfolio publicly available on the web you are in effect 'publishing' it, so need to observe copyright law. Plagiarism in anything you publish is illegal, and the penalties more severe than those for plagiarism in your coursework. Similarly, there are libel laws you might potentially break if you say something unjustifiably negative about someone else.

3

LEARNING, REFLECTIVE PRACTICE AND PROFESSIONAL DEVELOPMENT

Activity 3.11

Ask around in your Career Centre, or ask a Student Support representative to tell you about portfolio options available at your university. Then, conduct research online into external portfolio providers and see if any offer you a good storage solution as well as allows you to share the portfolio externally.

SUMMARY

This chapter has argued the following:

- Learning, in the sense of developing knowledge, skills and ways of thinking that will make you more effective both as a student and in your subsequent working life is clearly crucial in a world that is highly competitive and rapidly changing.

- Learning is usefully seen as a continuous process dependent on feedback. Seeking situations in which such feedback can be obtained, and using it, will increase learning.

- Learning to make sense of complex situations (as is expected of graduates) involves using existing theory, and building and testing new models in the light of experience.

- People tend to have preferred learning styles which emphasise some aspects of learning at the expense of others. Developing less preferred styles can make learning more effective.

- Reflection is a crucial element in learning, and a habit of reflective practice is essential for any professional.

- Reflection involves a dialogue, with yourself and/or others, in which you question your experiences and responses to them with a view to developing the way in which you think about them and your future practice.

- Learning will be most effective if it is managed, with learning needs identified and action plans drawn up for what needs to be done for the necessary learning to take place. These plans need to be implemented and progress reviewed, with adjustments made if need be.

- Explicit plans need to be supplemented by a constant alertness to the learning opportunities and a willingness to take some risks in order to learn.

- Organising relevant materials (plans, reflections, etc.) into some form of personal development file or ePortfolio is essential.

Further information

Andreas, S. and Faulkner, C. (1996) *NLP: The New Technology of Achievement*, Nicholas Brealey.

This provides a range of exercises designed to increase your motivation and accelerate your learning.

Bassot, B. (2013) *The Reflective Journal,* Palgrave Macmillan.

Honey, P. and Mumford, A. (1986) *The Manual of Learning Styles*, Peter Honey.

Krishnamurti, J. (1995) *The Book of Life*, HarperCollins. This is a useful introduction to Krishnamurti's thinking, containing extracts from his writings during the period 1933–68. It addresses 'learning for life' in a very different way from the present book, but this different perspective can sometimes sharpen your awareness of existing assumptions and preconceptions.

Moon, J.A. (1999) *Reflection in Learning and Professional Development*, RoutledgeFalmer.

www.cipd.co.uk for examples of CPD logs.

https://www.youtube.com/watch?v=6B3tujXlbdk introduction to ePortfolios.

http://vark-learn.com/the-vark-questionnaire/ to assess your VARK preference.

https://books.google.co.uk/books?id=K-4cBQAAQBAJ&pg=PA5&lpg=PA5&dq=netiquette+ for+online+dialogue&source=bl&ots=NipPONeIoh&sig=KKiTFcQ6bBi1s3f5v0DFo3eJchY&hl= en&sa=X&ei=J_8OVbqaBo3qOOnhgMgD&ved=0CC8Q6AEwBDgK#v=onepage&q=netiquette for further guidance on netiquette.

http://www.pebblepad.co.uk/cs_documentation/PP_V2_Getting%20Started.pdf for a description of how to use one of the popular VLE systems and links to examples.

3

LEARNING, REFLECTIVE PRACTICE AND PROFESSIONAL DEVELOPMENT

PART 2
ESSENTIAL LEARNING SKILLS

Introduction to Part 2 – Essential Learning Skills

The whole of this book is about skills for learning, but this part focuses particularly on skills that will help you to learn from, and score good marks in, your academic studies. Is such a section necessary in a book aimed at students in higher education? Surely people who have spent twelve years or more 'studying' will have developed their study skills to a high level.

Sadly few of the university students I have taught or examined demonstrate *all* of the skills they need to a sufficient level: many still have serious shortfalls in several areas. Such students often find their courses unrewarding and experience serious stress. They learn very little, may drop out, fail, or at best gain a poor degree. This part of the book will help you to avoid such a fate.

The next few chapters cover skills which will have an immediate impact on your studies: finding useful sources, reading them efficiently and critically, and taking good notes will help you both as a student and in employment. Similarly, basic mathematics and communicating in writing are employment skills as well as important for study. Coping with written and oral exams may seem a peculiarly academic skill, but many of the same skills will be useful in other situations, such as when you are being assessed, for a job or for membership of a professional body. So 'doing well in assessment' is also highly transferable. A quick glance at some of the chapters will probably reassure you that you are already skilled to a high degree in many of these areas. Indeed, these chapters may seem absurdly basic to you. If so, skip them! Concentrate your energies instead on those chapters where you have concerns about your level of competence.

A single book can do no more than cover the basics. But the basics are just that – an essential basis for all else. Lecturers may wrongly assume that you already have a basic understanding. But if you lack it, you will learn little from their teaching of more advanced material. Use this book to fill any gaps. If you understand the learning process and are now taking active control of your own learning, this should not be difficult. Take each chapter as the starting point for developing your skills to the necessary level.

To help you do this, each chapter aims to show why the skills it covers are important and to outline any basic ideas you need to 'demystify' the topic. Further readings are suggested in case you feel you need more intensive help. Common sense, with a small amount of hard work, should make you competent even in areas where you currently regard yourself as 'useless'.

The final chapter in this part aims to help you gain good marks in assessment. It is therefore about *showing* that you have learned, rather than about learning itself. You probably want your qualification to be as good as possible – a better class of degree will normally increase your employability. Your marks in any assessment will partly depend on how hard you have worked and how much you know. But your grades may be at least as strongly influenced by how you *use* what you know in order to satisfy those who are assessing you. It is therefore important to pay attention to the techniques required to convince assessors that you have learned what they intended.

All the skills addressed in this part will be of use in almost any job you are likely to be doing after graduation. Given the rate of change in technology, legislation, professional practice and other factors relevant to most careers, you are likely to need to absorb large amounts of information in any graduate-type job. For the foreseeable future, much of this information will come from *reading* – increasingly, online materials. Important information will be numerical, and you need to be able to understand the stories the numbers tell. *Communication* with a wide range of people, often in writing, will be equally important, as will be your ability to exploit information systems and technology at your disposal. There are obvious parallels between satisfying your tutors and examiners, and performance appraisal and assessment for professional qualifications.

4
CRITICAL READING AND NOTE TAKING

Learning outcomes

This chapter, together with *practise of* the skills covered, should make you better able to:

- find and select useful written resources, using appropriate search techniques

- use techniques that will help you to make most effective use of time

- take a critical approach to what you read, questioning evidence, assumptions and reasoning

- take useful notes when reading, in lectures, or when using online material

- keep a record of your references, using software as appropriate.

Introduction

Information is crucial to understanding situations and taking decisions about them. Any decision will be only as good as the information on which it is based. (It will also depend on how you *use* that information.) Today the easy availability of information online is both an advantage and a potential hazard. It is easy to find a mountain of information on almost any topic. It is far less easy to work out which of it is potentially useful, and assess its value for your particular purpose.

This chapter is designed to help you to scan a wide range of materials fairly quickly, select those which seem to offer the most, and then read them *critically*. This means assessing their usefulness for your particular purpose. Usefulness will depend on the relevance of the information, and its validity. Although much of what you read will be online, and cutting and pasting is easy, note-taking skills are important, both in helping you organise your thoughts about what you read, and for later reference. Most important of all, particularly in an academic context, is recording not only what you read, but where you read it. You may later want to use it in assignments, reports for an organisation, or articles for a professional journal. Your notes need to include details of your sources, and there is software available to help. Most universities will now provide this. The chapter covers general principles, and seeks to convince you to invest time in learning to use whatever bibliographic software you are offered.

This chapter focuses on choosing and using written resources. Since you will spend thousands of hours on this during your studies, and many thousands more during your career, it is well worth developing your skills in this area. (The next chapter looks at dealing with basic numerical information – developed further in Chapters 13 and 14. Chapter 15 looks at how to find and generate information to answer a specific research question.)

These skills will enable you to study more efficiently, and will be an asset throughout your career. The ability to find, assess and use information and ideas is increasingly important in a context where the importance of evidence is widely recognised, but where so much of what is offered as evidence has little if any value.

'Simple' Reading Skills

Given how much of our lives we spend reading, it is surprising that many of us read very slowly, and do not always understand and/or retain much of what we read. This does not matter when reading for pleasure, but can seriously affect your learning when reading for work or study.

Speed reading techniques are often suggested as a near-miraculous approach to reading more quickly. While claims tend to be over-stated, some of the techniques, with practice, can help you scan materials rapidly during an initial search for information. They may also help you become a little more efficient when reading selected materials more carefully and thoughtfully, as you will need to do with much of your reading for study.

One form of inefficiency in reading comes from allowing your eyes to move to slowly, or wander around the text. Speed-reading techniques include using a pointer to help you

Reading Speed Test

This requires you to time how long it takes to read the next section quickly but carefully, without stopping, aiming to remember any significant information contained in the text. There will be a short test to check how much you have absorbed. Read without a break until you are told to look at your watch again. Look at your watch *now* and note your starting time before reading on.

look at only two points (or even a single one) per line. To check your reading speed, do the following exercise. It is important that you do this before reading further.

Most readers are unaware of their eye movements while they read, assuming, if they think about it at all, that their eyes are moving steadily along each line before moving to the next. If this were the case, reading at one line per second (which most people would guess to be a reasonable speed) you would cover 600–700 words per minute. At this pace you would find you could easily cope with the volume of reading materials you are likely to encounter on your course. Eye movements when reading are far more complex, however. The eye makes a series of extremely rapid jumps along a line, with a significant pause, 0.25 to 1.5 seconds, between each jump. Furthermore, many readers do not move straight along a line, even in this jerky fashion. Instead, as Figure 4.1 shows, they indulge in frequent backward eye jumps, fixating for a second or even a third time on a previous word, and at intervals their eye may wander off the page altogether. With erratic eye movements like this and forward jumps from word to adjacent word, many readers achieve reading speeds of only 100 words per minute. At this rate of reading, the volume of work for your course, or that found in many jobs, is likely to prove an impossible task.

At the purely technical level, it is possible to achieve reading speeds of up to 1000 words per minute by:

- reducing the number of fixations per line, stopping every three to six words rather than every one
- eliminating backward movement and wandering
- reducing the duration of each fixation.

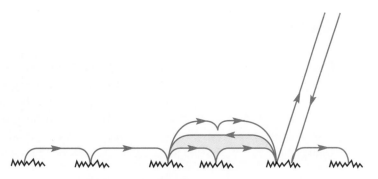

Figure 4.1 Typical eye movements while reading

It requires concentration and considerable practice to reach such speeds, and the method is designed for reading print rather than text on screen. But if it interests you, you might wish to experiment. If you are reading a lot of print, a reduction in eye movements could enable you to deal with reading printed material at work, or for your course, more quickly.

Furthermore, although you might expect comprehension to be reduced by more rapid reading, the reverse may well be the case. The pattern of a sentence and its meaning may emerge much more clearly and be more readily absorbed if the sentence is read in phrases rather than one word at a time. Your interest is more likely to be maintained if ideas are coming at you more quickly and your motivation will be higher if you feel you are making rapid progress, so the rewards of improved reading techniques are many.

You might ask why, given we read so much, most of us read so slowly. Remember that learning normally results from feedback. If there is no feedback to suggest the need for improvement, we are likely to establish bad habits more firmly, rather than to develop more rapid reading techniques. Breaking any habit is extremely difficult and takes considerable effort. Even when you have developed efficient reading techniques, you may still find that you have to make a point of consciously practising them at intervals, to prevent yourself from falling back into less efficient habits.

Reading Speed Calculation

Look at your watch again and note the time _____. Note how long it is since you last noted the time _____. There were approximately 590 words in that piece of text. Divide that figure by the number of minutes elapsed in order to find your reading speed in words per minute. Write this down _____.

As well as developing the ability to read at different speeds according to your purpose in reading, is the ability to 'read for sense'. This means actively thinking about what you are reading as you go along. Taking notes can be extremely helpful here, especially if your notes are more than a precis of what you have read, and impose some sort of structure on the ideas in the material, and the relationship between these ideas and other things you have read, or your own experience (see the section on note-taking later in this chapter).

Test Exercise 4.1

The activities you have carried out so far have not had 'right' answers, although sometimes the text which followed may have suggested the sort of thing that you might have written. The quiz which follows is the first exercise where your answers can be checked. Answers to test exercises are given at the end of the book.

Now check your comprehension and retention by answering the following questions, saying whether each statement is true or false according to the preceding text. Do not

➤

glance back at the text! Cover it so that you cannot. This is a check on what you have understood and can remember. Do the whole quiz before checking any of your answers. Remember, the information is for your use. It will tell you whether or not you need to do subsequent exercises. If you look back (or forward) before answering, you will lose this information.

True/false

1. Poor readers fixate once per word. ❑

2. With practice a poor reader can increase from a speed of 100 to 1000 words per minute. ❑

3. A speed reader will fixate only once per line. ❑

4. Once you have mastered speed reading techniques they will become second nature. ❑

5. The only drawback to rapid reading is that it tends to reduce comprehension. ❑

6. The duration of each fixation can range from as little as 0.25 of a second to as much as 1.5 seconds. ❑

The speed test and Test Exercise 4.1 will have given you some idea of your speed and comprehension/retention. If all your answers were right and you were reading at 250 words or more you may not need to work on your reading skills. If you do wish to invest time in developing your reading skills, use the online resource provided. It will give you practice in moving your eyes more efficiently in order to read faster and with less effort.

It is not enough to move our eyes efficiently. Text needs to be interpreted, so that the meaning and significance is understood and assessed.

Your interpretation of what your read will depend upon the context, on other things you have read or experienced, and on your judgement of its acceptability and potential usefulness. You can only interpret what is there, so it is important to be able to find suitable materials and select the most useful. Given the volume of information now available online, much of which may be irrelevant or invalid, you need to be able to 'search and assess' fairly quickly to select material that will be worth reading. If your reading skills are fine on paper, but you want to read more effectively from a screen, the following TECHSkills box may help.

TECHSkills 4.1 More effective reading from screen

If you are finding it hard to read something online, copy key text into a Word or similar document. You can then expand it or change the font to increase readability, cut out any ads, highlight parts of particular importance, or delete chunks that are not relevant.

> **Note: if saving this document ensure that you make clear it *is* a copy and note the url to avoid plagiarism.**
> Use your cursor as an eye guide, moving it steadily and following it with your eye.
>
> Alternatively, switch on your highlighter and drag highlight with cursor as you read. This acts to show the line you are reading, making it easy to follow, and if you stop reading you can 'save' the highlighted version, making it easy to resume at the point you stopped.
>
> Use your mouse to keep the line you are reading at the top of the screen to avoid eye-jumps backwards.
>
> If the text is really hard, look around for a more readable (though equally trustworthy) source; though beware of oversimplified consultants' offerings.

Selecting Materials and Choosing Reading Speeds

➤ **Ch 11**

➤ **Ch 2**

➤ **Ch 12**

A key skill is choosing material to read. Another is using an appropriate speed at which to read. Some lecturers provide long lists of books, articles and online resources. You may face a problem in knowing which will be most useful for an essay, and an even greater selection problem when doing a literature search for a dissertation. You may find it helpful to use a variant of the systematic approach to problem solving introduced earlier. You will find much more detail on how to search for and select information in Chapter 12.

Define your objectives

➤ **Ch 12**

What are you trying to achieve? Why do you want to read something on this topic? What do you really need to know? Are you seeking facts, ideas, theories or frameworks to help you develop your understanding? (More of this in the next section.) Are you looking for appropriate techniques or background information? Is the information something you may need for an examination? Is it necessary or potentially useful for a written assignment or clarification of something totally obscure from lectures? Is it merely for your own interest? Until you are clear what you want, you cannot start to look for it (though Chapter 12 explores some ways in which you may need to start with a vague idea and, through looking, find out enough to clarify your objectives).

Identify options

What sources exist? How easily can you access them? What does the library have in hard copy and what e-books and e-journals can you access? Until you are comfortable exploring by yourself, staff will usually be happy to help. Is a text sufficiently important to be worth buying? If so, is there a second-hand source? What does a bookshop have on the topic? Might there be something newer and cheaper than a suggested text that is as good or better. Ask teaching staff and other students for guidance, particularly before buying your own copy.

   If you are generating your own source list, look at references at the end of recent or key papers on the topic. See whether the library has copies of relevant theses or dissertations – they often have good reference lists or bibliographies. Search key words. Check whether there are relevant government publications – these tend to be available free of charge online. If relying on library books, do remember that others are likely to want the same ones at the same time. The early student gets the book!

Identify selection criteria

Obviously it is important that the book or paper covers the topic you are interested in. Are you only interested in reputable academic publications, or prepared to draw your net more widely? If so, you might choose to look only at information on government (.gov) or educational (.ac or .edu) sites. Are you interested only in recent publications or wanting to look further back in time? Are there particular areas of application (manufacturing? HR? public sector?) on which you would like to focus – or indeed exclude? Do you want to particularly include – or exclude – European, or US or Asian or other research? Are there any other factors which are important to your choice in this instance? Setting your criteria beforehand can help you focus your search more efficiently, as you can use appropriate search engines and search terms (see TECHSkills Box 4.2).

Searching for possible sources

You may have been given a list of things to read, but as your studies progress a reading list will increasingly become only a starting point. For a dissertation you will need to find suitable sources entirely by yourself. Once you have decided on your selection criteria you will want to search what is available as efficiently as possible. This means understanding the different places you can search, and how to use search engines effectively. Your university library is likely to offer most help here, and you can also find a wealth of tutorials online aimed at developing your search skills. TECHSkills 4.2 provides background information and suggestions that may help you make optimal use of such more in-depth resources.

➤ Ch 12

➤ Ch 12

> **TECHSkills 4.2** Searching online: the basics
>
> Given the plethora of online resources, efficient search techniques can save you many hours, and help you avoid missing important items. It may help to understand how some of the main tools can help you, what other places you can look, and the terms to use when searching.
>
> ### General search engines
>
> You will be familiar with using Google, Yahoo!, MSN or other search engines to find information online. These search engines have a database of web pages collected

4

CRITICAL READING AND NOTE TAKING

by computer programmes called 'spiders' which crawl around the web following links between pages. The search engine will select what the spiders have collected, and provide links to pages which match what you asked for. Note that because they are searching their 'copy' of what they have found, some of these links may not work when you try them. Note, too, that you may get different results with different search engines and from the same engine at different times as they order results according to popularity and financial factors.

Metasearch engines

These will search using several search engines and give you the combined result, thus partly getting around the issue of different results from different engines.

Specialist search engines

General search engines look at everything. A more specialised search engine will look at a more specific selection. Perhaps the most useful is Google Scholar, which searches only academic sources. It also gives information on 'cited by', which shows later papers which used the work – an indication of how influential it has been, and 'related articles' which may suggest additional useful search terms if your original search has been too narrow.

Library catalogues

You may find your university library's e-catalogue is easy to use, and your best way of finding relevant articles. However, some such catalogues are better suited to helping you find books or articles you have already identified as relevant. If this is the case, starting with Google Scholar to find a reference, and then going to your library catalogue, may be more efficient.

Specific journals

If you are interested in a specific area (e.g. LEAN manufacturing) check your library's list of journals on this or related topics and look at recent articles on your topic of interest. The reference lists at the end of any relevant articles will suggest further things you might like to scan.

Online repositories

Increasingly, universities offer free access to research by their staff (see, for example, the Open University's open research repository at http://oro.open.ac.uk/. Such repositories will be easily searchable by topic.

Author websites

If you are interested in work by a particular author you will often find useful information on this, and perhaps links to openly available resources, from the author's personal website.

Online 'digests'

There are now many online equivalents of textbooks which can provide a good starting point. An obvious staring (though not ending) point is Wikipedia. This is unreliable in that it can be altered by anyone and may not always be accurate, so you should never rely upon it, or cite it in your writing. But entries may provide a good starting point, often covering related ideas and listing references which can be helpful in your own search. Always check information against other sources.

More controlled versions of digests, where the provider commissions and 'publishes' content, often as a way in to paid-for training or resources are slightly more reliable. A useful example is http://www.businessballs.com/. Check whether tutors are happy with you citing such sources, or whether, as with Wikipedia, you should merely use them as background information.

Another source of useful information is professional institutes, such as the CIPD. Their website often has some useful and/or topical information openly available (though for more detail you may need to be a member). Such information is reliable enough to be cited, or can be used to extend or refine your search.

Online essays

You will find a plethora of essays available, free or for a modest price. Avoid these like the plague. They are of variable quality, and if you are tempted to use them you will be caught: universities have software that will easily detect such plagiarism.

Note 1: Whenever you find a relevant source, save the address, with a brief note of why it was useful and the date you accessed it. You will need to list the address just as you would any other reference when referring to the information in anything you write.

Note 2: When saving/copying material found online, remember to make it very clear that this is a copy, so that you do not inadvertently later use it as if it were your own, which would be plagiarism.

Selection

Once your search has found some potentially useful materials, you need to choose which to look at more carefully. For journal articles it may be enough to scan a summary of the article. Google Scholar, even if not giving you access to the whole article will give free access to such summaries. Your university catalogue will allow you to access the entire article, but even so, the summary is the place to start.

You will often be faced with many more sources than you have time to read. To select from these you can use the title, any summary, and a very fast scan of the whole article or chapter if it is available. It is worth remembering that in North America in particular, academic tenure depends largely on the length of an academic's publication list, so there is enormous pressure to publish regardless of the density of the ideas or the information contained in the book or article. It is all too easy to think that everything in print or e-journal is worthy of your attention, but this is far from the case. You need to form a judgement for yourself.

An important graduate skill is to know how to separate that which has value from that which is less so, whether because it is only slightly relevant to your topic, rather dated, from a doubtful source, based on weak evidence, or the logic seems flawed.

The section on critical reading later in the chapter addresses judging *content*.

Varying your reading speed

You can save time by varying your reading speed according to your purpose in reading. Sometimes you will be looking for a highly specific piece of information. Did this research use a particular technique? What sample was used? What does the author have to say on a particular point? If your purpose is to answer such questions use the index, plus rapid scanning of the material to identify the part you need to read in detail. Just as you can hear your name being mentioned at the other side of a crowded room, so you can bring selective attention to bear on written materials. While scanning the page too rapidly to read it, you can still notice the word or phrase you need. This will require serious concentration, however, and a refusal to be side-tracked, unless you can spare the time: interesting digressions are, after all, what true education is all about.

Use slightly slower, but still rapid reading to get a picture of the overall pattern of a book, chapter or article. For this, focus first on any contents list, then introductions and summaries, main headings and subheadings. Diagrams and tables of results are useful too. Several rapid passes may help you map the material better than a single slower one.

Speed reading at your fastest speed may be suitable for lengthy materials, where the level of relevance is fairly low, or for background reading. Your aim will be to absorb the main arguments and assess the extent to which these are based on relevant and reliable evidence.

Much of your study will, however, require a slower reading rate, since you will need to think really hard about the concepts and arguments contained. You will probably need to take notes, both to aid comprehension and for later recall. You may sometimes need to stop reading, think and perhaps consult other sources before proceeding.

You may find that once you have devoted time to understanding all the details, relationships and possible uses of material, you have in the process learned it. If not, and your memory is likely to be tested, try to devise a mnemonic, this is, something which is easier to remember than the thing itself. Acronyms or rhymes are good for this. You can probably already remember the requirements for objectives because SMART is so easy to remember and it is easy to go from that to what the letters stand for. The stages of group formation introduced in Chapter 9 are easily remembered as 'form, storm, norm, perform'. Sometimes rote learning may be useful, particularly if frequent fast recall is needed. This is the way multiplication tables were once taught, involving going over and over something until it sticks. Rote learning can decay rather more quickly than rhyme or acronym, so it needs occasional refreshing for anything you seldom need to recall.

➤ Ch 9

Reading Critically

➤ Ch 3 The idea of questioning the material you read was introduced in the previous chapter in the context of reflection on what you learned from reading. There, the focus was very much on how what you read related to *your* existing mental models, and whether it suggested that you might be able to enhance or improve them. Now you need to look critically at the material itself, and its author.

Critical thinking is a key graduate skill, and emphasised in the learning outcomes for many courses. So it is important to get a clear idea of what is meant. 'Critical' is not used in the sense of saying disparaging things about an author. Rather, it means engaging with the materials at a 'deep' level and making sure that you understand:

- the claims that are being made
- the arguments used
- the evidence that the author is using to support these claims
- how these claims relate to those made by other authors
- the context within which the author is writing.

There may be cultural, discipline-based or other assumptions which are never made explicit but which underpin the claims made. When you read critically you need to be alert to these assumptions, and prepared to question them.

It is also helpful to know *when* the author was writing. Some older books and papers offer splendid insights, and are often clearer than later 'improvements' to the ideas. But it is important to be aware that organisations and their contexts might have been very different at the time of writing, and to consider the implications of these differences if drawing conclusions about the present.

Theory and the nature of claims

Having established the context in which something was written, the next step to becoming a critical reader is to understand the sorts of claims being made. By claim I mean any idea which someone proposes as true or helpful. Usually they give reasons for this claim. The claim and its associated reasons constitute an argument. Before looking at arguments and how they are constructed, it is helpful to understand some of the terms used. In particular I should like to look at possible differences between concept, model, metaphor, framework and theory. I say 'possible' because these terms are used in different ways by different authors. Even though these words are distinguished differently on occasion, the distinctions themselves are worth noting.

Claims may be supported – or challenged by existing, generally accepted 'management theory'. They may be challenges to such theory, and/or propose new theory, so it is important to understand the nature of theory when checking or making claims in the academic domain.

The word is used very loosely in management: in science 'theory' is more narrowly defined. Figure 4.2 shows a possible ways of classifying management theory (classification

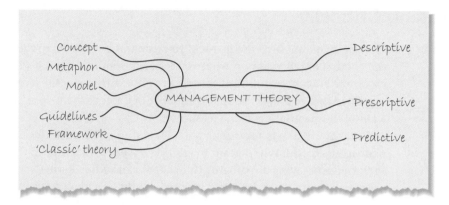

Figure 4.2 Possible typology of management theory

can be seen as a form of theory building). To the right are types of function, to the left types of content. Here concept can be seen as the building block of everything else save metaphor. Proposed relationships between concepts are the glue.

A *concept* is any abstract idea. 'Motivation' is a concept. 'Learning' is a concept. 'Hidden agenda' is a concept. Such concepts can be helpful in making you aware of an aspect of a situation and helping you to understand it. I can still remember my excitement when I first came upon the idea of hidden agendas, and started to look for the *real* objectives of people in meetings, something it had never occurred to me to consider before. In the previous chapter I mentioned 'cognitive housekeeping': adding a new concept is one of the ways you can improve your 'cognitive house'. When you are reading something, it is important to understand any concepts which the author uses and with which you are not familiar. Be particularly alert to 'everyday' words or phrases that seem to be being used in a non-everyday manner. ('Critical' is one such example in this chapter.) If you do not understand the specialist sense in which the word is being used then your reading will be of little benefit.

A *model* in everyday language is a simplified representation of something. Thus, the map of the London Underground is a model of one aspect of the system itself, namely the relationship between lines and stations on a line. An architect's 3D representation of a building they have designed is another type of model. When you are diagramming a situation you are creating a model of it, often concentrating on only one aspect of the situation. It is important to remember this uni-dimensionality when dealing with models, and not to confuse them with the reality: 'the map is not the territory'.

A *metaphor* is the use of a familiar term to describe something probably less familiar. It carries with it the suggestion that understanding the former will help you understand the latter. Examples include talking about an organisation as a 'well-oiled machine', or 'a tight ship'. Metaphors can usefully highlight key features of a situation. Morgan (1986) uses the spider plant as a striking metaphor for one form of organisational structure. But they are only as useful as the similarities contained. The comforting feeling of understanding that they give can be a dangerous illusion if you draw too many conclusions. As with models, you need to remember that metaphors only partially resemble the thing you are applying

➤ Ch 14   them to. Metaphors can, however, be a great aid to creativity, as discussed in Chapter 14.

Framework tends to be used to indicate a rather more organised abstraction. Frameworks are extremely common in management 'theory'. Thus you may well encounter the 4 (or 7) Ps in your marketing studies. Such frameworks tend to provide useful checklists for analysing a situation. If you wanted to look at the environment in which you were operating you might use STEEPLE (and look at sociological, technological, environmental (in the physical sense), economic, political, legal and ethical factors surrounding the organisation). You have already tried SWOT and SMART as frameworks for examining yourself and formulating your objectives.

'Management theory' is often used as a loose collective term to refer to any of the above, but it is more useful to think of *theory* as being an organised set of assumptions which allow you to make predictions about a situation. The STEEPLE framework alerts you to different categories of factors that might be important, but does not in itself allow you to predict anything. Expectancy *theory*, however, allows you to make a number of predictions. For example, it suggests that if you reduce the value of outcomes, or link them less closely to performance, or make it appear less likely that effort will produce performance then less effort is likely to be made. Management theories in this sense are rather less common than frameworks.

Management writing varies greatly. Sometimes the author may be proposing a new theory or a new framework, or may be critiquing some other theory. Or they might be describing a case study, or (in the case of some of the less academic publications) proposing the answer to life, the universe, and everything. When you are reading critically it is helpful to be clear whether the author is proposing – or drawing on – a theory or framework, or using metaphor. Some of the questions you would ask while reading will depend upon the nature of the claim.

Analysing the argument

In most papers you read, the author will be claiming that one or more statements are justified/true/useful, and providing arguments from evidence (which might be other theories, or research data or even armchair observations) to support this case. So before going further you need to work out the main claim that the author is making, and indeed any secondary claims. As an example of this sort of thinking I'll take another classic motivation theory, Herzberg's (1966) 'motivation–hygiene' theory: you are likely to encounter this at some point in your studies, and we have already introduced two other theories of motivation so it allows comparison. I shall abbreviate the argument here, for simplicity.

Herzberg claims that man has two sets of needs: one set concerns the need to avoid pain and the other concerns the specifically human need to grow psychologically. This claim is supported by the results of interviews with 200 engineers and accountants 'who represented a cross-section of Pittsburgh industry'. Interviewees were asked to think of a time when they had felt especially good about their jobs, and then to answer questions about why they had felt like that, and its impact on their performance, personal relationships and well-being. This process was then repeated for a time when they had negative feelings about their job. Five factors stood out as strong determinants of job satisfaction: achievement, recognition (for achievement), work itself, responsibility and advancement. Dissatisfaction was associated with company policy and administration, supervision, salary, interpersonal relations and working conditions. Thus satisfaction was associated with the person's relationship to what they do, dissatisfaction with the context within which they do it. A chart showing how responses are distributed is included, which broadly supports the 'two-factor' idea. Although most things are cited in the context of both satisfaction and dissatisfaction, mentions in the 'wrong' category are much less frequent than those in the 'right' one.

Remember the original claim: there are two categories of human need operating. The evidence to support it appears plausible. Different circumstances seemed to cause feeling good about your job, and feeling bad. But how adequate is the evidence? No detail is given about whether the 'theory' was already known to the person categorising the responses, or whether the experiment was done blind. There is room for subconscious bias in any subjective judgements: the paper I was reading (an extract from a book) did not make this clear, so I would need to go back to the original research paper to check the method. (At this point you would make an action note to do this.)

What about the sample of people interviewed? You could argue that two professional groups in a single US city is not really a representative sample. Would blue collar workers respond in the same fashion? Would poor people in other countries be similarly unmoved by money? Might people have different priorities and reactions today from those found in 1966?

Then what about the reasoning? Is the conclusion inevitable from this evidence? Would you get these results *only* if people had two different sets of needs? There is quite a lot of evidence to suggest that in other contexts we tend to take personal credit for good things that happen to us, and blame others for the bad. Herzberg's results could be explained equally well by this human tendency. Alternatively, as indeed Herzberg points out, the 'motivators' tend to be associated with performing the task, the 'dissatisfiers' with the context in which it is performed. Would not expectancy theory, which was being developed at around the same time, predict a similar result? And in a way that enabled further predictions to be made about ways in which strengthening the effort–outcome link could increase motivation?

The next question is the 'so what' one. At the time, Herzberg's theory had a profound influence on organisations. It proposed a whole new approach to improving employee motivation. Instead of pay rises, organisations found ways of increasing responsibility. A whole 'job enrichment' industry grew up, following a very prescriptive approach which Herzberg developed. (Indeed, this is still the thrust of many job redesign exercises today, although because the underpinning theory is less simplistic, the chances of success are arguably higher.)

Did it work? Sometimes. But in other cases the effort–performance link was already weak because the staff concerned did not have the skills to do what was required beforehand. Giving them additional responsibility actually made things worse, as expectancy theory would have predicted. It might have saved a lot of money in some of the organisations concerned if a more critical reading of Herzberg had been undertaken before job enrichment was embarked upon.

Mapping the argument

In looking at this particular, much quoted and, at the time, highly influential piece of writing, I was trying to do three things:

- identify the claim being made
- evaluate the evidence being used in support of the claim
- evaluate the reasoning used to link the evidence to the claim.

It can be helpful to approach this graphically. You can use an argument, as shown in Figure 4.3, or a mind map or spray diagram similar to that used in Figure 4.4. If using a spray diagram, you could use a branch for each 'reason' and twigs for the pieces of evidence that together form that reason.

Alternatively, branches might show different logical links. Thus, one set of twigs might 'prove' something, make it fairly likely to be the case, be consistent with it, be inconsistent with it, make it fairly unlikely, or actually disprove it. You could write the appropriate label on the branch. When you have a complex argument, unless there is actual proof – rare in management research – you will be faced with working out how much weight to give to the different reasons. This will depend upon the strength of the evidence itself, its consistency, and the strength of the evidence–claim links.

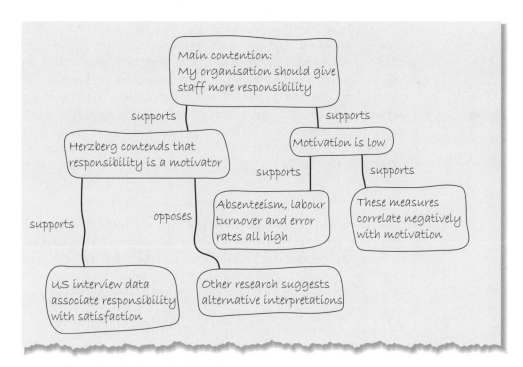

Figure 4.3 Example of an argument map

Although we have been talking about mapping other people's arguments, the technique is equally valuable for mapping your own reasoning when you are planning an essay answer. If you are planning a research project or dissertation it can also be invaluable to think about your potential evidence before you finalise your research design, and consider how it would relate to claims you might hope to make in your report.

➤ Ch 7, 15

Software packages which allow you to map arguments can be really useful if the argument is complex. And arguments can be *very* complex, with many reasons operating on several levels. In these cases each twig is in itself a claim, and has supporting reasons (premises), objections to reasons (rejoinders) and objections to objections (rebuttals). By teasing them apart it is possible to evaluate each chain of claim-supporting claim-evidence, by looking both at the logic involved and the evidence (and assumptions) to which this logic is applied. As in the example above, you may find that both the evidence and the reasoning leave something to be desired. If you are interested in this, you can find material online. It may be designed to support – and sell – a particular product, but in the process may provide more detailed teaching than there is room for here (try **www.austhink.com/reason/tutorials**).

Activity 4.2

Select an article from a business or management journal or professional magazine. Try to identify: the principle claim and any secondary claims. If applicable, it may help to decide whether theory, framework and/or metaphor are involved. Define any new concepts. Ask 'so what?' If the claim is true, what does it imply? If the implications are important enough to justify the effort, try to tease apart the arguments involved. What claims and/or evidence are used to support the claim(s) and what, if any, evidence is used to support any intermediate claims? What are the logical links used? Do they add up to a valid argument provided the evidence is sound (i.e. is the conclusion drawn the only possible one)? Is the evidence adequate? Are there any hidden assumptions being made? If so, how valid are these assumptions?

Hidden assumptions are difficult to identify but may be critical to an argument. There was a hidden assumption in the Herzberg case, which you may have seen once the alternative explanation was pointed out. This was that 'no other explanation is possible'. Once this assumption was queried, other possible explanations were looked for, and some found. So when a reason is offered it is always worth asking whether this reason is sufficient in itself to support the claim.

The other difficulty in business research is the complexity of most of the issues addressed, and the variety of contexts in which these issues arise. This makes it difficult to obtain convincing evidence and hard to know how far to generalise from it. Even if the evidence and argument were adequate in their context, would it be reasonable, for example, to draw conclusions about all employees from two professional groupings in one city? It was clear in the example above how difficult it was to interpret the subjective responses given by the professionals concerned. There is a real dilemma faced by many authors between seemingly 'scientific' quantitative data and the richer, but harder to interpret, qualitative information. More of this in Chapter 12.

➤ Ch 12

There are many other useful questions to ask when reading critically. A basic selection, including those already covered, is given in Box 4.1.

Box 4.1 Useful questions when reading critically

- When/where was this written and what was the author's purpose?
- What claims is the author making?
- What new concepts are introduced, and what do they mean?
- Are they really new, or merely a 're-badging' of existing ideas?
- How/when might they be useful?
- What new frameworks are introduced?
- What do they add to existing frameworks?
- How/when might the new frameworks be useful? Are there limitations to their application?
- Is there any new theory introduced?
- Do the 'organised assumptions' that make up the theory hang together logically?
- Does it extend an existing theory? (Sometimes quite small additions can be surprisingly useful.)
- Is it consistent with other theories that you already know? If not, what are the inconsistencies? Are they explained/justified?
- How/when might the new theory be useful? Are there limitations to its application?
- Are there ways in which this new theory might usefully be amended?
- Was the author arguing a case to which they were personally committed? (This can indicate potential for bias.)
- How good is the argument supporting the claim? Are there any shortcomings in the evidence or the logic, or any hidden assumptions which might be questioned?
- If there are inadequacies, is this because the paper is a shortened version of something else? If so, could you find more of the evidence by looking at other sources?

Notes and Annotations Using Words and Diagrams

Note taking is a crucial skill for both study and employment. Your notes help you remember something afterwards, but additionally are a key component in active learning. If you are one of those who learn best by writing, taking notes will be one of your best

Take notes for:

- concentration
- understanding
- retention
- reference
- revision.

'aids'. Although this chapter is mainly about written resources, note-taking skills will be helpful in lectures, interviews and at any other time when you need to capture the essence of something.

In writing good notes you are *organising* material, and therefore organising your thoughts. By extracting themes and key points, and jotting them down in a way that *makes sense* to you, you are interacting with the material. This interaction engages your mind. It stops your attention drifting off. It is *interesting*. It means that you will *absorb* the key points you have extracted, almost without effort. And good notes are likely to be far more useful to you in essay writing or revision than the original material.

'Good notes' are clearly more than a verbatim record of a lecturer's words or a section of text. Of course, there will be times when a diagram or piece of text is so important that you will want to copy or save the whole thing. Even if you do this, notes can still be helpful.

Whenever your notes include direct quotes it is absolutely essential to make this very clear, so that when you come back to them you know which parts are the author's words and which your own. There are two reasons for this. First, you may want to quote exactly what someone said when you are writing an essay or dissertation, so you need to know which words are a direct quotation – you will need to give the page number from which the quote is taken (see the guidance on referencing later in the chapter) so remember to note this against the quote. Second, and possibly even more important, if you quote without giving credit to an author, this is the deadly (in academic terms) sin of *plagiarism* (discussed shortly). If your notes do not make clear what is a direct quotation you are in danger of committing accidental plagiarism.

Because keeping track of references can be highly time-consuming, software has been developed to make the job (relatively) easy. TECHSkills 4.3 may help if you are not familiar with such software.

TECHSkills 4.3 Using bibliographic software

In any academic writing you will be expected to list your references, in the approved style. In the old days of print journals in libraries this often involved hours of frustrating searching if you were lazy about noting and then filing references when you were researching a topic, and hours of typing when you finally located them. Fortunately, electronic availability of materials now allows the whole process to be quick and painless if you use bibliographic software (RefWorks and EndNote are two such packages in common use). So useful are these tools that your university is likely to provide such software for students.

The advantages are that you no longer need to type in a reference – the software does it for you! As well as creating your own 'library of references' it will allow you to search them by author, topic, date, or many other fields, to insert the citation within an essay or paper, with a couple of clicks, and create the reference list at the end in an output style

➤

of your choice. Thus if your university required Harvard style references, but the journal to which you were sending a paper based on your essay required a different style, the programme would obligingly make the changes for you.

You may, however, lose access to the system a year or two after you leave the university, so would need to either sign up with the system in your own right, or export your library elsewhere.

Because different systems are in use, and because each is likely to provide comprehensive tutorials in how best to use it, there is little point in going into detail here. The main point is to find out what your university provides and invest time as soon as possible in learning to make efficient use of that system. If none is provided, consider subscribing to a system in your own right – some basic versions are available free. See, for example, http://endnote.com/product-details/basic and others which offer a free trial.

Notes and learning

As suggested earlier, the active process of organising material into notes can maintain your concentration and help you sort out the structure of what the author is saying (you might try mapping their arguments). Thus you learn at a deeper level, understand more and remember more than if you merely read passively.

Not only that, good notes can often be far more useful than the original material. They will be easier for you to understand, as you will have organised the material into a form which makes sense to you. You can also include cross-references to relevant material from other sources or other courses. If working on paper, you can use colour to emphasise structure and aid memory. Notes which are briefer than the originals are likely to be much easier to refer to and to revise from. This is particularly the case if you devise an indexing system which allows you to find related topics easily.

As with everything else, you need to be clear about *why* you are keeping notes. If you are working with borrowed materials which will be crucial for a major project later, you will need to keep more detailed notes and to copy quotations and key diagrams as well as any useful references that you may need to explore and/or quote. When accessing materials on the Internet there is a strong temptation merely to copy huge chunks. While such copies may have their uses, remember the advantages of notes just mentioned. Without active 'digestion', condensing and restructuring you are likely to miss major benefits. Keep a full copy for reference, but make brief notes to supplement this. The same applies to photocopying. Apart from the potential expense, copies of papers and chapters will not help you merely by sitting on your shelves. Indeed, if they give you a false sense of achievement they can be a hindrance. They are only any good when you *interact* with them. So how can you do this effectively?

Annotation

If you are working with your own hard copy of materials, the most basic form of note taking is annotation, highlighting key points or concepts and making brief marginal notes or inserted comments. This will ensure that you are *thinking* as you read, searching for the key ideas, and that you stay awake. When you return to the materials you will be able to extract key points from the highlighting, and the brief notes you have added will remind you of relevant examples from elsewhere or how you finally sorted out a point in the text that was confusing. If working from a Word document you can highlight, and/or use the <review> then <new comment> commands to insert comments into the margin to serve the same purpose.

Précis or summary

When you cannot annotate materials, or if you want more condensed notes, it can be helpful to make a précis or summary, where you write down key points made. If working from annotated materials, you may merely jot down your highlighted words plus marginal comments. But ideally you are aiming to say something more concise than the original *and in your own words*. The translation process will go far to making the meaning sink in. Normally, you will want your summary to be organised point by point, even if the original is less clear. Journal articles typically start with a summary, and it may be useful to save these. But they are no substitute for making your own summary, as cutting and pasting dose not engage your brain!

Diagrammatic notes

In taking notes you will often be looking for *relationships* – between ideas in a text or lecture, or between this material and some other. Diagrams are a particularly useful technique for representing relationships, with huge advantages over linear text for this purpose. A number of diagramming techniques are introduced at different points in the book: you have already encountered argument mapping. This is part of the same 'family' of diagrams as the more general mind-mapping technique, sometimes called brain patterns, described by Tony and Barry Buzan (2003). Variants of this basic form will appear in a variety of contexts and with different names. It is extremely versatile; note taking is just one of its applications.

In drawing a mind map, you start in the centre of the page, with a word or phrase indicating the main idea or central theme, then branch out from this, giving each sub-theme a separate branch. These branches divide further into sub-sub-themes. If you are exploring your own thoughts in this way it is called a mind map. If you are teasing out the content of something else, then it is often called a spray diagram. Figure 4.4 shows an example of a spray diagram on note taking. In the next chapter you will see how a similar diagram can be used to plan the structure of something that you are going to write. Software is readily available for drawing mind maps, and many students find this useful. Computer-drawn mind maps look much neater but they may be less memorable and can sometimes feel more constrained.

Buzan highlights the following advantages of this type of diagram over linear notes:

● The central idea is more clearly defined

● Position indicates relative importance – items near the centre are more significant than those nearer the periphery

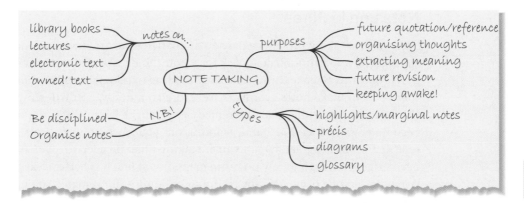

Figure 4.4 Diagrammatic notes on note taking

- Proximity and connections show links between key concepts
- Recall and review will be more rapid and more effective
- The structure allows for easy addition of new information
- Patterns will differ from each other, making them easier to remember
- (For divergent, creative use – covered later) the open-ended nature of the pattern helps the brain make new connections.

Thus you can see how mind maps help you with both the digesting and structuring of material you are studying and its later recall.

Activity 4.3

Return to whatever notes you took on Chapter 3 (or to the chapter itself if you did not take notes). Draw a mind map of the main points. Reflect on the extent to which this helped to make the structure clearer. If working with others compare diagrams and discuss both your diagrams and the extent to which they helped. Draw mind maps for the next five serious chapters or articles that you read. You should be hooked on the technique by then!

Activity 4.4

Prepare an exhibit showing that you can select, read and summarise in note form an appropriate chapter or paper. Your exhibit will need to document your objectives, the selection process used, the full reference of the text selected and your summary.

Notes on lectures

Lecture note-taking presents a particular challenge, as you have to go at the speed of the lecturer and cannot usually ask for a point to be repeated until you have grasped it. A few lecturers make things easy by providing handouts with the slides they use, so that you can make notes against these. More commonly, you will simply need to do the best you can at the time and remedy any deficits later. While you do not need to become proficient at shorthand, working out your own abbreviations for frequently repeated words is a great help. If you are taking notes on a lecture, you may eventually become good enough to rely on mind maps, but at first it is better to keep more narrative notes on one page, perhaps trying to build up a mind map in quiet moments on the facing page.

Some lecturers distribute their notes in hard copy. Does this mean you do not need to take notes during the lecture? It does rather depend upon your preferred learning mode. Some people who are strongly auditory may find that taking notes gets in the way, and if notes are to be provided it is best not to make their own. Most people, however, will find that note taking has the same benefits in lectures as it does when reading in terms of maintaining their concentration and forcing them to engage with the key points being made and the relationships between them. If relying on handed out notes, make sure you go through them soon after the lecture and note any additional thoughts you had, or queries you need to follow up.

As well as drawing mind maps, try using sketch diagrams. These can sometimes clarify meaning more quickly than words. Space is useful too – leave gaps for things you missed. Leave space, too, for things which will need expansion if they are ever to make sense to you three months later. Indicate as you go along all the points where your notes are not adequate. Then discipline yourself to make good the deficits *as soon as possible*. You will be able to do this relatively easily within 24 hours, while the event is still fresh in your mind. Check with others whose notes, memories or comprehension may be better than yours. If you wait more than a day, the task will be far more difficult, if not impossible.

Discipline and organisation

Whatever your note-taking and storage methods, it is vital that you have – and consistently use – a system for organising them. Well organised notes can be invaluable. Dozens of scruffy pieces of paper scattered around your flat or cryptically labelled documents strewn at random around your computer will not allow you to find what you need when you need it.

Title notes carefully. And build up a good index to your materials, so that you know what notes you have on which topics and can easily find both the original notes and any related materials.

Back up all your files at regular intervals, ideally to storage located well away from your machine so that you do not lose them in the same burglary or fire that destroyed the originals. Cloud storage is ideal, indeed your university may offer this facility, though you might need to remember to export everything you want to use after graduation *before* the university removes your access (which may be a year or two after you graduate.) You can also use Dropbox or Google docs for back up.

Alternatively, you can use a free app such as OneNote or Evernote, which is designed both to make it easy to take notes by better than in using Word and to store them in the Microsoft cloud. You can then easily access them from your phone or other devices and share them with others. It is easy to include links to web pages, or copy content from the web, or insert images you already have on file. The flexibility of the system for note taking is an advantage over other forms of cloud storage, and many students find this app invaluable. Again, you can access free tutorials in its use, so it is well worth at least trying this if you have not already done so.

If you still find paper notes help you think better, make sure that pages are titled and numbered so that if they get dropped or shuffled you can put them back together, and file them carefully.

> **For good note taking:**
>
> - use words and diagrams
> - 'organise' content
> - improve' within 24 hours
> - file systematically.

Organised and disciplined notes will have potential uses beyond the particular course to which they relate. (This is why the ability to search your references by topic as well as author is important.) Your notes (and references) may be a useful resource for a subsequent dissertation or project, or indeed help in a situation at work. Unless you are very pressed for space, it is therefore worth retaining them. It can be infuriating to need something and then realise you deleted it a year ago, or have since changed computer and failed to keep a back-up copy.

Similarly, you will have many occasions after your degree when you will need to take notes. Whether you are interviewing potential employees, listening to a speaker at a professional association, reading a lengthy report or sitting in a meeting, you will need similar skills so it is worth developing the skills – and the discipline – to take notes that will be of use after the event.

Avoiding Plagiarism

Plagiarism is the greatest academic sin you can commit. 'Stealing' someone else's ideas or words can cause you to fail a module, or in serious cases to fail the entire qualification. This is a deserved penalty when the plagiarism was a deliberate form of cheating. But sometimes it is because of carelessness in notetaking.

To avoid this you need to make very clear any content in your notes that is copied from elsewhere so that when you use it you either turn it into your own words, or put quotes around it and cite the author, date, and page reference (if there were page numbers). You then need to give a full list of references at the end, including the details of everything you cited in your essay or paper. This means that you need to keep a full reference list (use the format in the list of references at the end of this book if you have not been told to use something different) with your notes. If not, you may be condemned to hours of searching for the exact reference when, perhaps months or even years later, you need to use it for a paper or dissertation. It may seem a bother at the time, but it is more of a bother to resurrect an elusive reference when everything you can remember about it is insufficient to identify it. Fortunately, there is software available to make all this easy, as TECHSkills 4.3 described. You can find more on avoiding plagiarism in Chapter 7.

➤ Ch 7

SUMMARY

This chapter has argued the following:

- Improving your reading skills can make you a far more effective learner, and aid career success.
- Practice can significantly improve reading speeds.
- It is possible to increase your reading speed without loss of comprehension.
- Efficient reading requires you to think more clearly about what you need to read, and why, and about where to find it.
- Lecturers, library staff and other students can help you find and select appropriate reading material.
- Different reading speeds are appropriate for different purposes.
- When reading it is important to adopt a critical approach, asking a range of questions as you read.
- It is important to identify the claims the author is making and to evaluate their internal consistency and the strength of the evidence and reasoning given in support of these claims.
- Mapping the arguments can be a useful approach when evaluating a case.
- It is important to relate your reading to other materials on the same subject, to the author's purpose and to the context in which it was written.
- Taking notes will increase the effectiveness of your understanding and learning and give you something for future reference.
- Mind maps can form a useful part of your notes. It is essential to be disciplined in organising and storing your notes, and keeping back-up copies, ideally in a form which can be accessed from any device.
- You need to be equally disciplined about noting references for everything you read. Bibliographic software can help with this.

Further information

Buzan, T. (2003) *The Speed Reading Book*, BBC Publications.

Buzan, T. (2003) *Use Your Head*, BBC Publications.

Buzan, T. and Griffiths, C. (2014) *Mind Maps for Business: Using the Ultimate Thinking Tool to Revolutionise How You Think*, 2nd edn, Pearson.

Rose, C. and Nicholl, M.J. (1997) *Accelerated Learning for the 21st Century*, Piatkus.

4

CRITICAL READING AND NOTE TAKING

5
BASIC NUMBERS

Learning outcomes

By the end of this chapter you should:

- see why numbers are important

- understand some of the difficulties you may have had with using numbers in the past

- understand the 'language' of simple maths

- be able to use a calculator or spreadsheet to perform simple calculations

- be able to use estimations as a check on your calculations

- understand and have practiced how to rearrange equations

- feel relatively confident of your ability to do basic arithmetic and algebra.

Introduction

If you hate numbers, this chapter is for you. It should make you confident enough to benefit from courses with a quantitative element. If you are comfortable with basic maths, skip it!

Number skills are vital for business study (and many other subjects) and for many jobs. Whether you are analysing survey results, claiming your expenses, or project planning with a tight budget, you need numbers. Whether figuring out wallpaper requirements, or deciding between phone providers, you need basic arithmetic. Yet many people doubt their number skills, or are actually frightened of numbers and equations. This chapter aims to reduce such fears and address some of the basic uncertainties causing them. It can't take you from nothing to A level standard, But it can make the basic principles clear, act as revision of things you have forgotten, and build your confidence.

Once you have grasped the 'mechanics' of working with numbers, you will need to
➤ Ch 13 know how to interpret them. This is addressed in Chapter 13.

THE IMPORTANCE OF NUMBERS

It is difficult to overestimate the importance of numbers. Crosby (1997) argues that the amazing success of European imperialism can be explained only in terms of the shift from qualitative to quantitative perception during the late Middle Ages and Renaissance, the prime use of numbers being for measurement. He gives an interesting quotation (p. 109) in illustration:

> Wherefore in all great works are Clerks so much desired? Wherefore are Auditors so well fed? What causeth Geometricians so highly to be enhaunced? Why are Astronomers so greatly advanced? Because that by number such things they finde, which else would farre excell mans minde.

(Robert Recorde, 1540)

This might also explain something that puzzled me when I was a psychologist in the civil service – the fact that economists on equivalent grades to psychologists, and with equivalent qualifications, were paid significantly more. Consider how many highly paid professions today involve facility with numbers.

Of course, you should already have the basic ability to deal with numbers as a result of your secondary education. If this is the case, check that your judgement is correct by doing Test Exercise 5.1 and then move on to the next chapter. If you *can* cheerfully add, subtract, multiply and divide, can cope with fractions, decimals, ratios and percentages and do some basic algebra, you do not need this chapter.

But if you feel unsure about these things, if you hated maths at school, or somehow came to feel you were no good at it, do not worry. This chapter should take away some of your fears. It will redevelop some skills that may have atrophied through lack of use and fill gaps that your education may have left. This chapter is not intended to teach you maths, but rather to show that playing with numbers is not difficult, can often be fun and is an extremely useful skill. It should make you less nervous about any quantitative parts of your course and enable you to use sets of numbers you encounter at work without trauma. Drawing conclusions from numbers, rather than merely playing with them, is

➤ Ch 14   dealt with in Chapter 14.

This is one of the few topics where 'right' answers to exercises are possible. The answers to the test exercises are given at the end of the book. Write your own answer in the space provided, or on a separate piece of paper, *before* looking at the answer given. It is very easy to think that you know how to do something when in fact you only half know. Spending time on actually working out the examples given and writing down your answers will ensure that you really do master the skills involved. Resist any temptation to cut corners here!

Diagnostic Exercise

Test Exercise 5.1

In order to check whether you need to work through this chapter or can afford to move directly to the next one, answer the following questions, writing down your answers as you go. Do not use a calculator unless the question asks you to. Do not look at the answers given at the end of the book until you have finished the exercise.

(a)   Add 273 to 476 and 545, and divide your total by 5   _____

(b)   Multiply 27 by 45   _____

(c)   Divide 34 546 by 23   _____

(d)   Add 3^2 to 2^3 _____

(e)   Write 1234.5678 to two places of decimals   _____

(f)   Write 1234.5678 to three significant figures   _____

(g)   Write down 75% of 200   _____

(h)   Write down $^{13}/_{25}$ as a percentage   _____

(i)   If there are 6 tutors and 42 students, what is the ratio of staff to students?   _____

(j)   Divide $^2/_3$ by $^9/_{16}$ _____

(k)   Divide $(3a + 4b)(5c - 10d)$ by $5(a + b)(c - 2d)$ _____

(l)   How many tiles 10 cm square do you need to cover a room 2 m by 3 m?   _____

(m)   Use your calculator to work out $13^2 - 25 + 273 \times 5$ _____

Now check your answers and decide whether you need to study all of what follows, some of it, or can afford to move directly to the next chapter. If most of your answers were right but you feel it was as much by luck as good judgement, merely read what follows quickly, doing the examples only in the parts where you feel most uncertain.

➤ Ch 3

Activity 5.1

If you have decided as a result of the above that you do need to develop some of your mathematical skills, and have not yet compiled an 'exhibit' which demonstrates that you can manage your learning, this might be a good topic. Think about what you are likely to need to learn and about any evidence (in addition to answers to the above) of your learning needed in this area. Then you will need to set objectives, explore potential resources and so on, keeping a commentary as you go. Refer to Chapter 3 to remind yourself of the process.

The Importance of Mathematical Skills

If numbers are important, then the mathematical skills needed to deal with them are important too. There are many ways of thinking of mathematics. At its simplest it can be seen as a language with a set of symbols instead of words, and a set of rules for combining these symbols. These rules are equivalent to the grammar of a spoken language. At this level it can provide a clear, unambiguous and concise way of describing certain relationships. The section on 'mathematical vocabulary' will enable you to use the language to communicate in this way.

More often, though, you will want either to draw conclusions from numbers or to manipulate them in some way. To work out the cost of something made from several components, you need to manipulate numbers. To check expenditure against budget, you need numbers. To make sure that you have ordered enough meals for attenders at a conference when you know that a certain proportion of those registered will not arrive, you need numbers. Decisions about future actions in organisations will often involve cost–benefit or other calculations. Recently I asked a graduate employer what recruits needed number skills for. He replied: 'Just about everything.' Indeed, it is hard to see how you can measure, control, analyse, forecast or model, or make sense of the outputs of these processes, without feeling comfortable with basic maths.

Modelling

It is probably worth discussing one of these uses of maths in a little more detail. A model is something constructed for a particular purpose. It represents certain key aspects of the thing modelled in order to allow you to answer questions about it. Models may be used because they are smaller or simpler or cheaper or safer to play with than the real thing. To find out whether a dam design is going to be strong enough for a location you cannot build it and wait to see if it falls down. Nor do you put up a building in order to see whether people like the look of it. Architects make three-dimensional models of proposed buildings, or achieve the same effect on a computer screen. Their clients can decide from these whether something looks right. Engineers perform all sorts of calculations to decide whether the dam will be strong enough, given the strength of the materials, the way they are arranged and the water pressure expected. Even when deciding whether to fill up at this service station or wait until the next one, you will probably use a simple model. You relate the amount of fuel you estimate is left in the tank to the distance to the next service area, given the fuel consumption of your car at the rate you are likely to be travelling.

Very simple (or very complicated) mathematical equations can be used to give answers to all sorts of 'what if?' questions. What would be the staffing implications of this change in operations? or of that reduction in absence rates? If fixed costs are this, and variable costs are that, how many items do we need to sell at a given price to break even? What will the profit be if we sell so many hundred more? If interest rates are this, and expected return on investment is that, is it worth borrowing in order to invest? The maths will not tell you how many items you will sell, or what will happen to interest rates. Provided you have chosen appropriate equations to express the relationship between the relevant factors, it will tell you what is likely to happen in different sets of circumstances. One tool for doing

➤ Ch 7   this sort of fairly simple modelling easily is a spreadsheet (discussed in Chapter 7).

When doing this sort of simple modelling and using maths to answer real or hypothetical questions, we are going beyond descriptive language into using techniques derived from mathematics. Some of these techniques are extremely complex and will take you some time to learn. Unless you are going to use them regularly it is better to consult an expert. Others will be well within your grasp once you have learned the basics of arith-

➤ Ch 7   metic and algebra covered here. Spreadsheets, introduced in Chapter 7, make it easy to construct simple models on a PC and to use them to answer questions.

Sources of Difficulty

Most small children are perfectly comfortable with numbers once they have learned to count. They can make fairly sophisticated judgements about things like 'fair shares' or what their pocket money will buy. But for a significant proportion of these children something seems to go wrong once they are 'taught' maths. Either they fail to develop their skills further or they lose even those skills which they have. Furthermore, they develop almost a phobia about anything with a number or an equals sign in it. Even totally straightforward explanations of simple operations cannot penetrate. If you are one of these people, take frequent deep breaths as you move through this chapter!

Even if you are not disturbed by the sight of an equation, you may still have suffered from the shift in teaching methods before you entered education. It used to be the fashion to teach mathematics as a series of techniques. These were learned by rote rather than understood. Thus children learned to go through the mechanics of long multiplication or division, with absolutely no understanding of what they were doing. I remember being taught an incredibly complicated method for finding square roots by hand, even though any book of mathematical tables (before the calculator became an everyday item such tables were essential) had lists of square roots and we also knew how to find them from log tables in the same book.

Such a method of learning was difficult, boring and often pointless. But the endless calculations it required gave a great deal of practice in basic arithmetic. The ability to multiply or do long division without a calculator is still useful. It allows quick tests of the answers that your computer or calculator produces and means that you can afford to go out without a calculator on occasion.

The 'discovery' approach to maths teaching, which replaced the above, was intended to be more interesting. Unfortunately, it often left students feeling they were floundering in a foggy mathematical swamp, not knowing where they were going or how they would get there even if they did. At least with the old-fashioned method students were drilled in the basic techniques to such an extent that they would remember them for the rest of their lives.

Cartoon by Neill Cameron, neillcameron.com

What follows is an attempt at covering these basics. Some practice exercises are included but they are unlikely to be enough to remedy six or more years of poor teaching. If you are an extreme case, and if you need to pursue courses with a quantitative element, you are well advised to buy a basic maths book which contains lots of examples and answers at the back – and then work through it. Once you start getting things right it can be quite exciting. If, on the other hand, you are semi-confident, skim the more obvious bits that follow. Pause only on those sections where you feel less sure.

Basic Mathematical Signs, Symbols and Operations

This is where numberphobes may need a few deep breaths before progressing. Put on some relaxing music and then make sure that you understand the meaning of the following basic symbols:

You will know that in 5 + 3 the '+' is telling you to take the sum of 3 and 5, to add them together. For numbers in the thousands or more you might prefer to use a calculator. Note that in addition the order of terms does not matter: 5 + 3 is the same as 3 + 5.

You also know that 5 − 3, or 5 minus 3, means what you get when you take 3 away from 5. Again, even for large numbers, this is easy to do by pressing the right buttons on a calculator. But note, in this case the order *does* matter. If you have £300 in the bank and take out £500, you are not in the same position as if you have £500 and take out £300. In the second case your bank manager will be happy. In the first he or she will not, unless you had previously arranged an overdraft facility. You would have −£200. Negative sums of money, money owing, are often written in brackets; for example, '(£200)', in sets of accounts.

What do you do when you want to subtract something that is already negative, i.e. has a '−' sign in front of it? To 'take away' your overdraft, someone would have to give you £200 and, indeed, to subtract a number that is already negative you have to *add* it. Thus 5 − (−3) is 5 + 3, or 8. Note that basic calculators cannot cope with this. You need to apply this rule of signs for yourself and ask the calculator to *add* any negative numbers that are being subtracted.

This indicates multiplication. 5 × 3 means 5 lots of 3, or 15. Again, the obvious calculator buttons will produce the answer if you have forgotten your 'times tables'. As with addition, order does not matter: 5 × 3 is the same as 3 × 5. You need to be careful with negative numbers, however. As with subtraction, two minuses get you back to plus. So count the number of minus signs in the string of numbers you are multiplying. If there is only one of them, or any odd number, then the answer will be negative. If there are no minus signs, or two, or any even number, the result of the multiplication will be positive. A basic calculator will not read a minus sign as part of the multiplication. Instead it will think it has to subtract. So, if using a calculator, multiply all the numbers as if they were positive and put the appropriate sign in front of your answer, having worked this out for yourself by counting the number of minus signs.

Part of the difficulty in working with mixtures of signs on a calculator is that in a string of things to add, subtract, multiply and divide, the signs have different strengths, or priorities. If you see 5 + 3 × 2, this means that you should work out the 3 × 2 first, before adding the 5. Thus you get 11, not 16. Multiplication and division signs are stronger than addition and subtraction signs, so they must be worked out first. Sophisticated calculators are programmed with this rule, but cheap ones usually are not. Check to see whether yours is sophisticated enough by working out something like the example above, before relying on it.

Should you want to multiply large numbers by hand, you need to end up with a number of the right size. So 5 × 50 will be 250 and 500 × 50 will be 25 000. In the latter example there were two zeros in the first number, one in the second and three in the answer. If it is not already clear why this should be, you will understand when powers are discussed shortly. If you were multiplying numbers that were not merely hundreds or tens but had units as well (say 521 by 53), you would need to keep clear how many noughts would appear at any stage. So line the numbers up so that the units are underneath each other, thus:

$$521 \times$$
$$\underline{53}$$

Beneath the line, working with each digit at a time and making sure that the answer is in the right (units, tens or hundreds) column, multiply the whole first number by the first digit in the second number then add. So you multiply by the 5 in the 53 first. This is really 50, so place a 0 in the units column, then multiply the 1 above by the 5, then the 2 (this gives 10, so write down the zero and carry the 1 across to the next column, jotting it down to remember it). Next, 5 multiplied by 5 is 25. Add the 'carried' 1 to give 26 and write it down. In the line below, multiply the 1 by 3, then the 2, then the 5, working across from right to left. Then add the two numbers together. The resulting calculation, done by hand, looks like this:

$$521 \times \qquad 521 \times \qquad 521 \times$$
$$\underline{53} \qquad\qquad \underline{53} \qquad\qquad \underline{53}$$
$$26050 \qquad\quad 26050 \qquad\quad 26050$$
$$\qquad\qquad\qquad\quad 1563 \qquad\qquad 1563$$
$$\qquad\qquad\qquad\qquad\qquad\qquad\qquad 27613$$

$$\boxed{\div}$$

This indicates division: $5 \div 3$ means what you get when you divide 5 into 3 equal portions. If the second number goes into the first with no problems; for example, in the case of $6 \div 3$, life is simple. If you and your two flatmates have six pies, you can have two pies each. But if you have only five pies and want equal shares, you will be moving into the territory of fractions. You could divide each pie into three and share them out, ending up with five pieces, each ⅓ of a pie. Or you could take one pie each and cut up the two which remained. So you would have 1⅔ pies each. This shows that ⅗ and 1⅔ are simply different ways of writing the same thing. If you are dividing a large number by a smaller number, then you may not bother about the fraction. Instead, you may merely say what is left – the remainder. If you go out for a meal with six friends and the bill is £43, you might just say that is a bit over £7 each and offer to pay the £1 that is left over when you divide, adding it to your own £7 contribution.

Should you wish to do long division by hand, you need to write everything clearly in columns, just as you did when multiplying. However, instead of working right to left, you work left to right.

Suppose you are dividing 4737 by 21. Write it as:

$$21\overline{\smash{)}4737}$$

Now ask: 'Will 21 go into 4?' Clearly not. Will it go into 47? Yes, twice. So write a 2 above the 7. But it doesn't go exactly. What is left over? Two 21s are 42, so write this beneath the 47 and subtract. This gives you 5. (Note that this number is less than 21: if it had given you something bigger than 21, you would know you had made a mistake in the first number you wrote down since it should have been bigger.) This 5 is sitting in the hundreds column. It means 500. 'Bring down' the next available digit, the 3, and write it beside the 5. Don't worry that this is really 530. Treat it as 53. See how many 21s you can get into this. Two, again. So write down another 2, above the 3. This stands for 20 because it is in the tens column. That is why it didn't matter that it was 530. The columns mean that things end up standing for the right thing even though you conveniently forget what they stand for while working out the division. Write down the 42 and subtract from the 53. This gives you 11. 'Bring down' the final digit, the 7. How many 21s in 117? Five. So write down the 5 in the last place above the line and work out what 5 multiplied by 21 is: 105. Write this below 117 and subtract, giving you the remainder, which is 12. So the answer is 225 with a remainder of 12, or 225 and $\frac{12}{21}$ had you wanted an answer expressed as a fraction. The hand worked sum is shown below. You use the same principle, whatever the size of numbers involved.

$$
\begin{array}{r}
2 \\
21\overline{)4737} \\
42 \\
\hline
5
\end{array}
\qquad
\begin{array}{r}
22 \\
21\overline{)4737} \\
42 \\
\hline
53 \\
42 \\
\hline
11
\end{array}
\qquad
\begin{array}{r}
225 \\
21\overline{)4737} \\
42 \\
\hline
53 \\
42 \\
\hline
117 \\
105 \\
\hline
12 \; remainder
\end{array}
$$

$$\boxed{\;.\;}$$

This is a decimal point. (Note that this is not absolutely standard notation. There are some places where a comma rather than a full stop is used for this purpose.) You will be used to seeing figures written in decimals and know already that 1.5 is the same as 1½. The decimal point tells you where the whole number ends and the fraction starts. Adding fractions is quite difficult. How could you express the sum of $\frac{5}{7}$ and ¾, for example? (Answer – turn them both into 28ths and then add, which is possible, but a bit messy.) But if you express both as decimals then it is easy. Press $\boxed{5}\boxed{\div}\boxed{7}\boxed{=}$, and then $\boxed{3}\boxed{\div}\boxed{4}\boxed{=}$, on your calculator to see what each is as a decimal. Then add both on the calculator. (I get 1.4642857.) You will have noticed that ¾ used only two figures, whereas $\frac{5}{7}$ filled up your display with assorted numbers. This is because 100 can be divided equally into four parts, each of 25, but it does not divide equally into seven parts. For another nice display, divide 5 by 3 on your calculator to get the decimal solution to the pie problem.

In interpreting figures to the right of the decimal you use the same rule as for figures to the left. You know that the first place to the left of the point represents units, the next tens, the next hundreds, and so on. Starting at the point and moving right, you are still using a factor of ten with each move. The first figure to the right represents tenths, the next hundredths and so on.

If you are working with a calculator, all you need to do to work with decimals is to make sure that when you are entering a number and get to the decimal point you press the $\boxed{\cdot}$ key and then continue entering the decimal part of the number. The calculator is happy to work with such numbers. However, if you need to work out what the fraction is as a decimal first and then add or subtract, the calculator will get confused. You probably found this a minute ago. The trick is to use the memory. When the calculator has turned each fraction into a decimal press $\boxed{\text{M+}}$ (or $\boxed{\text{M−}}$ for a negative number). When you have entered all decimals in the memory press $\boxed{\text{MR}}$ to recall the total from the memory.

If you are adding by hand, you need to make sure that all the decimal points are lined up so that you start adding tens to tens, hundreds to hundreds and tenths to tenths. Thus, if adding 101.75 to 1.003, you would write:

$$\begin{array}{r} 101.75 \ + \\ 1.003 \\ \hline 102.753 \end{array}$$

This symbol means percentage or per cent, or a fraction expressed in 1/100ths. Thus 1 is 100/100 or 100% and half is 50/100 or 50% and so on. This is very similar to working in the first two numbers to the right of the decimal point and has the same advantages as using decimals. While it is very hard to see how $^{11}/_{13}$, $^{27}/_{31}$ and $^5/_7$ relate to each other, if you express them as percentages you can easily tell which is the biggest, or add or subtract them. You used your calculator before to find out what fractions were in decimals. You can do this again and take the first two figures. But it is much simpler to press, say, $\boxed{1}\boxed{\div}\boxed{4}\boxed{\%}$. Start with something you know, like ½, to check that this works on your calculator.

$$\boxed{=}$$

You have already been using this button on your calculator in the above examples. In a minute, when we look at simple algebra, we shall explore its meaning further. Equations always contain this equals sign. Basically it tells you that everything on one side of the sign is the same as everything on the other side.

This means to the power of 2, or squared. Numbers in small type, up in the air to the right of a number or letter, mean that it has been multiplied by itself, the number of terms in the multiplication being given by the small 'power' number. Thus, 2^2 means 2×2, and 3^2 means 3×3. We could call it '3 squared' or '3 to the power 2'. If the small number is a 3, we talk about something being 'cubed' or 'to the power 3': 4^3 is $4 \times 4 \times 4$, or 64. After cubed there are no more special terms, so we always talk of 'to the power'.

Now, think what happens when you multiply different powers of the same number. What do you think you will get if you multiply 10^2 by 10^3? Try it. This is 100 by 1000, or 100 000, or 10^5. Thus you could have got it by adding the powers, or indices, together. This always works. You can always write down the answer to a multiplication of two powers *of the same number* as that number to the sum of the powers. Thus, $3^2 \times 3^5 = 3^7$. Remember this. It has all sorts of uses. By the same token, you can divide a power of a number by another power of the same number by *subtracting* the second index from the first. Thus, $2^3 \div 2^2 = 2$ and $10^{12} \div 10^8 = 10^4$.

There are two curious indices, or powers: the power 0 and the power 1. Try to work out what these must mean, using as a clue the fact that to multiply powers you add indices. Raising a number to the power 1 must mean using that number as it stands. For example, 5^2 is the product of 5^1 and 5^1. And 5^3 is $5^2 \times 5$, or $5^2 \times 5^1$. By the same token, $5^0 \times 5^2$ gives you 5^2. The only number that will have this effect is 1, so any number to the power zero must mean 1.

This is a square root sign. A square root is the number which, when multiplied by itself, gives you the number in front of which you wrote the square root sign. Thus, $\sqrt{9}$ is the number which, when squared, gives 9, in other words it is 3. Press $\boxed{8}\,\boxed{1}\,\boxed{\sqrt{}}$ on your calculator to find the square root of 81. You should be able to work out the index number, or power, of a square root. Stop for a minute and try. (Some computers need $\boxed{\sqrt{}}\,\boxed{8}\,\boxed{1}$.)

If you are stuck, remember that to multiply two powers you *add* the index numbers. And the index for a number itself is ^{1}. The thing which you add to itself to get one is ½. Thus $\sqrt{4} \times \sqrt{4} = 4 = 4^{1/2} \times 4^{1/2}$.

Just as you can find squares, cubes, fourth powers, and so on, so you can find cube roots, fourth roots, etc. in a similar way to finding square roots. Cube roots are written or $^3\sqrt{}$ or $^{1/3}$ (the power ⅓), fourth roots as $^4\sqrt{}$. Work out $^4\sqrt{16}$ on your calculator.

There is no fourth root key. But you know that a fourth root is the square root of a square root, and can therefore press $\boxed{1}\,\boxed{6}\,\boxed{\sqrt{}}\,\boxed{\sqrt{}}$ giving the answer 2. If this still seems a bit confusing, set yourself some practice examples. Find some powers of numbers on your calculator by repeatedly multiplying the number by itself, counting how often so you know which power it is. Write yourself a question to find the appropriate root of this number, noting the answer separately. Put the questions to one side for a few days, then do them 'blind', checking the answer only when you have finished. Or forget about saving the answer and check on your calculator by multiplying up.

Other mathematical signs

The above list covers what a basic calculator can do. Scientific calculators will offer you a much wider range of options, including the ability to do mixed additions and multiplications without getting muddled and other things scientists do frequently. Financial calculators offer similar benefits in the area of accounting and finance. As well as costing more, these calculators require a time investment if you are to exploit their facilities fully. If you are going to do a lot of specialist calculations when away from a PC, the appropriate calculator (or even better, a palm-top computer) may be a good investment. But a simple calculator is probably best while you are developing your basic skills. It offers less to confuse you.

You will frequently meet the following signs in equations (or sometimes on more complex calculators).

$$\boxed{x}$$

This could be any other letter, usually italicised. This is referred to as a 'variable', and when it appears in an equation it represents something which can take a number of values, or whose value you do not know. Although you may be disconcerted to see an equation with a mixture of letters and numbers, the letters are very easy to deal with. You treat them just as you would numbers, moving them around in the same way (more of this later). Of course, if you want, say, to multiply 2 by x, you cannot simply write in a new number as you would if multiplying, say, 2 by 3. But you can write $2x$ and carry on quite happily like that. Indeed, it is really much simpler to play with letters than numbers, as well as far more useful on many occasions, which explains why you see them in equations so often. (More of this later, in the discussion of equations.)

$$\boxed{\Sigma}$$

This is the Greek capital letter sigma, used to indicate the sum of something. It is often written as $\sum_{n=1}^{r} x_n$. This means that x has a number of values, which have been called, for convenience, x_1 to x_r. You are to add all these values, from x_1 to x_r. Thus you could express a year's sales figures as the sum of the totals of month 1 to month 12, or x_1 to x_{12}. You would write this as $\sum_{n=1}^{12} x_n$. But if you were interested only in sales for the second quarter, you could write $\sum_{n=4}^{6} x_n$. This notation may look clumsy and forbidding (and is a nightmare when it comes to layout) but is often an extremely economical way of expressing something in an equation. And because it is a standard convention, anyone slightly familiar with mathematics will find it easy to understand.

$$\boxed{f}$$

This means 'function'. If we say $y = f(x)$ we mean that y varies in some way as x varies, or it is a function of x. Thus if the area of a carpet varies with both the width and the length of the piece, its area is a function of both of these dimensions. If you called the area a, the width w and the length l, you could write $a = f(l, w)$. If you knew that you were always buying from a roll that was 3 metres wide, the area would merely depend on the length bought, or $a = f(l)$. Indeed, it would have been perfectly correct to write $a = f(l)$ in the first case, too, because area does depend on the length. The fact that it also depends on width (or in another case, other variables) does not have to be mentioned. You might choose not to mention all the variables, for various reasons, or indeed might not know what some of them are.

This simply means 'not equal to'. If you write $x \neq y$ you are saying that x cannot take the same value as y, whatever else it may or may not be able to do.

This means 'less than'. If $x < y$ then it means that x must be less than y.

This means, not surprisingly, 'greater than'. So $x > y$ means x has to be greater than y. It is fairly easy to remember which sign is which: the fat side of the wedge points to the bigger number in both cases, and the thin side points to the smaller number.

This means 'less than or equal to'. Thus in $x \leq y$, x cannot be greater than y, but could be either the same as y or smaller.

Obviously, this means 'greater than or equal to'.

These are brackets and are extremely important in equations. If things are within a bracket, it means that they must be treated as a whole. For example, $2(7 + 6x + y)$ means $14 + 12x + 2y$ because you have to multiply every term within the bracket by the 2 outside.

The above constitutes a very basic mathematical vocabulary. Use the following test exercise to check your understanding of the points covered. Answers are given at the end of the book.

Where you have a wrong answer, work out why. Was it a careless error – when you do it again it actually gives the right answer? If so, take more care in future. But if this is not the case, and what you are doing gives the same (wrong) answer again, go back to the relevant definitions and examples and find out why.

5

BASIC NUMBERS

Test Exercise 5.2

(a) Write the following as decimals:

$\frac{3}{4}$ $\frac{21}{7}$ $1\frac{1}{3}$ $\frac{15}{7}$ $\frac{9}{11}$ $\frac{6}{8}$

————— ————— ————— ————— ————— —————

(b) Write the following as percentages:

2 $\frac{3}{4}$ $1\frac{1}{3}$ $\frac{10}{11}$ $\frac{1}{4}$ $\frac{2}{3}$

————— ————— ————— ————— ————— —————

(c) Write down the value of:

2^3 14^2 3^4 $3^2 \times 3^2$ 12^3 1^4 6^0

————— ————— ————— ————— ————— ————— —————

(d) Write as a power of a single number:

$2^2 \times 2^5$ $3^4 \times 3^2$ $10^3 \times 10^5 \div 10^8$ $17^6 \times 17^3$ $21^{21} \div 21^3$ $x^y \div x^2$ $x^3 \times x^2$ $z^{2x} \times z^{2y}$

————— ————— ——————————— ————— ————————— ————— ————— ———————

(e) Use your calculator to work out the following, writing your answer using only two places of decimals:

$\sqrt{16}$ $\sqrt{144}$ $\sqrt{36}$ $\sqrt{38}$ $\sqrt{2}$ $\sqrt{10}$

————— ————— ————— ————— ————— —————

(f) Write each of the following as a power of a number, rather than using a root sign:

$\sqrt{2^{16}}$ $\sqrt{10^4}$ $\sqrt[3]{3^2}$ $\sqrt{(x^2y^2)}$ $\sqrt[7]{z^{14}}$

————— ————— ————— —————

(g) If $x_1, x_2, x_3, \ldots, x_r$ represent the numbers 1, 2, 3, . . ., r, write down the value of

$\sum\limits_{r=1}^{3} x_r$ ————————————————————

(h) Which of the following are true?

(i) $7 \neq 7$ (ii) $3 \geq 1$ (iii) $5 > -5$ (iv) $3 < -5$ (v) $x^2 > x$ when $x = 1$

————— ————— ————— ————— —————

(i) Write each of the following in a way that does not use brackets:

$2(x + y)$ $3(x - y)$ $(x - y) - (x - y)$ $(x - y) - (x - 2y)$

————— ————— ——————————— ———————————

(j) Work out:

$5 + 2 \times 4$ $3 \times 6 - 5 + 4$ $x + x \times x \div y$ $1.2 \times 3.4 - 1.2 \div 6.1$

————— ————— ————— —————

Units

Numbers can indicate the quantity of almost anything. Even in a number, as you have already seen, the digits stand for different things depending on where they are placed in relation to the decimal point (or to the last digit if the number is whole). So '5' might mean five hundred, five million, five-tenths or whatever, as discussed above. Obviously, to make sense of any number you need to know what it stands for, and in doing things with the number, you need always to keep this in mind. You cannot add apples to oranges, though you can refer to both as pieces of fruit and come up with a meaningful answer. Thus in adding numbers 'by hand' you needed to be sure that you aligned them properly so that you were adding tens to tens, hundreds to hundreds and so on.

In dividing things by other things, it is just as important to be clear what units the answer is in. Thus, if you are concerned about fuel consumption you might use the imperial system and divide distance in miles by petrol used in gallons, and express your answer in miles per gallon. Or you might be resolutely metric and measure distance in kilometres and petrol in litres, and talk of kilometres per litre. But if you had done one, and your friend had done the other, you would not know which of you had the more efficient car (or driving style). And if a third friend had done the easiest calculation and divided miles (because that is what his car's instruments measured) by litres (because that is what the pump measures), producing a nasty hybrid unit, you could not relate his answer to either of yours.

In choosing units to work with, it makes sense to select those which are most straightforward to use and to communicate to others. Note that these may not always be the same. Metric systems are usually the easiest to use for measures because dividing by ten is so easy. But if you were selling cars to people who thought in miles per gallon, metric measures might not communicate best. Ease will depend on the size of units. You would use metres rather than centimetres as your main unit in measuring either carpets or short races because the number of metres will be manageable, whereas numbers of centimetres would be huge and kilometres would require you to be using fractions all the time. A marathon, however, would be measured in miles. Choice of unit will be important later, when you are manipulating numbers and representing them in ways that make their significance clear.

Estimating and Rounding

You have seen, in trying out basic arithmetic operations, that a calculator makes the whole thing absurdly easy. But it is very easy to press a wrong button in the middle of a calculation, or enter something wrongly in a spreadsheet.

If you have worked out very roughly what sort of answer you are likely to get, alarm bells will start to ring if the answer is wildly different from your rough guess. This will not alert you to faults where the answer is only slightly adrift, but it will save you from many an embarrassing situation.

The technique of getting a rough idea of what to expect is called *estimating*. For example, if you are adding up ten numbers, each of which is between 700 and 900, you might estimate that the answer will be about 8000. If it is more than 9000 or less than 7000 you know that something has gone wrong. Whatever calculation you are doing, it is worth getting a ballpark figure in your head, so that you know if some extra noughts have crept in somewhere, or you inadvertently inserted an unwanted decimal point, or pressed $\div$ rather than $-$.

Test Exercise 5.3

Estimate the value of the following before working them out on your calculator.

		Estimate	Answer
(a)	2734 + 5955	_____	_____
(b)	40 569 ÷ 9	_____	_____
(c)	25% of 39 400 113	_____	_____
(d)	95 + 15% of 113	_____	_____

To estimate you were probably working to the nearest hundred or thousand to get a rough idea of the expected answer. This technique, called *rounding*, is enormously useful. You will remember that when you used your calculator to work out 1⅔ it filled up its display capacity with 6s. You will not usually work to many places of decimals; total accuracy is seldom that important. It is not worth the inconvenience of working 1⅔ to many decimal places. Worse, to do this implies a spurious accuracy, which may cause people to doubt your grasp of what the results really mean.

Suppose that your project involved using a questionnaire to obtain a measure of job satisfaction. Respondents were asked to rate a number of aspects of their jobs on a scale of 1 to 5. If you wanted to work with average scores in this case it would be absurd to use more than one decimal place, as the ratings themselves are subjective and the scale crude.

When you have decided how many decimal places you want (or whether you are going to round to the nearest number of tens, or hundreds, or whatever) you need to decide the value of that last number, be it tens, tenths or millions, by looking at the first number that you are discarding. Thus if you want to round 178 to the nearest 10 you will be discarding the 8. But 8 is greater than 5 (the halfway point), so 178 is closer to 180 than to 170. You should therefore round 178 to 180. On the other hand, 172 would round to 170 – opinions differ about 175. Whether you round 175 up or down doesn't matter, but if you are rounding a set of numbers you should adopt the same principle throughout. Rounding fractional numbers is just the same: 21.178 would be 21.18 to two decimal places, or 21.2 to one decimal place.

Test Exercise 5.4

Round the following to two places of decimals:

(a) 1.2674   **(b)** 12.9763   **(c)** 129.763   **(d)** 129 763.557

_____   _____   _____   _____

You will see from the above exercise that rounding to, say, two decimal places does not make the same sort of sense with numbers of different orders of magnitude. If you are talking of numbers in the hundreds of thousands then decimal places will often be of little interest, whereas for a small number or a fraction they may make a huge difference. For example, 0.02 is twice as big as 0.01. Therefore, rather than rounding to a specific number of decimal places, or to tens or whatever, it may make more sense to give a specified number of *significant figures*. This is the number of figures from the first (non-zero in the case of decimals) digit to that which you round. Thus 673.457 is 670 to two significant figures, and 0.0050789 is 0.00508 to three significant figures, or 0.0051 to two significant figures.

Test Exercise 5.5

Give the following to three significant figures:

(a) 137.3   **(b)** 0.00078635   **(c)** 3976.77   **(d)** 1.0008762

_____   _____   _____   _____

Fractions, Ratios and Percentages

Decimals are a form of fraction, but a splendidly simple one to use. Decimal notation was not really worked out in systematic form until the sixteenth century. Before that, unwieldy fractions such as $^{197}/_{280}$, or worse (according to Crosby, 1997) $^{3345312}/_{4320864}$, made life exceedingly difficult. Indeed, Luca Pacioli, the famous Renaissance bookkeeper who popularised double-entry bookkeeping, said that 'many merchants disregard fractions in computing and give any money left over to the house'. There was clearly a need, from the customer's view at least, for a workable system for dealing with fractions.

The decimal system provides this. Working in tenths and hundredths is as easy as working with hundreds, tens and units, provided you take care to keep the decimal point in the right place. Percentages (i.e. hundredths) offer the same advantages of ease of working. As you saw with the case of ⅔, you cannot always express a fraction exactly as a decimal (or percentage), but by using enough places of decimals you can get as close as you want. Sometimes, however, you need to be given, or need to work with, the fractions themselves. A brief revision of these topics is therefore in order.

Test Exercise 5.6

To see how happy you are with percentages, try the following exercise.

The university bookshop is offering books at 80 per cent of their original selling price. You decide to buy two books, one of which costs £27.00 and the other £23.00. You also have an introductory voucher which offers you a 5 per cent reduction on anything you buy. What should you end up paying, and should you ask for your 5 per cent discount before or after the 20 per cent discount is deducted?

As you have already seen, it is easy to use a calculator to turn fractions into decimals, but this is no help if you are working with equations that include letters (we shall cover these shortly). And there are other times when you may not *want* to turn a fraction into a decimal. You therefore need to know the basic rules for dealing with fractions. Sometimes they will make a calculation so easy that you don't need your calculator.

Rule 1

You can multiply or divide the top and bottom of a fraction by the same thing, be it number, letter, or mixture of both, without changing the value of the fraction.

Imagine cutting a cake into two, four, six or eight pieces. How many pieces would constitute half the cake in each case? From this you can see that ½ is the same as ¾ or ⅜ or ⅝ or, for that matter, $^{600}/_{12000}$.

Similarly, when you start to play with equations, you can write $\dfrac{2x}{6x}$ as ⅓ or $\dfrac{2(3 + y)}{3(3 + y)}$ as ⅔. This operation is called *cancelling* and is extremely useful for simplifying fractions so that they are much easier to work with.

Test Exercise 5.7

Simplify the following fractions by dividing top and bottom by the same thing, i.e. by a factor common to both:

(a) $^{20}/_{30}$ _____

(b) $^{75}/_{100}$ _____

(c) $^{6}/_{9}$ _____

(d) $^{22}/_{11}$ _____

(e) $^{16}/_{12}$ _____

(f) $\dfrac{3x}{4x}$ _____

(g) $\dfrac{4(x + 1)}{8(x + 1)}$ _____

> ## Rule 2
>
> To multiply a series of fractions you multiply all the numbers (or letters or brackets) on top of the horizontal line to get the thing on top – known as the **numerator** – in your answer, and all the things underneath it to get the thing underneath – the **denominator**.

Thus $\frac{2}{3} \times \frac{4}{5} = \frac{8}{15}$ and $\frac{1}{2} \times \frac{3}{4} = \frac{3}{8}$. You can now see how cancelling comes in useful. You can cancel out numbers, letters or whole brackets wherever you see the same in one of the things on top of a line and one of the things below the line anywhere in a string of fractions to be multiplied. They do not have to appear in the same term. Thus $\frac{1}{2} \times \frac{4}{5}$ can be written as $\frac{2}{5}$ since you can divide both the 2 on the bottom and the 4 on the top by two.

Test Exercise 5.8

Use cancelling to simplify the following:

(a) $\frac{2}{3} \times \frac{3}{4} \times \frac{4}{5} \times \frac{1}{2}$ _____

(b) $\dfrac{1}{(n+1)} \times \dfrac{(n+1)}{3}$ _____

(c) $\dfrac{1}{xy} \times \dfrac{x}{(1+y)}$ _____

(d) $\frac{1}{2} \times {}^{50}\!/_{1000}$ _____

(e) $\dfrac{2y}{15} \times \dfrac{7}{xy}$ _____

(f) $\dfrac{2}{15} \times \dfrac{3x}{4y} \times \dfrac{y(y+1)}{x}$ _____

(g) $\dfrac{y}{x} \times \dfrac{7}{y} \times \dfrac{x^2y}{14}$ _____

Note that whether or not the bottom line of a fraction is written with brackets around it, you must treat it as if they were there. It would be quite correct to write $1+y$ in the denominator of (c) above, i.e. *without* a bracket, but you could not divide it by any y that appeared in the top line, as this would not go into the whole expression of $1+y$. However, if there were brackets containing $(1+y)$ in one of the top-line terms, you could cancel this with a $1+y$ term by itself, without (or with) brackets below the line somewhere or, indeed, with such a bracketed term multiplied by something else somewhere below the line.

Following the same rule, you can see that to square a fraction you square the number on the top to get the numerator, and the number below to get the denominator. Thus ½ squared is ¼, ⅔ cubed would have 2 × 2 × 2 on the top and 3 × 3 × 3 on the bottom, and so is 8⁄27. Or you could write this as 23 over 33. Thus there are different ways of writing the same thing. Whenever you are raising a fraction to some power, you have the choice of writing brackets around the whole fraction and putting the index number at the top right of the closing bracket, or putting an index number against each part of the fraction, or working the whole thing out. Thus the fifth power of 2⁄7 could be written as $(2/7)^5$ and the *n*th power of x/y could be written as $(x/y)^n$.

Test Exercise 5.9

Write out the value of $(x/y)^n$

(a) when x is 1, y is 2 and n is 3,

(b) when x is 2, y is 6 and n is 2.

Rule 3

To divide something by a fraction, turn that fraction upside down and multiply by the resulting inversion.

This rule may seem strange at first sight, but stop and think. You have to do something different as 4 ÷ 2 cannot be the same as 4 ÷ ½. The inversion does make sense. If 4 ÷ 2 means divide the 4 into two equal parts, then 4 ÷ ½ should mean divide 4 into half a part, in which case a whole part would be 8. English was not designed for mathematics, but you can see a sort of sense emerging.

So 4 ÷ ⅓ would be 12, and ½ ÷ ¾ would be 4⁄6 or ⅔ and $\frac{2(x+1)}{3} \div \frac{2}{x+1} = \frac{(x+1)^2}{3}$

Because you are converting a division into a multiplication by inverting it, you can string together multiplications and divisions of fractions without worry, provided you remember to invert all the things with a division sign in front and then multiply. So ½ × ¾ ÷ 5⁄7 × 1⁄14 ÷ ⅗ can be written as ½ × ¾ × 7⁄5 × 1⁄14 ÷ 5⁄3, which cancels down to 1⁄16.

Similarly,

$$\frac{(x+y)}{(2y+3)} \times \frac{3}{x} \div \frac{2(x+y)}{(2y+5)} \quad \text{becomes} \quad \frac{(x+y)}{(2y+3)} \times \frac{3}{x} \times \frac{(2y+5)}{2(x+y)}$$

which as you can divide both top and bottom by $(x + y)$, cancels down to:

$$\frac{3(2y+5)}{2x(2y+3)}$$

Test Exercise 5.10

Work out the following combined multiplications and divisions. Leave the brackets in as was done in the example above. Don't worry that we have not yet learned how to multiply them out.

(a) $\dfrac{1}{2} \times \dfrac{2(x + y)}{3} \div \dfrac{3(x + y)}{2}$ _____

(b) $\dfrac{x}{y} \times \dfrac{y}{x} \div \dfrac{x}{y} \div \dfrac{2}{3}$ _____

(c) $4 \div (x + 1) \times \dfrac{3}{4} \div \dfrac{(x + 2)}{(x + 4)}$ _____

(d) $\dfrac{3}{4} \div \dfrac{3}{5} \div \dfrac{x(x + 1)}{(y + 1)}$ _____

(e) $1\tfrac{1}{2} \times \dfrac{3}{4} \div \dfrac{y}{x}$ _____

Rule 4

You can add or subtract only fractions which share a common denominator.

Go back to your pies. It makes sense to talk about $\tfrac{1}{2} + \tfrac{1}{3}$ but you could not neatly include this expression in, say, a string of numbers to be multiplied. You cannot say that $\tfrac{1}{2} + \tfrac{1}{3}$ is $\tfrac{2}{5}$, $\tfrac{2}{3}$ or $\tfrac{2}{6}$. It isn't any of these things. In order to write the addition as something with a single number top and bottom, we need to turn each fraction into something comparable: $\tfrac{1}{2}$ can be written as $\tfrac{3}{6}$ and $\tfrac{1}{3}$ can be written as $\tfrac{2}{6}$. We can add sixths to sixths, as they are the same thing. So we end up with $\tfrac{5}{6}$. Similarly, $\tfrac{1}{2} - \tfrac{1}{3}$ could be written as $\tfrac{3}{6} - \tfrac{2}{6}$, or $\tfrac{1}{6}$.

If you have letters in your fractions, the principle is the same. If you wish to add $\tfrac{3}{5}$ and $\tfrac{5x}{y}$, you can turn both into fractions with $5y$ on the bottom line, by multiplying top and bottom of the first by y and top and bottom of the second by 5. This will give you the sum of $3y/5y$ and $25x/5y$ or $(3y + 25x)/5y$. (Turning everything into a percentage is another way of ensuring a common bottom line, or denominator – in this case 100.)

The only remaining thing to note is that you *cannot* cancel between different terms in an addition in the same way as you can for a multiplication. Note also that you cannot cancel between *part* of the numerator and *part* of the denominator unless that part is in brackets. Thus in the example just given you cannot get rid of either the 5 or the y in the answer above by dividing the $3y$ by y, or the $25x$ by 5. You have to be able to divide every term in the top line by something on the bottom line in order to be able to cancel. Thus if the top line had been $5y + 25x$, you would have been able to cancel the 5 in the bottom with the 5 in $5(y + 5x)$: an alternative way of writing the denominator.

Test Exercise 5.11

Write the following as single fractions.

(a) $\dfrac{3}{4} + \dfrac{7}{8}$ _____

(b) $\dfrac{2}{x} + \dfrac{4}{y}$ _____

(c) $\dfrac{5x}{y} - \dfrac{(2x + 1)}{y}$ _____

(d) $\dfrac{2}{3} + \dfrac{3x}{5}$ _____

(e) 50% of ¾ _____

(f) $\dfrac{y(5x + 1)}{x} + \dfrac{xy}{(5x + 1)}$ _____

(g) $\dfrac{5}{(x - 1)} - \dfrac{3}{(x - 2)}$ _____

Ratios

Now that you are comfortable with the basic rules for dealing with fractions, whether expressed in letters, numbers or a mixture, you can move on to another way of expressing what are essentially fractions – that is, ratios.

You use ratios when you are more interested in the relative sizes of things. That is, their proportions are of more interest than the absolute differences between them. To say that part A costs 20p more than part B may be more or less impressive depending on how much they both cost. If part A costs £200.20, the difference is very slight. If it costs 21p, the difference is huge. To say that you need 100 g more flour than fat in making shortcrust pastry would only be true if you were using 200 g of flour. It is far more useful to say that you need to use half as much fat (in weight) as flour. This is true whether you are catering for an army or cooking for yourself.

Ratios are obtained by dividing one thing by another. Thus in the above, if part A is 21p, the ratio of the cost of A to B is 21:1. If it is £200.20, the ratio is close to 1:1, that is, they cost almost the same. In shortcrust pastry, the ratio of flour to fat is 2:1. You obtain the ratio of A to B by dividing A by B. The ratio of fat to flour is 1:2, or ½. The thing you are finding the ratio *of* comes before the colon, or on top of the fraction. The thing you are finding the ratio of that *to* appears second, or as the denominator. While the colon way of writing ratios is very common if you merely want to say what a ratio *is*, if you want to include the ratio in an equation then writing it as a fraction will enable you to treat it as any other fraction. Since percentages are just another way of writing fractions you can, of course, express ratios as percentages if you want.

Test Exercise 5.12

Imagine that you work for a charity with a budget of £40 000, of which £12 800 is spent on advertising and fundraising.

(a) What percentage of the budget is spent on advertising and fundraising?

_____

(b) What is the ratio of this spending to the total budget?

_____

(c) What is the ratio of the advertising and fundraising budget to the money spent on everything else?

_____

If you are studying management or business, or if you become a senior manager, then you will meet many ratios. Because ratios deal in relative values rather than absolutes, they allow you to make meaningful comparisons between operations of different sizes. Particularly important is the use of certain key ratios to compare an organisation's performance from year to year and to identify emerging trends.

One key ratio of this kind is 'return on capital employed', or ROCE. This is sometimes called 'return on investment', or ROI, as it tells you precisely this. Obviously, if you make a huge investment and your profits are small, you will be less happy than if you get the same profits from a very small investment. The following exercise requires you to work out ROCE (or ROI) for a number of different organisations. For this you need to know what the ratio is:

$$\text{ROCE (or ROI)} = \frac{\text{Operating profit before interest and tax}}{\text{Capital employed}}$$

Remember, too, that figures may be written in brackets to show that they are negative. In such a case the figure in brackets is a loss, not a profit.

Test Exercise 5.13

Calculate ROCE (as a percentage) in the following cases (figures in £k).

	Operating profit	Capital employed	ROCE
(a)	500	4000	_____
(b)	164	83	_____
(c)	4.3	13	_____
(d)	(10)	256	_____

Using Equations

Equations have countless uses. Take a simple example: you want to borrow money at a certain rate of interest. Instead of paying the interest as it becomes due, you want to add it to the amount borrowed. This is called compound interest. Suppose you borrowed £1000 at 15 per cent interest for five years. At the end of the first year you would owe £1150. Or you could say that your debt at the end of year 1, call this D_1, will be 1.15 times the sum borrowed. At the end of the second year your debt (D_2) will be $D_1 \times 1.15$, or the original sum multiplied by 1.15 squared.

Test Exercise 5.14

Use your calculator to find the debt at the end of the second year and then the debt at the end of the third year.

————————   ————————

Now you can see why it is useful to replace numbers by letters. It enables us to write a general, all-purpose formula for how to calculate the amount owed without specifying actual figures. We can say that after any number of years, say n, the balance outstanding will be $(1.15)^n \times$ £1000. If you want the debt after ten years, it will be $(1.15)^{10} \times$ £1000, and so on.

We can make the formula more general by using a different letter, say A, for the original amount borrowed. It is even more general if we use a further letter, say r, for the interest rate. Thus if D_n is the debt at the end of year n, we can say that $D_n = A(1 + r)^n$.

Armed with this formula you can work out the debt for any loan, at any interest rate, for any length of time. You merely replace the letters by the numbers that apply in a particular case and work out the answer.

Test Exercise 5.15

Work out the amount which will be owed:

(a)   At the end of one year on a loan of £2000 at 13% interest.   ————————

(b)   At the end of two years on a loan of £1500 at 25% interest.   ————————

(c)   At the end of five years on a loan of £10 000 at 15% interest.   ————————

Thus far we have merely substituted values in a given formula in order to work out the amount owing. You can see that this is extremely useful. There are many formulae that will allow you to work out all sorts of things which might be important to you. But sometimes it is not simply a case of plugging in the numbers to get what you want.

You might find that, instead of sitting all by itself to the left of the equals sign, the 'thing' you are interested in finding the value of may be mixed up in the middle of an equation. Then you will need to move terms around to get the 'thing' by itself. Or, worse, you may wish to find the value of several terms which are all jumbled up in a single equation. In this case you will not be able to find a solution unless you have several equations.

Classical algebra relied heavily on x and y for its variables, but you can use any letter you want. It is usually easier to remember what stands for what if you use letters that relate in some way to what they stand for. Thus in the example above it was easy to remember that D stood for debt, r for rate of interest and A for amount borrowed initially. If you are working things out for yourself this can be a great help. (If working something out in an exam, use the letters in the formula as it was taught you or as it is given in the exam.)

To sort out equations into something that helps you work out what you want, you need to think a little more about just what an equation is. It is easiest if you visualise an equation as something where the two sets of things to be seen each side of the equals sign are in balance. For example, look at Figure 5.1.

Here, x on one side balances with $y + 1$ on the other, and we can write it as $x = y + 1$. Seeing it in this way makes it easy to understand what you can and cannot do to an equation. Obviously, if you added something to one pan the scales would be in balance only if you added the same thing to the other pan. So in this case you could write, for example, $x + 1 = y + 1 + 1 = y + 2$. Or $x + z = y + z + 1$. You could also take the same quantity from both sides and still be in balance. Thus you could write $x - z = y + 1 - z$, or $x - 1 = y$, or $x - y = 1$. (Can you begin to see how useful this fact is if you want to get one term all by itself on one side of the equals sign?)

Similarly, you can multiply both sides by the same thing, or divide by the same thing, and still be in balance. So,

$$2x = 2(y + 1), \quad zx = z(y + 1), \quad {}^{1}\!/_{2}x = {}^{1}\!/_{2}(y + 1) \quad \text{and} \quad x/(y + 1) = 1$$

Indeed, whatever you do, so long as you do the same thing to each side of the equation, you will still have a valid equation. But what you *cannot* do is to do something to one side

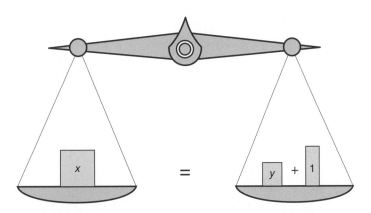

Figure 5.1 An equation as a balance

only, or to one side and only part of the other side. Thus you could not double the x and the y, but leave the 1 alone: $2x \neq 2y + 1$ in the example used above. To make sure that you do not inadvertently deal with only part of one side, put brackets around the whole thing before multiplying or dividing.

This is the main rule for manipulating equations. If you have now grasped it – and it is obvious when you think of the balance – you are in a position to do all sorts of things. Suppose you were working with the debt and compound interest example used earlier but you did not know how much had been borrowed, only the amount owed at the end of the period and the interest rate. You want to find out the original amount borrowed. Suppose that after four years at 20 per cent the debt was £4147.

You could experiment to get close to the answer. Guess at a loan and work out what the debt would be at the end of the period, using the formula as given. If it is too high, try it with a smaller loan and so on until you hit on a loan which is close enough for your purpose. When you cannot easily sort out an equation, this trial-and-error approach may be useful. But in this case there is a much easier way. All you need to do is to use what you know about equations to rearrange this one to give you what you want to know, A, on one side of the equals sign, with everything else on the other. Then you need to substitute the numbers which you know for the terms on that side to give you the value of A.

The original equation was

$$D_n = A(1 + r)^n$$

Don't worry that this looks much more complicated than the equation in the balance illustration: the principle of doing the same to each side is just the same. Here, we want to stop the A being multiplied by $(1 + r)^n$. If we divide that side of the equation by $(1 + r)^n$, then the two terms will cancel out, giving us A by itself. But remember, we need to divide *both* sides by the same thing, so we need to divide the D_n by $(1 + r)^n$ as well. This gives us the equally valid equation:

$$A = \frac{D_n}{(1 + r)^n}$$

This is a much more useful arrangement of the equation if A is what we are trying to find. We know the values of D, r and n, and can put these into the equation, giving $A = £4147$ divided by $(1.2)^4$, which your calculator should tell you is near enough to £2000. This is quicker and more accurate than the trial-and-error method.

We shall now do a similar thing with a different equation which looks more like those you find in a conventional algebra text. If you want to find x when you have the equation

$$y = 7 + 3x + \tfrac{1}{y}$$

you want to rearrange things to get the x on a different side from the 'y's, and from the 7. You can take 7 from both sides. And you can take $\tfrac{1}{y}$ from both sides. This gives you

$$y - 7 - \tfrac{1}{y} = 3x$$

It is usual to have the thing we are looking for on the left, so these two sides can be reversed

$$3x = y - 7 - \tfrac{1}{y}$$

The only thing remaining is to divide both sides by 3, to leave us with a single x on the left

$$x = \frac{y - 7 - \frac{1}{y}}{3}$$

This would be fine if you knew y and merely wanted to put in its value and work out x. But you might want to include this in a longer equation, where there could be a chance of cancelling some terms out and, with a messy-looking thing like this it would be quite hard to keep track of what you were doing. It could be tidied up into something with only one fraction. To get rid of the $\frac{1}{y}$ on the top, we need to turn all the terms into $y$ths. (Remember that with fractions you could multiply top and bottom by the same thing, or divide them by the same thing, without changing the value of a fraction: $\frac{1}{2} = \frac{2}{4} = \frac{10}{20}$ etc.). So y can be written as y^2/y, and 7 can be written as $7y/y$. Thus the whole numerator, the bracketed term, can equally well be written as

$$\frac{y^2 - 7y - 1}{y}$$

The whole equation can thus be written as

$$x = \frac{(y^2 - 7y - 1)}{3y}$$

This makes it easy to work out the value of x. It would be fairly easy to include this 'phrase' in a larger equation if you wished to work out something more complicated.

Test Exercise 5.16

Rearrange the following equations to get x on the left, then work out the values of x if
(i) $y = 2$, (ii) $y = -3$, (iii) $y = 0$

		(i)	(ii)	(iii)
(a)	$2y = x + 5$	_____	_____	_____
(b)	$y + 1 = 3x - 2$	_____	_____	_____
(c)	$y + 2x = y - x + 12$	_____	_____	_____
(d)	$\dfrac{y}{4} = \dfrac{x}{2} + 3$	_____	_____	_____
(e)	$xy = 3$	_____	_____	_____
(f)	$\dfrac{x}{y} = y + \dfrac{1}{2}$	_____	_____	_____
(g)	$\dfrac{y}{(x + 3)} = 4$	_____	_____	_____
(h)	$\dfrac{x}{(y + 2y + 1)} = y + 4$	_____	_____	_____

Using Brackets

In the above examples it was often necessary to use brackets to remind you that everything on the top or bottom of a fraction needed to be multiplied or divided by the same thing or that whatever you did to one side of an equation you needed to do to the other. In Test Exercise 5.11 above, you could handle the brackets by substituting numbers and working out the bracket before going further. Sometimes, though, you need to work with the brackets without substituting. This is less forbidding than it looks.

You have already seen that a simple multiplication, say $2(a + b)$ means multiplying *everything* in the bracket by the 2: here this simply gives you $2a + 2b$. In the slightly more complicated case of multiplying two brackets, the same underlying principle of multiplying everything in the bracket applies. So in $(a + b)(c + d)$ you need to multiply everything in the second bracket by a and add it to everything multiplied by b. Thus

$$(a + b)(c + d) = ac + ad + bc + bd$$

Note that wherever two brackets are written side by side like this it means that they are to be multiplied. There is no need to put a $\times$ sign to show this. Work out the value of each side of the above equation substituting $a = 1$, $b = 2$, $c = 3$ and $d = 4$, to check that they are indeed equal.

Test Exercise 5.17

Write without brackets:

(a) $2a(3b + 2c)$ _____

(b) $\dfrac{x(6y - 4z)}{2}$ _____

(c) $3r(s + 2t) + 3s(2r + t)$ _____

(d) $(2x + y)(y + 2)$ _____

(e) $\dfrac{(3z + 4y)(2y + z)}{2(4y + 2z)(a + b)}$ _____

Spreadsheets and Databases

Provided you *understand* how equations work, and can construct an equation to represent the relationship between different factors, you do not need to actually work it out, even using a calculator. Software exists to do this for you. Spreadsheets are now a near-universal basic business tool and have revolutionised simple financial (and other) modelling. Indeed, you may not even need to produce the tables, but you do need to understand them. Spreadsheets provide a useful secondary function of allowing you to produce charts and graphs which can easily be integrated into a report.

➤ Ch 13

Take every advantage your course offers to develop your skills in this area. You can use spreadsheets in many contexts where you want either to display information as a table or to do simple numerical modelling. Using packages such as these requires constant practice if you are to retain your skills. So look out for opportunities to use them.

> You don't think that your spreadsheet classes at university are remotely useful to anything – in fact these skills become key in a job, and far more interesting because of their relevance, than you ever dreamed.
>
> Biology graduate, managing databases for clinical trials of drugs

Databases are structured data sets of any sort. Relational databases, allow you to work in more dimensions than a simple spreadsheet, You can think of them as a series of linked spreadsheets, which allow you to put in relationships between as well as within spreadsheets, so that you can ask far more complex questions of your data. As with a single spreadsheet the database will update all relevant cells when anything is added or changed. Because of their greater complexity it takes a little more time to become competent in building and using databases. Unless you plan to collect a lot of complex data in your project you will probably find a spreadsheet is adequate.

As a student, and indeed in many jobs, it will be a great help if you are comfortable with using spreadsheets. The Microsoft version is called Excel, but other integrated office software packages will have an equivalent component. The TECHSkills Box 5.1 gives a brief description which will help if you have not yet used Excel or similar. Skip it if you are already competent with such software.

TECHSkills 5.1 Using spreadsheets

A spreadsheet is an arrangement of 'cells', i.e. spaces, arranged in rows and columns. You can enter text and/or numbers into any cell. You can also enter equations to calculate values from the contents of other cells. Obviously you need to specify which cells are to provide the terms in the equation. In Figure 5.2 the first column shows registration figures for the previous and current years for different courses. The appropriate equation is entered into the shaded cells (see how the cells are identified by column letter and row number). When you enter figures into the boxes, or change existing figures, the spreadsheet does all the necessary calculations.

You can enter text into any box to provide 'labels' (such as 'Last year', 'Accounting', or 'Total' that will make clear what the numbers mean. Obviously, you will not use these cells in any formula: they are there for clarity.

To summarise, cells can be used for **titles**, for the table as a whole, or a row or column, for **numbers**, representing data, or for an equation or **formula** (see shaded cells) used to calculate new values.

Once a spreadsheet has been set up with the correct formulae you can use it with different sets of numbers. For example, in 12 months you could delete last year's figures

	A	B	C	D
1		**Last year**	**This year**	**Percentages**
2	Accounting	100	109	= (C2/B2)* 100
3	Business studies	230	218	= (C3/B3)* 100
4	Computing	200	242	= (C4/B4)* 100
5	Design	50	46	= (C5/B5)* 100
6	**Total**	= B2+B3+B4+B5	= C2+C3+C4+C5	= (C6/B6)* 100

Figure 5.2 Example of a simple spreadsheet

and replace with this year's and then enter the new figures in the 'This year' column. Similarly you could add rows for additional courses you had introduced, and then simply enter their numbers.

Even with something as simple as the data in Figure 5.2, you can see the potential for saving time and reducing errors. For more complex data sets and formulae the time saved can be amazing. You will find spreadsheets useful in finance courses and for any project where you are collecting data and wish to relate different values to each other.

There are many shortcuts provided by the software. For example, the need to total a column or row is so common that Excel provides an Autosum function, which allows you to instruct a total to appear at a single mouse click (the equation for a sum is shown in Fig 5.2 as an example of how to sum without using this function). It is also extremely straightforward to calculate percentages, ignore negative values, round numbers to a given level, provide an average, or compute the rate of return on an investment, if you know present and future value. The 'chart wizard' produces a range of graphs from your data – another extremely useful feature.

If you feel you need to become more familiar with using spreadsheets and databases, use whatever training resources are at your disposal to develop your skills. Your university will probably offer training and/or learning resources. If not, there are many online tutorials available for software common use, so find an appropriate one that covers what you need to know.

Going Further

This chapter has introduced the basics of the maths that you are likely to need and should have made you less nervous about learning more. Once you grasp that the underlying principles are really remarkably simple, you should find that 'playing' with equations is fun. Chapter 13 'Making sense of data' will show you how you can understand the numbers that your equations or whatever produce, communicate this sense and use your results to aid decision taking. If you found this chapter both easy and interesting you might want to read Chapter 13 now. It also introduces the useful tool of calculus. Otherwise make a note to read it as soon as you begin to think about a module or dissertation or project involving any form of data collection.

This chapter has been a long one. Even so, it may be nowhere near as long as you may have felt was necessary! Perhaps you feel that you need more practice before you are really

➤ Ch 13

➤ Ch 13

comfortable with working things out and moving equations around. You may need more practice, too, in order to establish the skills sufficiently so that they will stay with you. There is no real substitute for practice – more practice than the limited number of exercises given here can provide.

So make up further equations for yourself, or for each other if working in a group. What equation will tell you how far a car will go on *g* gallons of petrol if it does 56 miles to the gallon? How many miles to the litre will it go if there are 4.5 litres in a gallon? Think of other such useful things to calculate, or ones which are not useful, but still good practice. Obtain one of the many books which offer examples (but make sure that it gives answers at the end). Some are suggested at the end of the chapter, and you can find some links to online teaching material in the web resources. Knowing that you are competent at manipulating numbers and equations in the simple ways described here will make you more confident in a huge range of situations. It is well worth the effort it may take to practise enough that the skills 'stick'.

SUMMARY

This chapter has argued the following:

- Mathematics offers a clear language for describing many relationships and for analysis and modelling in order to inform decisions.
- Being able to work with numbers and equations is an essential skill in a huge range of academic subjects and is needed for most graduate jobs.
- Although calculators or computers are wonderful for working things out, it is helpful to be able to get a rough idea of what the answer is. This acts as a check against faulty keying in of data or a flaw in the model.
- This means that you need to be able to do the basic operations by hand, working with simplified numbers of about the right size.
- Ratios, fractions and percentages can be used to indicate how parts relate to each other or to the whole.
- Ratios are particularly important in accounting and finance.
- Equations can be used to find unknown values, or to provide a general formula from which values can be calculated in specific cases.
- Equations can be simplified or rearranged using the basic rule that whatever you do to one side you must do to the other.
- Spreadsheets can be constructed to calculate new values from existing data, using equations.

Further information

Crosby, A.W. (1997) *The Measure of Reality*, Cambridge University Press. This will not teach you any techniques but is fascinating background reading, with discussion of the role of numbers and measurement in a wider historical context. Thus it covers not only mathematics and bookkeeping but also music and painting over the period 1250–1600.

GMAC (1015) *The Official Guide for GMAT Quantitative Review 2016.* John Wiley and Sons. This gives you a large number of test items from the GMAT test, with answers.

Graham, L. and Sargent, D. (1981) *Countdown to Mathematics*, Vol. 1, Addison-Wesley with the Open University Press. This covers much the same ground as this chapter but at greater length and with many more examples for you to work through, with answers.

Jaques, I. (2013) *Mathematics for Economics and Business, 7th edn,* Harlow: Pearson.

Morris, C. and Thanassoulis, E. (2007) *Essential Mathematics: For Business and Management*, Palgrave Macmillan. This also gives straightforward explanations of the topics covered here, together with statistics and calculus relevant to Chapter 13.

6
WRITING TO COMMUNICATE

Learning outcomes

By the end of this chapter you should:

- understand what is required for effective communication

- have assessed whether your grasp of written English is adequate for study and report writing

- be able to write a short letter communicating a particular message

- understand how to start planning a written assignment

- know how to structure a formal report.

Introduction

Communication is vital for employment, and written communications form a large part of communications in and with organisations. Improving your writing, whether of essays or management reports, will make you far more successful as a student and at work. This chapter explores a model relevant to any communication, before looking specifically at written communication skills.

If you can write clearly you have a great advantage in most situations over those who cannot. The written word is still a major channel for communication. Writing clearly, whether essays, letters, memos or reports, is a key skill, but a surprisingly rare one. Even native English speakers have difficulty with some of the basics of the English language. Mastering these can make you more confident, as well as more competent. Understanding the basic forms of written communication will help you to structure your essays or reports better. Improving your writing style will make your communication more persuasive. Your grades will benefit markedly, and your writing skills will also contribute to employability and career success – they are one of the key skills employers seek.

Note that there are two helpfiles at the end of this chapter. The first covers the basics of English grammar; the second is designed to give additional help if English is not your first language.

Writing As a Key Transferable Skill

Being able to get your message across by writing clearly is important in most aspects of life. As a student, you will probably be assessed on what you *write* rather than directly on what you *know*. It is your ability to *communicate* the extent of your knowledge and understanding to your assessor that determines your marks, rather than the extent of your knowledge. Expressing yourself in writing is therefore a critical skill for success as a student. It is equally important at work, and indeed in your non-work life.

You may need to write to a landlord about a problem with a flat, to the police explaining why you were parking in a residents' area without a permit, to a prospective employer to enquire about the sort of opportunity that might be available to you on graduation, or to your bank manager to explain why it would be a good idea for you to have a higher overdraft. In all such cases it is important to get your intended meaning across, and to create an appropriate impression so that the person receiving your communication responds as you hope.

I have seen many well-qualified applicants rejected without interview because of a badly written application. At work, an impressive report that you have written may bring you to the – favourable – notice of senior managers who may then remember you when an opportunity arises, whereas a confused, rambling or otherwise unimpressive report may create an equally lasting *unfavourable* impression. This impression can affect your subsequent promotion prospects. Poor communication with customers or other stakeholders can prove costly to an organisation, while good communication can win customers and convince others of the worth of any case you are making.

Elements of Communication

Think of written or spoken examples of communication that you have recently encountered and how you reacted. You were probably responding both to the content of the communication and to the way in which it was communicated. Sometimes you may have *misunderstood* a message, perhaps because of the way it was conveyed. The meaning you extracted from the 'message' was not the meaning intended by the person who was communicating with you. Look at the diagram in Figure 6.1, which makes these different elements in communication clear. This simple framework helps draw your attention to the four elements of communication, and to pay due attention to each.

Sender

When you are the sender, it is essential to be clear about your own objectives. What message(s) do you want to convey? Unless *you* are absolutely clear about this you are unlikely to achieve your objective. Are you aiming to impress, inform and/or influence?

To become better at communication you need to be aware of your strengths and weaknesses. Are you better at speaking than writing or vice versa? Do you tend to make things too involved or to skip over necessary detail? Do you unintentionally antagonise people? Or do you avoid necessary conflict? The more you know about your own characteristics as sender, the more likely you are to be able to achieve your (clarified) objectives. It is worth giving this aspect of your skills serious, and honest, consideration.

Receiver

Who is your message intended for? What are their objectives and characteristics? Are they happier with some forms of communication than others? Do they expect a particular format or level of language? Will they have particular expectations about you or your message that you need either to meet or to overcome? Different lecturers may demand different writing styles or have different attitudes to word limits. At work, one boss may expect you to put everything in writing whereas another is happier with a quick face-to-face meeting. Some managers refuse to read anything longer than one page, while others may want lots of detail.

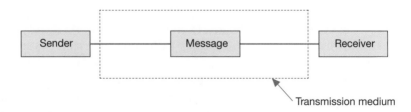

Figure 6.1 The elements of communication

At work, there is also often a question as to the best receiver(s) for a given message. Do you tell your boss or his or her senior? Or do you write to one copying it to the other? This whole area is fairly fraught and there is scope for making enemies by copying implicit criticism of one person to a number of others. On the other hand, you can waste considerable energy by communicating with those who choose to ignore you, or by failing to copy messages to people who need to know what you have said.

Message

Are you trying to communicate a simple piece of information or something more complex – perhaps an interpretation of and/or recommended response to that information? Do 'the facts' speak for themselves and, if so, which facts? Would numbers and tables support your argument? Would diagrams make things clearer? How much explanation do you need to give? In course assessments you are trying to convey the message that you know and understand and can apply relevant concepts and techniques and have the basic knowledge about your subject that your lecturer expects. You also need to show that you can use what you know as the basis for a clear analysis of situations. At work the 'meta-message' is likely to be slightly different: that you are capable of seeing clearly the essence of a situation and responding effectively, given the context in which it occurs.

Transmission medium

The medium, or channel, likely to be most effective will depend on the situation. A short, factual message could be conveyed equally well by email, telephone or face to face. A long, complicated argument, based on an analysis of large amounts of data, is likely to need a written report. A sensitive interpersonal issue is probably best handled face to face. A difficult communication which you do not wish to discuss might be easiest via email. Course assignments will usually specify the medium to be used.

Few channels are perfect. They tend to distort messages in various ways. A telephone line can make words inaudible. Poor handwriting in an exam can obscure your meaning. Your use of English may create further problems. As indicated earlier, a clear, well-presented piece of work will normally influence your marker to give a significantly higher grade than the same material badly presented. This is not a conscious 'mark for good presentation' effect, but an unconscious response to the meta-message. The well-presented work gives an impression of better content and better underlying understanding.

➤ Ch 10

Given the potential for loss in transmission, it is worth adopting strategies to minimise this. Underlining of key words, inclusion of diagrams or other illustrations to clarify and reinforce written points, and brief introductory statements of complex points you are about to make will all help. So too will summaries of points once made. These strategies are particularly important in verbal presentations (dealt with in Chapter 10). The formal report structure outlined shortly also serves to minimise this sort of transmission loss. So too, of course, does correct use of English.

Assessing Your Writing Skills

Writing can be a real strength or a weakness. This is an area where you can obtain some objective evidence of your abilities. First, look back at your SWOT analysis and your initial assessment. Then use the following activity to think further about how good your skills are in this area.

➤ Ch 1

Activity 6.1

Use the following questionnaire to help you to reassess your written communications skills. Say how often each of the following is true for you. (Score N for never, S for sometimes, O for often, A for always.)

	N	S	O	A
I enjoy having to do a piece of writing.	❏	❏	❏	❏
I think carefully about what I am trying to communicate before starting to write.	❏	❏	❏	❏
I choose words that will be easily understood by the person I am writing to.	❏	❏	❏	❏
I pay attention to the order of my sentences.	❏	❏	❏	❏
I group sentences carefully into paragraphs so each paragraph contains a single idea.	❏	❏	❏	❏
I make sure my writing is legible when handwriting.	❏	❏	❏	❏
I use the spell checker and grammar checker.	❏	❏	❏	❏
When I use these, very few mistakes are shown.	❏	❏	❏	❏
I leave generous margins and spaces between paragraphs to improve appearance and clarity.	❏	❏	❏	❏

6

WRITING TO COMMUNICATE

Cartoon by Neill Cameron, www.neillcameron.com

I use subheadings to break up long sections of text.	❏	❏	❏	❏
I use diagrams wherever possible to make my meaning clearer.	❏	❏	❏	❏
I re-read what I have written to check that there are no mistakes and my meaning is clear.	❏	❏	❏	❏
If I am writing something important I get someone to check it.	❏	❏	❏	❏
I really enjoy it when people are impressed by what I write.	❏	❏	❏	❏
I get praise from lecturers and others for my written work.	❏	❏	❏	❏

If you have lots of ticks under 'N' or 'S' you should work carefully through this chapter, and perhaps draw up an action plan to continue improving your skills thereafter. Even if your self-assessment suggests your skills are fine, check your competence by trying Test Exercise 6.1 before deciding that no further development is necessary. (A version of the above, which allows you to obtain a single 'score' and to reassess yourself at intervals, is available on the website.)

Activity 6.2

Collect copies of letters or other things you have written for a non-study and non-social purpose. If you do not have any, save copies of the next few such letters you write. Ideally, work with others to assess how well these are likely to convey the intended message, thinking about the message itself, the way it is expressed and the person for whom it is intended. Look out for possible *unintended* messages too. Try to redraft the content to be shorter and/or clearer and/or more likely to produce the response you want.

Basic English

Emphasis on teaching grammar and spelling in UK schools has changed over time. During the 1970s there was an increasing emphasis on creativity, and a corresponding move away from teaching language rules in case these should inhibit 'expression'. Government initiatives have now reversed this to some extent, but many still leave school in the UK feeling fairly insecure about their use of language. Those who have learned English as a second or subsequent language may also lack confidence in its use.

In either case, lecturers and employers may be frustrated by what they see either as an inability to express thoughts in writing or, worse, an inability to think at all. The following exercise will give you some idea of your own strengths and weaknesses in this area. (You may already have some idea of these from the comments teachers and lecturers have made!) Answers are given at the end of the book, but do the whole exercise before looking.

Test Exercise 6.1

The following sentences contain mistakes. Without using a dictionary or other reference source, write them out correctly. (This may give a different picture from your self-assessment.)

1. The father's going to take his children their, the mother is away on holiday.

   _____

2. The dog is compleatly disinterested in it's ball.

   _____

3. Studying english is very different to studying engineering.

   _____

4. When I recieved them the data surprised me.

   _____

5. The essay comprised of four separate parts.

   _____

6. He was very unique in having a choice between a career as a rock singer in a leading band or as a brain surgeon.

   _____

7. A range of statistics were available owing to there search of the literature.

   _____

8. I will probably come to see you and he tomorrow.

   _____

9. There were many mistakes in your letter. You're spelling and you're unskillful choice of words.

   _____

10. One can easily improve your writing by redrafting after an interval has elipsed.

    _____

If you had more than two mistakes in your 'correct' versions (either errors which you failed to correct or alterations to text that was already correct) you should probably work through the spelling and grammar helpfile at the end of this chapter. There are further text exercises on the website.

General Points on Style

Even if you write in perfectly correct English, the *style* of your writing may interfere with communication. Style is a difficult thing to define, and tastes in written style may differ almost as much as in styles of clothing. But just as all winter coats should keep out wind and rain, there are certain general points which can be made about written communication (rather than writing as art). Whether you are writing an essay, a formal letter or a report at work, you are likely to have the same need for simplicity, clarity and absence of emotionality. Other things will depend on the particular form of communication you are using and will be discussed in more detail in connection with that form.

Simplicity and clarity

While it is possible, if you are thoroughly confident in your use of English and can keep control of a whole sequence of subordinate clauses, some of which may describe elements of the main clause, others of which may describe phrases which are already subordinate clauses in themselves, without forgetting which verb belongs to which clause or omitting verbs altogether, to construct a long and complicated sentence that is grammatically correct, the overall effect of complexity is usually far from satisfactory, as the reader soon starts to lose track of the main idea, which may have been introduced several lines earlier, and by the end of the sentence it is extremely likely that he or she will have lost the thread altogether.

Is that clear? Although the last sentence was (I think) grammatically correct, you probably had to read it several times to extract its meaning. Yet many students write even longer sentences, and all too often their grammar falls apart in the process. If so, then no matter how often I re-read their work I cannot work out what they meant, and so I cannot give any marks for it.

Test Exercise 6.2

Try to identify the main clause in the first sentence of the last but one paragraph. How many subordinate clauses are there?

Imagine how much harder text is to read if long words are used as well as complex grammar. If you have a predilection for multi-syllabic words, habitually utilising these in preference to equivalent but briefer terms, intending possibly to enhance the impressiveness of your communication by demonstrating the extensiveness of your vocabulary, the capacity for obfuscation is multiplied significantly. So use short words and short sentences wherever possible.

As a rule of thumb, aim at sentences of less than 25 words, or two and a half lines. Sentences should be both grammatically complete and contain a single 'unit of meaning'. Unless your meaning is very complex you should be able to express it within 25 words. If you keep your sentences short you are also far more likely to keep control of nouns, verbs and objects. You will be less likely to put plural nouns with singular verbs. You will be less likely to omit verbs, subjects or objects altogether. Your meaning will be clearer both because shorter sentences are easier to read and because they are more likely to be grammatically correct.

Fog Index

There are several ways of measuring the clarity or otherwise of a piece of text. One of the best known is the 'Fog Index'. You can insert text into an online calculator to find the index, or work it out yourself. Select at least six sentences at random from your work – The longer the extract, the more reliable the index. To work out the index by hand, count the number of words in your selected sentences and find the average sentence length by dividing the number of words by the number of sentences. Count the number of words with three or more syllables, divide by the total number of words in the selected text and multiply by 100 to give the percentage of long words. Add your average sentence length to your percentage of long words and multiply the total by 0.4. The answer is the Fog Index for the text in question. If it is greater than 12, the text is 'foggy'; the larger the index, the less clear the text will normally be. (Your word processor may calculate readability statistics for you.)

Test Exercise 6.3

Calculate the Fog Index for the first paragraph in the section headed 'Simplicity and clarity', the sentence starting 'While it is possible . . .' in which it was difficult to find the main clause. The answer is given at the end of the book.

Activity 6.3

Calculate the Fog Index for your last three pieces of written work. If possible, compare notes with other people's writing, or perhaps swap work and calculate someone else's Fog Index while they work out yours. (If you are unsure about your number skills, do both, to see whether you come to the same answers.) Try to rewrite some of the work to reduce the index. Check whether you and others feel that this does indeed improve clarity.

If your work was 'foggy' check the index for future assignments before submitting them, and try to reduce it. Keep your sentences as short as possible, use subordinate clauses sparingly and use long words only when there is no shorter alternative. You may well find that your grades improve. Once this style is a habit, your writing will be clearer, even under pressure, such as exams.

Using paragraphs

As well as keeping sentences as short as possible, you need to think about how you split your text into paragraphs. Paragraphs serve to break your writing into units which the reader can absorb at one go. Ideally, a paragraph will be 75–100 words long. More importantly, it will relate to, and develop, a single topic or idea. Combining disjointed ideas in a single paragraph will confuse your reader.

> **Write clearly by using:**
>
> - short complete sentences
> - few subordinate clauses
> - one paragraph per idea
> - links between paragraphs.

If paragraphs are too short, your writing can seem disjointed or superficial. Check whether the offending paragraphs need to be expanded or perhaps combined (provided they are devoted to the same idea). The occasional short paragraph can be used to emphasise a point. But if your entire report or essay consists of very short paragraphs, you may not be developing your ideas sufficiently.

Overlong paragraphs make text seem heavy and forbidding, and are very hard to follow. See whether you can split them into shorter ones, each containing a single point or idea. A technical report can stand longer paragraphs than an email, and an essay probably falls somewhere between, so the ideal length will depend to some extent on what you are writing.

Thinking about carving text into paragraphs is another useful way of focusing on the points that you are trying to make and the exercise often generates significant improvements. When you start to think about what you were really trying to say, you can often find a way of saying it better.

However you split your paragraphs, it is important that you link them in some way so they flow from one to the other and you avoid disjointedness. The first part of the previous sentence is an example of such a link. It relates the idea of linking to the earlier idea of splitting. Linking needs to be done with a light touch. You do not want to spend half of each paragraph covering ground covered just before merely in order to establish a link.

At the same time, you need to avoid the floating 'this', one of the greatest enemies of clarity in the essays I mark. In the 'This means . . .' or 'This is . . .' type of link, it is unclear whether the 'this' is the whole previous paragraph, the last sentence or the subject (or even the object) of the last sentence. Whether you use 'this' to link sentences or paragraphs, you should always check that it is absolutely clear to the reader what 'this' is.

In summary, express yourself as simply and as clearly as possible, given the message that you wish to convey. If the ideas themselves are complex, they will need to be expressed in correspondingly complex language. The point is that you should not use *unnecessary* complexity, either in your course work or when writing something for your job.

Sensational or emotive language

While you want to make your writing as interesting as possible, avoid sounding like a cheap newspaper (unless, of course, you are writing for one). For example, if you had done a survey of health and safety in an organisation, it would be appropriate to describe the situation as 'worrying', 'thoroughly unsatisfactory' or 'in breach of legislation'. It would be inappropriate, whatever your personal feelings, to talk of 'a downright disgrace', 'a thoroughly immoral situation' or 'another example of capitalist managers exploiting the oppressed workers'. You can make your meaning perfectly clear while using restrained language, and may sound more credible. Indeed, whenever you encounter emotional rhetoric you should look particularly carefully at the strength of the supporting evidence and reasoning.

Use of the first person

You need to check the expectations of your audience here. For example, I have used the first person ('I') in this book to avoid sounding too distant. I find that 'the author' sounds uncomfortably pretentious, particularly as this book is not intended as an academically authoritative text. Rather, it is a collection of my suggestions for you to use where they seem helpful, and use of 'I' should serve to reinforce this.

The first person, used sparingly, is normally sensible in a letter, is acceptable in some (but by no means all) reports, and is essential for reflective writing. Check with your tutor or organisation how they feel about it before using 'I' in reports or essays. Knowing the expectations of your 'receiver' is important here.

Basic Written Forms

Using clear and correct English will always be important. Sometimes a particular form of writing will also be required. In writing to your bank manager or a potential employer, you will need to use a formal letter. For a job application you will often be asked to submit a *curriculum vitae* (CV). Your tutors may ask for essays. At work you may have to write emails and reports. If you are confident with these different forms, their structure can make it *easier* to write clearly. CVs are dealt with in the final chapter and the other forms are outlined below. How to decide the *content* within these forms will be dealt with in Chapter 7.

➤ Ch 16
➤ Ch 7

Presentation will always be important. Clear margins, clear font, good paper (if producing hard copy) and absence of errors will create a good impression – an important non-verbal aspect of many communications.

Formal Letters

Two possible layouts for formal letters are shown in Figure 6.2, one word-processed, one handwritten (although handwritten formal letters are now rare). In either case, you will see:

● careful layout on the page, so that there is space around and the effect is balanced

● sender's address and date of sending at the top right-hand corner (though some company letterheads vary)

● recipient's name and/or title with address below this and on the left of the page.

Addressee

Wherever possible, write to a named individual. This is particularly important if you are expecting some effort to be made on your behalf. Suppose that you are writing to enquire about a vacation job in a company that interests you or would like access to the company for research purposes. A letter that starts 'Dear Ms Fortescue' or whatever is far more likely to be read than one which starts 'Dear Sir'. It is usually possible to find out the name of the most appropriate recipient by telephoning first. Often the receptionist will tell you. If not, ask to speak to someone about vacation jobs (or whatever) and find out from them to whom you should address your letter. Check that you know how to spell the name and write it down straight away – such things seem impossible to forget, but believe me, they are not!

You can further increase your chances of success by speaking to that person on the telephone – they are then far more likely to read your letter when it arrives. Failing this, try to find out from the person what skills and experience are seen as important. This will enable you to slant your letter accordingly. If you cannot find a name, at least include an appropriate job title.

Starting your letter

If you are replying to an earlier letter, then it is usual to thank the person at the start, and to include any reference that the original letter quoted so that the earlier relevant correspondence can be easily found. If you are replying to an advertisement rather than a letter, then still quote the relevant reference. Start a new paragraph for the substance of your message.

Layout

Paragraphs can be separated either by indenting the first line or by leaving an extra line of space. With word-processed letters it is probably now more usual to space paragraphs, whereas with handwritten letters indentation is common. The examples given in Figure 6.2 show the effect of each.

It is common to leave a slightly larger space between the 'Dear . . .' line and subsequent text and again between text and 'Yours . . .'. Together with space between the addressee's details and the 'Dear . . .' line, this helps you to space the letter nicely on the page.

Epistolary (i.e. letter-writing) style

When writing a letter, as with other messages, you need to choose a style which suits both your recipient and your purpose in writing. You do not wish to sound arrogant, demanding or overfamiliar if you are writing formally to someone about a job or a favour of some kind. You *do* want to sound clear and to the point, as well as polite, so you will need to balance possibly conflicting demands between clarity and gratitude or whatever. If you are asking for something, it is usually enough to say 'I should be grateful if you would . . .' perhaps with some explanation of why you are making the request.

57 Variety Road
Tintown
Bucks
HB7 3RR
26.4.2016

Dr P. Tutor
Dept of Business Studies
University of Wight

Dear Dr Tutor,

<u>*Absence at start of term*</u>

I am afraid that I was bitten by a snake at the start of the vacation. It is getting better now, but my doctor says I shall not be able to return until the middle of the second week of term. I enclose a certificate from the doctor.

I should be very grateful if you could inform anyone who needs to know, and apologise to those who will be inconvenienced.

Your sincerely

ROBIN LEARNER

---

47 Sunny Avenue
Greenlands
Riverton
RV3 5PQ
Tel: 01222 575323
31.5.2016

Ms J. Jones
HR Department
Puddle Plastics
Industrial Estate
Maintown
M7 6FF

Vacancy for temporary general assistant

Dear Ms Jones

I should like to apply for the temporary general assistant post advertised in the *Maintown Courier*. I am a second-year student at Riverton University, but live in Maintown and am looking for vacation work in July and August.

Before going to university I worked for two years, and my experience includes clerical, secretarial, bar and reception work. I enclose a CV giving details of this and the names of two people willing to act as referees. I am currently studying for a business degree and as part of this have taken a computing course. I am now reasonably competent at both word processing and use of databases.

I shall be at the above address until the end of June, and thereafter living at home, at the address shown on my CV. If you need any further information, please let me know.

Yours sincerely

Chris Student

Chris Student

Figure 6.2 Possible layouts for a formal letter

Sincere or faithful?

If your computer wants you to use 'Yours truly', ignore it – unless you are in the USA or somewhere else where this is acceptable. Both 'Yours sincerely' and 'Yours faithfully' sound slightly archaic, but one or the other is expected and many people are uncertain as to which is right. If you are writing to a named person you should end your letter with 'Yours sincerely . . .'. If you have only a title, and therefore have had to start with 'Dear Sir or Madam', then you should end with 'Yours faithfully . . .'. Save more friendly endings, such as 'With best wishes . . .', for informal letters. Because most signatures are hard to decipher, you should type or print your name beneath your signature. If you are writing in an official capacity, write your position (for example, Chairman, University Debating Society) beneath your name.

Activity 6.4

Collect formal letters written to you and check them against the guidelines above. If you have copies of your replies, then check these too and redraft where you can see scope for improvement. (This may be easier if you swap letters with someone else and correct each other's.)

Activity 6.5

Prepare an exhibit for your portfolio based on two formal letters that you have written. Describe your objectives in writing them and comment on why you adopted the style and content shown. Include copies of the letters themselves and comment on their effectiveness in terms of the response they generated, noting any lessons learned.

Email

Email has become the dominant medium for internal organisational communication. The advantages are many:

- near instant transmission to any number of recipients and location
- the recipient need not be immediately available as with a phone
- zero cost
- automatic record of communication
- easy filing for future reference

There are also some disadvantages:

- messages can be missed or accidentally deleted
- absence of body language and tone of voice may lead to misunderstandings

If your main use of emails is social, you may need to think about the differences between informal and formal emails. This section looks at the formal use of email.

Formal emails need to be clear and to the point. Your recipient may receive dozens, or even hundreds of emails a day, and will necessarily read each very quickly. The title needs to succinctly convey the content of the email. The content itself needs to be clear and concise, with paragraphs clearly separated. Care is needed to avoid seeming terse and impersonal, unless that is what you intend.

It is worth noting that email can be a significant source of stress and ineffectiveness at work. Many people already receive 100–200 messages per day, and if they constantly respond to them it may disrupt their concentration. There is much you can do to reduce the stress potential of email. The following guidelines should help.

Guidelines for good email practice

Meet people if you can, and use the phone when it helps

Both telephone conversations and other virtual contacts are easier if you have already met the other person, so when possible, continue to meet people at intervals, rather than relying exclusively on email. Telephone may be better than email if you want to develop ideas together, or argue through a point, so may help for some interchanges when you cannot meet. Reserve email for those times when it is the most efficient medium.

Watch your language

Words alone can seem very impersonal, so care needs to be taken with the tone of a message. It is easy to give unintentional offence because there is no body language, no smile or tone of voice to show that your meaning is friendly. Words that you could say with a smile may have a very different effect if read from a screen. (I have noticed an increasing tendency to use 'Dear X', 'Yours . . .' or 'Best wishes' in emails, adopting something closer a letter style, even for work emails, and have also noticed that I respond far better to these messages than to those lacking such courtesies.)

If you are careless in your choice of words, email exchanges can become more and more heated – a process sometimes referred to as flaming. A particular hazard here is trying to email when you are in a hurry. Another is to email when you have been out for a drink. You may be trying to be helpful by sending a brief message late at night before leaving on a business trip, but the recipient will sense your haste rather than your intention to be helpful, so your reply may come across as terse or offhand (even if it is coherent).

Never be abusive or threatening on purpose

Messages can almost always be traced back to you and can easily be forwarded to people in authority if someone wants to complain. Even sarcasm is dangerous because of the possibility of misinterpretation. So . . .

Be careful what you send

What you write in confidence can easily be forwarded, deliberately or accidentally, perhaps to someone about whom you were being less than complimentary. It is therefore safest not to write anything that would be embarrassing or dangerous if it became public.

If someone does send you an injudicious email, assume that it was intended to be treated confidentially.

Be careful whom you mail

Address lists are both wonderfully convenient and highly dangerous. It is wonderfully convenient to be able to send a message to everyone it concerns by sending to an address list, or using 'Reply All' rather than needing to key in each name individually. It is *not* wonderful to receive dozens of irrelevant messages because a list has been used which contains people to whom the message is of little concern.

So target your message or reply carefully. Some systems default to 'Reply All', which can be a real hazard. Our entire system was once clogged up because of a message sent to all remote email users about a forthcoming change. This upset them greatly and, in their fury, about half of these hundreds of angry souls hit the 'Reply' key and sent their message to everyone on the original list. Recipients were then even angrier at the people who had replied to all and did the same thing themselves when complaining.

If people have not given permission for their email address to be made public, be careful to use blind copy (bcc) with your list, rather than using the regular copy (cc) function or simply addressing your message to everyone. If you do not, you are giving all addressees everyone else's email addresses, and this is a breach of confidence and has potential for abuse.

Make your meaning clear

It is very easy to reply to an email as if the sender has just spoken to you. But 'Fine by me' can be confusing if the question was sent some time previously, perhaps as one of several emails. Even if your system automatically appends the original message to the reply it is good practice to write a message which is self-explanatory. 'OK – see you Friday at 10.00 am' would not take you much longer to type and would make it much easier for the other person to understand. If someone has asked you several questions you may find it efficient to edit their original, putting replies after the questions, and then return it.

Always use the 'title' or 'subject' line to show what the message refers to when originating an exchange. Your recipient may have more emails than they have time to open, and use titles to select which to read. Locating an earlier email is also easier if the title gives a clear indication of the content. (Some skill is needed to convey your meaning in a few words: if your title is too long the end of it may not be displayed.)

Keep messages fairly short

Most recipients find it difficult to absorb more than one screen's worth of message. If a message is becoming overlong because you are trying to cover several topics, use a separate message for each. If it is long because it is complex, it is normally better to attach it as a file: it can then be easily saved and/or printed for consideration later. If word-processor compatibility is an issue, save your document as a rich text format (.rtf) file. If you want to send something in a form that will print well but cannot be edited, send it as a .pdf file.

Re-read before you send

Because of all the hazards above, it is important to read over your message before sending to check that it is clear and does not risk conveying meanings you did not intend. For particularly sensitive messages, or those you write when feeling emotional, it may be worth first sending the message to yourself in order to see how it comes across on a screen. Even if your system allows you to 'unsend' internal messages, it cannot 'undo' messages which have been opened already, or auto-forwarded to another address. Messages titled 'ignore last message' may even encourage people to look! There is also a strong tendency for recipients to plough through messages in the order in which they were received, and therefore, they could end up reading the mistaken message before the 'ignore' one.

Use an appropriate filing system for messages which you need to keep

It is tempting to treat email as a transient medium and delete all messages once answered. This is important to keep your mailbox from becoming full, and fine for social use but dangerous at work. It may be important to refer to the details of past messages or check the dates they were sent. Rather than leaving all your back mail to clog up the system, file all mail that you might conceivably need to refer to later on your own machine and/or cloud storage, and delete it from the mailing system. You need to be careful here – deleted items may stay on the system until you throw away deletions by 'emptying wastebasket' or whatever your system calls it. Do this regularly or you will be cluttering up the system unnecessarily.

Emphasise with care

Emails lack the paralinguistic elements of a spoken message, the speed, intonation and volume in speech which give emphasis. There is a temptation to use capitals and exclamation marks for emphasis instead. In an email, CAPITALS COME ACROSS AS SHOUTING. They can occasionally be useful for emphasis, but can easily give offence, so use with care. (Italics or bold are best avoided – they and other symbols can arrive as something very different on your receiver's machine.) Similarly, repeated exclamation marks are to be avoided, except when email your friends. Again, the occasional exclamation mark is acceptable in a formal email but use with care.

Emoticons or smileys

Since the beginning of email, users have tried to convey the emotions missing from text with combinations of symbols such as : - (for sadness. (Word now supports this to the extent of producing icons like: ☺.) Many such symbols are freely available for use on Facebook, etc. Smileys were once frowned on in non-social emails, but again, can be used with caution unless the message is very formal, or to a senior with whom you are not already on good personal terms.

Essays

➤ Ch 7

➤ Ch 15

This will be a short section as there are few 'rules' for the form of an essay. Content is of course more problematic and will be looked at in Chapter 7 when assessment requirements are covered. You will also find the material on report writing later in this chapter and towards the end of Chapter 15 helpful with essay writing. Box 6.1 highlights key points from all these chapters.

Box 6.1 Tips for writing good essays

- Start drafting early – do not procrastinate!
- Revisit and take note of feedback on past essays
- Make sure you understand (all) the question
- Research your subject
- Work out the case you want to make
- Structure your answer clearly
- Make clear the evidence and reasoning that support your case
- Write clearly in an appropriate style
- Edit your essay carefully
- Avoid plagiarism like the plague
- Submit work on time.

This chapter addresses the few formal elements needed for a good essay, namely:

- The *title*, which may be given by the person setting the assignment or, if not, chosen by you to reflect the content.

- An *introduction*, which may not be headed as such but which should clearly 'set the scene' and arouse the reader's interest. Normally, it helps to enlarge slightly on the title, so that the topic and scope are clear, explain your objectives in writing the essay, outline the approach you intend to take and briefly preview key points to be covered. (It is a waste of space to use your introduction merely to restate the question to which your essay is an answer. You need to expand or build on it in some way.)

- Any *background information*, if brief, may be included in the introduction. If longer, it could be a separate section immediately after. If very extensive it could be summarised briefly, with the full version appended, although appendices are not usually expected in essays.

- The *main section of your essay*, in which you make the points you feel are necessary in order to address the topic of the title. In making these points you will need to include your arguments and describe any evidence on which they are based.

- Your *conclusions*, which provide a satisfactory feeling of completion. This section should briefly look back over what you have said, showing how the points raised answer the question or provide a specific perspective on the title (to which the conclusion needs to refer).

- The *references (which are allowed to be headed 'References')* which you used in your work, in alphabetical order of first author, giving date and full title of the publication. (More detailed guidelines on referencing are given at the end of this chapter.)

- A *structure* – which is an equally important, though less visible, element of your essay. Mind maps may be useful in planning this, as the main branches can represent sections of your essay, each made up of paragraphs dealing with its twigs. Your arguments should be balanced, giving due weight to both sides of whatever question you are addressing. They should also lead firmly and directly from the initial question implicit in the title through to your conclusions. (It may help to try to map your argument, as described in

➤ **Ch 4**   Chapter 4, to check that it is sound.)

Essay style

All the earlier general points about written communication are important. You need to be clear about your objectives and meet them by writing in good English and using convincing arguments and evidence. You should avoid colloquialisms and emotive or sensational language, repetition, rambling, pomposity and over-complex or jargon-ridden

➤ **Ch 7**   expression. Planning the structure of your essay is dealt with in more detail in Chapter 7.

Writing concisely is good stylistically. It also helps you cover all the points expected within any word limit for an essay, or time available for writing an exam. Rambling, long-winded writing will mean you cover only a small fraction of what is expected in the words (or time) allowed, or before your boss's patience runs out. Penalties for going over the word limit will vary from course to course. Penalties for not covering expected ground in an exam are fairly universal.

Views on use of headings in essays vary. Some feel that an essay should always consist of continuous, smoothly flowing prose, uninterrupted by any headings. Others think that for a longer essay it is helpful to use headings for the introduction, the subject of the main body and conclusion and even appropriate subheadings within the main part of the essay if it contains two or more distinct sections. There will be variations according to subject, as well as personal preference. Scientific or technical essays may need subdivisions whereas essays on arts topics may not. Business studies lecturers, accustomed to report formats, normally find subheadings useful. Ask the person setting the essay for their preferences.

Lists and very short numbered points are seldom suited to essays. Again, there will be variations depending on subject matter and tutor preferences. Sometimes a short list may be very helpful. But normally it will be better to develop each point as you make it (a paragraph for each?) aiming for a flow from one to the next.

Diagrams, tables and other illustrations are also frowned upon in some subjects but considered essential in others. In some essays a diagram may be necessary for your readers' understanding. If you were using a particular model such as Porter's value chain as a framework for your analysis, a diagram included at the relevant point (rather than placed at the end as an appendix) might be extremely helpful. Given that few marks are given for straight copying of diagrams it makes sense to annotate it to show relevance to your particular argument. Whatever you do, be guided by what is likely to be best for the reader/tutor, who will want to follow your arguments as easily as possible, without interruption.

Reports

Most substantial communications within organisations are reports of some form or other. Consultants realise that the report they write is often the only tangible output of their expensive work, so the impression it creates is extremely important. Government departments and professional institutes produce many reports.

The purpose of a report (it may be called a paper) might be to inform or to persuade, or sometimes a mixture of both. The exact structure adopted will depend to some extent on the conventions used in an organisation, and on the purpose of the report. Graduate recruits may be asked to investigate an issue and write a report on it as part of their induction. Such reports may be read by senior managers: thus your report writing skills may attract favourable (or unfavourable) notice early in your career.

 My boss really noticed the first report I wrote. I was pretty proud of the analysis I'd done, but it was the presentation and graphics that seemed to make the biggest impression on him.

(Graduate in first management position)

All the earlier points about clear writing, appropriate style and good presentation are important in determining how good an impression your report creates.

> **Reports should normally have:**
>
> - a clear descriptive title
> - author and recipient(s)
> - the date
> - a summary
> - a contents list
> - clear subheadings
> - a list of references used.

If your course requires a project or dissertation you will normally need to submit a written report for assessment. The structure required will probably be very similar to a management report. The underlying form in either case is similar to that of an essay, but with the additional key features listed above, which make the structure much clearer to the reader:

Managers are busy people and do not want to spend time wading through undifferentiated text, only to find at the end that the whole thing was irrelevant. The title page, contents list and summary allow for a fast decision as to whether to read the full report.

By establishing the skeleton of the report in the reader's mind, the summary also makes it easier for the reader to grasp the possibly complex arguments which follow and key conclusions and/or recommendations. Subheadings serve to keep the structure clear. (They also serve a useful function in helping the *writer* keep the structure under control.) Detail on the functions of the different parts of a report follows.

Summary (or abstract)

For all save very short reports a summary is useful. For a dissertation or thesis a summary is normally a formal requirement. The summary should come either at the start or finish.

Many organisations insist on an executive summary at the start, making it easy for the busy manager to decide whether or not to read the report. The 'orientation' role of a summary is also better served if it is at the start. A summary at the end may help reinforce what the reader has read (though the conclusions should already have done this).

Wherever you place your summary, clearly, you will *write* it last. It should normally summarise the whole report, rather than merely the recommendations. You should therefore include a brief statement of the original problem, its importance, and the main arguments and evidence leading to your conclusions. You cannot do this until the report is finished. The summary should be complete in that it should make sense when read as a stand-alone document. Indeed, for longer reports the summary may have a wide circulation, with the full report going to a much smaller group. The summary is normally deemed to be outside the report, so not listed under contents, and not counted towards any assignment word limit.

Title page

The title is important, and needs to be as descriptive as possible. In any catalogue or listing of reports, potential readers may select on the basis of title alone, so the title needs to allow them to make a decision on relevance. A title page needs to show the report's author(s) and their role or title, if relevant. It will normally also include the intended recipients (with roles/titles if relevant) and the date the report was circulated. All these provide important information for someone seeking a relevant report for their own purposes. For short reports, or those for close colleagues only, the basic information (To: ..., From: ..., Report title, Date) can instead be put at the start.

For more formal reports, especially if presented in hard copy, the title page creates a strong first impression which may influence judgement of the rest of the report, so attention to design is important. An example of a very basic title page is given in Figure 6.3.

Contents list

The contents list should show major and minor section headings, preferably numbered. A numbering system such as that used in Figure 6.3 shows which are major sections and which minor. It makes it easy for people discussing the report, or wishing to query some part of it, to identify the part they mean. It also makes cross-referencing within the report easier.

You can see how such a contents list provides a clear indication of what is to come, as well as serving as an index to someone interested in only a part of the report. Page numbers help here, although for a short report they are not essential. Some (often government) organisations prefer to number paragraphs rather than sections. This helps with referencing particular parts but does little to reinforce the structure.

Introduction

The introduction to a report is identical in function to the introduction to an essay, but because reports are often longer and more complex, and the topic was not 'set' by the

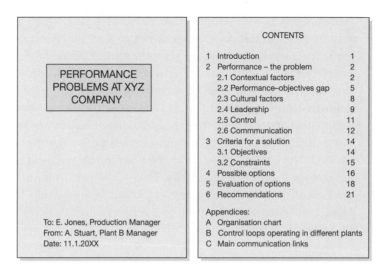

Figure 6.3 Example of student title and contents page

reader, their introductions may have to work harder to achieve their aims. Your reader will usually come to a report with a number of questions:

- Why is this topic important/potentially relevant to my concerns?
- What was the remit of the report writer?
- What method was used (for research)?
- What is the main argument/finding/conclusion?
- On what evidence is this based?
- What are the implications/recommendations?

If your introduction can answer these questions, at least in outline, your reader will both be more interested in your report and follow your arguments with greater ease.

Background information

As with an essay, you may have to provide background information. If readers need a lot of background information it may help to include this in a separate section following your introduction. Otherwise, mention key background points briefly where they are relevant, with reference to an appendix where more detailed background information can be found for those who want it.

Literature search

You need some basis for your arguments, and some of this will usually be rooted in what others have written on the subject. If your report is a research report, perhaps for a dissertation, you will need to conduct an extensive search of existing research before refining your topic and your approach and devote a section of your report to this. Chapters 4 and 12 give guidance on searching the literature. This section should aim to make clear the importance of the literature surveyed to your own investigation. Note that your report should include only the relevant literature, namely that which directly influenced your choice of topic and approach. Do not try to summarise everything that anybody ever wrote that has any connection, no matter how remote, with the broad area in which your topic is located.

➤ Ch 12

Research method

Again, this section is only necessary for dissertations or other research reports or papers. For these it is absolutely essential. Your reader will wish to know precisely how you went about collecting your data and why, in order to be able to judge the validity of what follows. In justifying your choice of approach you may well need to discuss alternative methodologies that you might have used.

Main section(s) – needs to be titled to reflect the content of the section

As with an essay, this is the main substance of your communication. How you write it will depend on your objectives. If you are writing a report on something which has happened, then a suitable structure might be merely to describe the events in logical sequence. If you are writing a progress report, then you might outline achievements to date, and describe work which remains to be done. Cover any problems encountered thus far and ways in which they have been, or will be, overcome, and outline the significance of any deviation from planned timescales. If you are writing a position paper, you might want to outline current policy, explain any changes in circumstances since the policy was established and make a case for any change in policy which you think might be required as a consequence. If you are proposing action, you may wish to start with your proposals and then justify them. For a research report you may need to survey prior research, outline and justify your own research design, give the results of your research and then your analysis. (More guidance on planning your structure is given in Chapter 7.)

Whatever structure is appropriate for your objectives, you need to use a system of subheadings to make this structure clear, whether or not you are using a list of contents. If the report is a long one, then it may be helpful to include a short introduction to each main section and possibly a summary concluding statement to each as well. For a longer section you may need secondary headings within the main headed sections.

(Note: while 'Introduction' is a valid heading 'Main Section' is not. Choose an appropriate main heading appropriate to the content of your particular report.)

In a report, you should think carefully about how to reinforce the arguments in your text with diagrams, graphical representations of data, such as graphs and charts, and raw data. When deciding how much non-textual material to use, and where to put it, the ques-

➤ Ch 8

tion is always 'How will it work best to convince my reader?'. If you are unlikely to be believed without evidence, then this evidence needs to be included wherever it will best support your argument.

If the non-textual material is essential for the argument to be understood, then it (or a summary of it) normally needs to go into the text. If your argument can be understood but may not be accepted without the data, then it may still be necessary to include some of the data in the text, although the bulk of it may be better relegated to an appendix. If a point can be reinforced or made more persuasive by some illustrative material, then again you may be advised to put the illustration in the text. Readers find it inconvenient and annoying to have to keep turning to the end to refer to necessary diagrams. It is even more irritating if there is no mention of the diagram in the text and it is only discovered when the end is reached, far too late for it to be helpful.

Spreadsheets now make it easy to include graphics derived from numbers, and it is also relatively easy to insert other illustrations into your text (see TECHSkills 6.1). Always think about how you can best use illustrations to communicate with, and convince your reader.

A further advantage of including at least some diagrams in the text is that this breaks up the words, making the text look more attractive and less forbidding. However, diagrams should always serve a valid purpose in their own right. Diagrams used purely for decorative purposes may distract or even annoy your reader.

Diagrams should be appended (rather than included) only when they are extremely detailed and of interest only to the most dedicated or critical reader, or are working diagrams produced en route to final versions. (Working diagrams may show your tutor your thought processes, but they would not normally be relevant in a management report.)

Other appendices might include detailed mathematical arguments or equations, so that mathematically minded sceptics among your readers can convince themselves, while those who are happy with your condensed version of the data can follow your overall argument without interruption.

Conclusions

Conclusions should follow naturally from the arguments in the main body of your report. There should be no new material introduced at this stage, nor should any of your conclusions come as a surprise to your readers. You are not a magician, producing rabbits from your hat at this stage. Instead, conclusions should draw together the arguments you developed in your main section and clarify their implications. It can be difficult to distinguish between conclusions and recommendations. Some reports which are not primarily action-oriented combine them in a single section. But there *is* a distinction: conclusions may be thought of as having to do with the logical outcomes of your arguments, whereas recommendations concern actions suggested in the light of these conclusions and of the conditions prevailing in the real world.

Conclusions should:

- flow naturally from earlier arguments
- draw these arguments together
- clarify their implications.

Recommendations

As with the summary, there is debate as to the best location for recommendations. Action-oriented managers often prefer them at the front: 'Tell me what you want me to do then convince me!' For a more analytical report they may be better placed at the end, as they follow naturally from your analysis and conclusions. If your summary includes a brief statement of your main recommendations, with more detailed recommendations at the end, you should be safe, but check with the report's recipients whether they have preferences.

> **Recommendations should:**
>
> - flow naturally from analysis and conclusions
> - be clear proposals for action
> - be sensible and realistic.

In a management report, recommendations should be clearly prioritised and the priorities justified. There may not be the resources to implement all of them, and those evaluating your report will be checking that your priorities are justified, and realistic, given the prevailing situation.

References and bibliographies

➤ Ch 4

In a report you are likely to draw on a range of sources for ideas, data and methods. Whether these are printed, electronic or even personal communications, they need to be clearly referenced. This will avoid charges of plagiarism, and will enable your reader to go to the original sources for more information (or to check that you have interpreted them correctly). It will also convince your readers that you are familiar with other work on a topic and that your conclusions are therefore likely to add something to existing debates.

Sometimes you will want to quote directly from your sources (though remember the caution on this earlier in the chapter). If so, you may need to indicate the page you are quoting from, as well as the reference itself. Usually, you will want to convey their content in your own words. But it is always important to attribute ideas, methods or theories, as well as showing where secondary information was found. You need to do this briefly, efficiently and consistently within your text. Give fuller information, which allows your reader to locate the original if required, in a list of references at the end. One well worked out system for this, widely used in academic writing but acceptable elsewhere, is the Harvard system. It is the system followed in this book, with the exception of location of publisher, which has been omitted. The following guidelines outline how the Harvard system works. Note the importance of mentioning the date you accessed electronic materials. This is because they may be updated frequently. If you have been using bibliographic software you can choose the approved referencing system, which makes it easy to please your tutors.

➤ Ch 4

Note that a list of references includes only those sources which you have specifically referenced in your text. For dissertations and some other more academic forms of writing you may be asked for a bibliography instead of or as well as your list of references. A bibliography is a more extensive list of all the reading which influenced your work, even that which you have not explicitly referred to.

Guidelines for in-text references

- When referring to something in your text, give author name and date. Thus: 'It has been shown that . . . (Graveson, 1998)' or 'According to Graveson (1998) . . . '.

- If referring generally to several different authors on a topic, refer to them in alphabetical order, thus: 'The theory's generalisability may also be tested in other contexts (Glaser and Straus, 1967; Corbin and Straus, 1990)'.

- If referring to something by two authors give both, as in Corbin and Straus above.

- If referring to something by more than two authors use 'et al.' (from Latin for 'and others'), as in 'Buchanan et al., 1988'.

- If referring to corporate authors, such as a company report, follow the style of 'Hanson Trust plc, 1990'.

- If referring to something with no obvious author, such as a government publication, give the title, e.g. 'Employment Gazette, 1992'.

- If referring to works by the same author in different years, order by date, earliest first, thus 'Handy, 1987, 1993'.

- If referring to works by the same author in the same year, use a, b, etc. to differentiate, thus 'Handy, 1987a' and, for the next, 'Handy, 1987b'.

- If referring to something you have read about, in some other book, without actually going back to the original, then make this clear, as in 'Glaser and Straus, 1967, cited by Saunders et al., 1997'.

- You need not use initials for in-text references unless you have to distinguish between two different authors with the same surname.

- If quoting word for word, put the quotation in inverted commas and give author surname, date, page number from which quote was taken, as in

  '. . . business and management research involves undertaking systematic research to find out about business and management . . .'

  (Saunders et al., 1997: 1)

  though here you might like to reflect on the wisdom of quoting something like this.

- To save giving the same information repeatedly, especially if you are using footnotes as well as references, two common abbreviations are used:
  - op. cit. – this is from the Latin for 'in the work cited', so that if you have already given a full reference and wish to refer to the same publication again, you could merely say 'Jones, op. cit.'.
  - ibid. – again from the Latin, this means the same work and refers to the work referenced immediately before.

Guidelines for 'Reference' section at the end

- Reference lists should normally include only those sources which have been directly referred to in your text. It is not normal in a report to include other sources which might interest a reader but which have not been referred to. Should you, exceptionally, wish to do this, it is normal to call the list 'Bibliography'.

- References should be in alphabetical order.

- If you have several references by the same author, they should be ordered by date of publication, earliest first.

- If you have used a, b, etc. to differentiate publications by the same author in the same year, then you need to use them in your reference list as well, making sure that they correspond to the articles you intended in your text.

- Give first author, initials, any subsequent authors each with initials, date (in brackets) then:

  - for papers, give title of paper in inverted commas, *title of publication in which paper appeared in italics*, journal volume and number (with a colon separating them) then page numbers of paper

  - for a chapter in a book where chapters are written by different people, you would similarly give title in quotes, the word 'in' followed by name(s) of book editor(s), book title in italics, location of publisher, publisher's name, page numbers of chapter

  - for a book you merely give title in italics, location of publisher, publisher's name. Thus:

    > Dooley, D., Rook, K. and Catalano, R. (1987) 'Job and non-job stressors and their moderators', *Journal of Occupational Psychology*, 60: 2, 115–32.
    > Craig, P.B. (1991) 'Designing and using mail questionnaires', in Smith, N.C. and Dainty, P. (eds) *The Management Research Handbook*, London, Routledge, pp.181–9.
    > Saunders, M., Lewis, P. and Thornhill, A. (1997) *Research Methods for Business Students*, London, Pitman Publishing.

- If referencing an online source you should indicate that this was the source, give the date of access and the full Internet address. Thus:

  > Jenkins, M. and Bailey, L. (1995) 'The role of learning centre staff in supporting student learning', *Journal of Learning and Teaching*, 1:1, Spring [online] [cited 29 Mar 1996] Available from the Internet <http://www.chelt.ac.uk/cwis/pubs/jolt/issue 1.1/page2.htm>.

6

WRITING TO COMMUNICATE

Appendices

As indicated, detailed supporting evidence or background information can be placed in appendices. Thus you might append a copy of a questionnaire or interview schedule used to collect data, or full monthly production figures for all departments studied, or detailed organisation charts. Where you do this, you normally need to provide a summary of the information in the text and refer to the fuller version so that the interested reader knows where to find it.

Appendices are sometimes used by students as a way of getting around the word limit. Because they are 'optional' to the reader they may not be counted in the length. This is not a good strategy. If material is essential to your argument it should not be in an appendix. The report needs to be capable of standing alone. If including essential material in your text makes your report overlong, consider whether the style is too verbose or the scope of the report too wide.

In the interests of clarity, since numbers are used to identify parts of the report, letters or Roman numerals are often used to identify appendices. (If you have more than 26 appendices, think carefully about whether they are *all* essential before moving on to AA, etc.)

The Serious Sin of Plagiarism

Remember that whatever style you adopt, and whatever form you are writing in, it is essential to avoid plagiarism. This was discussed in Chapter 4 but is repeated here because it is SO important. Plagiarism means passing off the work of others as your own, and is regarded as a serious offence in universities. You are deemed to be 'copying' if the material used is essentially the same as the original, even if you make minor changes to the text. Rearranging paragraphs or changing a few words is not enough to render the material

➤ Ch 4   your own.

So ensure that the words you use are *your own*, unless you are explicitly quoting from a named source and making this very clear. Universities use software to detect any plagiarism, and penalise students severely if it is found. 'Copying' without attribution, whether from another student's work or from something you found on the Internet, can lead to zero marks or, in the worst cases, to expulsion from your university without a qualification and with little likelihood of getting a good reference from your tutors.

Plagiarism is seen by academics as dishonesty of the worst kind – stealing other people's thoughts and ideas. If students were not penalised heavily for this, degrees would come to be worthless, negating all the hard work most students put into gaining their (deserved) qualification. It is for this reason that you need to be absolutely clear what plagiarism means, and avoid it at all costs, no matter how behind you are, or how tempted for any other reason. Every university will have a clearly stated policy on plagiarism. Make sure that you fully understand your own university's policy and do not infringe it. Many universities are now using software to detect work that is not your own, so you are increasingly likely to be found out.

There are many possible reasons for plagiarism. These include:

- being unsure of your understanding of an idea, so copying the original rather than putting it in your own words

- getting behind, having no time to write an assignment, so 'borrowing' one from a friend or colleague

- getting low grades, so submitting work from a better student or material copied from the web
- laziness – it is easier to use someone else's work
- misunderstanding what is required – if you have studied overseas, it is possible that in your last educational system reproducing the (appropriate) original material was usual
- being plagiarised yourself – it is possible to be suspected of plagiarism if someone else uses your work, so avoid this by not giving them the opportunity.

> **To avoid plagiarism:**
>
> - use your own words whenever possible
> - quote other people only when necessary
> - always indicate clearly that you are quoting
> - always give the reference for the material quoted
> - never, NEVER use other people's text as if your own
> - never let other students have a copy of your work.

None of these reasons is acceptable. It is your responsibility to find out what is allowable in your own university (though it is unlikely to differ much from what is said here), and to ensure that others do not have the opportunity to copy from you.

Apart from the risk of being expelled, plagiarism robs you of learning opportunities. You are being asked to write essays to develop and demonstrate your understanding, and to improve your writing skills. Extended use of other people's work will serve neither of these purposes. So use quotations only when necessary to support your argument or if the quotation itself is something that you want to analyse. Do not quote authors when they are saying totally self-evident things. It is not necessary to say things like: 'As Cameron (2008) points out, "Students go to university for many reasons".' This might have been a reasonable point for me to make as part of an introduction to an exploration of these reasons; it is certainly not worth quoting in its own right. (As light relief, you might wish to play 'spot the unnecessary quote' when reading something overzealously academic and turgid.)

When deliberately quoting, use quotation marks to show the extent of what is being quoted and give the author of the quotation and its date immediately before or after, with the full reference to the source, including page number for an extended quote, in the list of references at the end of your essay. If you are not referring to other works and therefore do not need a list of references at the end, then the complete reference may be given immediately after the quote, or in a footnote on that page.

> Remember: copying chunks of other people's work, without saying so, is blatant plagiarism, whether you are quoting published authors, other students' work, or something you bought from an essay service. All are unethical. All will violate university's plagiarism policy and may cost you your degree.

Similarly, you should never claim credit for an idea which originated elsewhere. Although you may not wish to quote the original author exactly, you should still attribute the idea to the relevant publication in your list of references. 'Combobulation theory (Blobbs,

2014) suggests . . .', 'Blobbs's (2014) ideas about combobulation . . .', or 'As Blobbs (2014) found . . .', are examples of ways of doing this. Where you have not read the original paper, merely the description of Blobb in a textbook by Digester, it is good practice to say 'Blobbs (2014) as cited by Digester (2015)', and list the Digester reference.

Writing to Look Good

The key to good presentation without spending hours on it (apart from everything already discussed) is to use those features of your word processor that contribute most to the essays and reports expected of you. Basic touch-typing and editing skills can save you many hours over your degree, and contribute substantially to the appearance of your work, thus influencing your tutors, without their even realising it, to give you higher grades. Use the following activity to assess whether you might benefit from TECHSkills 6.1 on basic wordprocessing.

Activity 6.6

Rate your skills in the following basic areas. Score 5 if you think you are really good, 4 if you are fairly good, 3 if a lot of people seem better than you, 2 if you are at a really basic level, and 1 if you are completely incompetent.

Keyboard – touch typing, speed and accuracy	___
Keyboard – inserting fancy symbols/subscripts/superscripts	___
Editing – moving sections of text within a document	___
Editing – retrieving text deleted in error	___
Editing – using word count, spell and grammar checker	___
Formatting – changing font, paragraph spacing, columns of selected text	___
Formatting – presenting text in the form of a table	___
Formatting – highlighting areas of text using borders and shading	___
Formatting – numbering pages, adding headers and footers	___
Graphics – importing diagrams from other applications into a report	___
Graphics – using a 'draw' or 'paint' facility to generate diagrams in text	___
Filing – storing in systematically named files and folders	___

Total score

A web version is available to allow repeated assessment and filing.

If you scored less than 48 on the above activity, or had very low scores on any particular items, consider making an action plan for improving your text processing skills. (This might form the basis for portfolio evidence of both managing learning and IT skills) Use TECHSkills 6.1 to help.

TECHSkills 6.1: Basic wordprocessing

Keyboard skills, the ability to edit and format text, awareness of the tools available and a good filing habit can all help you produce better written work. If most of your recent 'typing' has been emails and texts, you may need to develop your basic e-writing skills in order to cut down the time you need for writing assignments and improve the presentation of your work.

Note: The example commands below are for Microsoft Office Word 10. You will need to find their equivalent if working with different software.

Fast accurate typing will greatly help when writing assignments or taking part in text-based online discussions. You may also find it easier to delete text, and replace it with something better if the typing itself is easy. (The ability to delete work in order to improve it is a key self-editing skill.)

Rearranging text by cutting (Ctrl + X) and then pasting it where it would work better (Ctrl + V) is very easy and can help you improve the structure of your writing if you find that related points are scattered in your text. However, beware of simply copying (Ctrl + C) text into its new place while leaving the original in place: this results in duplication.

Whenever you have moved or changed text it is essential to re-read the whole thing, as you may find that other changes are needed for the change to work.

Get into the habit of using the extremely helpful tools your software provides. Take notice of the warnings given by spell-checker (red wavy line under text) and grammar checker (green ditto). If you see spelling being autocorrected, check that the computer has correctly guessed what you meant to type. Sometimes it gets it comically wrong. Use the word count tool to check you are not breaking a word limit.

Alter font and font size to increase readability. If your work is submitted and read electronically choose a san serif (i.e. no curly bits) font such as Ariel or Calibri from the drop down font menu, and a font size that will not tax your tutor's eyes, which may be older than yours. By using the spell and grammar checker you can reduce errors, which again will make it easier for your tutor to understand what you have written.

By setting reasonably wide margins, choosing suitable fonts and sizes for both headings and text, and paying attention to the design of your title page, you can easily and impressively improve the appearance your work. You can further improve your presentation (and strengthen your arguments) by incorporating figures and tables from a spreadsheet or other sources (remember to attribute these). The presentational skills you develop for assignments will allow you to produce a more impressive CV and application when applying for a job, and more impressive written communications once in that job.

If you find reading from a screen difficult, and do not yet have voice recognition software to make this unnecessary, ask whether your university can provide this, or if not, where you can get help with obtaining it.

I hope this has motivated you to explore the features of your own software, and to find – and practice using – those which will be most helpful to you. If you need further help ask what support your university provides, or explore the many tutorials available online (some suggestions are available in the web resources).

6

WRITING TO COMMUNICATE

SUMMARY

This chapter has argued the following:

- Effective written communication requires clarity concerning your objectives in communication, understanding of your recipient's needs and expectations and choice of appropriate content, style and form.

- Correct spelling and grammar and good presentation will create a good impression and make it more likely that your message will be understood and accepted.

- Your writing is more likely to be clear if you keep your language as simple as the complexity of your message allows.

- You are likely to be able to improve your writing considerably if you set your first draft aside for a day or two before editing/redrafting.

- Although there is some agreement as to the correct form for emails, essays and reports, there is also some variation in preferred style among tutors and organisations. You should check with your intended recipient to find out their preferences.

- Careful and correct referencing is essential.

- It is essential to avoid any charge of plagiarism.

- Spending a little time becoming familiar with your word-processing software will allow you to greatly improve the appearance of your work.

Further information

Atkinson, I. (2011) *FT Essential Guide to Basic Writing: How to Engage, Persuade, and Sell*, Pearson.

Blamires, H. (2000) *The Penguin Guide to Plain English*, Penguin.

Bowden, J. (2011) *Writing a Report*, 9th edn, Howtobooks.

Burchfield, R.W. (ed.) (2004) *Fowler's Modern English Usage*, 3rd edn, Oxford University Press. A classic – Fowler's first edition appeared in 1926 – a sort of enlarged dictionary with hints on how to pronounce and use the words included. A mine of information.

Gowers, E. (2014) *The Complete Plain Words*, HMSO - 232 Celsius, Kindle edition. This is *the* classic work on the use of English. It has been regularly updated even since the author's death and is well worth acquiring.

Gravett, S. (2003) *The Right Way to Write Reports*, Elliot Right Way Books.

Truss, L. (2003) *Eats, Shoots and Leaves: The Zero Tolerance Approach to Punctuation*, Profile Books. An amusing defence of appropriate punctuation.

http://gunning-fog-index.com/fog.cgi (accessed 18/5/15) to calculate the fog index of any text.

http://www.usingenglish.com/glossary/fog-index.html on fog index in general (accessed 18/15/15).

http://www.gcflearnfree.org/word2010 for a series of tutorials on using Word 10 – but there are many others, and many tutorials for other common word-processing programmes.

http://www.open.edu/openlearn/education/english-skills-learning/content-section-overview for a free OpenLearn course in English for students.

Explore MOOC (Massive Open Online Course) providers like Coursera, edX and Openlearn for more free courses that start every few weeks and allow you to earn a certificate, test yourself and make new connections with other students around the world.

HELPFILE 1
GRAMMAR AND SPELLING

Elements of grammar

Obviously, it is beyond the scope of this chapter to teach you all the complexities of English grammar. But the following rapid overview may help you to avoid some of the more common mistakes and to feel more secure in expressing yourself. You may find it helpful, first, to become more familiar with a number of different parts of speech, serving various functions in a sentence. The most basic (with examples in *italics*) are:

- A **noun**, which names a person, thing or quality (*James, essay, incompetence*).

- A **pronoun**, which stands in for a noun, to save repeating it (*it, he, them*).

- A **verb**, which expresses an action or state of being, past, present, future or possible (*ran, is, will go*).

- An **adjective**, which describes a noun or pronoun (*unhappy, my own, incompetent*).

- An **adverb**, which modifies a verb, adjective or other adverb (ran *quickly*, *deeply* unhappy, *extremely* well).

- A **conjunction**, which joins or relates words or clauses (rich *and* famous, poor *but* happy, working *despite* his illness).

- A **preposition**, which introduces a phrase and is followed by a noun or pronoun which it 'governs' (put it *in* my pigeonhole, *between* you and me).

Nouns

Nouns can be subjects (the thing 'doing' something) or direct objects (the thing affected by the action). In 'You wrote your essay', *you* is the subject and *essay* is the object. With the verb 'to be' the noun is a complement, i.e. completes the sense of the verb, as in 'You are *a student*'.

Phrases

A phrase is a group of two or more words that acts as a noun, adjective or adverb. (*To write well* requires a basic knowledge of grammar. Students *ignorant of this* will do poorly. You need to learn *every day*.)

Sentences

Sentences need to be complete. Simple sentences contain one finite verb, i.e. a verb with its subject. The finite verb may, depending on its tense (past, future, etc.), be several words. And it may have an object, adjectives or adverbs. (I [subject] *should have written* [finite verb] more clearly [adverb].)

Clauses

A clause is a group of words containing a finite verb that forms part of a sentence. The main clause is the backbone of the sentence and could often be used as a sentence in its own right. The subordinate clause, like a phrase, acts as adjective, adverb or noun and depends on the main clause. For example (subordinate clause in *italics*):

- The person *who marks my essays* is not my tutor [adjectival clause, describing person].

- I was very unhappy *when I received that really low grade* [adverb, saying when].

- I worked really hard *so that I would get a good exam mark* [adverb, describing purpose].

- *Why I found it so difficult* is beyond me [noun, subject of 'is'].

- I do not know *whether I shall pass* [noun, object of 'know'].

- The idea *that I might have misinterpreted the question* never entered my head [noun, enlarging on 'idea'].

Spelling (the right word)

Misspelling can sometimes totally alter the meaning of a sentence, occasionally with comical effect. Even if the meaning is still clear, spelling mistakes prevent you from creating a good impression on your readers and may make them less likely to accept the message which you are trying to convey. Fortunately, dictionaries and spell checkers exist to help. Use them! This chapter is not intended to save you the expense of a dictionary or the hassle of using the spell checker once you have completed a piece of work. But many spelling errors are correct spellings in themselves, but of a different word from the one you intended. Your spell checker will not identify these as errors. What follows is a list of some of the most common words which are misspelled as other valid words.

accept – except

The first means to receive, the second to omit or exclude.

advice – advise

The noun has a *c*, the verb an *s*. It is clear from the pronunciation which is which in this case, but this does not seem to prevent frequent mistakes. In similar pairs, e.g.

practice – practise, the pronunciation is no help. You may like to use the 'advice – advise' pair to guide you in such cases.

affect – effect

To affect something is to change it or to have an effect on it. As a noun, affect is used by psychologists to mean 'mood'. As a verb, to effect something means to bring it about. Thus: 'In order to affect the way recruiters treat minority groups, it may be necessary to effect new legislation. The effect of the legislation might, however, be minimal.'

already – all ready

Already means by this time, whereas all ready, not surprisingly, means that all are ready. Thus: 'Are you all ready? It is lunch time already.'

bare – bear

You bare (or uncover) your head or soul, whereas a bear has four legs or is a verb meaning to carry.

complement – compliment

A complement completes something, as in cream complementing strawberries. If you are telling someone they are wonderful, it is a compliment. If the strawberries and cream were free with the entry ticket, they were complimentary.

council (councillor) – counsel (counsellor)

Council is an assembly, as in student council, whereas counsel is advice or the legal person who provides it. Thus if you are worried or depressed you might arrange an interview with a counsellor, but if you are protesting about a local authority decision you might write to your elected councillor.

currant – current

Currants grow on bushes and are used in baking. Currents are found in rivers. Current practice means the practice now.

definitely – defiantly

You are much more likely to want to be definite than defiant when writing, but if you mis-type, your computer may miscorrect so watch out for any unwanted defiance.

disinterested – uninterested

Not so much a spelling mistake as use of an incorrect word. Disinterested means impartial or unbiased (related to the use of interest in 'interested party'). Uninterested means showing no interest in something. This improper usage is extremely common but irritates many readers who do know the correct meanings of the words.

ensure – insure

To ensure means to make sure, whereas to insure means to take (or make) out an insurance policy.

hear – here

Hear has to do with ears, whereas here means in this place (as in 'here, there and everywhere').

imply – infer

More confusion rather than misspelling. Imply means to hint at. It is done by the 'sender'. Infer means to draw a conclusion or inference and is done by the 'receiver'.

i.e. – e.g. – etc.

These are all abbreviations of Latin phrases: i.e. means 'that is', e.g. means 'for example' and etc. means 'and so on'. They are frequently interchanged, incorrectly. Even if used correctly, etc. is best used sparingly. It can suggest that you haven't bothered to think an argument through. There is a fairly common school of thought (particularly among editors) that none of these abbreviations should be used unless absolutely necessary.

its – it's

This is probably the commonest confusion of all. It's is short for 'it is' – the apostrophe stands for the missing letter. Its means 'belonging to it', i.e. indicates possession. The confusion arises because most possessives have an apostrophe, as in 'The cat's ball'. But these are there because the old English possessive used to be 'The cat his ball', which was shortened to cat's, with the apostrophe, as in other contractions such as 'don't', standing for missing letters. But in the possessive its there are no missing letters, so no apostrophe.

lead – led

The metal is lead, as is the present of the verb: 'I lead a blameless life now'. Led is the past: 'Until I became a student I led a blameless life.'

loose – lose

Loose means 'to unfasten' or 'not tight'. Lose refers to misplacing something or not winning.

moral – morale

When you talk of job satisfaction or the mood of the troops, you mean morale. Every time moral is used in this context (and it very commonly is) it conjures up visions of defrauding the customer, or carryings on behind filing cabinets. Morals have to do with beliefs about right and wrong and with morality.

oral – aural – verbal

Oral has to do with the mouth, so refers to speaking or swallowing medicine. Aural has to do with the ears, whereas verbal has to do with words, which might be written or spoken.

personal – personnel

Personal means belonging to one or private. Personnel are people, such as employees.

principal – principle

Principal means most important, or head of something like a college. Principle means an idea, or truth, or code of conduct.

stationary – stationery

You buy stationery at a stationer's. Stationary means not moving.

there – their – they're

There is the place (here, there, etc.). Their indicates possession (there is nothing missing when this is in the form 'theirs', so no apostrophes are needed). They're is short for 'they are', hence the apostrophe.

to – too – two

The only times you don't use to are when you mean excessive (too) or when you mean the number (two). So: 'Two of us are going to be too late.'

were – we're – where

Were is the past tense, we're is the shortened version of 'we are', where is the place – think of it getting the answer 'here'.

who's – whose

Another muddling case like its, where you have a possessive without an apostrophe, whose. Who's is short for who is.

your – you're

Again, you're is short for you are, whereas your indicates that you possess whatever it is.

You will see that by remembering the simple rule that an apostrophe stands for the letters left out, many of the most common errors will be prevented. For the rest, you need either to learn the correct spellings by rote or to use mnemonics. For all other words that cause you doubt, use your dictionary. And always use your spell checker too, to check for mistypes as well as misspellings.

Punctuation

Once your spelling is under control, the only thing left to worry about is getting the punctuation right. Grammar checks on your word processor are some help here, but the following comments might also be useful. Keeping your sentences as short as possible (see the section on style earlier in the chapter) will make correct punctuation easier, but even with short sentences you are likely to need most of the following. The following digest may help. For more, see the hugely popular Truss (2003).

Full stops (.)

You will need one of these at the end of each sentence. Check that the sentence is complete before putting in the full stop. Occasionally, a sentence may be a single word, such as: 'No.' But normally you will want to check that the sentence has a verb, that the verb has a noun as subject and another as object (or clauses serving as subject and object) and that the sentence makes sense.

A series of stops (. . .) can be used to indicate either that you are breaking off before finishing something or that you are omitting part of a quotation. This is called an ellipsis.

A full stop is also used to indicate an abbreviation, as in Co., though it is not needed if the abbreviation ends with the last letter of the shortened word, as in Dr or many other titles.

Question marks (?)

These are used instead of a full stop at the end of any sentence which asks a direct question, such as: 'What do you want to do when you graduate?' They are not needed if the question is reported, rather than direct: 'Many students wonder what they will do when they graduate.'

Exclamation marks (!)

These can be used (sparingly) to denote excitement or amazement, or to indicate humour or sarcasm.

Commas (,)

These are used to split up parts of a sentence to make the meaning clearer and allow the reader to draw mental breath. They may split strings of nouns, such as: 'Students need clear objectives, time-management skills and constant reviews of progress if they are to do well.' It would be equally acceptable to have another comma before the final 'and'. In a longer list this would probably be preferable. Commas may also split lists of adjectives or verbs. For example: 'You need to work quickly, efficiently, thoroughly and with sustained concentration.'

Commas are also used to split the clauses in a complex sentence. I shall not give you an example of this: the book is full of them. No matter how hard I try to practise what I preach, many of my sentences end up being fairly complicated: someone once described it as 'an unfortunate tendency towards the baroque'.

When using commas it is essential to check that you have not placed a comma between a verb and its subject. For example, you should not write: 'The courses I am studying, include accountancy and marketing.' In this case courses is the subject of the verb include. An exception to this is when you need to separate off a clause: 'The courses I am studying, particularly those taught by some of the professors in the business school, are extremely interesting.' This is fine and indeed would be hard to understand without the commas.

Inverted commas or quotation marks ("...") or ('...')

Use these whenever you are quoting, whether speech or a section of text. You can use single or double inverted commas, but you should be consistent. Single ones do not require use of the shift key, which may explain their common usage. If you have a quotation within a quotation; for example, if a passage of text you quote itself includes a quotation, use double quotation marks for the inner quote if you normally use single, or vice versa, so that the two are distinct. Quotation marks may also be used to denote titles of books or articles, although it is equally common to use italics (or underlining, if in a manuscript).

Apostrophes (')

As has been stressed already, these indicate where a word has been shortened by omitting letters, e.g. 'didn't'. An apostrophe is also used to indicate possession where *s* is added to a normal word, as in 'a dog's breakfast'. For plurals, when an *s* is there already, the apostrophe is added after the *s*, as in 'eight weeks' work'. Note that for odd plurals (those where the plural is different from the singular rather than merely the singular with an *s* added) where you do need to add an *s* to indicate possession, as in 'men's', or 'women's', you put the apostrophe before the added *s*, just as with singular possessives where you are adding an *s*. Remember that where there is a special word to indicate a possessive, there is no apostrophe. After all, you would never write 'hi's', so don't do the equivalent with 'yours', 'theirs', 'its' or 'hers'.

Brackets or parentheses

These are used to separate off something that is an addition or insertion (such as an aside which casts light on what you have said). When they occur as the last part of a sentence, as above, close the bracket *before* adding the full stop. (When a bracket encloses a complete sentence, as here, put the full stop *inside* the bracket.)

Dashes (– . . . –)

These can be used instead of brackets to separate off the same sort of thing or used singly to indicate a break in the train of thought – those occasions when inspiration strikes in mid-sentence.

Semi-colon (;)

This is a weaker form of a full stop. It is used to separate things which could be separate sentences but which are closely linked, thus making the writing less abrupt. Always check before using a semi-colon that what follows it could stand as a sentence in its own right; if it does not, you should probably have used a comma. You can also use semi-colons to separate the items in a list, provided you started the list with a colon. You can use it before the final item in the list, even where this is preceded by 'and', as in: 'You will need many resources for successful study: access to a good library; access to a PC; good tutors; a quiet place to work; and sufficient time.'

Colon (:)

This can be used to introduce a list as in the example above, or in a way similar to a semi-colon to link two clauses that could stand as sentences in their own right. A colon is preferable if the second clause explains the first, if you want to highlight a strong contrast between them or if you are trying to draw particular attention to the connection between them. For example: 'He had no trouble getting on to the course: his father was head of department.'

Capital letters

These are used at the start of each sentence, for names (people, places, months etc.) or for the adjectives derived from them (Elizabethan, French, Mancunian). They are also used for the first and main words of a book or film title (The Business Student's Handbook, The Good, the Bad and the Ugly).

Common grammatical mistakes

It would be impossible to list all the grammatical mistakes I have seen cropping up in assignments, but the following are some of the most common and it is worth learning how to avoid them.

Mixed plurality

A single noun should have an appropriate verb. 'We is' or 'he are' is clearly wrong. Yet this sort of mixing of singular verbs with plural subjects or vice versa is all too common, particularly in cases where a singular noun refers to, or is linked with, a group of some sort. You should say 'one of the students *was* late' and 'the group *was* annoyed' (although 'group' refers to several people, the word itself is singular – 'groups' is the plural). Purists still hold that 'data', being a Latin plural (singular 'datum'), should be treated as a plural, but it is so often used as singular (data is available …) that it is almost acceptable. 'A data' still sounds pretty dreadful, though, so if you feel 'datum' is unacceptable, talk of 'a piece of information' or 'an item of data'.

Incorrect prepositions

Another fault is using incorrect prepositions. It should be 'different *from*' not 'to', 'anxious *about*' not 'of', 'bored *with*' not 'of' and 'centre *on*' not 'round'.

Will I or shall I?

Confusing 'shall' and 'will' is also common. The normal future is 'I shall, you will, he will, we shall, they will'. 'I will' indicates strong determination, as in: 'I shall take several exams next month. I will work very hard between now and then.'

Can I or may I?

'Can' and 'may' are often confused. 'Can' refers to being able to. 'May' means either being permitted or that something is moderately likely to happen. 'I can swim,' that is, I have the necessary skill. 'I may swim here as it is a public beach.' 'It may rain tomorrow.' 'Might' means less likely, but still possible: 'If it rains tomorrow there might be a flood, but I am not expecting it.'

Due or owing?

'Due to' and 'owing to' are problematic. 'Owing to' means because of and usually comes at the start of a sentence. 'Due to' means caused by and usually comes after the verb 'to be'. 'Owing to confusion over meanings, words are often used incorrectly. This is often due to poor teaching of English at school.'

HELPFILE 2
IF ENGLISH IS NOT YOUR NATIVE LANGUAGE . . .

If you are about to study in English for the first time, you may be worried about your abilities. This worry is reasonable but may not be justified. Many students who are non-native English speakers write far better English than many native speakers. However, even if your chosen institution does not insist upon it, it is worth taking one of the standard English tests available to check that you are likely to be able to cope with university-level study in the language.

Three areas of competence will be important:

- **Reading** – you will need to read, and understand, a considerable volume of fairly difficult materials.
- **Speaking** – you will need to be able to follow, and contribute to, group discussions.
- **Writing** – you will need to be able to express yourself in written English in assignments and, under pressure, in examinations.

I shall focus here on written English, although improving this will impact upon speaking and writing too, and one of the ways of improving your writing is to read as extensively as possible.

To improve your written English you need to improve your vocabulary and your grammar.

Vocabulary

Although students often worry about vocabulary, the problem is seldom that the students do not use a wide enough range of words. More often, the words are used in a way that leaves their meaning ambiguous. Part of the reason for this lies in the difference between *active* and *passive* vocabulary. Words you use easily are active. Your passive vocabulary is made up of words which you understand when reading them in context, but which you would not readily use yourself. (A similar distinction applies to grammatical structures.) It is likely that you will need to extend and consolidate your active, and perhaps also your passive, vocabulary.

To focus your efforts you need to concentrate on:

- *Frequently used words*: clearly, words which you encounter frequently in your reading and in lectures are ones which you need to know, and probably need to be able to use easily. Log any such words where you are unsure of the meaning, check with dictionaries and native speakers to be sure that you do understand, note down and learn them!

- *Terms that resemble words in your own language*. For example, the common word 'sensible' in English now means 'showing good sense' (as in 'sensible shoes', i.e. ones that are comfortable for walking in). Yet the similar looking Spanish *'sensible'* or Italian *sensibile* means 'sensitive' a meaning which the English word lost shortly after the time of Jane Austen. If something is not making sense it may be because you are assuming an equivalence that no longer exists.

- *Colloquial terms*: dictionaries are not a lot of help here, though online dictionaries may be better than print ones. While many lecturers avoid using colloquial terms, you may find some who revel in using such terms in assignments, perhaps in the interests of making a scenario sound 'real'. For example, a recent reference to 'mothballing' a factory (closing it down, but in a way that it can be opened later if there is a need for it) puzzled one of my (French) students (though www.businessdictionary.com was up to the task). If you cannot find a dictionary meaning which makes sense, ask a native English speaker for help.

➤ Ch 7

- *Specialist words*: these are words that have special meanings in a particular discipline or in a university context. Words which appear in assignments are of particular importance. You must be absolutely sure that you understand what the assignment requires. There is a helpfile at the end of Chapter 7, which provides a good starting point, but always check any word in an assignment if you are unsure exactly what it means. And make sure that you *learn* the meaning of such words. They may well appear in examinations.

Many of the words or phrases you encounter will be specialist terms. Some will have originated in the study of management or related subjects, but most will be everyday words that are given a specific meaning when combined (such as transaction costs or value chain). Standard dictionaries are of limited use here – but you should be given definitions for such terms, and you will be on an equal footing with other students, as such specialist terms will be new to them too. You may well not know the equivalent term in your own language (though if you have a management text from home you should easily be able to find it).

To extend your vocabulary, Giles and Hedge (1994) suggest the following:

- Write down words and phrases rather than merely repeating them in your head – this will help them to stick in your memory.

- Try to learn vocabulary in context, so write new words and phrases into a sentence to learn the way they are used.

- Try to group new words with other words that frequently occur with them – for example, 'personnel' might be grouped with: personnel manager; personnel department; military personnel; 'all personnel should receive health and safety training'.

- Set aside regular 'slots' in your study schedule for learning vocabulary. Don't make these too long. Little and often is more effective.

- Work out a system for recording your new vocabulary – for example, 'groupings' could be shown diagrammatically on cards, to be easily carried around.

- Read for language acquisition – this is different from reading for information (also important). Identify problematic words, check the meaning, and if they seem important (in terms of frequency or utility) ensure that you have a correct definition and start a 'grouping' card for them.

- If your course has not yet started, use an introductory management text, together with an interesting book by a 'guru' and the *Financial Times* and/or *The Economist* as the basis for your 'reading for language acquisition'.

➤ Ch 8

- Take advantage of any language support offered by your university, and/or explore what is available, often free and online to help develop your skills in writing English. Some suggestions are available in the web resources for this chapter.

Grammar

English grammar is complex and the guidelines above provide the barest starting point. To go further is beyond the scope of this book. It is poorly understood by many in the UK who were educated in the 1970s and 1980s, when grammar was seldom taught in state schools. Study this chapter and the helpfile carefully. If possible, ask someone who is good at English to read your assignments before you submit them. Where they think grammar could be improved, make sure that they explain (if they can) what is wrong and why, so that you understand how to improve things. And ask tutors for as much feedback as possible. Some are reluctant to correct grammar for fear of seeming petty, but will do so if you show that you genuinely want their help.

If you are uncertain about your grammar it is particularly important to keep the structure of your sentences simple.

US versus UK 'English'

A number of words are spelled differently in US and UK English, while some words have completely different meanings.

Spelling differences:

If you learned US English as a second or subsequent language, check whether your tutor is happy for you to continue using this. If so, it will not be a problem.

If you are searching online, you will probably be able to search by either form of English. Since most engines offer you an 'or similar' option when searching, and the two forms are normally similar, you may not even need to do this. However, to avoid being caught out, you may need to be aware of the following differences in spellings of words commonly used in business and management.

There are three common shifts: UK words ending in 'our', such as 'labour' lose the u in US English, becoming, for example, 'labor'.

UK words ending in 'ise' or 'yse' replace the s by z in US English, hence organise becomes organize, organisation becomes organization, and analyse becomes 'analyze'.

US English often simplifies spellings, thus dialogue and catalogue may appear as dialog and catalog.

For more on UK/US differences see http://www.oxforddictionaries.com/words/british-and-american-terms (accessed 18/5/15).

7
IMPRESSING ASSESSORS

Learning outcomes

By the end of this chapter you should:

- understand what is involved in the activity of assessing

- appreciate the perspective of those doing the assessment

- be better able to use feedback on assessment to do better in future assignments

- be aware of some of the common causes of student failure

- appreciate the importance of taking action immediately there is a threat to success

- be better able to interpret assessment questions correctly

- be better able to plan a structured answer

- be better able to use analytical and critical reasoning skills in your answers

- compile a portfolio demonstrating your competence.

Introduction

As a student you want the highest marks possible. In a job interview you will want to be judged the best candidate. At work, your promotion prospects will depend on how your seniors assess you. In each case, two things will influence the resulting judgement. The first is your knowledge/skills/performance, or whatever else is being assessed. The second – and equally important – is how well you communicate this to your assessors. While the main focus of this chapter is improving your marks while a student, you will find that much of what you learn will be relevant throughout your career.

➤ Ch 6   The general ability to communicate in writing (addressed in Chapter 6) is essential to gaining good marks. Some skills are more specific to assessment. One is the ability to understand precisely what is being asked and answer *that question*. Another, for most university assignments, will be to demonstrate your conceptual skills. Tutors will be looking for the ability to analyse a situation in the light of both its context and the theory which you have learned. They will often want you to construct a balanced and well-reasoned argument for action on the basis of your analysis. Job interviews may be seeking similar analytical and reasoning skills, and the ability to communicate your thinking.

This chapter looks at interpreting questions and planning the content and structure of a good answer. It looks at meeting assignment requirements in the context of essays, reports, written exams, portfolio assessment and viva voce examinations. It also discusses some forms of assessment you may encounter once working, such as annual performance appraisal and seeking professional accreditation.

The Aims of Assessment

For any communication it is essential to understand your *receiver*. What are their objectives? What criteria are they using? Why are particular assessment methods being used? When marking essays or exams, I am assessing how well the student has met a specific set of

➤ Ch 6   requirements. Try to put yourself into the shoes (or head) of the person doing the assessing.

Activity 7.1

Select one of the modules you are currently studying. If you were the lecturer, what do you think you would be trying to achieve when you set and marked assignments? Write down what you think your objectives would be and, if possible, discuss them with one or two fellow students on that course. Discuss, too, how sure you would be about your judgements when marking and what might make them more, or less, reliable.

What follows is based on many years of setting and marking assignments and exams, chairing exam boards, and acting as an external examiner for other institutions. Despite this experience I cannot guarantee to speak for all examiners everywhere. You need to check what I say against the views of your own assessors.

My main objective is fairly simple: I want to check that students have learned enough from the course to be able to move on to subsequent courses without difficulty. I am also concerned to 'maintain standards': students who pass our courses should not reflect badly on the institution or qualification because of their ignorance or lack of competence after graduation. If students who are incompetent, or seem to know little gain a qualification, employers and other universities will cease to value our degree. This would be a disaster for other students, who have worked hard and performed well to gain their degree.

By 'learning' I do not mean merely the ability to regurgitate what has been taught. Examinees need to use ideas and techniques appropriately in a given context in order to come to a better understanding of the situation and, usually, of how to respond to it. My final objective is to distinguish between those who have barely learned enough and those

➤ Ch 3   who have a high level of mastery of the subject.

Another objective of assessment is to help learning to take place. The act of writing an assignment can lead to a deeper understanding of the material covered and the ways in which it can be used. (It also helps to develop skills in written communication.) Examinations will exert pressure on students to learn the material so that they retain it and can draw on it when necessary long after the course has finished.

Assessment is difficult, as I am painfully aware. Assessing this deeper form of learning in subjects such as business and management is inevitably subjective. It is easy to test whether someone can correctly define a particular concept, or remembers the author of a particular theory. It is fairly easy to see whether a person can use a particular formula correctly. It is much harder to judge whether someone can use relevant concepts appropriately, even creatively, in a particular situation.

Unless a lengthy case study is used, the context will be described so briefly that it will probably be fairly obvious which concept to use. Word or time limits will work against answers that go into depth. It is easy to be over-impressed by clear writing (rather than particularly clear thinking) and by a high level of word-processing skills. (This is why it is important to develop these skills.) It is even easier to underrate an assignment that looks rushed and scrappy. It may be impossible to make any judgement about the knowledge of someone who totally misinterprets a question.

Much of what follows is intended to help you avoid these difficulties, or even to exploit

➤ Ch 6   them to your advantage.

Why Students Fail

Failure is seldom due to intellectual inadequacy. Some people may have to work harder than others, but almost all those selected for a place on a course should have the ability to pass. Some, however, will lack the ability to manage their learning. A very small number have problems, such as illness or difficulties in their private life, which puts success at risk. Figure 7.1 is a composite multiple cause diagram for the most common causes of failure, showing how factors can interact.

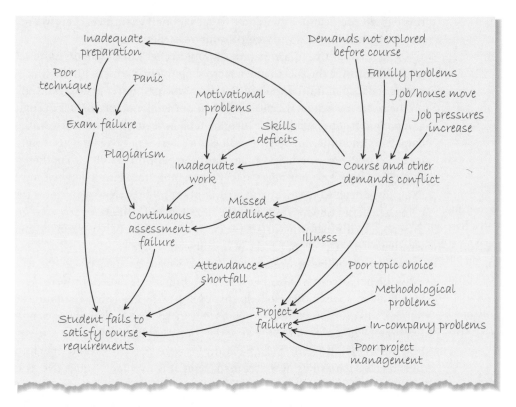

Figure 7.1 Common causes of student failure (a composite multiple cause diagram)

Activity 7.2

Think about factors which you feel might threaten your own success. If you cannot find them on Figure 7.1, add them at appropriate points. Highlight all the factors which you think are particularly relevant to you.

The factors shown, and probably those you have added as well, fall into three categories: some factors are beyond your control, some you might be able to do something about with the aid of this book or other assistance, and for some factors you already know the remedy.

Coping with factors beyond your control

Sometimes your success is put at risk by factors beyond your control. You might fall seriously ill, or all your revision notes might be in your car when it is stolen. If so, you need to take steps to minimise the effect of the disaster. An essential first step will be to let the system know. Tell your personal tutor, or someone else in authority. They can help you work out how best to cope with the situation, whether by asking for special consideration, extensions to deadlines, or changing your study plans. They can also help you make sure that any relevant forms are filled in, and evidence of your problems provided. Most institutions are prepared to make considerable allowances for students who meet with misfortune of one kind or another. But they are not psychic, so need to be told of your problems, often in the correct way, by a specified deadline, and with particular evidence. Such disasters are rare, so there is no point worrying about them in advance. Just remember the need to take urgent action and seek help if you are unlucky enough to experience such a problem.

Things you can control

Many students experience problems which should have been within their control but somehow got beyond them. The commonest cause is poor time management. If, in the self-assessment activity above, you highlighted this as a threat, and you have not yet developed the skills covered in Chapter 2, you need to work on them urgently before you fall irremediably behind. You will note from Figure 7.1 that dissertation failure forms a major causal strand. If your course requires a dissertation, and your time management is already giving you problems this may be a serious risk factor. Use Chapter 2 now to start improving your time management skills so that they are well established before you start your dissertation. You will also need to pay careful attention to Chapter 15 on managing projects. You also, of course, need to avoid plagiarism.

➤ Ch 2

➤ Ch 6

➤ Ch 15

If 'potentially controllable' factors get beyond control, it is again imperative that you seek help from your supervisor, personal tutor or other member of staff. It is far better to alert them to a possible problem and, with their help, to avert it, than to persist in denying that things could go wrong until the situation is beyond remedy. Sticking your head in the sand may feel good at the time, but sooner or later you will feel very much worse.

Activity 7.3

Should things look like getting out of control, see it as an opportunity! Set a specific objective for averting disaster, develop an objectives tree and then develop an action plan for achieving your objective. If you also document the circumstances, the help you seek, remedial actions taken and the outcomes, you will have the basis of an excellent 'exhibit' for the part of your portfolio devoted to 'managing your own learning'.

Motivational problems

Time problems are one major cause of failure, whether generated by circumstances beyond your control or poor management on your part. Motivational problems are another. Indeed, the two may be closely interlinked: either can cause the other. Expectancy theory suggests that poor motivation is likely if you feel that:

➤ Ch 3

- no matter how hard you try, your grades do not improve – effort does not produce performance – whether because of poor study skills (if so revisit Chapter 3), or poor assessment technique

● performance does not produce rewards (perhaps your long-term objectives have changed or there are too few shorter-term rewards).

A further possible reason, not covered by the model, is that:

● you are depressed generally and have little motivation for anything. (If so, try the normal remedies of sleep, healthy food, exercise/yoga and talking to friends. If these don't help within a week or two, or you cannot find the motivation even for these steps, seek medical help.)

The main sources of motivational 'recharging' are your teachers, your friends on the course, and yourself. If these fail you then you may need to seek professional help. Institutions vary greatly in the support they offer students, but most will assign students to some sort of personal counsellor or academic advisor, with a back-up counselling service for more serious cases. If you experience motivational, or indeed any sort of problems, you should not hesitate to take advantage of whatever help is available. This will not be held against you, or affect your grades in any way other than positively (as your advisor can argue for your circumstances to be taken into consideration when your final marks are decided).

> **Motivational resources:**
>
> * your teachers
> * friends
> * fellow students
> * your academic advisor
> * yourself.

Improving Your Assessment Technique

Success in assessment requires skills in learning, critical thinking, number, reasoning and writing, plus some techniques specific to the academic context. These are covered in the remainder of the chapter. If you work hard and understand the subject matter but your marks do not seem to reflect this, study what follows carefully. Remember that most assessment in business and management is closer to an art than a science. Your assessors are *making inferences from* what you write in response to a specific question. There is a technique of responding in such a way that they will infer that you are competent. This technique will also help you in interviews and when you get a request for a report on a topic of interest to management. It is therefore well worth developing.

➤ **Ch 3, 5, 6, 11**

Interpreting questions

A key factor in good exam technique is the art of question interpretation. A common cause of exam failure is that a student appears to have answered a question that bears little resemblance to that which was asked. Perhaps the question, following a description of a particular organisational scenario in, shall we say, Case Study and Co., was:

Analyse the motivational problems in the customer billing department of Case Study and Co. and suggest action which the organisation might take to reduce labour turnover.

Activity 7.4

Jot down possible headings and subheadings for an answer to the above.

_____

_____

_____

When a question similar to this was set, many students lost marks through poor 'question interpretation' skills. Some seemed to have read the question as 'Tell me everything you know about motivation' and regurgitated all they could remember of the lecture on the subject. Others read it as 'What symptoms are there of low motivation in the above description?' and repeated all the bits of the scenario, in only slightly different words, that relate to motivation. Some realised that they had to *analyse* the situation, but got so carried away by this that they forgot all about the need to offer suggestions for remedial action. Some made lots of assertions as to what would improve the situation without giving any underlying reasoning or evidence. (An approach to case-study-based assessment is given in Chapter 11.) Check that your headings in Activity 7.4 avoided these traps.

➤ Ch 11

Any misinterpretation of a question can cause huge loss of marks. This is *much* more common in exams because of the pressure you are under. If feedback on your assignments suggests that you sometimes miss parts of a question, or misinterpret them, you need to address this as soon as possible, and well in advance of any exam.

Make absolutely sure that you now understand where you missed something, and why, whenever you received such feedback. This is probably the most critical thing for you to address of all those covered in the book because it can seriously reduce your grades and even mean failure. It will also cause you to waste a huge amount of time and effort in directions that not only gain you few marks but also contribute little to the learning your tutor intended.

Refer to the helpfile at the end of this chapter if you meet terms you are not sure about, or even to check that you are correctly interpreting those you think you understand. If you encounter a term which is not on the list, or have doubts about the meaning of one which is but seems curious in the context, check its intended meaning with the person setting the assignment. If you are unsure about the meaning of a term used in an examination, avoid that question if you can. If you have to answer that question, say at the outset how you are defining the problematic word. Your markers may accept your interpretation and mark you in the light of that meaning. If you are not explicit in this way, they may merely think that you have not answered the question very well.

Deconstructing Questions and Planning Answers

Answering exactly the question asked demands more than merely being sure of the meaning of the words used. It is important to identify all the separate parts of the question and plan an outline answer covering all of these before planning the answer in more detail.

For simple questions this is not a problem. But questions are often complex and you may need to practise teasing apart the separate 'building blocks' of which they are composed. A couple of examples follow of questions that might be asked about the content of this book. There are additional practice interpretation questions on the website. Spend some time on Activity 7.5 and look at real questions drawn from your own course.

Activity 7.5

Before reading on, highlight the key words in the following question and jot down possible headings and subheadings in an answer.

Discuss the adequacy of the control model as a framework for understanding poor student performance. Suggest three steps which you might take to improve your own performance, drawing on this or other appropriate theory.

_____

_____

_____

There are two clear parts to the question: the evaluation of the control model and the suggested steps for improvement. Within each there are implicit sub-parts. To evaluate the control model you need to establish what it is – it would be almost essential to include a diagram here, but you would need to describe it in words as well. You would also have to establish what you meant by 'poor performance'. Note that there are different ways in which

➤ Ch 2   performance can fail to meet required standards – Figure 7.1 would be a good starting point.

Once you have established these two bases, you can start to examine the extent to which the control model helps with the different causes of poor performance. You would probably argue that for some sorts of poor performance the model could add considerably to your understanding of the shortfall, as some part of the control loop (establishing standards, perhaps, or monitoring performance against these standards) is usually at fault when this sort of shortfall occurs. But for other causes of poor performance (poor motivation, say, or serious illness), the control loop might be of limited or no usefulness. Again you would need to say *why*.

The second part of the question requires you to draw on the first, but also to link it to your own situation. Thus you could start by identifying the three ways in which your own performance could most be improved. Perhaps you are poor at managing your time. You tend to hand work in late after a rushed last-minute effort and your 'clear writing' skills are poor. Note that while your example has to be plausible, you will not be judged on its 'truth'. In an exam it would make sense to pick something that allowed you to show fairly easily that you could apply the ideas, rather than agonising over what were your real performance problems.

You could then show what the control loop would suggest – perhaps the need for interim deadlines to address the time management issue. Then you could refer back to the first part of your answer to establish that some of your shortfall could not be understood in control loop terms and briefly establish some other theory – showing the breadth of your knowledge – which might help. Suppose that you wanted to say that part of the problem was that you couldn't be bothered to practise good time management or work hard at written work. This could be understood in terms of expectancy theory – because you lacked the ability to write well, you knew that effort would not translate into performance anyway. Therefore to improve your performance you would need to work on your writing skills and strengthen this link in the motivational chain.

Given that you are asked only for three suggestions, you might be able to make these based on strengthening various parts of the control loop. But if you had been asked for more, then drawing on at least one other theory would have been advisable. Note that for each suggestion you would need to make it clear how it addressed an underlying reason suggested by the model or theory. Thus to address the second part of the question merely by saying: 'The three steps I would take are to work harder, hand in my work on time and try to be neater', would probably gain you no marks at all.

Figure 7.2 shows a mind map for a possible answer to the question in Activity 7.5.

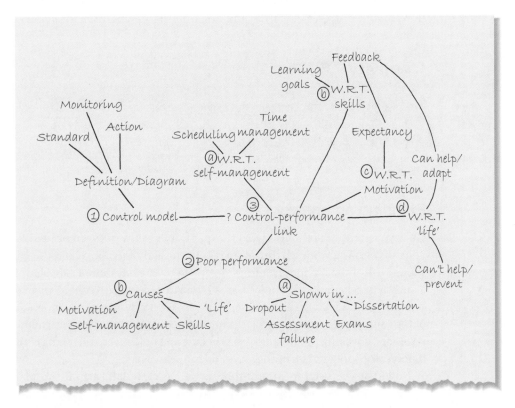

Figure 7.2 Mind map based on 'deconstruction' of a question about student performance and control

Let's take a second example, albeit more briefly. Think briefly about how you would approach this before reading the analysis which follows.

> 'Organisations today are likely to recruit graduates primarily because of the knowledge that they have gained during their degree studies.' To what extent do you agree with this statement?

This question is asking you to demonstrate your understanding of relevant factors in organisations today and link these to employer views about graduates as potential employees. It is also checking your understanding of the whole idea of transferable skills, even though these are not mentioned. Any student who restricted their answer to knowledge, and made no mention of skills, would probably fail.

The other implicit instruction is to give a *reasoned* conclusion for agreeing or disagreeing with the question, so you are also being tested on your ability to argue from evidence. You can find plenty of evidence in Chapter 1. In building your argument you might want to think about the principles of argument mapping introduced in Chapter 4. Most assessments will expect you to look at arguments for and against whatever conclusion is being presented in a balanced way, taking all the evidence into consideration.

➤ Ch 1
➤ Ch 4

Many assignments will require *analysis*. Some will require you to analyse a case. All the issues discussed in this chapter are relevant to this, but you will also need to understand how to work with cases. Analysis and case working are discussed in Chapter 11.

➤ Ch 11

Activity 7.6

Collect samples of assignment and exam questions from your own course(s) – lecturers should be able to provide these if you do not already have them. Working with one or two other people if possible, first highlight the 'instruction' words (explain, compare, etc.), then try to break the questions down into their constituent parts.

➤ Ch 2

Planning an answer

Once you are absolutely clear what the question is asking for, you need to start planning your answer. You were starting to do this in the activities above, but there is more to do than think of the obvious headings suggested by the question. Essay planning is ideally a fairly leisurely process: your ideas need time to develop and cohere. In an exam, time is seriously limited. But in either case, planning is an essential stage. Indeed, all the stages of the control loop – setting or clarifying objectives, planning to meet them, marshalling resources, checking progress against schedule and objectives and taking corrective action if necessary – are vital for both essays and exam answers.

➤ Ch 2

Note that you need to control time as well as material. Part of your planning therefore has to involve a work schedule, and an essential part of your control will be directed towards ensuring that you keep to this schedule. If possible, spread both your planning and writing over several days to allow a 'fallow' time between first and final draft of both plan and assignment. During this gap you may find that your subconscious develops your ideas considerably without effort on your part. You will also find it easier to spot logical inconsistencies and poor English if you edit your essay after a decent interval, rather than on completion.

Planning your time for exams is equally important. If you finish early, use any spare time to re-read earlier answers checking they do answer the question, and adding anything else that improves them.

There are two popular approaches to planning the content of an essay or report. The first is to collect together all the possibly relevant things you might wish to cover and then to organise these into some kind of structure. The other is to develop the structure first and then search for the appropriate material to flesh it out. Sometimes it may be worth adopting a mixed approach, starting with either a rough structure or reading a few relevant materials and then moving to the other approach, which may then prompt developments or additions to the first, and so on. If you are already completely happy with how you go about planning (and your grades are as high as you want), stick with what works. Otherwise, experiment with each approach first, before trying the mixed one.

> ➤ Ch 4 In either case, remember the importance (outlined in Chapter 4) of selecting your material carefully with a view to relevance and currency, keeping careful notes as you read, and making sure that you keep a record of the full reference of anything you are at all likely to use, as an integral part of your notes. (References are of little use if you cannot marry them up with the relevant notes.)

In an exam you will normally need to keep any 'collecting of materials' to the minimum. Some students find it helpful to jot down single words or short phrases to 'capture' everything they can remember that may be relevant to an answer before it is driven out of their heads by the first thing they start to write. But such notes need to be written very quickly so as not to use time that might be better devoted to analysing the question, planning the structure of your answer and *writing* it.

Assignment planning involves:

- noting deadline
- clarifying question requirements
- identifying resources needed
- scheduling activities to:
  - acquire resources
  - extract information
  - plan assignment structure
  - write it
  - review what you have written
- monitoring progress.

Mind maps for planning

> ➤ Ch 4 Whichever approach you adopt, you will find that mind maps (mentioned in Chapter 4 and used in the deconstruction example above) can be invaluable. If you have collected notes on a number of relevant books and articles, you can use a mind map to organise the content of these. If you are starting with structure you can represent this as a mind map. In either case, once you have your main 'branches' and 'twigs' established, all that remains is to order the branches in the best way and then for each branch to order the twigs. This gives you the outline of your essay plan. If structure came first, you will then need to search for relevant sources. You may find that these cast new light on the subject. If so, you may need to do some reordering or alter the groupings. If your structure was

developed from notes, you may be ready to start writing once you have ordered the branches on your map.

In an exam, a mind map can be a useful way to establish, very quickly, the structure of your answer. While you write, use it as a reference point against which to check your progress. It is a good idea to number the branches in the order you intend to cover them. Sometimes it can be useful to cross off branches when they have been completed. (If you prefer to generate mind maps for essays on a computer, affordable, or sometimes free, software is readily available.)

Your resulting essay plan, however derived, needs to be as brief as possible – a list of section headings or a diagram (with order indicated) is usually enough. Remember to include an introduction and conclusions and, if relevant, recommendations, as well as the structure of the main section. Writing a good answer is much easier if all you have to do is work your way through the stages you have set out for yourself. It is easy to check your plan against the question, to ensure that all the parts you have deconstructed are covered. It is easy to see whether the order you have planned is logical and likely to flow well. It is easy to check your answer, at intervals, against the plan. Writing without a plan and subsequently trying to check your full answer for flow and completeness is far more difficult. You should still, for safety's sake, perform a direct check of answer against question at some mid-point and again at the end, to ensure that you answer the question, the whole question and nothing but the question! If you keep this requirement in mind while you perform both the check via plan and the direct check, you should end up with a good, clear, relevant answer.

Test Exercise 7.1

Draw a mind map and brief essay plan based on the 'reasons for graduate recruitment' question used to exemplify deconstruction of a question.

Rough drafts

Are you prone to procrastination, or more severe 'writer's block'? Do you find it hard to put pen to paper or finger to key? If so, you may find it liberating to write a deliberately rough first draft. Resistance to writing often stems from a fear of not being able to do it well enough, or dread at the sheer size of the task. This latter is a particular problem with long essays or reports. Setting yourself to write something that may be total rubbish removes this fear.

So set yourself an interim task of completing a quick, *very* rough draft well in advance of the deadline. This has several advantages:

- The draft will clarify your thoughts greatly, highlighting points where your structure or arguments are weak, or evidence is lacking.

- It will give you raw material to work with. You can then craft this into something far better than you could ever have produced at a first draft.

- It will stir your subconscious into action, as mentioned.

- If you come down with flu or suffer some other disaster, you will have something which you can hand in with an explanatory note if asking for an extended deadline is not a good option.

Once you have a draft it is usually fairly painless to turn it into something good. It can even be enjoyable – but only if you are prepared to treat the draft as an interim stage in your thoughts and do not become attached to it. Read it in 'critical bystander' mode and discard or seriously modify those parts which do not work. Refer back to Chapter 6 if you are unhappy with the quality of your writing, rather than the quality of your thought. Use Part 4 of this book if the content is the problem.

➤ Ch 6

Box 7.1 Checklist for final drafts

When you have polished your draft into something that you are reasonably happy with, it is still worth performing a final check. Ask yourself:

- Does the introduction serve to orient the reader adequately?

- Is there a logical flow through the essay?

- Are argument chains clear?

- Is the language clear and appropriate?

- Have you covered all the parts of the question?

- Is the proportion of your answer devoted to each part reasonable, given the way the question was phrased?

- Have you provided enough evidence and clear arguments to convince your reader of each of the points you wanted to make?

- Have you made use of diagrams or graphs where these really help make your points?

- Have you used relevant concepts from the course to develop your answer wherever possible?

- Is there any material which could be deleted as less than fully relevant or necessary?

- Does your conclusion flow naturally from the points you have made earlier?

- Are you (just) within the word limit?

- Is your reference list complete in that all the sources you cited in your answer are included?

A version of this list is available on the website, for convenience.

You may also find it helpful to ask a friend on a related course to read the essay and tell you of any points that she or he is unhappy about. (If you swap essays with someone on the same course for this purpose, you may find it very difficult not to swap good ideas too, so that your essays come to resemble each other more closely than is safe. Remember, cheating and plagiarism will attract severe penalties.)

Learning from feedback

Feedback from a friend before submitting can be extremely helpful in pointing out areas that lack clarity. Feedback from your tutor can be even more helpful. Universities (and tutors) vary in the amount and specificity of feedback given, but you need to make sure that you understand what would have improved your mark, and how you can do better next time.

There will always be a tendency to become defensive when faced with a low mark or what may seem harsh criticism. Defensive reactions include refusing to read any comments, or brushing them off as 'rubbish'. It is important to treat all criticism as relating to your *work*, rather than as something personal. Try to see it as a gift from your tutor, who may have spent time thinking about how to explain where you went wrong. Where the tutor has said you went right, think about how to build on the strength identified in future assignments.

There is more on both giving and receiving feedback in the next chapter, where the focus is on spoken feedback. The following guidelines relate particularly to written feedback, but apply also to any verbal feedback you receive on your assignments.

➤ Ch 8

Guidelines for dealing with feedback

- Take a deep breath and relax.
- Read feedback carefully, checking that you can see why the tutor said what she or he did.
- If having read the comments you don't understand why your mark was not higher, or cannot see how the comments will help you to do better next time, ask your tutor for help in understanding them.
- Reflect on your work in the light of comments and make notes of any actions you need to take (such as allowing more time, reading questions more carefully, making clearer use of concepts, or using chapters from this book to help with basic maths or whatever weakness has been identified).
- Plan actions, carry out, and monitor.
- Re-read comments before your next assignment to make sure that work will not attract similar comments!

Doing Well in Examinations

Once you are good at writing essays to a plan, with a clear structure, and ensuring that you answer all of the questions, you are halfway to doing well in examinations. 'All' you need do beyond that is to manage your time so that you prepare adequately. Part of that preparation

> **Causes of exam failure include:**
>
> - inadequate preparation
> - poor time management
> - answering too few questions
> - missing out parts of questions
> - misinterpreting the question
> - not using course ideas.

may be to practise relaxation techniques so that you control any tendency to panic in the exam. You also need to manage your time carefully during the exam itself. Answer the correct number of questions, giving each part of each question an appropriate amount of attention. The basic principles involved are those already covered in the context of managing your learning and written communication. What follows is merely a brief outline of the key points as they relate to the specific context of examinations.

Exam preparation

In one sense, you are preparing for the exam from the moment you begin to study a course. Think about what you are learning, aim for 'deep learning' and take notes in a form that will be useful for revision and half your work is already done. However, at some point prior to the exam you will need to focus more specifically on revision and on developing a strategy for gaining good marks. As with much of what is suggested in this book, the action needed is straightforward. But it does require careful planning and good time management. You will probably

➤ Ch 3, 4   find the following stages helpful for managing your preparation.

Identify requirements

As with all management, you need to clarify your objectives, in this case by becoming as clear as possible about what will be required of you. Analysing past papers is one of the best means of doing this, unless it is a new course or the exam has changed recently. Look for the type of questions asked and the most popular topics. Try to put yourself in the examiner's position. It may be easier to set questions on some topics than others. Some topics may be so central to understanding a subject that it is highly likely that they will be included, directly or indirectly, in the exam.

Make sure that you know the likely format of the paper. How many questions are there usually? How many of these do you need to answer? Are they equally weighted in terms of marks allowed? How many topics does this mean you can afford not to revise? With a little research you should be able to identify areas of the course which it would be dangerous not to know and some which, if pushed, you could more safely afford to revise less thoroughly. But *always* allow a margin. It is extremely dangerous to think that you can completely predict an exam's content, and to revise only the portion of the course you are 'sure' will come up.

Find out from your tutors what *level* of knowledge they expect. Is it fine detail or broad principles? Do you need to remember formulae or will any necessary ones be provided? Find out, too, for subjects where it is an issue, the balance expected between theory and its application. Tailor your revision accordingly.

Find out what you can bring into the exam room and make sure it is in working order. If you are required to handwrite your paper and need a set of coloured pens, pencil and rubber, invest in new ones: during the exam your mind should be on what you are drawing

> **To prepare for exam success:**
>
> - identify requirements
> - prepare a revision plan
> - revise actively
> - practise writing answers
> - get in good physical shape
> - ensure that you know the time and place of each exam.

or writing, not on whether your pens work. Make sure you have a fresh battery in your calculator or perhaps even a spare machine. I apologise if this sounds patronisingly obvious. It is. But many people still omit these simple precautions, with tragic results.

If you have an 'open book' exam and are allowed to take notes or books into the room, think very carefully about the preparation you need in order to make good use of these materials. You will gain no marks for time spent searching through books for the relevant pages.

Produce an index of best references for likely topics. If you are allowed to annotate books, use this facility to make points briefly in margins. Text which is copied is unlikely to gain you any marks at all, but if you copy a relevant note of your own, the examiner will not know.

Prepare a revision plan

Plan carefully, and realistically. A revision plan will help you to balance your efforts and make revision more rewarding, keeping your motivation high. Clarify your objectives and decide on how much revision you need to do. Think about the time you have available and the time you estimate you will need. (Remember to build in a contingency factor in case of the unexpected.)

How are you going to revise? Clearly, you cannot read all the books again. Allow extra time to revise topics you found difficult or material you still do not fully understand. If you have already become used to planning your work actively, this stage should be almost second nature to you by now.

Prepare a chart showing when you will work on each part of the course. You can do this well in advance, but once actual dates are announced you may need to reschedule to take into account the timing of specific exams. Remember to allow time at the end for overall preparation and for practice with past papers or other dummy questions. Avoid scheduling revision the night before the exam. There are better uses for that time. Your chart should have spaces for you to tick off topics as you progress. This helps to sustain your motivation.

Revise actively

Once you have scheduled your time you need to use it to derive maximum benefit. Mere passive reading of books and notes is unlikely to help. Instead, you need to bear the following questions in mind as you tackle each topic:

- What do I need to *learn by heart* (i.e. be able to reproduce from memory – formulae and diagrams, for example)?
- What do I need to *know* (e.g. concepts, principles and techniques and their significance)?
- What do I need to be able to *do* with the above and in what contexts?

You should already have the answers to these questions, but you need to keep them in mind as you work through your notes and other materials.

Even if your notes were taken with revision in mind, you will still need to take further notes as part of your revision. You may find it helpful to extract on to cards those things which you need to be able to reproduce from memory, and learn them (on the bus, in the bath, or wherever you have suitable time at your disposal).

For everything other than rote learning, you should be aiming to *interact* with the materials in as many ways as possible. Draw diagrams of text. Describe diagrams in words. Try to represent relationships with equations. Try to describe equations in words. List possible uses of various techniques. Summarise key parts of the course from memory, then go back to see whether there is anything significant that you have left out. Draw mind maps of possible answers to past questions. Try to invent questions as if you were setting the exam. Then construct outline answers for these. Practise the analysis of requirements and planning of your answer, as suggested earlier for essays.

Aim to do all this fairly quickly. It will keep your brain alert and give you valuable practice in organising your thoughts quickly – a key exam skill. Then go back to course materials and 'mark' your attempts, seeing what you left out and spotting any errors. If you *work* at your revision in this way, rather than sitting in front of your notes and letting your eyes move over them, or merely copying things from one piece of paper to another, you will find that the process is fairly interesting and, more importantly, results in far more learning.

Practise

Unless you are provided with a word processor for the exam there is one very basic skill you may need to practise: that of writing, quickly, for long periods of time, with a pen. If all your writing is at a keyboard, the connection between brain and pen may have withered. This makes it very hard to write fluently in an exam. Your muscles may cramp, and your thoughts will limp along. Prevent this with 'writing practice'. Pick up a pen and write a diary, letters, or first drafts of essays in order to re-establish your skills.

The next thing to practise is writing for as long as an exam, in order to maintain concentration. Unless you habitually write essays in long stretches and by hand, set yourself 'mock exams'. Draft answers to past papers or to questions you set yourself, allowing the same length of time as you will have in the exam. Start, if you like, with single questions and the time that would be allowed for them, before working up to the whole paper. This gives you a good feel for time and the amount you can write in it and will make time management in the exam somewhat easier.

Feedback on your performance is important here, as with everything else. You can check timing easily. You can if necessary mark your own work, putting it aside for a while so that you come to it fresh. Better still, exchange answers with someone else and mark each other's.

Other preparation

Your final task is to be in good shape for the exam. If you are on the verge of caffeine poisoning, have worked through the night or have subsisted on biscuits for a week beforehand, you cannot expect your brain to do you justice in the exam. So it is essential to plan to get enough sleep and exercise during the whole revision period. In particular, use the evening before the exam to do something relaxing and have a reasonably early night. (Walk, hot bath, hot milk, bed is a good sequence.) You can waste all your earlier efforts by not taking your body's needs into account.

Do check, too, that you have the time and place of the exam correct. Someone very near to me arrived in the afternoon for a morning exam, an error which prevented him from getting the 'first' he might otherwise have expected.

> **To do well in the exam:**
>
> - read the paper carefully
> - budget time carefully
> - choose questions you understand
> - read each question very carefully
> - plan your answer
> - monitor progress against question
> - move to next question on schedule
> - relax!

During the examination

If you have followed the above advice, have checked the time of the exam carefully and arrived in time to relax before entering the room, you should be in good shape during the exam. You merely need to remember the following points.

Read the paper carefully

Check that the number of questions you have to answer is what you expected. If you have a choice, read all the questions carefully enough to understand what is required before making your choice. It is often better to answer a question you fully understand about something you more or less know than to attack a question on a topic you have revised extensively but where you really are not sure what the question wants you to do. Totally open-ended questions are hazardous: they leave you to guess at an appropriate structure for your answer, with the possibility that you will get it wrong. Questions with a number of parts clearly spelled out make it easier for you to feel confident that you understand what the examiner requires.

Manage your time

Work out how much time you can afford to allow for each question and monitor your time usage. You must be disciplined about this. More people have failed because they spent too much time on one question and totally failed to answer one or more others than for any other reason. Remember the Pareto principle: here it suggests that you will get 80 per cent of the marks for a question for 20 per cent of the effort that full marks would require. So keeping to time is far more important than aiming for perfection. Move on to the next question when you have used your 'ration' for the current question. You can leave space and come back if you do not use all the time allocated to a subsequent question. Even if you feel forced to choose a question or two on topics where you know your revision to have been inadequate, you should still budget a reasonable time for your attempts. You can gain a surprising number of marks for fairly scant knowledge, if carefully applied to the question. Check your watch and your schedule at frequent intervals to ensure that you allocate your time as intended.

Read each selected question very carefully

Remember the techniques covered earlier for deconstructing questions. You will need to do this fairly quickly, but it is essential that you identify and understand the instruction words and that you separate out *all* the implicit parts of the question. Any part that you miss will cost you a significant chunk of marks, as it will get zero out of whatever was allowed for that part of the question in the marking scheme.

Plan your answer

There is a strong temptation, knowing how scarce time is, to leap straight into answering, without any plan. But this is dangerous. It is easy to miss essential dimensions of an answer or to end up with something which lacks much structure, is out of balance and fails to convince the marker of your grasp of the topic. While you cannot afford the leisurely, 'collect everything of potential relevance' approach that may work for essays, you *can* do a quick 'brain dump' of key concepts and points that seem important, each encapsulated in a single word or very short phrase. This captures them so that they do not retreat into the inaccessible parts of your brain once you start writing about something else. You can then spend a few minutes arranging these into a mind map or set of headings and subheadings. Writing your answer will be so much easier once you have done this, and you will more than gain back the time you have spent. (This is provided you did not overindulge in planning – 20 per cent of the available time would seem a reasonable limit for this in most cases.)

A clear structure, with introduction and conclusion and a logical and connected flow between, is essential. It can help to leave space at the start of your answer and add your introduction after you have written the rest. Diagrams may be well worth including. (They need to be clear rather than artistic, so do not spend too much time on making them pretty.)

If you *are* running short of time, do not cross out your notes until your answer is completed. Markers are usually prevented from giving marks for crossed-out work, but will not penalise for notes which are clearly headed as such and *not* crossed out: in case of disaster they may give you some credit for them.

Remember to monitor progress at intervals

The control loop only works if 'outputs' are sampled often enough that you can take corrective action in time to prevent disaster. This means checking your time management every page or so and also checking that you are still answering the question asked. (Questions have a nasty habit of silently rewriting themselves inside your head into something you would prefer to answer; frequent checking against the original is essential.)

One of your objectives is to demonstrate academic competence, so part of the checking should be that you have noted relevant authors and dates wherever appropriate.

Above all, DON'T PANIC

Most people pass exams. Almost everyone could have passed by following the guidance above. So if anything feels as if it is going wrong, take a few deep breaths and consciously relax your body while reminding yourself of this. Your brain will probably unscramble itself enough to proceed. If you really cannot answer a question then write *something* that has some tenuous relevance. If you run out of clearly relevant things to say and have not used the time, write something more that has at least some bearing on the subject. If you are running out of time despite everything above, stop and jot down some notes in answer to the remaining questions. And if your problems were because of illness on the day, see a doctor as soon as the exam is over, get a certificate and send it in.

Viva Voce Examinations

Oral assessment was the earliest examination form of all. In the UK it is uncommon at undergraduate level, though sometimes used for dissertations. It is sometimes used when examiners cannot decide your result from your written papers, perhaps because you were ill and so unable to do yourself justice on the day of an exam. Sometimes a few other people are summoned to a viva to help examiners establish the range of expected standards. You may well need to meet your examiner and discuss your portfolio if you are pursuing an NVQ or other work-based assessment. Such examinations can be tailored to the needs of an individual candidate, but are also very expensive. It is hard to ensure uniformity of standards, so institutions may seek to keep their use to a minimum.

Any viva can be seen as good practice for job and appraisal interviews, so you may like to read what follows with this in mind if you are not expecting a viva.

Preparing for a viva

Your first requirement is to know *why* you are being examined, and therefore what people are likely to be looking for. You will probably not be told exactly but may be able get some indication at least. Knowing reasons can help you prepare, and may make you less anxious if, for example, the viva is because your work was so good the examiners wish to reassure themselves that you produced it unaided.

> **To do well in a viva:**
> - find out why you are being examined
> - prepare accordingly
> - check that you understand each question
> - allow yourself time to think
> - answer clearly and honestly
> - watch responses to your answers
> - check you have been understood.

If the viva is to give you a chance to improve on the marks you gained in a written exam, then you should revise in much the same way as you did for the exam itself, as this is another form of test of the same knowledge. You could also usefully reflect on any exam questions you know you answered badly. It is likely that your examiners will focus on the areas where they think you are weak. Furthermore, if you can demonstrate to them that you are aware of where you went wrong, it will count in your favour. Do not restrict your revision to such areas, however. You may be questioned on any part of the course and, indeed, may not have judged your shortcomings correctly.

If the exam is a routine one in support of a project or thesis, then little preparation should be needed beyond reminding yourself of its contents. If you have sweated blood over writing it, these will probably be indelibly etched in your mind anyway. You might, however, wish to think about your 'reflections' section on lessons learned (assuming there was one – if not, reflect anyway) and about any areas where you know the research was weak so that you can say what you would do about this, given a chance. But much of the exam will probably be directed towards establishing that the work was your own, by looking for the sort of in-depth knowledge you could only have if this were the case.

For a non-routine project viva, or in the case of a borderline written exam, try to find out what the concern was, either from your project supervisor or tutor or from your own reflection. Think of ways in which you can reassure your examiner(s) that such weaknesses either were unavoidable or would be avoided in future because you now fully understand how they arose.

Answering questions

A viva is an example of a spoken exchange where you will be aiming to determine the examiner's concerns and address them concisely. Your goal is to demonstrate your understanding of the material in question. Thus you need the talking and listening skills addressed in Chapter 8. Revisit that chapter before your exam (or interview).

➤ **Ch 8**

Careful listening is crucial. If you fail to understand a question, you will do yourself as much harm as if you misread a question in a written exam. In a viva you have the chance to check the meaning of a question with the examiner. Take advantage of this. Clarify the meaning and check that your understanding is correct if you are in any doubt.

Thinking is vital too. Do not feel you have to answer a question the instant the examiner stops asking it. It is perfectly reasonable to spend a short time thinking about how to answer it. If this seems odd, ask: 'Can I think about that for a moment?' You will almost always be told that you can. Be honest. If there is a weakness in your project, or you answer something and then realise that your answer was inadequate, say so and then go on to do what you can to make good the shortcomings you have revealed. This is far safer than hoping that the examiner didn't notice. Examiners notice a great deal: that is their job.

Take your cues on formality from the examiner. Some are more informal than others. Aim to match their chosen level. But above all, remember that anything you can do to help the *process* of the interview will help. Look directly at the examiner when talking or listening. You can smile where appropriate. The occasion is one for communication, so treat it as such. Check that you have received the right (question) message. Check that your answer is clear to your examiner. If you are at all unsure, ask whether what you have said is enough, or if there is another angle the examiner would like you to explore, or something which should be covered in more depth. They may not always tell you. But often they will and this will enable you to give a more satisfactory answer.

Portfolio Assessment

The importance of reflection in learning is now widely recognised and both universities and professional bodies may assess some of your learning and development on the basis of

➤ **Ch 3**
personal development files including learning logs, learning journals and other evidence of planning and managing learning. This was discussed in Chapter 3, and if you follow the guidance there, together with that given by your university, and use an appropriate portfolio management system, you should not find compiling this evidence difficult.

If your course includes an element of competence-based assessment, or if you seek such a qualification later in your career, you are likely to be required to produce a more systematic portfolio demonstrating that you have the full range of competences covered in that qualification. Your portfolio will consist of a number of 'exhibits' which demonstrate your skills in some way. Your work on the book thus far should have generated some exhibits. Additionally, you might need to include letters or reports you have written, work schedules you have drawn up, interview plans and/or reports of the interview, training plans, audio or video recordings of interactions of one kind or another, testimonials from people for whom you have worked, examples of things you have made, and so forth. The list is endless, and what is required will depend on the particular qual-
➤ **Ch 1**
ification which you are seeking.

The *principles* of portfolio assessment are fairly uniform:

- You need to address all, or most of, the aspects of the relevant performance standards.
- Exhibits need to be relevant, fairly recent and to demonstrate your own competence rather than that of other people.
- You need to have organised, indexed, cross-referenced or linked and justified your contents.

In summary, it needs to be easy for the examiner to find the relevant and convincing evidence for each relevant standard.

Having studied the relevant competence framework, the contexts in which assessors want competences to be displayed and the sorts of evidence they want, you can put together suitable materials, together with a 'story' which explains your situation and the contexts in which the competences are used and an index which clearly links exhibits to competences. This is important because a carefully chosen exhibit can often evidence a number of different competences. A project, for example, could show self-management skills, project management skills, written communication skills, information handling skills and possibly others as well. But you cannot merely hand your project in and expect the assessor to work this out. You need to explain which exhibit shows which competence(s) and why, referencing relevant parts of any lengthy exhibit.

If you have been constructing exhibits as instructed in the exercises, you should already be getting a feel for how to do this. You should also be building a collection of evidence which could help you gain qualifications after graduation. It is a good habit to treat everything you do which shows you have mastered a new skill, or can use it in a new context, as a potential exhibit. You will find it helps to consolidate your learning to write your case around the material. Leafing through the portfolio can also be a powerful antidote to depression. When you are depressed it is easy to underestimate yourself. A solid portfolio can counteract this.

SUMMARY

This chapter has argued the following:

- Doing well in assessment requires clarity of objectives, planning, monitoring and use of feedback wherever possible. It thus closely resembles management in other contexts.

- All assessments can usefully be regarded as communication, so written or spoken communication skills are vital.

- Use of ideas, images or words originated by others, without giving the originators the credit, constitutes plagiarism. Universities exact severe penalties for this, so it is important to clearly indicate and attribute any material which you did not generate yourself.

- Understanding objectives requires that you deconstruct a question and identify its constituent parts, then plan an answer which addresses all parts of a question, in a reasonable sequence.

- Understanding and using tutor feedback can help you improve your marks.

- Both essays and reports need an introduction and a conclusion and clear arguments based on valid evidence between the two.

- Time management is crucial for both written assignments and exams.

- For exams you need a clear revision plan based on identification of the material that it is important to cover. Revision needs to be active and to include frequent tests of recall and of ability to draft outline answers to possible questions.

- During an exam it is important to read questions carefully before selecting, to plan your answers and regularly check both your time usage and the continued relevance of what you write to the actual question asked.

- Should anything go wrong to threaten your success, obtain evidence of the problem where possible and notify the authorities as soon as possible.

Further information

Race, P. (2007) *How to Get a Good Degree (2nd edition)*, Open University Press.

HELPFILE
TERMS COMMONLY USED
IN ASSESSMENT

Analyse

To examine part by part. Thus if you are asked to analyse a problem situation you would be looking for the roots of the problem rather than merely describing the symptoms which are presented. You would normally be expected to draw heavily on ideas and frameworks in the course being assessed in order to identify the root causes. The analysis may be the basis for suggesting possible ways forward and deciding among them.

Assess

To judge the importance of something, or say what it is worth, giving your reasons for your verdict.

Comment

This terse instruction may appear after a quotation or other statement. You are required to respond in a way that shows that you understand the topic to which the statement refers. Thus you might need to define any terms contained, explain the significance of the statement and possibly evaluate it (see below), or state the extent to which you agree and disagree and give your reasons for this.

Compare

This means that you should look for both similarities and differences between the (usually) two things mentioned. It is very easy to forget one or the other, thus potentially losing half the available marks. It is safest always to think of 'compare' as shorthand for 'compare and contrast'. Sometimes you will be expected to come down in favour of one of the things compared. One possible approach to comparison is to construct a table with one column for each of the items compared and rows for each relevant aspect. This gives an 'at a glance' impression of aspects where entries are the same and those where there are differences. It will not, however, allow much space for discussion and may need to be complemented by a paragraph or two highlighting the significance of key similarities and differences which appear in the table.

Consider

This has a similar meaning to comment, though the emphasis on evaluation is likely to be higher.

Contrast

A subset of 'compare' (see above), requiring you to focus only on differences between the things mentioned.

Criticise/critically evaluate

To judge the merit of a statement or theory, making clear the basis for your judgement. This might be in terms of the evidence on which the statement or theory is based, the likely validity of any assumptions made, the internal consistency of the statement, or its theoretical, logical or factual underpinning.

Define

To state, precisely, the meaning of a concept. Normally this will be a definition that you have been given in your course. Sometimes there may be competing definitions, in which case you may need to give both (or all, if more than two), and discuss the differences between them. You will often be asked to include examples of the thing to be defined. Even if not asked for, an example may help to convey to the marker that you understand the meaning of the term in question.

Demonstrate

This means you need to show something, usually by giving relevant examples, in order to convince the marker of your understanding of something or of its relevance or importance.

Describe

To give a detailed account of the thing referred to, again with a view to establishing that you know what is being referred to and understand its significance. Diagrams can often help you to describe something and should be included if they add something to your words.

Differentiate

This is similar to 'contrast', again requiring you to describe the differences between the things mentioned.

Discuss

To extract the different themes in a subject and to describe and evaluate them. What are the key factors/aspects? What are the arguments in favour of, and against, each aspect? What evidence is there supporting each side of the argument? What is the significance of each aspect?

Evaluate

This means much the same as 'assess'. If you were asked to evaluate a theory, for example, you would look both at the evidence supporting the theory and at the theory's usefulness.

Examine

This means much the same as 'analyse', though it might require a slightly higher proportion of description in relation to evaluation.

Explain

This can mean to make something clear or to give reasons for something, depending on the context. Frequently, you would need to do both in order to answer a question. Remember that your explanation, as with all assessments, is intended to demonstrate to your assessor your understanding of a concept or argument.

Illustrate

This is similar to 'demonstrate'. It requires you to make clear your understanding of an idea or term by giving concrete examples, or by using a diagram or other figure to add to the word(s) and convey the message that you know what you are talking about.

Interpret

This normally means to make sense of something, to make it clear, usually giving your judgement of the significance of the thing to be interpreted. You might be asked to interpret a set of figures or a graph, in which case you would need to describe in words the significant features, or messages, contained therein.

Justify

This means you must give good reason for something, in terms of logic or evidence. It helps to think of the main objections to whatever it is and then show why they are not valid, as well as thinking of the plus points.

List

This needs to be treated with caution. Strictly it means to give single words or phrases. But sometimes the assessor wants you to give a brief description rather than merely a single word. If in doubt, ask, if it is a written assignment. In an exam, make a reasoned guess from the proportion of the marks allocated to this part of the question and any subsequent instructions. For example, 'List ... Select two items from your list and describe them in detail' clearly does mean a list pure and simple.

Outline

To give a brief description of the most important features of whatever it is.

Refute

The converse of 'justify', requiring you to make the case *against* something.

Review

To go over a subject carefully, giving as much as you can remember or unearth of what is relevant, though as concisely as is appropriate.

Summarise

Write briefly the main points of something – very similar to 'outline'.

Trace

This requires you to track a sequence of events which led to a specified state. (Multiple cause diagrams may be helpful here if there is more than a single 'track'.)

. . . ?

By this I mean questions which seem to invite the answer yes or no, such as 'Do you agree?' after a statement. It is extremely rare for the assessor to expect such a simple answer. Far more often the expectation is that you will discuss the statement and evaluate it.

PART 3
WORKING WITH OTHERS

Introduction to Part 3

For almost everyone, work means working with others and therefore involves communication and collaboration. Organisations are increasingly structured around teams, sometimes widely scattered ones, which has increased both the amount and the variety of interaction needed. Team work is one of the skills employers look for in graduates, and your subsequent career success will depend on how effectively you interact with colleagues.

Much of the deep learning this book is seeking to help you develop also depends on interactions with others. Your studies will give you many opportunities to practise working and learning with others, and these skills will help you understand more about organisational situations, and further develop your team skills.

While task-related communication is clearly important at work and in group learning, wider aspects of relationships can have even more impact. Many decisions at work are not purely rational. They are influenced by relationships and feelings. If you have a good relationship with someone, they are likely to view your proposals more positively and to go out of their way to be cooperative. When compromise is inevitable, it will be achieved more easily. If someone stands you up, you are far more likely to forgive them if they are a good friend. If someone asks you to do them a favour, again you are more likely to help them if you get on well with them. This partly explains why networking skills are important for management success.

The impact of relationships at work goes far beyond issues of success. A job can be one of the most satisfying parts of your life, or it can be sheer purgatory. The quality of relationships between those who work together can in large part determine which. When reading a case for promotion recently, I was struck by the following phrase from one of the candidate's referees:

He's a pleasure to work with – a crucial, yet frequently overlooked attribute of the modern manager.

Your ability to work well with others affects their lives as well as your own.

Given all this, it is not surprising that one of the attributes sought by employers of graduates is 'interactive attributes' (Harvey *et al.,* 1997) or 'networking skills' (QAA, 2015) Both relate to the ability to *communicate* formally and informally with a wide range of people and to *relate* to these people and to work effectively in *teams*.

Look at the graduate recruitment section of any major daily newspaper or website and you are likely to find organisations seeking graduates who are 'enthusiastic, self-motivated and have excellent communication skills . . .', 'are self-starters with the ability to communicate . . .', 'have excellent communication and interpersonal skills . . .' and 'have the kind of personality that helps them get on harmoniously and productively with colleagues . . .', to quote but a few of those I found when doing this.

Clearly, then, interpersonal skills can have a major impact on both your enjoyment of work and your success both in gaining and being successful in a job. After all, humans have evolved as highly social animals. It is not, therefore, surprising that most selection processes are heavily weighted, intentionally or not, towards assessing interpersonal skills.

Good interpersonal skills will help you to benefit from tutors and advisors and from feedback from fellow students, to do well in group projects, and to make rewarding friendships. You have started to think about elements of communication to improve your writing skills. This part of the book develops these ideas in the context of spoken communication, group working and talking to a group.

The first chapter in this part therefore looks at talking and listening, skills which you will use in almost all group working. As part of this, you will explore how to be assertive rather than aggressive or defensive: assertiveness helps you resolve differences of either opinion or objectives. The subsequent chapter looks at the sorts of behaviours which contribute to effective team working. The final chapter looks at formal presentation skills.

8
TALKING AND LISTENING

Learning outcomes

By the end of this chapter you should:

- have a clearer idea of your own strengths in the area of one-to-one communication and be able to convey this to a prospective employer

- be developing your talking and listening skills

- be becoming more assertive when necessary

- be better at influencing others

- be starting to network

- have developed the habit of reflecting on your interpersonal effectiveness

- be developing your interpersonal skills through reflection on experience.

Cartoon by Neill Cameron, www.neillcameron.com

Introduction

The spoken word is perhaps the most powerful communication channel, yet many people are poor talkers and poorer listeners. This chapter shows you how to become better at both, developing skills that will make you a better learner, a better team worker, and more effective in almost all areas of your life. Better communication can transform all your relationships, and greatly increase your employability and promotion prospects.

Most relationships, whether at work or elsewhere, are based on talking and listening. *Real* learning, rather than merely accumulating 'book knowledge', involves discussing ideas with others. It involves being able to listen to, and absorb feedback. You can find out a lot about a situation by talking to the people involved. To convince someone to take action, you may need to talk them through the arguments. You may need to negotiate with people to get what you want. Small wonder that the Quality Assurance Agency (QAA, 2015) list of skills of particular relevance for business and management includes 'Networking: an awareness of the interpersonal skills of effective listening, negotiating, persuasion and presentation and their use in generating business contacts.'

As with reading, many people communicate poorly despite decades of experience. They may say something without thinking about its impact on the other person. They may come across as aggressive, and therefore generate a negative response. Some are so afraid of saying the wrong thing, or of offending the listener, that they do not say what they mean.

Since communication is a two-way process, listening skills are as important as talking skills. Feedback on your own communication can help you improve your listening, as well as talking skills, thus increase your ability to communicate effectively. This will improve the quality of all your interpersonal relationships, as well as your ability to learn from and with others and be more effective in any job.

The Importance of Interpersonal Skills

In most jobs, interaction with others is crucial. Many organisations have restructured around flexible working groups as the main unit, and team work is essential for success.

Even if you work on an individual task you will still usually need to interact with others. As a friend who is responsible for systems design for a major US bank said to me:

> You are always going to have to sell your ideas to your boss, to argue for resources, and to let people know what you have done and why it is important.

➤ Ch 9

In almost any job you will be more successful if you can talk clearly and confidently, can be assertive, can influence people and can negotiate effectively. Whether dealing with clients or customers, your boss or those whom you yourself manage, you have to be able to communicate effectively face to face.

Activity 8.1

Look back at your initial SWOT analysis. Did you include communication skills as a potential strength? Reassess yourself using the questions below. If you have any doubts about your skills in this area, reassess yourself at the end of the chapter (a version is available on the website), and develop an action plan for developing your skills. Score each item 1 if it is usually the case, 2 if quite often, 3 if sometimes, 4 if seldom the case, and 5 if almost never.

➤ Ch 1

When I meet new people, much of my attention is on planning my reply
rather than really listening to what they are saying   _____

Most people I talk to seem to be rather boring   _____

I find it quite difficult to network with other people   _____

In a group, I don't feel that my contributions have much impact   _____

I tend to get into arguments if people don't see my point of view   _____

I may sound defensive if people give me negative feedback, although it
may be because they haven't understood my reasons   _____

I tend to focus more on a person's words than their non-verbal signals   _____

I have no hesitation in telling people they are bad at something   _____

People seem not to hear what I am saying   _____

I feel uncomfortable in social or group work situations   _____

I find it hard to create a good impression in an interview   _____

I find it almost impossible not to interrupt if something someone says
prompts a really good idea   _____

Total   _____

Note: this is a very crude questionnaire, but it will act as a starting point for thinking about your interpersonal skills. If you were being strictly honest you are unlikely to get a score much above 50 (unless you are very unaware of your shortcomings). Above 40 is good but shows room for improvement – file your score if you are planning to work on this area.

You are likely to experience many job interviews during your career. In an interview your talking and listening skills will strongly influence how interviewers judge you. Thus these skills will help you to get a job, as well as to be effective once you have got it. Appraisal interviews are a major part of the system for assessing performance in most large organisations. Again, your talking and listening skills will be essential. They are essential for the effective team work, which is a feature of so many jobs and which will be explored in

➤ Ch 9

more detail in the next chapter. Many jobs will involve daily communication with clients and internal and external customers. Good communication with those who work for you is essential to being an effective manager. It would be hard to overestimate the impact of improving your talking and listening skills on your career success.

Since daily communication with those around you is an essential element in your life, improving your communication skills can improve not just your work, but every aspect of your life.

Active Listening

Do you ever feel that the person you are talking to is not really listening? They may forget, or misremember what you have said, or interrupt you in mid-sentence with some barely related statement that they have obviously been dying to make for some time. Or they may be looking over your shoulder and not showing any response to what you say. Now, be honest with yourself and think about how often you do exactly the same thing to others. Active listening will help you avoid this. The basic communication model from

➤ Ch 6

Chapter 6 showed sender, message, communication channel and receiver as key elements. If someone is talking to you, perhaps very clearly and cogently, but you are not really listening, then communication has failed because the receiver is not functioning.

Activity 8.2

Think of a recent social situation at which you were present and at which people were not listening to each other. If possible, think also of a work-related situation (job or study) in which, again, communication was failing because you or someone else was not listening. Why do people seemingly persist in such non-communication? List as many reasons as you can for the talker continuing to talk, and the listener not listening, in the situation(s) you have just identified. If you are working through this chapter with others, once you have written your lists compare them with those made by one or two other people and discuss any similarities and differences.

Activity 8.2 may well have given you some difficulty. Why would people so persistently not communicate? Your list might include:

- failure to realise that the other person is not listening
- a desire to be seen by others to be talking – this can make you seem a lively person at a party

- enjoyment of the sound of your own voice

- the conviction that the other person must find what you are saying riveting

- the realisation that *you* are sorting out your thoughts by talking, even if you are having no effect on the thought processes of the other person

- a wish to stop the other person from talking – they may be boring, or you don't understand them and don't like to be found out in this

- a simple lack of interest in the other person

- a desire to be the centre of attention

- the dread of silence.

You may have come up with many of the above, plus a variety of other reasons. Your list and mine can probably be broken down into a small number of categories. Some reasons represent more or less sensible behaviour, such as trying to avoid boredom or exploring your own thoughts and where they lead. Some are defensive, such as avoiding being made to look stupid by not understanding. Some are aggressive, such as exerting your will on others. Some represent lack of perception. Some have to do with communicating something other than the message contained in the words spoken.

The skill of being heard when speaking, rather than having your words fall on unreceptive ears or minds, is dealt with shortly. First, we shall look in more detail at the motivations for not listening.

Your list of possible reasons for 'people hearing without listening' or, more accurately if less poetically, *not* hearing because of this might include:

- lack of interest in either the person speaking or what they are saying

- fear about how to respond, and thoughts about this taking up most of your awareness

- inability to concentrate

- inability to understand what is being said, or to perceive the emotions leading to its expression

- desire *not* to hear – for example, things that reflect badly on the listener or are inconsistent with strongly held ideas.

'Not listening' wastes time and energy – both the speaker's and yours. It makes for negative feelings between you. It may cause you to miss a real opportunity to find out something useful or interesting. You may lose the chance to build a good relationship or to give or receive support (both of which can be rewarding). You will also, of course, be wasting the opportunity to develop your listening skills.

Identifying purposes

If you wish to avoid these negative aspects and use one-to-one exchanges to good effect, then you need first to think about the purpose of the exchange, what the positive outcomes might be and then how you can develop the skills needed to achieve these.

Activity 8.3

Think about some *good* conversations that you have recently had and the sorts of benefits which you were deriving from them. List these. Now think about exchanges which you have had which have been unsatisfactory. Aim for about six such conversations. Split these into those which might have been useful or rewarding if they had gone differently and those which were probably doomed to be a waste of time from the start. Reflect on this, and consider whether talking and listening is an area which you need to work on. If so, develop an action plan for your file.

Active listening helps you:

- build relationships
- learn
- develop ideas
- work better together.

You should have been able to identify positive potential in at least some of the bad experiences. Few of us know so much that we have nothing to learn from someone else or cannot derive comfort from support and sympathy. Most of us find it intellectually stimulating to exchange ideas and explore areas of disagreement. Of course, it does take two to play. Very occasionally you will meet people who seem incapable of ever taking part in a two-way conversation. In such cases, it may be best to cut your losses and find a tactful way of stopping the exchange. But take care not to do this too soon. Some of the most unpromising beginnings turn into useful exchanges.

For conversations which were rewarding, or which had the potential to be so, the outcomes might have included:

- enjoyment at sharing ideas
- discovering new information
- agreement to some future action on your part
- laughter
- an increased sense of self-worth
- a clearer understanding of one or more of your own ideas
- a possible way of resolving a problem
- reduced worry about something that was troubling you
- satisfaction at feeling that you have helped someone
- plans to do things together in future
- a clearer sense of purpose regarding a shared task.

The list could be much longer. You probably identified outcomes that were not on the list, as the range of possible interchanges is almost infinite. But again, a smaller number of broad categories will probably contain most, if not all, of your outcomes. The first is *satisfaction of social needs*: you will remember from Chapter 2 that these form an important part of human motivation and contribute to your feelings of well-being.

➤ Ch 2

The second category will concern *information transfer*. We learn a great deal from conversations with other people. This is one of the reasons that networking is so important. The information could include simple facts, names of further contacts or other potentially useful resources you might be able to access. But more tenuous information can be just as useful. You may get a better idea of what is important to someone, and find out what is likely to upset them. You may discover their position on some issue of future concern to you.

The third category has to do with *developing ideas*. While much of this can be done in a solitary fashion, most people enjoy testing ideas against other people. Apart from the fun, this is an important way of identifying unconscious assumptions which you have made. These may seem so obviously true to you that you do not question them; they may be far less obviously true to others. Inappropriate assumptions may be leading you astray. If the ideas need to be accepted by a group of people, then developing them in the group is important. More of this in Part 4.

➤ Ch 11, 12, 14, 15

The fourth category has to do with *task planning and management*, for which communication is essential, whether at work or in relation to study. For shared tasks the need is obvious. For solitary ones, you will still almost certainly need to communicate – often by talking – to make sure that you understand the task fully. You will also need to renegotiate deadlines or resources if things turn out differently from what is expected.

Listening skills

To achieve any of the above four categories of outcomes from conversations, both participants need to be skilled listeners. If you are listening actively you will do the following.

To listen better:

- suspend judgement
- concentrate on the speaker
- watch body language
- avoid interruptions
- seek clarification
- acknowledge feelings
- allow silence
- encourage and prompt
- avoid opinions
- don't offer your 'solutions'
- show you value the speaker.

Suspend judgement

It is vital to keep an open mind while you are listening. If you have already judged a situation and come to an opinion you are likely to hear only those things which are consistent with your existing opinion. This will severely restrict what you learn from the exchange. Instead, try hard to approach the situation as one where what the other person knows and says is the important thing.

Concentrate on the speaker

Focus on what the speaker is saying and how they are saying it. This will take all your attention – you cannot afford to think about their hair, the weather, what you are going to say next, or anything else. Is there a logical thread? Are there inconsistencies? If something sounds wrong to you, is it because you and the speaker have different basic assumptions? If the speaker is giving 'facts' what is the evidence for these? Similarly, what underlies opinions? What feelings are being expressed?

Watch their body language

This can tell you as much as the words. Unease may be expressed, for example, by restless hand or body movements, looking away or inappropriate smiling. Where words and body are at odds, remember this for later probing. (When speakers are having a good conversation you will often find that their body language becomes similar, so that one mirrors the other. Two people may face each other over a bar, one with their left elbow resting on it, the other with their right elbow. Or if seated opposite each other they may cross their legs at roughly the same time, one the left leg, one the right, so that again one looks like the mirror image of the other. (One way of building rapid rapport with someone else is to actively mirror their body language.)

Show your interest

Eye contact, smiles and an 'open' posture help. Don't cross your arms or legs – this shows a degree of 'closedness' to the other person. Nods and expressions of agreement from time to time help to demonstrate interest. But it is possible to do all of these without hearing a word the other person is saying. Reinforce these general cues, therefore, by more specific ones. Paraphrasing what the other person has said at key points shows that content has registered with you. 'So what you are saying is . . .' or 'It sounds as if . . .' shows that something has registered. It also allows you to check that you are receiving the message intended. Such reflections are useful for the speaker too. Sometimes they may not have realised just what they *were* saying, or perhaps were unaware of some of its implications.

Avoid interruptions

This is really an extension of the point above. If you are interested, you will interrupt only when the thing said is so interesting that you cannot control your excitement. But interruptions are such a frequent way in which listening fails that they are worth separate mention. Note that talking into a silence, but still breaking the speaker's 'train of thought', is a form of interruption.

Seek clarification

If you are not sure that you understand what someone is saying, or if what they are saying seems inconsistent with something said earlier, ask questions exploring this. Use questions such as 'Do you mean . . .?' or 'How does this fit with . . .?' or 'I don't quite understand why . . .' to help clarify things.

Recognise feelings

Feelings are an important component in communications. It can be useful to show the other person that you are aware of how they feel. 'I can see how angry this makes you . . .'

or 'Yes, it is quite scary when . . .' or 'That really upset you, didn't it . . .' can convey that you have heard, and accepted, the feelings that are being communicated as well as the words. If, for example, you are trying to give support to someone who is worried or who has had a bad experience, it is very important to accept, and show that you have accepted, their feelings.

Allow silence

If the speaker is trying to say something difficult, or they are using talking as a way of developing their thoughts, they may need time to think. Many people feel uncomfortable with silences in conversation, but it is important that you do not rush in because you find the situation embarrassing. Instead, show by your body language that you are comfortable with the silence, and allow the person the thinking time they need. (You can usually see that they are indeed thinking, as their eyes will wander round the room rather than looking at you.) A good interviewer will always allow a candidate this thinking time.

Encourage and prompt

If a person *is* finding things difficult, and a pause does not seem to be the answer, you might want to ask a gently probing question: 'That's really interesting. What happened next?' or 'How did you feel about that?' or 'So what options do you think you have?'

Direct the conversation only when necessary

If you are trying to listen, to learn and perhaps to help the speaker, then taking charge of the conversation should be done only with caution. Sometimes the speaker will be going round in circles. If so, you may need to summarise the argument in question and suggest another avenue. Sometimes the conversation will raise a question or issue that had not previously occurred to you. If so you may want to lead into this topic. It is usually better to steer with a light hand. Being too directive will carry the message that you are more concerned with your perspective than that of the speaker. (Of course, in a more formal interview, where you have a clear agenda, you *will* need to be rather more directive.)

Avoid expressing you own opinions and judgements

There is another important reason for suspending judgement. It stops you expressing opinions. If someone feels that you are making negative judgements they will soon stop talking. Being too full of praise is not always helpful either. While support is good, agreeing with everything a person says may make them less likely to question their perspective. Helping someone to see things differently might be a positive outcome of a conversation. There is a further hazard. We almost all have a strong need for approval. Expressing judgement will slant the conversation even if it does not stop it. The speaker will start to say things in order to gain your approval, which is unlikely to be helpful. This

➤ Ch 11

is particularly likely if the listener has a higher status than the speaker, if you are listening to someone who reports to you at work, for example.

Be wary of suggesting solutions

➤ Ch 11

If the conversation is a joint problem-solving situation there will be a time when suggested solutions may be helpful. Even then it is possible to start looking for solutions too soon, before the problem is fully understood. (When you have read Chapter 11 the reasons for this will be clearer.) If you are trying to help someone else to solve their problem, suggested solutions, even if asked for, are likely to get a 'Yes, but . . . ' response. This will be followed by a series of reasons why the solution is impossible or inappropriate. It is more useful to help the other person to find their own solution. This will be one which they will accept and therefore have the motivation to implement.

Show that you value the speaker

A 'good' exchange can increase the self-esteem of those involved. Your active listening will already show the speaker that you value them through your concentration on what they are saying, your efforts to understand their exact meaning and your encouragement when they find it difficult to put something into words. You can further help their self-esteem, and build a positive relationship with them, by showing your appreciation of their input. So at the end of a talking–listening exchange, it is useful to tell the speaker that you valued their input, perhaps saying what in particular you found useful about talking and listening with them, or what you enjoyed.

This somewhat lengthy list should make it clear why listening demands skill and a high level of concentration. Becoming a proficient listener takes practice and time. You may need to break the bad habits of a lifetime, and breaking any habits is extremely difficult. To become a better listener, first become much more aware of the dimensions of listening. Only then can you start reflecting actively on how you score on these dimensions – a difficult task when listening itself leaves little if any spare brain capacity.

Activity 8.4

Increase your awareness of the various dimensions by listening carefully to other people's conversations. Make a rough assessment of how well they are communicating. Watch their body language and listen for a little while before coming to this judgement. Then try to find out what is contributing to the effectiveness or otherwise of the interchange. Score the participants on the dimensions described above. Are they expressing interest? How? How is lack of interest being communicated? How are silences handled? What sort of probes seem to be effective in encouraging the speaker? You can do this on a bus, in a pub, at a party or anywhere that people interact. If several of you are doing it, compare notes afterwards.

Activity 8.5

Once you are more aware of the aspects of effective listening, start to observe your own behaviour by reflecting on conversations as soon as possible after they take place. Once you become aware of some of your bad habits, identify some purposeful exchanges where you know in advance that listening will be important. Think about your objectives in the exchange and those of the other person. Try to think before you speak and to avoid bad habits such as interruption or passing judgement. Try to use more 'good' listening behaviour, such as encouragement, close concentration, paraphrasing or recognition of feelings.

Attentive listening is a variant on active listening that can give you useful 'listening' practice. It can be useful in a range of situations from resolving conflict to developing your thoughts by 'thinking aloud' while someone listens. *Attentive listening* relies on attending very closely to the talker, without prompting, clarifying or in any other way directing the conversation. At its simplest, the talker talks and the listener listens, all the while looking at, and concentrating fully on the talker.

When you disagree with someone, it can be useful to agree to take 2- or 3-minute turns, and to alternate talking and attentive listening. If you are part of a group trying to work something out, you can similarly split into pairs and each have a timed talk and listen before feeding any new thoughts back into the group. In each case the listener remains silent. (Kline (1999) has developed this approach for a wide range of applications in organisations.)

Activity 8.6

Practise attentive listening with a partner. Using a timer, take turns listening while the other talks about something of current concern. Afterwards, compare notes on how it felt to listen and be listened to.

Giving and Receiving Feedback

Giving and receiving feedback is an important interpersonal – and learning – skill. Feedback is a core element in the control loop, and essential for both learning and motivation. Much of this feedback will come from other people.

Fellow team members can give you useful feedback on your performance as a team member. Tutors will give you feedback on assignments. Some students improve their marks considerably by taking notice of this feedback. Others seem to ignore it completely, and never improve. Seeking feedback if you are not shortlisted for a job, or do not get it at interview can help you strengthen your next application, and/or do better in interviews.

➤ Ch 7

At work you will often need to be guided by informal feedback from a superior or to help your own subordinates improve by use of constructive comment. Performance appraisal interviews provide more formal feedback. In many organisations these will be linked to both pay and career prospects.

➤ Ch 9

Talking and listening are essential to much feedback, and improving your general communication skills will help. There are, however, some factors which are particularly important for feedback to be effective. One of these is getting feedback on how well you give and receive feedback. So what helps and hinders effective use of feedback?

One point you need to be aware of is that we typically find it very hard to accept criticism – a common response is to deny or explain away any problems. The more insecure people feel the stronger will be this tendency. Some people simply do not seem to *hear* criticism. They will claim never to have been told that anything was wrong, though their superior might strongly deny this. Many people in the UK culture find it equally difficult to give feedback, often finding it as difficult to praise as to point out where improvements would help.

Guidelines for giving feedback

> **To give useful feedback:**
>
> - avoid appearing superior
> - emphasise good points
> - focus on behaviour, not person
> - be specific.

The following good practice guidelines should help overcome the difficulties of giving feedback. The examples are drawn from situations where feedback is being given on contributions to a discussion group (see next chapter), but the principles themselves apply in any feedback situation. To give effective feedback you should do the following.

Avoid appearing superior

Good feedback is a reciprocal process, where *each* party has something to learn. You do not need to be 'better' than the person to whom you offer feedback. You merely offer a different perspective.

Focus on good points as well as bad

It is often suggested that there should be two things to praise for every point made suggesting a need for improvement. This makes the whole exchange more positive and reduces the tendency to reject suggestions because of insecurity. Also, people are not necessarily aware of some of their strengths and it is important that in trying to change their behaviour they do not lose these.

Focus on the behaviour, not the person

Focusing on the behaviour makes the feedback less personal and therefore less threatening. Do not say 'You are bad at . . .' but 'Your comment about . . . seemed to make . . . look uneasy.' Rather than 'You are incredibly talkative', say 'According to my log, you were talking for roughly half of the time.' Rather than say 'You are a really aggressive person', say 'When you said . . . I felt as if I was being personally attacked.'

Be as specific as possible

Say things like 'Did you realise that you interrupted Robin 15 times?' or 'Were you aware that each time someone interrupted you, you stopped talking, and that after the first ten minutes you made no further contribution?', or 'When there was that long silence, you showed you were comfortable by smiling and by your relaxed posture.' If you are focusing on behaviour not the person, you will almost inevitably find that you are being more specific, but give as much information as you can if you want to be as helpful as possible.

Guidelines for receiving and using feedback

In receiving feedback you are exercising your skills very much for your own benefit. To benefit from feedback you need to do the following.

> **To benefit from feedback:**
> - listen actively
> - appreciate the help
> - clarify what is meant
> - use several sources
> - accept imperfections
> - identify steps forward
> - monitor progress.

Listen carefully

Listen to what is being said, rather than immediately trying to think of excuses. Watch out for any responses you make which start with 'Yes, but . . .' You are trying to learn from the feedback rather than justify your normal way of operating.

Be appreciative

Remember that the person giving the feedback may be finding it very difficult and that they are doing it for your benefit.

Seek clarification

Seeking clarification is necessary if you are unclear about quite what is being said (but in a positive, not confrontational way). Say 'That's interesting. But I'm not quite sure if you mean . . .'

Use several sources

Remember that observing and giving feedback is a subjective activity. There may be different opinions. No one person is necessarily right (or wrong). But if several are saying the same thing, then what they are saying is worth taking seriously. Try to find other sorts of information to support (or otherwise) the view of the person giving feedback.

Accept your imperfections

No one is perfect, so there is no need for you to pretend to yourself or others that you are. Such pretending can take a lot of effort, makes it harder for others to work with you, and eventually may cost you their respect. By being open about your areas of uncertainty or low skill levels, seeking feedback and then taking it seriously you can become very much better.

Try to identify positive steps you can take to improve

Simply giving yourself a mental slap across the wrists every time you interrupt might be one way. Disciplining yourself to check your understanding of the previous point by giving a brief summary before making a new point might be another. Obviously, you would not want to do things like this for ever, but doing it each time you talk until the habit is established can help you to do it on appropriate occasions thereafter.

Activity 8.7

Work out a detailed action plan for improving your spoken communication skills, remembering to include target and review dates, and place in the appropriate section of your file. Remember to check progress at intervals.

Check your progress at intervals

Either repeat the observation exercise in Activity 8.5 to see whether you are developing your targeted skills, or make a habit of reflecting, perhaps weekly, and noting progress (or lack of it) in your learning file. If you feel you are not getting better at this important skill, seek feedback from others.

Activity 8.8

In reflecting on your own practice, you are working with feedback gained through the filter of your own (imperfect) perceptions and judgement. This can be usefully supplemented by feedback from others. Find someone willing to have a session where you will focus on listening and take turns at being the listener. Think of a topic which would be helpful to talk through but which is not too sensitive or emotionally painful. Examples might include where to live next year, what industrial placement to pursue or whether to stand for office in a society. Or some of the ideas introduced earlier: your work expectations; your progress towards developing key skills thus far; learning objectives for your degree and any blocks encountered on the way to achieving them.

Agree that for a specific time – say, 10 minutes – the listener will aim to help the speaker in sorting out their thoughts by active listening. Then at the end of that period, discuss the effectiveness of the listening. How helpful did the speaker find it? What was most and what least helpful in the listener's behaviour? Were there points at which either of you felt uncomfortable? Why was this? After the discussion, exchange roles and start again. (You might like to reflect on similarities and differences between the experiences of active and attentive listening.)

Activity 8.9

As giving feedback and receiving it are skills in themselves, you need to extend the previous activity. Once you have done it often enough to feel comfortable with the feedback aspect, add a further level of 'feedback on feedback', with the speaker and the listener giving observers feedback on their comments. Again, the goal will be to identify useful and less useful aspects of behaviour.

A note of caution

Observing and giving feedback is highly subjective and requires considerable skill. If you do it without sensitivity you may hurt, or even damage the recipient, so you need to be careful how you do it. Activity 8.9 is therefore an important one. When you are *receiving* feedback, remember that it is one person's subjective view. Being defensive doesn't help, but remember the need for using multiple sources. Rather than believing every word of feedback, take it as information for your use, to be combined with the opinions of others and any other relevant information – for example, your own reflections on situations and exchanges in the past and their outcomes and your observations of other exchanges.

Talking

The simple act of talking to another person is one in which a huge range of skills can be observed. Many of the dimensions will have been implicit in the discussion of listening, but briefly they are as follows.

Talking clearly – audibility

The need for audibility is self-evident; yet three friends of mine spring to mind. One mumbles so that the ends of words are totally inaudible. I frequently have to guess at the meaning or ask for a sentence to be repeated. Another has such an exaggerated accent (this is someone who is a native English speaker) that again I am concentrating so much on what the words are that I lose the meaning of the sentence. The third speaks so fast that my brain cannot keep up. Conversation with any of these is exhausting for me, probably unsatisfactory for them, and I am sure that there are many points that I miss. It is worth checking that your speech itself is an adequate channel for your message.

Talking clearly – content

Again, clear content is fairly obvious. If your message is muddled it has little chance of communicating anything. A colleague of mine, let us call him Albert, speaks at great length and with a huge degree of enthusiasm. Unfortunately, I seldom know what he is saying as he never finishes a sentence, leaving me trying to unravel a long string of half-ideas. Another colleague explained that the problem was that Albert's brain is always a minute ahead of his mouth, which is struggling to keep up. Listeners struggle more.

> **A good 'talker':**
> - speaks clearly
> - checks listener's reactions
> - meets listener's needs
> - listens.

If English is not your mother tongue you may worry about others understanding you, whether because of your accent or because you lack the words. If your accent is unfamiliar to your listener it is even more important to speak as clearly as you can, and slowly, so that their brains have time to 'decode' your speech. It will be even more important to check their understanding at regular intervals. It is equally important – and harder – for those with English as their first language to remember to do the same when speaking to you – you may need to give them feedback on how successfully they are adapting to your needs as receiver.

It is also important not to be discouraged from speaking because of fears about your language skills. The more you practice, the better you will become. And it is possible to communicate very clearly without using a wide vocabulary. Everyone on your course will be learning slightly new meanings of key words like 'environment', 'strategy' and 'market' so if anything you may be at an advantage with unfamiliar words – you will not need to unlearn their everyday sense.

When talking to someone who is less familiar with English than you are, remember the extra work they have to do to decode *your* speech, and again be careful to speak slowly, avoid unnecessarily difficult words or idioms, and check understanding regularly.

A bigger threat to clarity of speech is unclear thinking. This is not a problem if the whole point of the conversation is to try to clarify something. But if in speaking you are attempting to convey something specific, then it is a serious impediment. If there *is* a message which you are trying to communicate, make sure that you have sorted out just what it is before starting.

Checking you are being heard

Watch your listener's reactions. If there are signs that their attention is wandering, try to find out why and adjust your talking accordingly.

Being alert to the listener's objectives

Even if you are speaking to pass on straightforward information, your success will depend on how well you make the other person want to receive it. This will in turn depend on how well you relate what you are saying to your listener's objectives. Links which are clear to you may be far less evident to them. If the exchange is less one-directional it is even more important to be sensitive to the other person's objectives and to make sure that they are meeting these to the same extent as you are serving your own needs. Note that the listener will probably be hoping to get social rewards as well as information from the conversation: smiles, explicit verbal 'strokes' (such as genuine compliments which make a person feel good) and other social rewards are important.

Listening as well as talking

The above points mean that listening is crucial. It is unlikely that you will be able to see how a person is responding, adjust what you are saying accordingly, perceive or meet your listener's objectives very well or achieve anything at all if you do not listen.

Activity 8.10

Repeat the listening activities with and without observers, and with feedback on feedback, with the focus of your observation and discussion shifted to talking rather than listening.

Assertiveness

Often you will find yourself in a situation where you and the person with whom you are talking want quite different things. Your friend wants to go to see a film, while you are keen on a concert. Your flatmates are planning to move out without giving agreed notice, while you want them to stay – or at least to keep paying their share of the rent until suitable replacements can be found. Your landlord suddenly demands a contribution to maintenance when nothing was said about this when you moved in. Your tutor gives you an assignment without making quite clear what is required.

> **To become more assertive:**
> - believe in your rights
> - express them calmly but firmly
> - prepare for any likely conflict.

One option in any of these situations is to get really angry and shout or be rude. Another is to agree meekly but feel very unhappy about the situation. How do you tend to react in such situations? Neither approach is ideal. If you take the aggressive line, you may find that the other person also becomes aggressive and the situation can escalate. Even if you eventually get what you want, future relations with the other person may be soured or even broken off. With a departing flatmate, this may not matter. If the disagreement is with someone at work with whom you need to cooperate in future, such an outcome may be disastrous.

If you take the 'avoid conflict at all costs' line and go along with the other person's wishes or demands, life may be more peaceful but it is still far from ideal. If you end up seeing a film that doesn't appeal to you, it is not the end of the world. But if you submit quietly to your landlord's demands, you may be seriously out of pocket and may find yourself being asked for even more in future. If you accept the assignment without query, you may spend hours worrying about it, or working on something that is not at all what was wanted. If you fail to make your feelings known at work, you may end up overloaded, doing work for which you have not had the necessary training, missing out on the chance of working on a project that really appeals to you, or taking the blame for things which were nothing to do with you. You may also spend a lot of your time seething with resentment, something which can be bad for your health in the long term. Avoidance can be as counterproductive as aggression.

Self-esteem

Assertiveness is about dealing with differences in what people want from a situation in such a way that both parties' rights are respected. How you *perceive* these rights is crucial. A classic book on interpersonal skills is Harris's (1973) *I'm OK, You're OK*. This was based on Berne's transactional analysis approach to psychiatry. The title reflects the position that we can see both ourselves and others as either 'OK' or 'not OK'. These perceptions will have a profound effect on how we interact with others. If we see ourselves as 'not OK', and others as 'OK', we may be over compliant and avoid the slightest hint of conflict. This is because we are trying to persuade others that we *are* worthy of their approval. The belief that 'I'm OK, you're not OK' may lead to aggression and domination. The belief that 'I'm not OK, you're not OK' can lead to either aggression or withdrawal. Only the 'I'm OK, you're OK' position allows for assertion. Figure 8.1 shows this graphically.

This makes the point very clearly that self-esteem and esteem for others is crucial to assertiveness. You will remember that esteem was one of the five major need categories identified by Maslow. It may be helpful at this point to think about your own level of self-esteem. It will affect your interpersonal skills generally, and influence how others view you.

	You're not OK	You're OK
I'm OK	**Aggression and dominance**	**Assertion**
I'm not OK	**Aggression or withdrawal**	**Overcompliance**

Figure 8.1 Assertion and OK-ness

Activity 8.11

Check the extent to which you agree or disagree with the following statements:

	Strongly disagree				*Strongly agree*
	1	2	3	4	5
1. Most people are more confident than I am.	❑	❑	❑	❑	❑
2. Although I'm not perfect, I'm pretty good.	❑	❑	❑	❑	❑
3. If I were more attractive people would think more of me.	❑	❑	❑	❑	❑
4. I wish I had a better brain.	❑	❑	❑	❑	❑
5. Most people seem to know more than I do.	❑	❑	❑	❑	❑
6. If I disagree with someone, I'm probably right.	❑	❑	❑	❑	❑
7. I think that I'm likely to be as successful as most of my friends.	❑	❑	❑	❑	❑
8. I am uneasy about talking to strangers as they are unlikely to be interested in anything I say.	❑	❑	❑	❑	❑
9. If someone insults me I feel dreadful.	❑	❑	❑	❑	❑
10. In class I tend to avoid saying anything in case I'm wrong.	❑	❑	❑	❑	❑
11. There are some people I'd like as friends, but I don't think they would want to be friends with me.	❑	❑	❑	❑	❑
12. If I want to get to know someone better I suggest that we do something together.	❑	❑	❑	❑	❑

For questions 2, 6, 7 and 12 reverse the scoring, thus 1 becomes 5, and 2 becomes 4 and vice versa. Then add up your scores. The higher your score, the lower your self-esteem. If it is above 30, you might want to think about how you could reduce it. You may be making lots of assumptions about yourself that are *wrong*. Try getting your friends to say how they would expect you to score, given how *they* regard you. This may help!

Assertion or aggression?

Where there *are* inevitable differences in interest, you need to learn to be assertive, rather than either aggressive or avoiding. An assertive approach requires that you accept that there actually is a conflict. Having accepted this, you neither try to impose your needs or views on the other person through verbal aggression, nor simply accept the views of the other person perhaps because they are being aggressive. Instead, you state *your* perspective and *your* needs, because you believe that these are as valuable as those of the person with whom you are in disagreement. A balanced negotiation can then take place. Of course, this is rather less simple than it sounds, but the benefits of assertion are sufficiently great that it is worth putting in the necessary practice.

Few of us respond well to aggression. It is all too easy either to become aggressive yourself or to back down completely. There will be some situations where it is very hard to believe that your perspective *is* as valuable as the other person's. They may be more experienced, more senior, seem so much more confident, or apparently feel so much more strongly about something than you do. In order to develop assertiveness skills you need first to start believing in your own rights. The section which follows will help you with this. Once you have come to believe in your own needs, you need to practise saying the sorts of things that will express your perspective in a clear, firm but non-aggressive way. Assertiveness is a skill which can be learned, but as with any skill you need practice and feedback on your performance. The chapter concludes with exercises which will help.

Before going further, you need to check that you have understood the difference between aggression, assertion and avoidance and thought about your own most frequent response to conflict.

Test Exercise 8.1

Classify each of the following responses as aggression, assertion or avoidance.

1. You always blame me for not washing up. It was you who last cooked a meal.

2. Of course I don't mind. I'll see if I can find something you can use as an ashtray.

3. Why are you always so critical?

4. I feel really fed up that I have to wash your dishes every day before I can cook. I have someone coming to supper tonight. I'd feel much less fraught if you washed your things up before they come.

5. Well, if you all want to buy a video I suppose I'll pay my share.

6. I'd love to go out with you. But I only have £20 to last the month. So we'd have to go somewhere very cheap.

7. OK. If you all think the answer is to increase the marketing budget, I guess I'll go along with that.

8. I'm afraid I am still not sure who the notional addressee of this report is supposed to be, or quite what they would use it for. Could you explain a bit more?

9. If you are all too busy to do any of the work for this group project, I suppose I'll have to find the time for it.

10. No, that's all right. You borrow it. I'll find something else to wear to the party.

11. You are right. I didn't realise that I interrupt so often. I must be more alert to that in future.

12. What do you mean, I always interrupt? You should hear how often *you* do it!

13. No, I'll work late Saturday night. My flight doesn't go until seven the following morning.

You should be able to see from the few examples in the exercise how wide a range of situations offer scope for assertiveness. Now you need to think about how you react to such situations.

Activity 8.12

Think of about five recent situations in which you wanted something different from what others wanted. Jot down each of the situations. Now think about whether you got what you wanted or whether you had to compromise or give in totally to the other person's wishes. Think about how happy or otherwise you were in each case. Classify your behaviour as aggressive, assertive or avoiding in each instance. Discuss with others if possible, to see whether there are some sorts of situations where aggression or avoidance seems particularly likely and why this might be.

Activity 8.12 should have given you an idea of how much you might benefit from becoming more assertive. You should have seen how often you are not as assertive as you might be and become aware of some of the disadvantages of an aggressive or avoiding response. For example, although you may have in the end gained your point by aggression, this may have damaged your relationship with the person concerned and make future disagreements both more likely and more heated. Or the other person may have become defensive and failed to point out something you needed to know. Avoidance may have led to resentment on your part and reduced your chances of getting your own needs met in future, as well as on the occasion in question. If the disagreement was over an approach to a problem and you had a clearer view of the situation than did others, avoidance may well have led to a worse solution for everyone than if you had persisted until your position was appreciated.

So how can you become more assertive? How can you, first of all, realise what your rights are and then behave in a way that ensures that they are taken into account?

Believing in your rights

Too many of us undervalue our rights and underestimate the worth of our own contributions. If you wish to become more assertive, you need to *believe* that you do indeed have rights such as the following. Thinking hard about them may help your self-esteem.

Believe in your rights to:

- ask for what you want
- be listened to and respected
- not know/understand
- make mistakes
- change your mind.

The right to ask for what you want or to make clear what you do not want

Your wants and needs in a situation, whether for housework to be fairly shared or for a point in a lecture to be explained so that you understand it, are valid information. Suppose that at work you feel unfairly overloaded with routine work, so unable to exercise your particular skills. Others may be completely unaware that you feel this if you say nothing. Even if they have some idea that you are dissatisfied, they will find it much easier to ignore your rights if you do not state them.

The right to be listened to and respected

There is no reason why you should be of less worth than anyone else. Others may *sound* confident and knowledgeable but in reality know less than you do. If someone fails to give you respect then it is not because you do not deserve it. It is more likely to be because of failure on their part. One of the great benefits of team working, as a student or in a job, is that it brings together a range of perspectives. If you do not listen to some of these perspectives, or if others do not listen to you, then part of this valuable diversity is lost. So do not keep quiet because your view seems to be different from others: this is the very reason that you should contribute.

The right not to know or not to understand

No one is omniscient. People who think they know everything, but don't, tend to be a danger. It is far better to recognise areas of ignorance or lack of understanding explain your position and ask for help from those who do know. Sometimes you may be the only person to admit to general ignorance. Or you may have seen a flaw in others' reasoning or have queried an unwarranted assumption. Sometimes when something has been clarified for you, you may be the one who can take a new perspective on the information, precisely because you are less familiar with it than others were.

The right to make mistakes

Infallibility is as unlikely as omniscience. Trying to conceal mistakes can take considerable effort and sometimes make things even worse. Instead, face up to them and learn from them. Some enlightened organisations have as their motto 'It is OK to make mistakes – once.' They realise that mistakes are an inevitable part of learning.

The right to change your mind

All too often people stick to their initial position come what may, feeling in some way that it would show weakness to change. But this point is linked to the previous one. If you are genuinely pushing forward your understanding of a problem, you may realise that an earlier interpretation was wrong, perhaps because you now have new information. A group can be blocked, and never move on, if a position is defended to the death by its original protagonists, regardless of subsequent debate. Sometimes you can make a major contribution to a group simply by changing your position and explaining why. Whether this happens when you are working with other students, or in a team once you start a job, such change is a sign of strength, not of weakness.

Activity 8.13

Go back to the situations identified in Activity 8.12, in which you were dissatisfied with the outcome. Try to identify which rights you had undervalued in each case.

Speaking assertively

Believing in your rights is a large part of becoming more assertive, but finding ways of expressing them is essential if this belief is to be turned into action. Some of this expression has to do with the form of words used. Assertive speech tends to be characterised by:

- clarity
- acceptance of feelings as valid data
- calmness, rather than emotion
- firmness
- refusal to be side-tracked
- pursuit of a positive and constructive solution rather than a 'win'.

Look back at the responses which you classified as assertive or otherwise in Test Exercise 9.1, and at any past examples where you were assertive yourself to see the extent to which they indeed showed these features.

Guidelines for assertiveness

To be more assertive you should aim to:
- use phrases such as 'I think . . .' or 'I prefer . . .' rather than 'You . . .' or 'He . . .'
- use words such as 'could' and 'might' rather than 'can't' or 'shouldn't'
- check that you have understood before responding (remember active listening) – 'I think your argument is . . .'
- ask for more detail if you are unsure – 'Could you give me another example?'
- acknowledge the other person's feelings – 'I know that you are unhappy about . . .'
- say what you feel – 'I feel really frustrated about . . .'

- calmly repeat things, possibly using the same words each time, when it is clear that you are not being listened to (try it – it is amazingly effective)
- avoid apology (unless justified).

Activity 8.14

Go back to the examples you identified in Activities 8.12 and 8.13 and choose two or three where you were less assertive than in retrospect you would have liked to be. 'Rewrite the script', showing how the exchange might have gone, using phrases similar to those in the guidelines above. If working with a group, act out some of these scripts to see how they 'feel' and comment on the extent to which the words come across as assertive rather than aggressive. File your reflections on this activity.

Acting assertively

As with all talking and listening, body language is important. If you avoid eye contact, if you hide your mouth with your hand and slump back in your chair or lean away from the other person, you will find it very hard to use assertive forms of words. Even if you do, their effect will be lessened. If you raise your voice, glare at the other person, clench your fists or thump the table, or get too close to the person, the effect will be one of aggression no matter how carefully you choose your words. So make sure that your body language matches your words in being straightforward, confident, open and unthreatening.

Activity 8.15

Observe people in conflict situations. (You may find that you have disagreements in group discussions that provide material for observation, but shops, pubs and society meetings can often be a rich source of further instances to observe.) Focus on the body language used, note examples of assertive, aggressive and avoiding postures and gestures and observe the amount of eye contact.

Preparing to be assertive

Sometimes you will unexpectedly find yourself in a situation where you need to be assertive, if so, you will need to rely on skills and habits developed earlier. Even then, you may want time to think. It is often acceptable, and extremely useful, to ask for thinking time so that you prepare yourself a little, rather than saying things while in a state of mild shock. A response such as, 'This is a total surprise. I had no idea you were feeling like this. Can you give me five minutes to think about it?', can lead to a much more constructive outcome to the encounter.

Sometimes you will know in advance that a situation will need to be confronted or that conflict is inevitable. If so, it is important that you prepare yourself. Think clearly about what you want to achieve and why. If you know that you tend to undervalue your rights, discuss the situation with a friend or supportive colleague (if at work) to reinforce your beliefs. Think about how the other person may perceive the situation, and their likely wants. Given this, what might be their response and how might you react to this? If possible, act out the encounter with your friend or colleague beforehand, trying a range of approaches but aiming always to be calm and assertive and to face up to issues without aggression.

Assertiveness skills take time to develop. So does the skill of knowing when to be assertive. Aggression has its (limited) place and sometimes avoidance has too. But there will be a wide range of situations where the firm but cool, assertive response will be the most effective. If you have prepared beforehand (if possible), if you use the sorts of phrases outlined and if you *think* about it afterwards, reflecting on your success or otherwise with a view to further improvement in future, you should be well on the way to developing an important interpersonal skill, of use in most areas of your life.

Because learning to be assertive is so important, you may want to read further on the subject. Suggested readings are at the end of the chapter. Because it is very much a skill, and therefore benefits from practice and feedback, you may wish to consider a short practical course if you feel you are seriously unassertive. Certainly, this is one area where you could usefully include materials in your portfolio. A common question in interviews is: 'Think about a time when you were in conflict or disagreed with someone. How did you handle this?' If you have some examples in your portfolio of positive outcomes of conflict that arose because you handled the conflict in an assertive way, with details of how you did this, you should be well placed to answer such questions.

Activity 8.16

During the next month or so, note carefully the situations where assertiveness is appropriate and describe them for your portfolio. Detail the situation and the aims of the parties involved. If you had a chance to prepare, describe how you did this. Give a brief summary of the exchange, including examples of assertive phrases used and any body language noted. Include your reflections on the extent to which you succeeded, not in terms of winning regardless, but in terms of your views having contributed to the outcome and a feeling that the outcome was fair to both parties. Note any things which you wish you had done or said differently. Repeat the exercise in three months to note progress.

Negotiation

Assertiveness skills are often used in the context of negotiation. Negotiation is a process of seeking agreement when there are incompatible objectives and some compromise is needed. For example, in a classic wage negotiation the employers might want to agree a 1per cent increase, and the union might want a 7 per cent increase. The union might, however, be secretly willing to accept an increase as low as 3per cent, but anything less would be totally unacceptable. The employers might secretly be willing to pay up to 4.5per cent, but absolutely no more. Each would have their aim and their sticking point or 'no deal' position at which they would walk away from the table. The space for compromise exists between each party's sticking point. The point at which agreement is reached will depend upon the general interpersonal and specific negotiating skills of each party, their attitudes, motivation and preparation.

Figure 8.2 shows the 'space' within which this compromise can be reached.

Sometimes there is no gap – in the wages case the lowest increase the union would accept might be higher than the employers could afford, and thus above their sticking point.

Fisher and Ury (1983) in a classic book on negotiation called this sort of negotiation 'positional bargaining' and suggested it was inefficient. People tended to focus on their own requirements, and to stick stubbornly to their position, without seeking to understand the other party's needs, or look for more creative solutions.

Not all negotiations are as formal as a wages dispute. For example a friend was trying to arrange a family holiday with one family member unwilling to fly, another who gets seasick, and a third interested only in a holiday on another continent. There are also many conflicts of interest at work that do not involve pay.

Successful negotiations may not give each party everything they want, but they should end up with people feeling that the resolution was fair, and that their needs in the situation were respected. Fisher and Ury's principles for successful negotiation are still relevant. They suggest first that – as in giving feedback or in assertiveness – you focus on the problem not the people. Then focus not on positions, but on interests – it may be that actual interests are less in conflict than people at first think. Thirdly, look for a creative range of possible ways forward, using this understanding of what people really want. Finally, as with any problem solving, try to find objective criteria for a solution. (The third and fourth might be reversed to avoid criteria being influenced by what someone already prefers as an option.)

To negotiate successfully:

- Focus on problem not people
- Focus on interests not positions
- Seek objective criteria
- Be creative

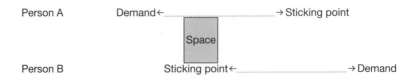

Figure 8.2 'Space' for a negotiated agreement

Imagine that your brother has just announced he is getting married in five weeks. This is a weekend when you are scheduled to work. Your new boss says it is not his problem, and refuses to give you the time off. This could end badly – perhaps you take the time off anyway and things go badly wrong at work and you lose your job without a reference. Both you and your boss end up with bigger problems. On the other hand, you might realise that your already highly stressed boss simply cannot face the extra stress of finding someone to change at short notice. If so, you might find someone willing to swap weekends before approaching your boss, and perhaps also offer to cover at Easter, when no-one wants to work. This way both of you would be able to achieve what is important to you.

There may be far more scope for a 'good' resolution of conflict than people believe, provided the negotiation is approached as shared problem solving rather than a conflict in which someone has to win, while the other person loses.

Networking

Networking in this context refers to the activity of making, maintaining and using personal contacts for professional purposes. Such contacts are invaluable for *all* areas of life. Think about how often you have discovered something important from someone you knew, rather than through official channels. I found my house not through an estate agent but via a friend who told me that a friend of hers was thinking of moving and it sounded like an ideal house. A recent graduate found his (very good) present job by talking to someone in a café. In a pub conversation someone said that they wanted a room to rent and someone else said, 'I don't think Sandy has found a new lodger yet.'

> Networking is strongly associated with management success.

Most jobs are advertised and specified selection procedures are followed. Yet they frequently go to someone who knew of the vacancy in advance and who had contacted relevant people, or exploited existing contacts, before the interview. And despite equal opportunities legislation, not all jobs are advertised. There are many ways of starting to work for an organisation which may grow into jobs if the original project is well handled. For those who are, as is increasingly the case, working for small organisations or for themselves, these informal routes are often the most important ones. One writer on networking (Hart, 1996) claims, though without giving the evidence for this, that networking can be twelve times as effective in getting a new job as answering advertisements.

Networking is valued differently in different cultures. In the UK, some people see it as slightly 'unsporting' actively to develop and exploit personal relationships. In Japan, it is seen as a vital activity in business. Indeed, Japanese managers in the 1980s were sent to major US business schools to study for an MBA not because their superiors felt that the Americans could teach them anything about business, but because of the contacts that they would make with future senior US managers.

➤ **Ch 1**

Networking is not limited to finding new jobs. It also seems to be of value in progressing within an organisation once you have found the job. The US study by Luthans *et al.* (1988), referred to in Chapter 1, showed that those managers who were *effective* (i.e. who had satisfied subordinates that performed well) were not necessarily the same as those managers who were *successful* (i.e. who were promoted rapidly).

Indeed, only 10 per cent of managers were in the top one-third on both counts, slightly less than you would expect if the two factors were totally unrelated to each other. If organisational life in the US resembles that elsewhere, and if being successful is something worth aiming for, it is worth looking at the key characteristics associated with success in this study.

The successful managers devoted more time to interacting with outsiders, chatting, joking, passing on rumours, complaining, paying attention to both customers and suppliers, attending external meetings and taking part in activities in the local community. In other words, they spent a lot of time on developing networks of primarily social contacts way beyond their immediate work group but clearly of value to their careers. Note that these exchanges do not need to involve face-to-face contact all the time, though this helps at the start. The telephone can be a useful channel, email is often used in this way to sustain a relationship once established, and even letters can sometimes be used.

So how can you develop networking skills while you are studying? There is a heavy overlap with the skills of talking, listening and the 'valuing yourself' aspect of assertiveness. These lie at the heart of networking, and thus in developing these skills you will inevitably be starting to build a network. By making a point of trying to practise these skills with as many people as possible, you will be starting to maximise the networking potential of your time as a student and to build the foundation of a network that you can develop after graduating. This will be greatly helped if you appreciate just how important networking is. After all, other people will be succeeding because they are networking and may well be including you in their networks. As it is ideally a mutual activity rather than exploitation in the bad sense, you should overcome any inhibitions you may have about becoming good at networking yourself.

Activity 8.17

Start by establishing the extent of your current potential network. List all the people you know well enough to ask for information on something like accommodation or holiday or job opportunities. (It doesn't matter if they would be likely to know the answer, just whether you would feel comfortable asking them for neutral information of such a kind.) If you are working with a group, compare lists and see whether this prompts any additions. Check that you have included people you know at home, as well as where you are studying, and those you know through all the activities in which you take part. File this list, in order to refer to it at intervals and add to it.

Activity 8.18

Test the assertion that such networks are more useful than official channels is right. Think of some information that would be useful to you and select from your list of potential network members those who might be able to give that information, or might know people who could. This does not have to be information about a job – it could be anything which you could, in theory, find from an advertisement. See how quickly you can get the same (or better) information just by talking to people.

Activity 8.19

Draw up an action plan for maintaining your network. Think about opportunities for developing your relationships with people on your list. Could you make a point of having an exchange with them the next time you see them? Remember, Luthans *et al.* (1988) listed joking, social chat, exchanging rumours and complaining among effective networking behaviours. List the people you might have a chance to talk to in the next two weeks. List those you do manage to talk to. (You will be practising your talking and listening skills in the process.) Reflect after each contact on how effective the interaction was in strengthening your relationship and what else you might need to do. Add these comments to your list.

Activity 8.20

Draw up an action plan for developing your network by making new contacts. Think about activities you can take part in and people you can get to know in order that your net spreads more widely. Members of your network need to be aware of your interests and strengths, so that they will think of you if asked about suitable candidates for an opportunity, or hear something that might interest you. This may help them as well as you. Similarly, you need to know as much as possible about them – the more mutual such relationships are, the stronger and more effective they will be. Again, log thoughts and compare progress with your list and notes already made.

Activity 8.21

Identify opportunities to use your network. In future, whenever you need to find something out, think about who in your network can help, and approach them. Also, help any people who approach you as best you can. Log your reflections on the process. If your network needs extending, think about who else you need to be able to talk to and deliberately approach them. You will be surprised how often people who do not know you at the start will be willing to tell you things if you make clear why you are asking and that their help would be appreciated. Once they have helped you they will be part of your network.

Activity 8.22

Monitor your progress. Refer to your list at intervals. If working in a study group discuss your progress with other members and try to help each other to become more effective in this way. Until you have developed the networking habit, checks will need to be fairly frequent. Later you will need to check that you have not neglected anyone and have had at least some contact with them (even if only sending them a Christmas card) during the last year.

Activity 8.23

Now that you are more aware of the components of effective interpersonal skills, you are ready to reassess your own skills level. Revisit Activity 8.1 and reassess yourself. Then draw up an overall action plan to become more effective in this area.

SUMMARY

This chapter has argued the following:

- Spoken communication is an essential part of virtually all aspects of life and work.
- It serves to satisfy social needs, for information transfer, for developing ideas and for planning and managing shared tasks.
- Speaking and listening skills are equally important. Understanding and practice with feedback are necessary to develop these.
- Giving and receiving feedback skills depend on speaking and listening. They are vital for learning.
- Assertiveness, rather than avoidance or aggression, is important in the resolution of conflicting objectives. Assertiveness depends on knowing (and believing in) your own rights and speaking and acting in a way which asserts them. Again, practice is important.
- Networking is making, maintaining and using personal contacts, usually for professional purposes. The skills involved overlap heavily with those of talking, listening and assertiveness.

Further information

Andreas, S. and Faulkner, C. (1996) *NLP: The New Technology of Achievement*, Nicholas Brealey. This contains useful ideas for effective listening and establishing rapport.

Back, K. and Back, K. (1999) *Assertiveness at Work*, 3rd edn, McGraw-Hill.

Connolly, S. (2013) *Effective Networking*. Marshall Cavendish International.

Fisher, R. and Ury, W. (1983) *Getting to Yes: Negotiating Agreement Without Giving In*, New York: Penguin Books.

Potts, C. and Potts, S. (2013) *How to Be Strong in Every Situation*. Capstone.

8

TALKING AND LISTENING

9

TEAM WORK AND LEADERSHIP

Learning outcomes

By the end of this chapter you should:

- appreciate the importance of team working

- have identified your strengths and weaknesses as a team member and identified any development needs

- be able to identify the roles and behaviours needed to manage group tasks and processes

- understand the importance of clear group objectives

- be aware of the importance of motivation in group work

- be able to identify things that may go wrong in groups and take avoiding action

- be able to make an effective contribution to both formal and informal group discussions

- understand the need to monitor group progress

- understand how to become influential in a group

- be able to demonstrate the contributions that you have made to a group project or endeavour.

Introduction

The Quality Assurance Agency (QAA, 2015) puts 'People management: to include communications, team building, leadership and motivating others' first in their list of skills of particular relevance to graduates in business and management. Team skills are likely to feature in ads for almost any job you are likely to want, with 'leadership' potential as a close second. These skills are vital for employability and career success. As a student, team skills are equally important. They will help you learn in informal groups, and to make a valuable contribution to group projects. Leadership potential is similarly something that employers are looking for, as a simple search on 'graduate leadership programme' will show. This chapter will help you acquire the skills you need to be an effective team member, and help you maximise your learning in group contexts. It will also look at how you can become more influential in teams and exercise leadership.

Most work in organisations is done in a team context. Many, probably most decisions are taken in meetings. If team members do not work well together a project can fail, or at best produce poor work and demotivate team members. A bad meeting can take decisions that are expensively wrong: at worst they can ruin an organisation. No wonder employers are looking for team skills and see leadership potential as important.

Your course will almost certainly give you opportunities to study the theory of teams and leadership, and to practise team skills in discussion groups, and group assignments. Case study work (discussed in Chapter 11) and projects (Chapter 15) will almost certainly involve group work, so team-working skills will help you to get better grades, and to learn more effectively. If you are studying by distance learning you may be part of a 'virtual' student group and also need skills specific to virtual team work. These are highly transferable as organisations become more global.

➤ Chs 11, 15

Because team skills are so crucial for both study and employment it is important to grasp the opportunities your course offers for developing them. Also, take advantage of other interactions, whether in your social life or work placements and vacation jobs to practise these skills, and reflect on your team experiences.

Team Working in Organisations

There are many different sorts of groups which form in organisations. While many use 'team' and 'group' to mean the same thing, much of the academic literature sees teams as a particular subset of groups. In this view teams

- are deliberately formed for a purpose, to perform particular tasks or projects
- have a common goal, which cannot be pursued unless the team members work together.

Teams are essential when inputs from a number of different perspectives or different skills are necessary and where commitment to outcome is important. Teams can be given a considerable degree of autonomy – output may be specified and measured by higher management, but the team left free to decide how best to achieve that output. This way of working offers considerable flexibility, as a team with this freedom can respond to local changes far more rapidly than one waiting for a decision to be taken higher in the organisation. (Decisions taken only after reference up (and up) the chain of command, can be very slow.) Autonomous team working also provides ideal conditions for high levels of motivation, so it is little wonder team working is so widely adopted.

Even autonomous teams vary widely, as their goals will be different, requiring different members and ways of working. A committee is charged with taking decisions and perhaps seeing that those decisions are implemented. A work group might have the task of producing a particular component or providing a specified service. A project team might be charged with developing an original idea into concrete plans, or with putting those plans into action.

Responsibility within the team will also vary. Some teams may have a specified leader who may or may not also have managerial authority. (While many organisations use 'leader' to mean manager there is a distinction, which will be explored later in this chapter). Other teams may have no obvious leader. Some teams will contain a wide variety of expertise, whereas others may consist of people with very similar skills.

Whatever the team structure and membership, and regardless of whether the task is sharing information and negotiating a decision, gathering information and making plans, or performing a physical task that requires the skills or labour of more than one person, effective working together is essential for success. And while the relative importance of the skills required depends on the situation, the requirements for success are remarkably similar across the spectrum. Success will depend on:

- clarity of goals and acceptance of these among team members
- agreement over ways of working towards these goals
- effective communication between team members
- support and cooperation between team members, rather than competition
- arrangements for monitoring progress and taking corrective action if necessary.

> **Successful team working needs:**
>
> - clear, shared goals
> - agreed ways of working
> - effective communication
> - support and cooperation between members
> - monitoring of progress.

These factors are not, of course, always present. Simply calling a group a 'team' does not guarantee success. 'Team' is an emotionally loaded word, standing for all sorts of positive things. By relabelling groups of people as 'teams' organisations often think that they have solved a problem. If you have already experienced a rocky time in some of the groups you work with in class, you know that the label is not enough. Thought needs to be given to the success factors above, and to ensuring that 'team' members have the understanding and skills needed for this form of working.

Key factors in team success

Looking at the list above, it is clear that the elements contributing to success can be grouped into three broad classes of factors, as has been done in Figure 9.1 (see later in this chapter). Three sets of skills are important:

- **Managing the task** – clear objectives, monitoring progress towards them and taking corrective action are as important for team working as for managing yourself. The principles are just the same, although applied in a group context.

- **Managing the process** – this is the part that is new. People need to stay committed to the team's goals and motivated to contribute to achieving them. Attention therefore needs to be paid to their support and encouragement. This will be a major topic in this chapter.

- **Communication** – this will be vital for managing both task and process. You have already developed the basic skills of talking and listening (and being assertive where necessary). Their application in a group context is very similar to their use one to one. By practising communication skills in group work, you will become better at communicating in other contexts.

➤ Ch 1, 2
➤ Ch 8

Whatever the type of task a team is addressing, success will depend upon a combination of communication skills (especially talking and listening) and management skills relating to both the task and process. The emphasis will differ depending on the nature of the task, as the following exploration of the different contexts for group working shows.

Discussion Groups

Because they are a natural extension of the previous chapter, and because almost any group will at times need to have informal discussions about the task, it makes sense to focus first on informal group discussions. You will probably be familiar with these from seminar or study groups.

Activity 9.1

Reflect on a recent group discussion in which you found it satisfactory to take part and another which you have not enjoyed and/or to which you felt you made little contribution. List at least three ways in which the 'good' group differed from the 'bad' group. If thinking of a discussion on your course, try to compare your list with the lists of other people involved in the discussion, If not, sharing lists with others will still be useful, even if you are considering a variety of different discussions.

You will probably find that some of your 'bad' experiences have to do with poor task management. Quotes overheard after experiences like this include those in Figure 9.1.

Other 'bad' experiences may have had more to do with poor process management – lack of attention to group needs, perhaps conflict or even aggression between some members. Such meetings produce reactions like those in Figure 9.2.

Informal discussion groups do not necessarily have a 'leader'. All members of the group may be on an equal footing and between them need to ensure that the discussion goes somewhere and that members are involved. But a good chair would have avoided some of the issues reflected in the quotes in Figure 9.1. Informal groups without chairs will only work well if most of the members play their part in contributing to both task needs

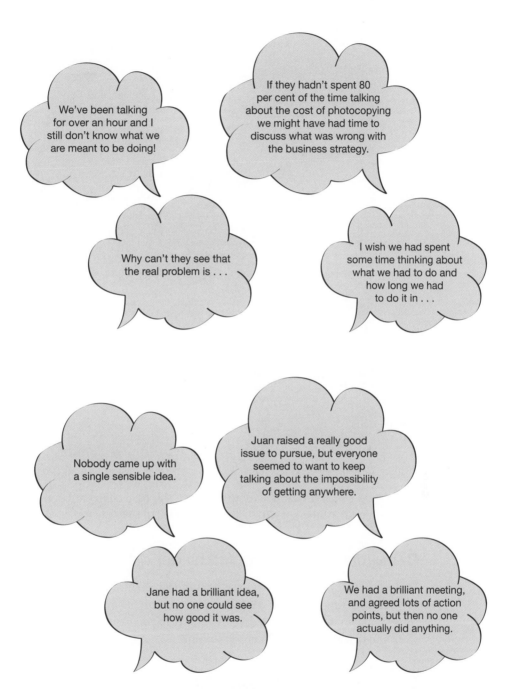

Figure 9.1 Quotes overheard after 'bad' experiences related to poor task management

and group needs, and avoiding behaviours which get in their way. This means keeping a focus on what the group is trying to do, contributing to this yourself and helping others to make a contribution, valuing other members and their contributions and not letting your own or others' needs unrelated to the task (for attention, dominance or whatever) get

9

TEAM WORK AND LEADERSHIP

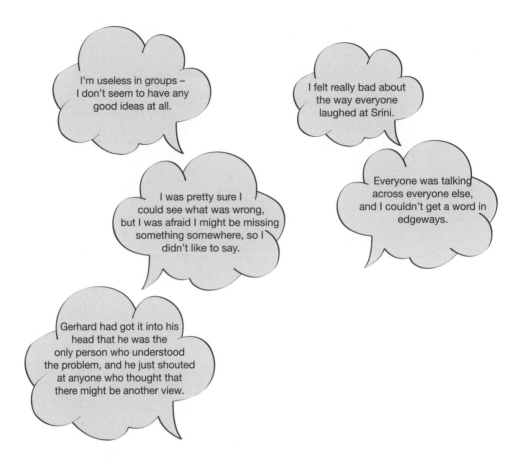

Figure 9.2 Quotes overheard after 'bad' experiences related to poor process management

in the way of what the group is doing. (Even if there is a chair, and especially if the chair is not particularly skilled, it will help if you behave in this way.)

Behaviours which help and hinder discussion groups

If you are aware of which behaviours help and which hinder, you will become more aware of your own strengths and weaknesses in this context. The following lists of the most important behaviours in each category may help you reflect on the part you play in group work and to become more effective in future.

Behaviours serving task needs

- *Clarifying objectives* – unless everyone in the group is clear about what the group is trying to achieve the group cannot be fully effective.
- *Seeking information from group members* – often people are asked to join a group because they know something of particular relevance, or have a particular perspec-

tive. If they are naturally quiet or diffident they may not offer this unless they are specifically asked.

- *Giving relevant information* – this may apply to you, so if you offer any relevant information which you have this will progress the task.

- *Proposing ideas* – these might be ideas about how to address the group task or ideas about possible solutions to a problem under discussion.

- *Building on ideas or proposals contributed by others* – the real advantage in groups is not that members bring lots of ideas but that these ideas can then spark new ones or be developed by others, so that there is a synergy between members' thinking. Acknowledging the person whose idea you are building on is really helpful, as it makes them feel valued rather than inadequate – 'John, that's a really good idea – it would let us do X. But you've got me thinking – if we did Y as well, we could actually achieve this, this and this . . .'

- *Summarising progress so far* – this can be extremely useful in stopping people from covering the same ground over and over, as it helps the group realise what progress has been made. It also helps any note taker.

- *Evaluating progress against objectives* – once progress has been summarised it is easier to see what is left to be done, and plan to achieve it.

- *Time keeping* – most groups usually have a time limit, so it is important to manage the activity to ensure that it is completed within this time.

- *Allocating responsibility for any actions* – all too often a group has wonderful ideas and members go away feeling it was a great meeting, but feel no obligation to actually do anything themselves. Agreed actions are far more likely to be taken if individuals commit, in the meeting, to taking them.

- *Setting up review mechanisms* – if actions will go on for some time after the meeting, some way is needed of reviewing progress and taking corrective action where necessary.

Behaviours serving group needs

- *Encouraging members to contribute* – this is linked to the task need of eliciting information, but also helps individuals to feel part of the group. (Some members will need more encouragement than others.)

- *Rewarding contributions with praise or agreement* – again, this is helpful in making people feel that they are valued members of the group, thus increasing their commitment to the group's collective activity.

- *Checking understanding* – it is important to be sure that you understand any contribution, but particularly helpful to check that you have understood a point by summarising that understanding in your own words before giving reasons for disagreeing. Many disagreements are rooted in misunderstandings but become heated before this is discovered.

- *Helping to resolve conflicts positively* – in any group, conflicts are inevitable, and by exploring the reasons for conflict a group may uncover crucial information, but this needs to be done in a way that avoids either party feeling rejected.

- *Changing your own position in the light of arguments or information given by others* – many people see hanging on to their original position as a high priority, but this can greatly reduce the ability of a group to make any sort of progress.

- *Helping to control those who talk too much* – there is often someone in a group who just loves to talk. Since this prevents others from contributing, sometimes a way needs to be found of making space for others. Ideally, this needs to be done in a positive way, so that the talker feels appreciated rather than rejected. 'John – I think your point is important, but we really don't have time to go into it in enough depth here, so perhaps some of us could go into it in more depth after the meeting . . .'

- *Praising group progress* towards objectives – if group members feel that they are getting somewhere they will feel motivated to keep working, so 'celebrating' progress in some way can make an important contribution.

- *Dissuading group members from negative behaviours* – again, in a positive way if possible (see below).

Behaviours interfering with task or group needs

- *Talking too much* – or otherwise focusing attention on your for the sake of it.

- *Reacting emotionally* – while emotions may be an important element in a discussion, and it may be worth saying how you feel about something, contributions driven by anger or other emotions are usually unhelpful.

- *Attacking others' points by ridicule or other unreasoned statement* – attacks (e.g. 'it won't work') tend to be directed at individuals and are different from reasoned disagreement, which is aimed at a point made and which can be extremely valuable.

- *Not listening to others* – this is unhelpful for obvious reasons.

- *Interrupting others* or talking at the same time as them.

- *Introducing a totally different point* in the midst of productive discussion of something else.

- Chatting with others privately during the meeting – a form of not listening.

- *Using humour to excess* – this can distract the group from the task, though a little humour can 'oil the wheels' and contribute to positive handling of conflict.

- *Introducing red herrings* – by this I mean wilful distractions rather than genuinely suggesting something that turns out to be irrelevant.

- *Withdrawing ostentatiously from the group* – for example, by turning away, pushing chair back, crossing arms, determined silence. This can make others in the group feel uncomfortable, and generally reduces effectiveness.

How do you behave?

The lists above are quite long as they cover much of what helps and hinders group discussion. You will find it difficult at first to keep all the behaviours in mind, but a checklist such as that shown (completed) in Figure 9.3 will help. A blank checklist is available online.

The more aware you are of others' use of these behaviours, the easier it will be to notice – and improve – your own behaviour. A useful first step is to observe discussions without taking part in them. (If you cannot officially act as observer, choose a meeting in which it will not matter if you adopt a low profile and take notes surreptitiously.) Use the checklist as the basis for your observations. At first you may find it easiest to concentrate on one category of behaviour. Two other people might observe the remaining categories. Alternatively, you might observe only one or two people each.

	JEFF	SABINE	LING PEI	ASAD	YIANI	CLARK	JO
Clarifying objectives							✔✔✔✔
Giving/seeking info.						✔✔✔✔✔	
Proposing/developing			✔✔✔	✔✔✔		✔✔✔✔	
Summarising	✔						✔✔✔✔✔
Timekeeping	✔✔✔						✔
Encouraging/rewarding							
Conflict reduction		✔✔✔✔					✔✔✔
'Gatekeeping'							✔✔✔✔✔
Interrupting/speaking over			✔✔✔✔ ✔✔✔	✔✔✔✔✔✔		✔✔✔✔	
Attack/defence			✔✔	✔✔✔			
Changing the subject					✔✔		
Excessive humour		✔✔				✔✔	
Withdrawal		✔			✔		

Figure 9.3 Example of a simplified form used in recording behaviours in a group

Activity 9.2

Use a form such as that provided online to record the sorts of contributions members make to a discussion. Reflect on the extent to which the pattern of ticks which emerges explains the effectiveness or otherwise of the group.

Activity 9.3

Ask someone else to record *your* contribution to group work and give you feedback on the sorts of behaviours you used most. Reflect together on your effectiveness in the light of this. Such feedback can be a powerful tool in helping you become a more valuable and influential team member. If any of the desirable behaviours seem lacking, practise using them in subsequent meetings. For example, decide that you will try to ensure that even the quietest members are encouraged enough to make a contribution, or make a point of summarising the discussion each time progress seems to have been made so that points are not lost. If you are behaving in a way which interferes with the group, think about why you may be doing this and try to notice (and silently rebuke yourself) each time you do this in future. It should eventually become less frequent. Devise an action plan for becoming more effective.

Activity 9.4

After a while, perhaps a few months, repeat Activity 9.3 to see whether you have shifted your behaviours in the intended direction. File your comments for future review.

Formal Meetings

Many managers complain that they spend far too much time in meetings. Formal meetings may seem intimidating until you are used to them. There are rituals to do with approving minutes, making remarks through the chair and identifying 'voting members'. You may feel unwilling to contribute because you feel unsure about the 'rules' or wonder how on earth to take minutes if charged with this task. However, the 'rules' are really only an attempt to avoid some of the things that commonly go wrong in informal discussions. The actual skills involved are much the same, as becomes clear when you understand what the ritual is intended to serve.

Membership lists

When a meeting is intended to take significant decisions (about costs, policy, progress on an important contract and so on), the informality of a discussion group is not enough.

Cartoon by Neill Cameron, www.neillcomeron.com

It is important that the right people are at the meeting, so a formal membership list will need to be agreed. Otherwise there may be complaints that the decision was improperly taken. Indeed, if key players are not there to contribute their information, bad decisions may be taken.

Attendance

Since there was a reason for members to be on the list, it is important that they attend. Normally the minutes of the meeting will log those present so that they cannot later disclaim responsibility for decisions. Absentees, who should have given apologies in advance, can also be contacted by anyone who feels the need to 'fill them in' on something which happened. The secretary may also wish to arrange for absentees to send a representative in their place. (This representative would not usually be able to vote and would be minuted as 'in attendance' rather than 'present'.)

Chair

In an *informal group,* members usually share responsibility for the behaviours necessary to progress the task and manage the process. They are expected to exercise self-discipline and avoid the unhelpful behaviours listed above.

In *formal meetings,* the overall responsibility for all this is vested in the person chairing the meeting. With a skilled chair this can work wonderfully. People are asked to make contributions at relevant points, the discussion is gently 'managed' to ensure that it is kept to the point, progress is summarised at intervals, conflicts are tactfully explored and resolved and, when as much progress has been made as is likely, the point is drawn to a close and the next item on the agenda is taken so that the meeting finishes on time, with all items having been properly covered.

Unfortunately, not all chairs have the skill to achieve this. (They may have been chosen for their seniority rather than their skills.) Provided other group members quietly adopt the necessary behaviours to fill the gap, this does not matter. If they sit back and cheerfully take no responsibility, the meeting can be a disaster.

Agenda

People need to know in advance what will be discussed so that they can consult with those they represent, gather any necessary information and have thought about the issues involved. An agenda lists the time and place of the meeting and the items to be discussed in the order in which they will be addressed. It should be sent to all members well in advance of the meeting. The chair of the meeting is normally responsible for putting together the agenda and will need to think about how long items are likely to take. Too long an agenda is to be avoided. Items will be given insufficient attention or the meeting may go on beyond the point at which those present are capable of thinking straight. (Most people cannot concentrate fully for more than two hours.) As meetings take some time to warm up, one or two short items at the start of the agenda may be a good idea. But the most important items should follow immediately after this, when people are most alert. Beware the really important item which appears at the very end of a long agenda. This will be one where the chair is hoping to get a decision to go in a particular way and is more likely to achieve this when everyone is exhausted and hungry. It is possible in this case to ask for the item to be taken earlier on the agenda. If you suggest this, giving your reasons, and others present support you, the chair may have to agree.

Papers

In assembling an agenda it is important to think about how much preparatory infor-mation members need beforehand. Small items may not need supporting papers. Their proponents can make a verbal case at the meeting and this will be an adequate basis for discussion. For any complex case, however, where there are reasons for and against a proposal and information which people need to have absorbed before they can discuss it,

➤ Ch 6

supporting papers need to be written (the report format discussed earlier is helpful here).

These papers need to be circulated to members sufficiently in advance of the meeting (ideally with the agenda) for them to be able to study their content in detail. If you are asked to write a paper for a meeting, remember that you are trying to make a clear and fair case without giving unnecessary information. Write as succinctly as if you have a word limit. If a paper is too long, it risks not being read properly.

Preparation

Assuming that the chair and secretary have circulated agenda and papers in good time, you have an obligation to prepare yourself. This means setting aside sufficient time to read papers thoroughly, think about them, discuss them with others who may be involved, gathering all the information you can that might help the meeting, working out what points you would like to make, and how best to make them, given the likely points of view and counter-arguments of others who will be there.

You may not actually make these points, or not in these words, as you will need to respond to the discussion as it develops. Meetings are not best seen as a collection of set speeches. But you will be much more effective if you have worked out what is important for you (and those you represent), and how best to convince others of its importance. This preparation will help you achieve your (task) objectives for the meeting. It will also mean that you appear coherent, focused and well prepared to any senior people there, thus raising your profile (in a good way). Going into a meeting unprepared not only damages your own reputation, but risks wasting the time of everyone present.

Discussion style

Because the chair is officially responsible for the progress of the meeting, members are normally expected to catch the chair's eye and gain permission to speak. In large meetings this is essential. In smaller ones, provided conduct is reasonably orderly, the chair may let people discuss without this hindrance. (She or he will, intervene only if discussion is becoming disorganised or someone is talking too much, or someone else is contributing nothing on an item on which they would be expected to have useful information to offer.)

The more formal the meeting, the more formal the language that tends to be used in making contributions, but the basics of talking and listening still apply: paying full attention to what others are saying and making sure that you do not undervalue it because of prejudice; 'rewarding' their contributions with agreement; expressing your points clearly; avoiding getting emotional about issues; being sufficiently assertive to make points that have a fair chance of being valid and to make them in a positive enough way that they will be heard and avoiding time wasting of any kind.

Minutes

Because it is important to know what decisions were reached, and who was involved in reaching them, minutes are usually taken. In addition to listing those present, minutes need to log the basic reasons for a decision, actions agreed and responsibility for progress on these actions. Minutes should be circulated soon after a meeting so that any inaccuracies can be spotted, and the corrected minutes are then approved at the start of the next meeting. As the agreed record of decisions, these minutes are extremely important. There can, in theory, be no ambiguity about what is now agreed policy and it is clear whose responsibility it is to implement it.

The practice, alas, may fall short of this. The person charged with taking the minutes often feels that they need to transcribe every word said, so that the minutes become so long that no one has time to read them. Perhaps because of this, the minutes may be put off as an unimportant or difficult job and appear on the day of the next meeting, by which time no one can really remember what happened and some of those who were supposed to have taken action will have totally forgotten about it. Or the minutes may be circulated late on purpose and record what the chair and secretary wanted to have happened, rather than what really did happen. 'Managing by minutes' can be a very effective tool, if an undemocratic one. Indeed, in an episode of the television comedy *Yes, Minister* it was suggested that the minutes should be written *before* the meeting. If you are taking minutes for the first time, model them on previous minutes. Once you are confident with this, discuss with the chair whether there might be better ways of doing it.

Action notes

For slightly less formal or more task-oriented meetings, a scaled-down version of minutes may be taken. These will note who was present and log actions agreed and responsibilities for these actions, but no more. Because they are briefer and focus on action, they can be written extremely quickly, even during the meeting, and people can be given a clear statement of their responsibilities the next day.

Activity 9.5

Review the formal groups to which you belong. (If you don't belong to any, try to join at least one during the next few months so that you can practise these skills.) List them and note against each how effective the formal structure is in progressing the group's objectives. If elements seem to be ritualistic rather than serve their intended purpose, think about ways in which you might be able to contribute to their effectiveness. Draw up a plan for doing this and check your success against this after each meeting you attend.

Activity 9.6

Find a way of taking at least some responsibility for a meeting. This might be by chairing it (volunteers for this role are often very welcome), acting as secretary or as assistant, joining in agenda-setting discussions and taking some of the responsibility for ensuring that the meeting progresses as desired. Put together an 'exhibit' for your file which describes the purpose of the meeting and the ways in which you contributed to achieving this. An annotated agenda showing which items you suggested and why, any papers you wrote and comments on the interventions you made, together with the minutes and a statement from the chair saying how he or she perceived your contribution, might form a clear demonstration of your ability to function in this context.

Activity 9.7

Chairing a meeting, at least until you get used to it requires you to think of more things at once than most brains can handle. You will be so involved in task and process that you will have little brain capacity for reflecting on your own performance. If at all possible, the first few times you act as chair ask someone attending the meeting to act as observer for you and to give you feedback afterwards. This can feel very risky but may be encouraging. You may feel that you totally messed things up, but the observer may have noticed a number of things that you did well. If they *do* see weaknesses, surely it

➤

is better to be aware of them and work at improving them. You would not want everyone else to know about them while you remain in blissful ignorance. Such feedback is best given a short while after the meeting, rather than immediately. Chairing is exhausting and frequently traumatic, at least at first, and you are unlikely to be fit for anything, certainly not for constructive feedback, until you have had a recovery period. It can be helpful to write down your own reflections on your performance – what contributed to success and what might, on reflection, have been handled differently – as soon as you feel strong enough and to file these. Comparing your own reactions with feedback from an observer can make future reflection more effective as you will become aware of blind spots, or areas of over- or under-sensitivity.

Task Groups

Task groups are one of the building blocks of organisations. Teams are formed which contain all the skills needed to progress a specific task. Some task groups have a designated leader. In others, responsibility for the work is shared equally among members. The former is the classic 'supervisor responsible for a group of subordinates' structure. It has the apparent merits of clarity of responsibility and of power. If things go wrong, the supervisor will have to answer to his or her superior. But because the supervisor can, in theory at least, discipline any member of the team not pulling their weight, things should not go wrong in the first place.

There are less apparent, but equally real, drawbacks which parallel issues raised in the discussion of the chairing role above. If 'team' members see all the responsibility as lying with the designated leader they will feel none themselves. Their goal may be to avoid getting into trouble, rather than progressing in the work.

The concept of 'autonomous working groups' (AWGs) was one of the organisational breakthroughs of the 1960s, seen as avoiding many of the problems of assembly lines. AWGs were given collective responsibility for a specified task (in one of the classic experiments Sandberg (2007) describes how small teams working without supervision assembled entire Volvos. With AWGs, supervisors no longer need to coordinate the efforts of individuals, but instead serve as resources available for consultation or are removed altogether. At Volvo all decisions (including the holiday rota) were the responsibility of the group as a whole. These autonomous groups became very committed to the task and produced measurably higher-quality work. Absenteeism was much lower. There were queues of people wanting to work in this fashion.

There were costs, of course. Assembly lines are a very efficient way of operating: tooling up for group assembly was much more expensive; there was more work in progress at any one time; the training of multi-skilled employees was initially costly. But above all, management felt threatened by the autonomy which the workforce had under this arrangement, even though managers had their roles redefined rather than being made redundant. (The original Volvo plant at Kalmar, which pioneered AWGs in the 1970s, and the Uddevalla plant designed around this approach in the early 1990s were both closed by 1995.)

In the harsher 1990s the revolution in information technology meant that neither work groups at the bottom of the organisation nor senior management at the top needed layers of intervening managers to filter information up and down. They could now have direct access to it themselves. Such layers were therefore drastically pruned, or removed altogether, and fairly autonomous work groups came into favour again, variously entitled 'flexible work teams', 'cells' or 'high-performance teams', and have remained a common structure. In professional organisations this has always been a common way of working.

You should have plenty of opportunities to work in task groups while you are a student. Even groups formed to discuss case studies and present conclusions to the class as a whole are task groups as well as discussion groups if some of the work needs to be subdivided between group members. Collective work on an experiment, or on data collection for a topic, offers further possibilities. Project groups of any nature are likely to share many features with

➤ Ch 11

➤ Ch 15

semi-autonomous working groups in organisations and offer excellent scope for practising the necessary skills. (There is more specifically on project work in Chapter 15.)

Outside university you may find opportunities to develop your team skills through things like raising funds for a good cause, organising a social event or planning an expedition to a remote part of the globe. If you are doing any of these things with other people the general principles underlying success are the same as those for a group discussion. All group members need to understand the group's objectives, communication will be vital both at this and at every subsequent stage, progress needs to be monitored, and so on. Unless a formal leader is chosen, group members will need to find some way of ensuring that these aspects are covered all the time.

Additionally, there will need to be discussion about how to split up the work. What sub-tasks can be progressed independently and how should responsibilities for these be allocated to make best use of the group's resources? If group members can take on tasks which interest them and which they feel play to their strengths the output is likely to be better. This may require a degree of negotiation or even a rearrangement of sub-tasks if some jobs prove much more popular than others. People will need to understand their responsibilities (see comments on action notes in the previous section), will need to use self-management skills to progress their own part of the task (including taking corrective action, perhaps in the form of letting people know if there is a problem and seeking help), and will always need to remember to communicate anything which comes up in the course of their work which would be useful for others to know. This is often problematic: as

➤ Ch 8

one's own task assumes great importance it is easy to forget the wider group and its needs.

Activity 9.8

List the task groups of which you are already a member and use the ideas above as a basis for reviewing their effectiveness. Note whether you are clear about group objectives and whether others share your interpretation of these (could you all draw up the same list of what would constitute success and failure?). Similarly, how clear are you about your personal (or subgroup) objectives? Do you know whether or not you are on

➤

target? If you know you have done less than you should have, do you know why? Does anyone else know you are behind? Might they be able to help if they did? Do you feel committed to the group and the task? Note down ways in which the group as a whole, and you individually as a member of the group, could be more effective

Activity 9.9

In the light of the previous activity, try to improve the effectiveness of a group and document the experience as an exhibit. You will need to address the following.

- **Understanding of collective goals** – who set the goals, what constitutes success and what failure, what the constraints are, what the timescales are, how closely group members agree on the goals. (Note that it is important to explore reasons for disagreement: the minority view might be the right one.)

- **Allocation of responsibility for sub-tasks** – what was done to maximise the extent to which these fit people's strengths and preferences, how the group checked that people understood and agreed to their tasks, whether people were clear on interim goals and the timing for these, whether there are arrangements for checking progress and sharing information on an ongoing basis.

- **Support and encouragement** – are there ways of ensuring that people can seek help from others if things go wrong and can 'reward' each other for interim successes? Particularly for long-term projects, such motivational aspects are extremely important.

Your exhibit might include notes of discussions, highlighting your contributions, quotes from others (including your tutor) on the effectiveness of your own efforts, any plans you drew up for group or individual work with progress noted on them, notes of any corrective action or adaptation of plans which was necessary and reasons for this, and of course, if appropriate, the finished product or tutor comments on this.

Virtual Teams

In global organisations teams are often widely dispersed geographically and need to 'meet' electronically as to meet face to face would be far too expensive and take too much time and energy. Students on distance learning programmes may be similarly dispersed, and teaching and discussions may be mainly or completely online.

Virtual meetings

Online 'meetings' rely on the same group skills as any other meeting, but some aspects may require more care because of the nature of the medium. You need to understand not only the technical aspects of doing whatever your chosen system allows, but also the ways in which you can improve effectiveness by modifying aspects of your behaviour.

Systems for virtual working range from simple text-based online chat rooms and audio conferences through to simulations of meeting rooms or classrooms allowing most of the features of the face to face situation. There are therefore several dimensions to consider:

- Is the conference synchronous or asynchronous?
- Is the medium text, audio and/or vision?
- Does the system include features to help with managing process?
- What limitations does the system have?

The effectiveness of any virtual 'meeting' will depend on the general task and process skills of participants, the suitability of the channel and system to the task of the meeting, and the degree to which participants have the skills needed to exploit the strengths of the system they are using and minimise its disadvantages. Table 9.1 shows some of the systems you are likely to encounter, and factors to consider when using them. You will almost certainly have experience with using some of these, so can check your own experience against the table.

All the systems listed have the advantage of not needing travel, with its attendant costs, so this is not mentioned on the table. Similarly all real-time systems require people to be free at the same time, which may present diary problems and be difficult in some time zones. In contrast, asynchronous systems allow people to contribute at times that are convenient to them (helpful for a time that spans different time zones). Asynchronous systems also mean you can take time to consider all previous contributions in relation to your own thoughts before responding. The corresponding cost is that asynchronous work needs a period of time, and unless this is strictly limited, the discussion may lose momentum. Asynchronous work is not usually suited to anything needing an urgent response. Again these common features are not shown on the table, but need to be remembered if you are comparing systems.

The extent to which you meet 'virtually' with fellow students will depend on how dispersed you are and the extent to which you are involved in collaborative work. If you live with/are regularly in classes with/have coffee and lunch with others on your course you may not need to do more than occasionally text them. But if this is not the case, consider whether you might find up to four others interested in forming a virtual study group to discuss course ideas in the light of your disparate experiences (aim for as diverse a group as possible) and to offer each other help when someone finds something difficult to understand, but to others it is not at all difficult.

If your university has its own system to allow such interactions, use it. If not, experiment with shared email lists, blogs, Skype, etc. to find what works best for you. The support such a group gives can improve everyone's grade markedly, as well as making study much more fun.

The following guidelines for asynchronous conferencing may be helpful if you choose a text-based asynchronous system. Note, in particular, the need to pay attention to making people feel valued members of the group when you lack the body language (and the beer or coffee) that make people feel welcome and appreciated.

Table 9.1 Strengths and weaknesses of some commonly used virtual meeting systems.

System and Features	Strengths	Potential Limitations
1. Text-based asynchronous forum (such as university conferencing system, chat room, blog or Facebook group).	Cheap. Can allow discussion to be organised into separate 'threads' for different topics. May suit those with stronger written than spoken English. History of contributions is clear and can be stored. Messages can have documents or other files attached, and can include links to relevant websites.	Text is relatively impoverished as a communication channel – it carries the same risks of misunderstanding etc. as email, so a facilitator/ moderator who can delete unhelpful posts, and more things to better threads, and summarise at intervals is a good idea. (A blog will normally be 'owned' by someone with this role.)
2. Audio conferences via phone system or internet.	Relatively cheap. Real time so can conclude meeting quickly, and participants can 'spark off' each other. Conveys 'paralinguistics' so richer than mere words.	People need to be free at same time. May be hard to know who is speaking. System may cut out all save loudest speaker if people talk at once.
3. Simple video conferences, e.g. via Skype, or Microsoft's Lync.	Can be very cheap or free May allow screen sharing. Allows body language as well as tone of voice and words.	Some systems can be expensive. Low grade video can be a distraction rather than a help.
4. Virtual classrooms – may include a video component but this makes high bandwidth demands.	Designed to replicate key features of a classroom, allowing the tutor to put up slides, write on whiteboard, set instant tests to check understanding, and divide students into breakout rooms for small group work. Students can put up a hand to indicate they want to talk (or in a small group just say something), can move work on a whiteboard back into main forum for plenary, and 'vote' to show views or understanding. Sessions can be recorded for absentees or revision.	The more complex the system, the more the tutor may need to focus on system aspects. A helper can free the tutor to concentrate on the task and process. Students may need time to become comfortable with the mechanics of the system.
5. Virtual meeting systems designed to make people in different locations feel as if they are all in the same room.	Can simulate a shared location so effectively that people really feel as if they are in the same room, and can hold a meeting as easily as if they were genuinely face to face.	Very expensive! May need technical back-up. Usually linked to specific locations, e.g. head offices on different continents.

9

TEAM WORK AND LEADERSHIP

TECHSkills 9.1 Guidelines for asynchronous conferencing

- Meet face to face if at all possible, in order to get to know group members and to start to build trust.
- If you cannot meet, allow some 'social' time in the conference for people to feel comfortable together.
- At the same time, post résumés so that people can check who you are if they forget.
- Include a photo if you can.
- Obtain members' explicit agreement on what is needed to achieve the group task, and how it will be most effective to operate (times of logging on, deadlines for contributions and so on).
- Break tasks down into constituent parts with deadlines, and be absolutely clear who is responsible for doing what.
- Ensure that someone accepts responsibility for reminding people of incipient deadlines.
- Be particularly careful to give feedback in a constructive and supportive way – and pay attention to making people feel their contributions are valued.
- Summarise discussion at regular intervals and check on progress.

It can help to set aside some short periods when people will all try to log on at once and respond quickly to each other – this can be a useful antidote to the more disconnected and 'measured' asynchronous communication.

Working collaboratively on a shared document

You may find virtual meetings extremely useful as a study group, or when working on a group project. They can help you agree on how to progress the project, allocate tasks and share reports on progress. Once the work is done, you may need to produce a shared report. You can do this via email, sharing and commenting on drafts, or by attaching drafts in an online text-based forum, with the message explaining why a draft is as it is, what needs still to be done, and/or explaining edits to a previous draft.

TECHSkills 9.2 Working with google docs

You will probably have seen, or worked on, a Google file in your study. These correspond broadly to the standard applications from the Microsoft Office package. Google Sheets works like Excel, Google Docs like Word and Google Slides like PowerPoint. Their key advantages are:

➤

- Access any time, any place – it doesn't matter if you're on campus or at home, or at a friend's house – you can always access your documents. This comes in particularly handy when you need to deliver a presentation in class, or print something – no need to remember to save a copy on a USB stick, an internet connection is all you need to bring a document up on any screen.

- Automatic saving of changes – so you don't have to worry about losing your work.

- Multiple collaborators/viewers – you can work on the same document with a number of people, including editing it at the same time. This great feature allows you to collaborate in real time, which is key for time-sensitive projects. You can also give 'view only' or 'comment only' access to others, e.g. your lecturer or even potential employers, without worrying that they edit your version.

- You can upload standard files (like .doc) into Google Docs and create an editable version (likewise for the other apps) – and you can download a version that can be opened in standard programmes. Note, however, that you should always check such files for formatting – some features are specific to the applications the files originated in, hence you may need to update fonts, effects or sizing to suit your needs.

- Best of all – so far, access to Google apps is free – so you can be sure that anyone working on those with you is operating within copyright.

(written by Natalia Jaszczuk)

An alternative approach is to set up a wiki. In a forum or blog messages cannot usually be edited (apart from being deleted by the moderator). A wiki uses software that makes it very easy for collaborative working, as all participants can add to, or amend a document that has been posted. It also allows a series of pages which have been so authored to be linked. This allows for rapid production of a document by a group – 'Wiki' comes from the Hawaiian word for fast. Your university will probably provide you with wiki facilities.

A wiki system means people can write and/or change parts of the document until everyone is happy. The best known user of such software is Wikipedia. The collaborative authorship is what makes academics wary of using Wikipedia as a main source. But its collaborative nature can give it a richness that is valuable when you are starting to explore a topic, provided you use it critically, and as a signpost to more reliable sources.

Challenges of Online Collaboration

Despite the availability of a wide range of software for online collaboration, some aspects still present particular challenges. It may be harder for members to be clear on, and committed to, the team objectives, yet this is as important as with face-to-face teams, as is the need to continue to feel involved. You cannot make someone feel better with a smile or tone of voice if using a text-based system.

If you are conferencing in real time while sharing screens, you will need to work hard at ensuring that 'airtime' is shared fairly. Gatekeeping is essential, and even if you do not have a formal chair you will almost certainly need to designate someone to manage the turn-taking element. In an asynchronous conference this is less of a problem, but it is easy for people to feel 'distanced' and withdraw, so particular attention needs to be paid to process and making people feel involved.

When working remotely the early stages of teambuilding may need particular attention. Clarifying objectives, deciding on the roles members will play and agreeing ways of working may take more effort as it is less easy to thrash out complex issues and explore areas of disagreement remotely. Nor is it easy to develop the sense of membership and mutual support essential for effective team working.

It helps if virtual teams can go through these early and crucial stages face to face. Once members feel they 'know' each other it is much easier to sustain subsequent progress while working remotely. If this is not possible, care needs to be paid to achieving this online. Familiarity with remote working also makes things easier. If you get the chance to work in this way during your course you should use the opportunity to develop your remote team-working skills as they may increase your employability.

Developing Effective Groups

Some of the classic research on groups is still helpful if you are trying to put together an effective team, regardless of the nature of the task. In case you have not covered this research in a social psychology course, some commonly used frameworks are outlined here. These relate to selection of group members, to the stages which groups go through when they first form and to two main hazards of an established group: groupthink and scapegoating. If you are aware of these aspects of group working, it will increase your chances of being a member of an effective group.

Assembling an effective group

You may well have found that your 'bad' group experiences listed at the start of the chapter arose at least partly because the group seemed 'wrong' in some way. It may have been too big or too small to do the task effectively. Some key skills or perspectives may have been lacking. Perhaps the group got on *too* well and developed its own view of the world which was out of kilter with that of other groups working on a wider task. Or perhaps the group got off to a bad start and people dropped out because it wasn't working. You need to understand some of the features common to groups in order to comprehend and avoid such hazards.

Group size

The optimum size of group will depend on the task. If a large number of perspectives or skills need to be included, or a great deal of work is needed within a short timescale, then obviously a large group will be needed. But the larger the discussion group, the less the scope for individual contributions, and the larger the task group, the greater the task of coordination. Larger groups can also present logistical problems as members find it difficult to identify times when they are all free. As a general rule of thumb, if you can do the job with between four and eight people, then stick with a group of this size.

Expertise

Linked to the point above is the need to ensure that the group includes the necessary range of expertise. If you are choosing a group to work with on a project, this can be an important point. Again, you may feel most comfortable with like-minded people, but the task may be better done if you deliberately choose to work with a more varied group, with a wider range of backgrounds and knowledge.

Motivation

In forming groups, it is important to maximise the extent to which people *want* to do the task. At work they may not have much choice, but even then there will be issues that seem of burning importance to some and insignificant to others. Where possible, the more commitment you have to a task at the outset, the better the group is likely to perform. If you are choosing a group to work with on an assessed project, it is important to try to find others who have similar goals to your own. If you want to get top marks, you will be very unhappy in a group where no one else cares about doing more than scraping a pass. If you want merely to pass, you may feel out of place in a group of people aiming for a first.

Individual behavioural differences

When you looked at the behaviours that were shown in a group and who was using those behaviours, you may well have found some quite clear patterns. Some people often behaved in certain ways and seldom, if ever, in others. You might, for example, be very good at proposing ideas, but never get involved with making sure that they are implemented. Someone else might be quite the reverse, or do these activities some-times but spend much more time on, say, clarifying objectives and checking progress. Although if you are aware of the behaviours needed you can make a conscious effort to fill any gaps, you are likely to have natural preferences and to be able to behave in these ways without effort.

Noting this variation, Belbin (1981) suggested that, for a group to be fully successful, a number of roles were needed. He was working with groups doing real tasks in organi-sations, so although there are clear links with the behaviours seen in group discussions, you will also notice some differences. He originally suggested that eight roles could be identified, as Box 9.1 shows. Later he added a ninth role, that of *specialist.*

Box 9.1 Belbin's team roles

- Chair, who acts as coordinator, working primarily through others. The role calls for discipline and balance.
- Plant, who comes up with original ideas, is imaginative and usually very intelligent, but can be careless of detail and resent criticism.
- Shaper, who stimulates others to act.
- Monitor–evaluator, who assesses ideas or proposals.
- Resource investigator, who brings in resources and ideas from outside. While usually extroverted and relaxed, this person is not usually original. Nor is she or he a driver, relying on the team to take up and develop his or her contributions.
- Team worker, who works on process, holding the team together.
- Company worker, who is strong on practical organisation, administration and turning ideas into manageable tasks.
- Completer–finisher, who does the essential (if unpopular) work of checking details and chasing when deadlines approach.

It is fairly clear that for most tasks to be progressed all these roles will be needed. You will probably be able to think of people who seem to be particularly good at some and less good at others. You may even have a clear idea of your own tendencies. (If not, Belbin includes a questionnaire that, by asking you about your approaches to and feelings about certain situations, enables you to identify your perceived preferred roles. Your tutor may have access to the questionnaire, or you can obtain it from the Belbin website, although you need to pay to get it scored. Other free team role tests are available online, some using more recent frameworks of roles.

If you have the luxury of choosing members of a group according to their preferred Belbin (or other) team roles, then there is considerable evidence to suggest that it is worth doing this. But the fact that you cannot is no excuse for poor performance. Regardless of preferred behaviours, the roles are necessary and the group will have to find ways of ensuring that there is attention to process and that details *are* checked, even if this means, say, that one or two people who do not score highly on 'finisher' or 'team worker' have to make a conscious effort to take these responsibilities.

Myers–Briggs typing

Belbin's is but one of a large number of approaches to classifying people. One typology which is widely used by organisations for selection and/or team formation is the Myers–Briggs Type Indicator (MBTI). This is based on thinking by Jung, a contemporary of Freud, and uses a fairly complex questionnaire. Your tutor may be able to administer this so that you can locate yourself on the four dimensions shown in Box 9.2, and thus identify your 'type'. Again, a variety of online testing options are available if you want to pursue this, or you can be tested by a qualified Myers–Briggs tester.

Box 9.2 Myers–Briggs dimensions

- **E or I:** Extravert vs Introvert – this assesses whether you are externally or internally driven. In the first case, as an 'E' you will react to things and people, acting before you think. In the second, as an 'I' you will be more internally focused, more reflective.

- **S or N:** Sensing vs iNtuition – this looks at what you pay attention to. If you are an 'S' this will be your normal five senses, you will focus on the 'real', take a pragmatic approach. If an 'N' you will use your 'sixth' sense, and be more future-oriented, more of a theorist.

- **T or F:** Thinking vs Feeling – this reflects the way you tend to decide or judge. If at the 'T' end, you will reason from principles, using a logical system. If an 'F' you will use heart rather than head, subjectively emphasising values, preferring compassion to justice.

- **J or P:** Judgement vs Perception – this looks at the way you live and work. A 'J' will adopt the planned approach, organised, controlled and with clear goals. A 'P' will be more spontaneous, preferring to 'go with the flow'.

Since the dimensions are independent, this gives sixteen different types, each of which has distinct characteristics. You will hear people proudly declaiming their 'MBTI type'. Many organisations have found this information useful in helping people to understand why they are finding it difficult to work together. For example, if you are an ISTJ person, you might find an ENFP person to be hopelessly disorganised, whereas they might find you hopelessly unimaginative and unadventurous. MBTI types can also be used to help assemble a suitable team for a particular purpose – you would not want all Js on a project requiring high creativity – though you might need one on the team to increase the chances of an output.

Activity 9.10

If you have not been 'typed', estimate where you might lie on each dimension. Now think of two people with whom you find it difficult to work in a group. Where do you think they might lie? Can you attribute some of this difficulty to their being different 'types' from you? If so, try to think about the strengths their type might contribute and see whether it helps you to work together more effectively in future.

If you have not done the questionnaire, or if you would like to gain further information, it is possible to find many questionnaires online that will give you an indication (of varying reliability) of your characteristics and their impact on team behaviour. You might like to explore the possibilities and compare your results on one or more of these with the results of other group members.

List the task groups of which you are already a member and use the ideas above as a basis for reviewing their effectiveness.

Group life cycles

Often when groups first work together they are far from effective. Sometimes (perhaps if there are no team workers and lots of plants) arguments can become very heated and destructive. Some members may withdraw from the group altogether, either physically if membership is voluntary or mentally if they have to be there but hate every minute of it. There may be disagreements about objectives and about how the group is to work, two or three people all wanting to be 'in charge' of the group, some people behaving in ways that others find unacceptable. Tuckman (1965) found that groups commonly go through a sequence of stages in becoming effective. Knowing that this is normal may make the stages easier to bear and enable you to find ways of minimising any negative effects.

The stages nicely rhyme (this may in part account for the continued use of this framework):

- **Forming** – this is when individuals are trying to establish their identity within the group and find out what the 'rules' are. Behaviour is often tentative at this stage and extreme politeness may prevail, with no one saying what they really mean. A leadership pattern may start to emerge.

- **Storming** – the politeness vanishes and all positions established earlier are challenged. Personal agendas emerge and there may be fierce status battles. This can be an uncomfortable time in a group: sometimes the group may disintegrate totally. But if the conflict is constructive it may generate greater cohesion, a realistic commitment to objectives and trust between members.

- **Norming** – out of the storm, more enduring norms emerge for how the group will operate, and what is acceptable behaviour within the group is established.

- **Performing** – provided that the necessary roles are being filled, the group can now really start to perform well.

Some people suggest that it is important to recognise a fifth stage. For groups that have worked closely together there can be unhappiness, even distress, when the group stops working together. Indeed, some groups keep going long after they have achieved their original goals. It is therefore helpful to talk about a stage of:

- **Adjourning** – here the process of group dissolution needs to be handled with care so that members can move on to other things.

Managing Diversity and Conflict

A major advantage of teams is that they can draw on a range of expertise and different sets of assumptions and perspectives. But to exploit this advantage you need to be prepared to work constructively with people whose world view is very different from yours. This diversity can stem from 'type', but also from cultural and other differences. In diverse groups, conflicts will sometimes arise, and you need also to have the skills to manage these.

Workforces (and students) are increasingly diverse. Many organisations now operate around the globe. Many workforces even within a single location draw upon an ethnically diverse workforce. You are likely to work with people from a wide range of backgrounds during your career. Furthermore, different professions have different 'cultures' too – different values and different ways of working. Yet many work teams are interdisciplinary, as are most customer groups. An ability to work effectively in diverse groups is a crucial management skill.

Most people are fairly tribal, and easily adopt an 'us' and 'them' position: 'We are OK, they are not.' This is the comfortable view as it preserves familiar ways of thinking and doing. It is probably barely conscious. I was once assessing teaching quality in the Midlands and commented afterwards that it seemed odd to see students working in such unmixed subgroups. The four West Indian boys worked together. The three West Indian girls, the five Asians and the three slightly older white women formed the other three groups. The lecturer seemed surprised I'd mentioned it. 'But they always do that,' she said.

Yet this micro-segregation was a hugely wasted learning opportunity. Each of these different groups was bringing different viewpoints, assumptions, values and experiences to the task. But because these were not being exchanged and debated, there was no learning about how others see the world. None of the students was finding out what was important to other people, or realising how their own perspectives might be limited. Nor were they learning how to manage the inevitable differences of opinion. Given concerns about global warming, it is a great pity not to exploit the opportunity to understand other people's ways of thinking without impacting upon your carbon footprint.

Working in mixed groups takes more effort. It becomes even more vital to check understanding at every stage than it is with a homogeneous group. Words may mean slightly different things within different cultures. Some cultures are less assertive than others: their 'agreement' may be mere politeness. Some cultures express themselves very directly, in ways that may seem almost offensive to others but are just the 'normal' way of saying things to those concerned. Some cultures treat deadlines differently from others.

If you get the opportunity to work in groups from a range of backgrounds, seize it. The potential for learning about others, and about yourself, is great. But to realise this potential you will probably need to make 'understanding each other's viewpoints and backgrounds' an explicit team objective, and to check progress on this regularly. You will also need to pay particular attention to setting 'group rules' – agreed ways of operating. These may need to include procedures for ensuring that less assertive members contribute at regular intervals, and regular checks on how people are *feeling* about how other members respond to their contributions. (Many of the indications of potential for learning will be at the implicit 'feeling' level.) You will also need to accept and examine explicit conflict.

When conflict *does* arise you need to handle it as a phenomenon to be explored rather than as a personal threat. Be assertive, not aggressive. In particular, aim to explore the situation rather than judge right and wrong. What exactly is the *nature* of the disagreement? Are people perceiving *facts* differently, disagreeing about *ways of working*, operating with conflicting *values* or bringing different sets of *assumptions* to the situation? If the latter, are these assumptions based on different experiences, perhaps in different contexts? By exploring questions such as these you may as a team come to a much more comprehensive understanding of the task and its context.

It may also be useful to explore why people feel so strongly about a point on which they disagree. This is a potential minefield, so you need to tread carefully. Think honestly about your own feelings first. Do you feel threatened? Undervalued? Are cherished values being called into question? Do you carry 'baggage' in the form of ingrained negative attitudes about certain groups of people? Where possible, check your feelings against the facts. For example, 'You are always saying my contributions are rubbish,' might not match the perception of others in the group. Could you have an observer sit outside a discussion and check how your contributions are actually received?

By exploring such issues for yourself you may come to a much clearer understanding of your own attitudes. By exploring the issues – carefully – with others, you may come to see both how they perceive you, and the strengths and weaknesses of their, and your own, ways of thinking.

Feelings are dangerous territory. But an ability to appreciate how others are feeling, and how they are *likely* to feel if you say or do something, is an important management skill, and a key component in 'emotional intelligence', described shortly. You can go a long way towards increasing your interpersonal sensitivity by treating conflict within groups as a learning experience. Use your talking listening and assertiveness skills, focus on the behaviour not the person, refuse to 'give up' until an issue is dealt with, and accept that your view may not always be the only, or even the best one. Check your progress at regular intervals as a group, and try to capture what the various members feel they have learned.

➤ Ch 8

Developing Your Leadership Skills

A favourite interview question is 'Describe a time when you showed leadership.' While many organisations use 'management' and 'leadership' to mean the same thing, it can be helpful to think of management as exercising authority (given by the organisation), and leadership as exercising influence which does not derive from position, formal power and/or authority.

As part of a team carrying out a project, or working in a group on a case study, you are unlikely to have a formally designated leader. If you use the opportunity to exercise your (non-authority derived) influence, you will be demonstrating your leadership skills. Developing confidence in taking the lead on such occasions, and knowing how to increase the chances that others will want to follow your lead, will help you show leadership in work and other contexts.

A vast amount has been written on leadership (check out how many items Amazon.com currently lists on 'leadership'), but there is still a lack of agreement over a definition of leadership, and how it differs – if it does – from management. The distinction in terms of authority versus other influence is now fairly common in the academic literature. This sees management as exercising influence from position, aimed at achieving conformity and control. Leadership, in contrast, is seen as influencing by other means and has to do with inspiring people to change.

The emphasis on 'leadership skills' for people in positions of authority is therefore interesting. If it is more than mere fashion, it suggests a growing awareness of the importance of internal motivation rather than 'sticks and carrots' – a form of motivation consistent with a team-based organisational structure.

So what skills does leadership demand? Goleman (1998) claims that his research 'clearly shows that emotional intelligence (EI) is the *sine qua non* of leadership'. (Note that he is clearly taking 'leaders' to mean senior managers, here.) He identifies five components of EI at work:

- **Self-awareness** – the ability to recognise your own emotions and drives and their impact on others, to be honest with oneself and others.
- **Self-regulation** – the ability to control impulses and moods, to suspend judgement, to think before acting.
- **Self-motivation** – a passion for the work itself, and energy and enthusiasm to pursue goals.
- **Empathy** – the ability to treat people according to their emotional reactions (rather than your own).
- **Social skills** – proficiency in managing relationships and building networks.

If you are working through the activities in this book you should be developing most of these components. Reflective learning, as outlined in Chapter 3, should be increasing your self-awareness, and if you are including reflection on feelings, will also impact upon self-regulation. Your work on planning and on motivation will help with self-motivation. So, too, will ongoing emphasis on the need for clarity of objectives. This chapter and the previous one, together with the feedback you manage to gather on your own impact, will help with developing social skills.

If you have the emotional sensitivity Goleman describes, you will be well on the way to being able to influence people by making them *want* to follow your lead. I would argue that understanding their motivation is also important for this, and being able to make them feel good about the group task. (The process-oriented group behaviours are a big help here, while being able to listen, both attentively and actively, will help greatly in one-to-one situations.)

A number of writers on leadership emphasise 'authenticity' as a key component. This is a combination of the self-awareness that Goleman lists, and the willingness to be honest with other group members about your own feelings, possible inadequacies and mistakes. If you are working in a group, this kind of honesty can help to build trust with other group members. If you are all honest about your shortcomings and your worries about being able to do a task well enough or to meet deadlines, the group will be much better placed to exercise control in the sense of planning to cope with the problem so that objectives are met despite any deviation from the original plan.

Other dimensions to leadership concern the task and the environment. As a student, using the task behaviours listed earlier will help you to exercise an influence on a group. At work it will help to be the one who can see what is needed to meet changes in the wider organisation, or its competitive or wider environment. Part 4 of this book addresses many of the relevant conceptual skills, though you will be developing these throughout your degree course.

➤ Ch 3

➤ Ch 2

➤ Ch 8

➤ Ch 11, 12, 13, 14

9

TEAM WORK AND LEADERSHIP

Activity 9.11

Consider the extent to which you currently influence a team of which you are a member. What are your 'leadership strengths'? List those factors which you think are helping you to exercise leadership – perhaps you are good at making others feel part of the team and wanting to contribute to the task, or good at organising meetings. Make an action plan to become even more effective through these strengths. Look at any possible reasons for your influence being less than it might be. (Feedback from fellow team members can be really useful here.) Make an action plan to develop your skills in these areas too.

Activity 9.12

Look for an area where you can demonstrate leadership. Ideally, this should be something which you already feel passionate about, whether a hobby or a charity. Aim during your degree to have devised a project within this area, got together a group to work on it, and acted as explicit leader. Log the experience in your learning journal and reflect on it as a basis for further learning. Write up a version of it that could form the basis of answers to 'give an example of when you have exercised leadership' on an application form or in an interview.

Potential Hazards of Team Work

Much of this chapter has looked at how to make teams effective. Can a team be *too* cohesive? If the group *process* is going well, and teams become really close, then there are three related things that can go wrong with the *task*. All are variants of the hazard hinted at earlier: the team becomes the main focus, and the wider task vanishes from awareness.

Dominance of sub-objectives

If sub-objectives predominate, the team may end up in competition with other teams working towards the same wider objective. If the team becomes too committed to its own task and to 'winning' in some way (for example, getting the highest production output), it may forget that it is part of a wider endeavour, and competition (rather than necessary collaboration) may get in the way of achieving the overall objective. (There is more of this in Chapter 11 when systems ideas are discussed.)

➤ Ch 11

Groupthink

Where 'groupthink' exists the group develops such a good feeling about itself, with members reinforcing each other's good opinion, that all indications that anything is wrong are disregarded. Any member brave enough to suggest that there is a problem will be made to feel a traitor to the group. This phenomenon is common in organisations. You will often find a board of a company refusing to believe that the signs of major problems are more than temporary blips, even though it is blindingly obvious to everyone outside this group that there is a significant disaster looming. You may find the same thing in project groups, where members get on very well together and are sure that they are doing brilliantly despite evidence to the contrary. If they know what 'groupthink' is, you may be able to make progress by asking if they think it is happening. But the tendency to deny it is a strong one.

Scapegoating

If things do go wrong, and this is finally so obvious that the group has to accept it, its members may still try to preserve their positive feelings about the group by finding one individual to accept all the blame. A group that realises that its presentation on a case study was the worst in the class may blame something outside the group – the tutor for giving unclear instructions, or a task that was harder than that given to other groups, or a single member of the group (perhaps the one who was trying to alert them to problems earlier).

There are two negative consequences of scapegoating. First, the scapegoat, if she or he is a group member, may be unhappy and lose self-confidence. Second, the group will not learn what went wrong if it does not accept responsibility for there having been a problem. This is common in work situations. A single person will be sacked when a problem arises. Yet often it is the system that is at fault and many people in that position would have behaved in the same way. Indeed, they will go on to behave in that way in future if the real cause of problems is not investigated.

Guidelines for effective team working

- Select members with appropriate skills, knowledge, and, if possible, a mix of preferred team roles and types.
- If working remotely, try to have an early face-to-face meeting.
- Ensure that all members understand and accept the objectives.
- Pay attention to both task and process.

- Accept that feelings may run high during early storming, and when working in a mixed group.
- Explore the reasons for disagreements and conflict.
- Value all contributions.
- Review both task progress and group process at regular intervals.
- Reward success.

SUMMARY

This chapter has argued the following:

- Team-working skills are essential in employment, aid learning, and can be developed in many ways while you are a student.
- All teams need to manage both task and process, and good communication is essential.
- To work effectively in a team, you need to apply your personal management and communication skills in a group context and understand the requirements for effective teams.
- To be effective in a formal group, you need to understand the role of agendas, minutes and a formal chair. This understanding is also relevant to informal groups.
- In establishing a group, group members should be chosen to cover the necessary range of expertise and of roles. Sometimes it will be necessary to agree ways of dealing with missing expertise or handling non-preferred roles.
- A new group can feel uncomfortable, but later performance will actually benefit from early conflict, provided that this is firmly faced and prevented from being damaging.
- Virtual teams are increasingly common in global organisations. Group process may need particular attention when meeting virtually.
- A 'mixed' group can produce better task outcomes and help you increase your interpersonal sensitivity.
- It can sometimes be helpful to designate a group leader, or to allocate responsibility for different aspects of leadership to team members.
- Leadership skills are increasingly valued by employers, and team working gives you an opportunity to develop your skills.
- Key tasks for leaders include identifying requirements, task management and process management, particularly making individuals feel valued and motivated. Relevant skills include 'emotional intelligence' and conceptual skills for problem identification and clarification.
- Groups are at risk of becoming too cohesive and inward looking losing track of the wider goal, 'scapegoating' and/or showing 'groupthink' when things go wrong. Team working is a rich and varied area of activity, with many dimensions. You will need to observe

others and yourself in groups and ask others to observe you and give feedback if you are to develop your skills.

Further information

Belbin, R.M. (2010) *Team Roles at Work, 2nd edn*, Routledge.

Harvard Business Review (2014) *Running Meetings*, HBR Press.

Maginn, M. (2004) *Making Teams Work*, McGraw-Hill.

West, M.A. (2012) *Effective Teamwork*, Blackwell.

10 PRESENTING TO AN AUDIENCE

Learning outcomes

By the end of this chapter you should:

- be alert to the things that can go wrong with presentations

- have assessed your own strengths and weaknesses in this area

- be able to structure a presentation in a way that is appropriate to your audience

- be developing your delivery technique

- be using appropriate software and other visual aids to good effect

- be confident in handling questions from your audience

- be able to control nervousness.

Introduction

Most managers will need to give talks or make presentations as part of their job, and such presentations are often an opportunity to raise your profile in an organisation. Your presentation skills may be tested at a job interview. Becoming better at making presentations can therefore make you more employable, and accelerate your career, as well as being useful to you as a student. Many people are terrified of public speaking at first, yet, with practice, most come to enjoy it, though usually with an element of nervousness. This chapter looks at the necessary skills and suggests ways in which you can improve your skills as a presenter. You may not become brilliant at it – such people are rare – but you can become good enough to get high marks on your course and impress potential employers.

The final face-to-face communication skill you need is that of making a presentation to a group. Poor presentations can be an ordeal for speaker and audience; good ones can be a delight for both. Furthermore, both good and bad presentations are *remembered*. Whether you are presenting your research results to a group of potential collaborators, talking to a group of senior managers in your own organisation, making a pitch to a potential major client or giving an after-dinner speech for a professional association, it is important to make a good impression. You may pay an invisible price for years to come if you do not. On the other hand, if you do well, unexpected opportunities may come your way in the future. You will also have an immediate feeling of power and euphoria from having had your audience exactly where you want them.

This chapter addresses the problem of nervousness and the skills that you need to make a good presentation. Again, these overlap with skills already covered. Being clear about your objectives, understanding your listeners' (albeit now in the plural) needs, expressing yourself appropriately and clearly and checking understanding will be as important as in one-to-one talking or in making a contribution to a group discussion. But additionally, you need to know how to ensure that your audience can see and hear you, to gain and hold their attention and to use visual aids to good effect. The bulk of the chapter looks at presenting formally to a captive audience. However, there is a short section on presenting

➤ Ch 2, 6, 8   more informally via a poster display with a passing audience.

The Risks in Presentation

Presentations, like written papers or reports, showcase you to a wider audience so it is important to do all you can to avoid the risks of anything going wrong. Because you are operating in real time, the risks of this may be greater than for a written report. If something is difficult to express in writing, you can keep trying until you get it right. If your reader finds that concentration has lapsed, they can go and make a cup of tea, then try reading again from where they 'switched off'. In a live presentation, neither presenter nor

➤ Ch 6   audience has a second chance.

There is normally less interchange between speaker and listeners in a formal presentation than in one-to-one or group discussion. Keeping the audience awake, interested and involved is therefore a considerable challenge. You probably know all too well how easy it is to stop concentrating in a lecture and have found sitting still and being 'talked at' a fairly stressful experience. Unfortunately, the older you get, the harder it becomes to be a member of an audience.

As in other areas, the best way to become more aware of what is required is to look at what other people do less than well. You can then look at how those who are more competent do the same thing. Once you are more alert to the different dimensions required, you will be better able to reflect on, and develop, your own skills.

Activity 10.1

Think of an unsatisfactory presentation that you have attended recently (lectures are fair game here, as well as presentations by fellow students). List all the factors which contributed to your dissatisfaction. Now think of an experience of a good presentation. List any additional features which distinguished this. (You can go on to do this again at the next presentation you attend.)

Good features: _____

_____

Bad features: _____

_____

If your experience is anything like mine, your list of bad practice might include occasions when the speaker did some or even all of the following:

- read a prepared speech in 'written' rather than 'spoken' English
- mumbled, whispered, went too fast or was otherwise inaudible
- used illegible visual aids – perhaps with far too much text in the smallest font
- faced away from you, perhaps while writing on the board or flipchart
- used a hypnotic monotone making sleep irresistible, probably with no visual aids at all
- distributed handouts during the presentation, so that you read these rather than listened
- was muddled incomprehensible, or said nothing you did not already know
- 'lost the thread' by responding at length to barely relevant questions
- went on long beyond the scheduled end
- got into an argument with a single member of the audience.

The remainder of the chapter addresses these common faults as well as covering features which may well have appeared on your list of 'good' points.

Activity 10.2

➤ **Ch 1**

Did you mention presentation skills as a strength in your SWOT in Chapter 1? If not, use the following questionnaire to assess your skill level (score 5 if the statement is completely true, 4 if mostly true, 3 if it is neither true nor untrue, 2 if it is not very true, and 1 if it is totally untrue)

I have lots of experience in giving presentations _____

The presentations I give are usually very well received _____

I always think carefully about what I need to communicate, and how best to do it to any particular audience _____

I am good at thinking of how to use visual aids to reinforce my message _____

I am confident in using PowerPoint to produce effective overheads _____

I think it is really important to watch the audience, and modify a presentation if it does not seem to be working _____

Total _____

If your score is 25 or above you should not need this chapter – assuming your assessment of your skills is accurate. Below this, you might think about developing an action plan to improve aspects of your skills.

Structure

A clear structure is perhaps even more important in a presentation than a written report. It is very easy for your audience to lose the thread of what you are saying and very hard for them to find it again if they do. They cannot go back and read the difficult bit again. So the classic advice of 'Say what you are going to say, say it, then tell them what you have said' still holds good.

> **Good presentations:**
> - have a clear structure
> - are clearly signposted
> - are clearly delivered
> - use varied visual aids
> - interest the audience throughout
> - do not overrun.

Introduction

At the beginning you need to settle your audience, so say who you are, what you are aiming to achieve, how long you will be talking and how you plan to operate. Do you want to save all questions except those for clarification to the end, for example, or are you happy to take questions at any point? Will you be handing out copies of your overhead transparencies (OHTs) at the end or do people need to take notes? Once the ground rules have been established, you then need to outline the main points that you will be covering during your presentation. If you can say something that catches your audience's attention at the outset and makes them *want* to hear what follows, then the presentation is likely to go well.

Main presentation

As with a written report, you need to make clear what situation or topic you are addressing and use evidence to support the arguments you are making. Because of the difficulty of following a spoken argument, you need to make your structure absolutely clear and give your audience as much help as possible on this: 'What I have established thus far is . . . (brief summary). The next point I want to make is . . .' If you give such pointers at regular intervals, perhaps with slides or other visual aids to reinforce them, your audience will find it easier to maintain concentration and to stay with your argument.

Conclusion

This is the 'tell them what you have said' section. You need to summarise the points you have made, again using visual aids to reinforce them if possible. If you are making a proposal, then it is worth emphasising the main points of this again. It is also good practice to thank the audience for their patience and to invite questions or discussion.

Delivery Technique

If you do come across good presenters, study them carefully to see if there are ways in which you could improve your own performance. Even if you are not exposed to skilled practitioners, the following guidelines will give you a good foundation.

Relate to your audience

How well do you relate to a speaker who seems to be talking to a point on the back wall, in a monotone? Try to sound human in your introduction. Look at people. Say things in the way that they are most likely to understand. Check with them that you are on the right lines: 'Was that point clear?' 'Can you all see this slide?' 'Am I going too fast?'

Make it easy for people to hear

Speak clearly, not too fast, and vary your tone. Use short sentences and straightforward language, avoiding unnecessary jargon. Use 'spoken language' not 'written language'. If you have ever heard someone (literally) read a paper they have written, you will probably be all too aware of the difference. If not, try reading part of a journal article out loud, and then rephrase it using words you would normally use in talking. Avoid turning your back on your audience (whiteboards are a real hazard here) or being hidden by equipment.

Try to be interesting

Vary your pace and use a variety of visual aids if there are appropriate ones; showing something as simple as showing a pile of books on a subject can reinforce the point that there has been a lot written on it. Occasional humour can be useful, but don't overdo it (unless you are making an after-dinner speech, when a high proportion of jokes seem to be the norm). Above all, make the relevance of what you are saying clear. It may be less obvious to your audience why something is significant than it is to you: you need to *work* at making sure that they see it too.

Beware of becoming bogged down in detail

It is far harder to absorb detail from a spoken presentation than from a written report. Indeed, detail is likely to obscure the main point. Try to give only as much detail as you need to make your point. If a fine detail is crucial, it is probably better to give this as a handout. (If you are doing this at the end, let people know so that they do not take unnecessary notes.)

Avoid giving handouts while you speak

If you give out handouts while you are talking it distracts people, and you will lose your audience; everyone will be reading rather than listening. It doesn't matter how often you say of a handout 'don't read this now' – the temptation to look at it immediately seems universally irresistible. If you distribute handouts before you start, early arrivals will have something to do while they wait. It will also be clear to them how many additional notes (if any) they need to take. Handouts distributed at the end can be a good way of concluding, but you need to tell people at the outset that you are going to do this; otherwise they can feel annoyed if they have taken careful notes which the handout makes superfluous.

Keep your notes brief

Particularly if you are new to giving presentations, it is tempting to write out – and then read – the whole thing. Such a script can be reassuring as you know that if you dry up you can simply read the rest. But resort to reading only as an emergency measure. And if you do write out a full-text version, write briefer notes from which, barring the onset of total panic, you will actually speak.

These notes should indicate the key points to be made, in order. Hard copy notes are ideally made on index cards, numbered and joined with a treasury tag or similar in case you drop them. (Trying to reorder a hopeless jumble of cards while facing an audience can be deeply embarrassing.) Alternatively use a phone or small tablet – this is better than staring at a laptop. Indicate in your notes each point at which you need to use a visual aid. And cross-refer to your transcript so that you can easily switch to that if necessary. (After a few presentations, when you have never used the full notes, you will probably feel confident enough to dispense with them.)

It may seem obvious to use your slides as notes. But what will help your audience grasp and remember key points from your presentation is likely to be very different from what will help you remember what to say next. Slides should serve the first purpose!

Watch your audience

You need feedback on your delivery as you go along, so that you can adjust accordingly. People may not tell you in words, but their body language will speak volumes. If a glaze of incomprehension is stealing over your audience you may need to slow down and explain more, or perhaps check understanding by asking a question. If eyelids are drooping, you may be going too slowly already or have underestimated the prior knowledge of people there. Or you may need to vary your delivery more. If people are tense, tapping feet or fingers with restrained force, you are seriously getting on their nerves. You need to find out why. Unless you are fairly sure what you are doing wrong, *ask* what the problem is – and adapt your presentation in the light of the answers.

Be honest

Trying to fool people seldom works. If there is a weakness in your case, admit it rather than hoping that no one will notice. If they do notice, they will not think well of you for seemingly failing to spot the weakness yourself. But if you admit to it and have formed a good relationship with your audience, they may help you to strengthen the point. Similarly, pretending to know something when in fact you don't may make you look foolish. But admitting your ignorance may allow someone in the audience who does know to contribute their knowledge – to everyone's advantage.

Manage your time

Inexperienced presenters are often surprised at how little it is possible to communicate in a specified time. This is because they do not allow for speech being slower than reading, for questions of clarification, for introductions, for interim summaries or for use of visual aids. Do a 'dry run' in front of a friend to judge how long a presentation will take and adjust it if your guess is wrong. Aim to undershoot slightly. It is generally better to risk allowing slightly too long for questions than to run out of time, and to stop before you have said everything necessary.

Effective Visual Aids

Communication will be far more effective in either writing or speaking if you use images to reinforce your words. Visual aids have already been mentioned several times: this should have indicated that they are essential in formal presentations of any length or complexity. Such aids have three main functions: they can help the audience *understand* a point; they can help the audience *remember* a point and they can keep your audience

➤ Ch 5, 6, 11

> **Visual aids can:**
> - reinforce key points
> - clarify meaning
> - aid retention
> - keep audience awake.

awake. To make good use of visual aids, you need to think about how each of your points could be reinforced by an action, an object or a picture, and then how best to achieve this reinforcement. The best visual aid to use will depend on both the point you are making and the audience to whom you are making it.

Some things can be conveyed far more effectively by means other than words alone. Relationships are more clearly shown in diagrams, whereas trends are clearly demonstrated in graphs. Video clips can provide powerful and memorable examples. Other chapters cover representing data visually and diagramming other aspects of a situation. You can incorporate such visuals into your presentation as you would in a written report. The same principles apply, though within the restrictions of what can be seen from a distance. Revise these principles if you are in doubt. But although you will probably use visual aids similar to those suitable for a report for most of your points, your scope in a spoken presentation is potentially far wider.

Video clips of products, processes, people or places can be hugely effective. Concrete objects can also make a lasting impression. To take an example, when running open events to attract potential Open University students, I needed to explain how distance learning works, especially for a subject like management. *Showing* the audience a course pack, with written units, and print-outs of course assignments covered in teaching comments from the tutor, together with extracts from teaching videos or a video of a seminar (or recording of an online event) conveyed far more about the course than would a mere spoken description.

I have seen speakers hold up broken items to make a point about quality, or a new product to make a different point. Cognitive psychologist Stephen Pinker held up a comb to make a point about the innate distastefulness of using a comb to stir coffee. Such images make a lasting impression – though the point they demonstrated is not always clearly remembered. If the image is too strong, then it may overshadow the point (what *was* the significance of the comb-related distaste?). Even for points which might be adequately made in words, an appropriate visual aid might help people remember the point.

It is also important to incorporate variety to keep people awake and interested. For any presentation longer than, say, half an hour, it is worth using a range of visual aids for this reason alone. You can mix PowerPoint or Prezi slides with diagrams you draw on a board or flipchart at an appropriate point (do this quickly and avoid talking while drawing), and add photos and video clips to enliven your presentation. Because visual aids can be so powerful it is important to make sure that any you use will reinforce rather than distract from your message.

If your talk is short, you do not need to work so hard at keeping people's attention, and too much variety in visual aids can be counterproductive. It is better to reserve them for points that are best made visually, plus those which you really wish to emphasise.

TECHSkills 10.1 Choosing and using presentation software

It is now normal to use presentation software: PowerPoint is perhaps the most widely used, as it comes as part of Microsoft Office, but there are several other popular options. PowerPoint is basically designed to deliver a series of slides, stored on your own device, downloaded onto a data stick for portability, or stored a cloud for access from anywhere with internet access. Similar tools include Apple's Keynote, and for those with a Gmail or Google account, the web driven Google Drive slides, which since they exist on the Google cloud can be shared with 'friends'.

A popular alternative for those who find PowerPoint or comparable systems too linear is Prezi. Instead of a series of discrete slides, Prezi allows you to assemble your presentation on something akin to a giant board, constructing frames at different places and then zooming in and out from the big picture to individual frames as you give your presentation. The 'track' of the focus is pre-programmed, so you decide on the order the frames will appear beforehand, just as you decide on the order of your slides in PowerPoint, but what the audience sees is much more dynamic and visually interesting that a series of discrete PowerPoint slides.

Prezi provides a much wider range of templates, too, and makes it easy to use frames for pictures, video clips or other non-textual material to add variety, and to resize, move or rotate frames. The ability to see the 'big picture' is the visual equivalent of the summary in a report, and zooming out at intervals enable the structure of the presentation to be clear. A basic version of Prezi is (at the time of writing) free and there are many free tutorials online (see online resources for suggestions). This basic version should be adequate for your use until presentations become a key part of your job, at which point their hope is that you will purchase the more advanced system, which offers far more features.

If you want something even more different from PowerPoint, PowToon is another popular system. This allows you to create animated presentations, and if you love graphics you may enjoy playing with it.

As well as software that helps you directly create the visual aspect of your presentation, there are programmes such as SlideDog, which help you create the equivalent of a playlist of videos, documents or other things you might want to use in a presentation, and then link them to Prezi or other presentation software.

In recent years the range of options has increased hugely, and your choice of presentation software becomes correspondingly harder. What is best for you will depend on answers to a number of questions:

- What packages do you already have? (For example, PowerPoint comes as part of Microsoft Office, and your university might provide other options.)
- Do you want to be able to access slides or the whole presentation remotely?

10

PRESENTING TO AN AUDIENCE

- How important is it to create a good impression with your visual aids?
- How much time (and money) do you want to spend on acquiring new software and the skills to use it? (Though as noted, there are often free basic versions available usually offering only a limited number of features, and therefore perhaps less learning time.)

You will find online reviews of the main presentation software packages, and may like to check some of these out (see online resources for a suggestion). Check who is writing the review. If it written by the company selling one of the packages being reviewed you might expect a degree of bias!

Whatever presentation software and other visual aids you are using, it is important to consider how to use these to engage your audience and convey your message in a way they will understand, be convinced by and remember. Your aim is to communicate, and your visual aids are a tool for this, not something to be considered in isolation.

Resist using the features of your system just because you can. While it is important to know what the system can do, you need to choose those features which will best serve your objectives for the presentation. Only use features that are impressive in their own right rather than there to make your message more powerful if your main aim is to show your technical competence rather than to communicate a more substantive message.

If using PowerPoint or a similar system you need to be careful it does not constrain your presentation to an endless series of bullet points. As Naughton (2003) pointed out, Power-Point was conceived in a software sales environment, so it tends to turn everything into a sales pitch. There was a version of the Gettysburg address doing the email rounds a while ago that demonstrated this limitation (see **www.norvig.com/Gettysburg** for some light relief on this topic, or explore versions fitting the actual speech to the slides or critiquing PowerPoint, which you can easily find online).

Tufte, a Yale professor and expert on visual communication argues that PowerPoint's ready-made templates tend to weaken verbal and spatial reasoning and corrupt statistical analysis. He attributes the Columbia space shuttle disaster to a slide that led Nasa to overlook the destructive potential of the crucial loose tile (see 'PowerPoint does rocket science', on Tuft's website **www.edwardtufte.com**). His analysis may also add to your understanding of the idea of argument mapping outlined in Chapter 4.

➤ Ch 4

General requirements for visual aids

There is often a temptation to cram too much onto a slide. The amount of effective information people can absorb from any one screen is surprisingly small. Before finalising your visual aids, check that they will be visible to the normal eye from the same distance as the back of the room in which you will make your presentation. A good rule of thumb is to aim at no more than four points per slide.

Colour can either enhance or hinder clarity. Think about how you use it. I have seen tasteful but totally useless slides in shades of blue on blue, the words invisible from more than three paces. Use both colour and light/dark contrast to enhance legibility and emphasise key points. And be careful about fancy backgrounds and too much animation of slides: they may look good in themselves but they can distract, and obscure your message.

For 'transient' presentations, for example on group work, where all you are seeking is to convey your thought processes to fellow students, it is fine to use flip charts. But it is still important that you manage the amount of information per chart, and ensure that charts will be legible from the farthest seat. (Avoid using red pen, or any light colour, as these are not easily visible at a distance.) You can prepare flipchart sheets in the same way as slides and ask a fellow student to be responsible for displaying the right one on cue. (Trying to talk and manage a flipchart is possible but not easy. It helps considerably to split the responsibility.)

Activity 10.3

You can easily assemble an exhibit for your portfolio that addresses both your ability to use images and your ability to read and respond to materials. Take as the basis for this a presentation you make in class, perhaps summarising something you have studied. The exhibit should include the notes for your talk and copies of the images used, together with a description of how you selected the content and images, any feedback on their effectiveness from tutor and other students, and your reflections on what you would do differently next time.

Handling Questions

Sometimes questions are helpful, but I have seen them wreck a presentation completely. Until you are fairly experienced, it is safer to take substantive questions at the end. Make it clear at the outset that during your presentation you will deal only with requests for clarification and that there will be time for questions at the end.

Otherwise, you risk being completely sidetracked from your main argument or disconcerted by challenges to what you are saying before you have completed your case. If you want to postpone a question, either take a note of it so that you do not forget or, better still, ask the questioner to ask it again at the end. This means that your brain is not distracted by trying to remember the question while giving the talk.

When you do accept a question, your listening skills will be important. It is hard to listen carefully when you are nervous, particularly if someone is asking a complex question with many, perhaps not closely related parts. If this happens, jot down the key parts of the question, otherwise it is easy to answer the first part and forget all the rest. If you are at all uncertain what the question means, clarify this with the questioner. You may feel that it makes you look stupid if you don't understand. But if the questioner is far from clear it is sensible to pick up on this. You may tie yourself in knots if you try to answer a question that you have only partially understood: this does not look all that impressive either.

If a question challenges what you have said, resist the temptation to become either defensive or aggressive. Take their view seriously, looking for ways to develop your position in the light of it, unless you are convinced that the questioner really has missed or misunderstood your point or is misinformed. If the point has been missed by the questioner, others may have missed it too, so it is worth trying to repeat it in a slightly different way. If you cannot quickly satisfy the questioner, suggest that you discuss it after the presentation is finished. This avoids getting into an argument that will be of little interest to most of the audience.

People ask questions for many reasons. In work presentations, there will be some who are trying to make an impression on the audience, perhaps with a view to establishing themselves as a rival expert or advertising their own business. Or they may simply like being the centre of attention. Where questions are clearly being asked in the questioner's personal interest, it is simplest to thank them for raising their point, agree with as much of the point as you can, perhaps suggest a discussion outside the meeting and move on to the next question.

If questions reveal a genuine weakness in your presentation, it is usually better to accept this and ask for suggestions from the questioner and the audience for ways around the difficulty. You may find that someone can suggest a way forward. If, however, the difficulty seems to you to be much less significant than the questioner is suggesting, you will need to make sure that the audience does not end up devaluing the bulk of what you have said.

Virtual Presentations and Podcasts

Virtual presentations are becoming increasingly common for reasons similar to those driving growth in virtual meetings. Again they may be take place in real time, with scope for some at least of the scattered audience to email or phone in questions. Such presentations are often recorded to allow access by people not available at the time of the podcast, or there may be no live version, only a recording. Such presentations may be 'broadcast' through a conferencing system or made available (via Dropbox or Google Drive) for people to access on demand.

If you are studying online using a 'virtual classroom' you may be asked to make presentations on group work within this system. If not, you may well need to make virtual presentations at some point in your career, so can usefully think about any modifications that may be needed. If you are presenting privately, the general principles above may be enough, although it is worth using any 'voting' or other option to check understanding as you go along.

If you are 'broadcasting' your presentation on a public platform you will need to think about copyright implications. Video clips, music, quotations and images copied from elsewhere are all likely to be subject to copyright legislation, so should not be used without permission. You can find some music which is not copyrighted, but need to hunt for it. Podcasting is an excellent form of advertising if you eventually choose to set up your own business. A wealth of podcasting tips are available online should you wish to develop your skills in this direction.

Poster Presentations

Thus far the chapter has addressed formal presentations to a (normally) seated audience. At conferences it is common to supplement the formal presentation programme with less formal poster presentations. A large space will be made available, and each presenter will be allocated wall space for a poster. The audience will wander round the room, looking at the various displays and stopping to discuss those of particular interest with the 'presenter', who will be standing by the poster ready to answer questions.

This allows participants to access a much greater number of presenters than would otherwise be the case, and is often used to allow students to present their research. If you are doing a dissertation you may have the opportunity to take part in a poster session within the university or at a larger conference. This sort of presentation is also sometimes used in organisational contexts, at meetings between members of different project groups, so it is worth extending your presentation skills to include this format. In either case the poster presentation tends to be aimed primarily at peers and/or colleagues.

Poster presentations present different communication challenges to the presenter. The 'talking' part tends to be less intimidating: you are talking to people individually or in very small groups. On the other hand, these conversations are equivalent to the 'questions' part of a formal presentation, which is in many respects the most challenging part as much of the control passes to the questioner.

The real challenge for most, however, is in poster design. Typically you will have a space 1 metre high, and 1.5–1.75 metres wide. This space has to work hard for you. As with any communication, your first task is to clarify your objectives. What do you want the poster to achieve? Clearly this will depend on what you are presenting upon and the context in which you are presenting. Are you simply aiming to inform as many participants as possible? If so, what are the key points you are trying to get across? Are you trying to sell yourself or your research, and if so, to whom? Are you aiming to engage colleagues in conversation? If so, what would you particularly like to talk with them about? Are you seeking like-minded people from other universities with whom to network? If so, what would be most likely to interest such people? This is not an exhaustive list. It merely indicates the sort of objectives you might have. You need to be absolutely clear of your objectives on each occasion.

> **Posters aim to:**
> - attract
> - inform
> - start conversations
> - advertise your work
> - summarise achievements.

Clarity is paramount because 1.5 square metres is not very big, and anything within this space has to be visible from around 1.5 metres away. So every word needs to count, and you need to use pictures (or graphs or whatever) as much as possible. Aim to 'show' rather than 'tell'. A good rule of thumb is 20 per cent text, 40 per cent graphics and 40 per cent space. Do not underestimate the importance of this white space, on slides, as well as in posters. It is what gives the other 60% its impact.

Given overall space limitations, and the need to include a lot of white space, you need to think very carefully about what to include. Useful questions to answer include.

- What are your (very few) key points?
- How can you convey these graphically?
- How can you lay these out on a poster so that they will communicate to someone walking past at a distance of up to 2 metres?

Remember, you may be in competition with dozens of other posters, and participants will not look in any detail at more than a small proportion of these. You will not have time to talk to everybody even if you attract them. So, how can you ensure that you engage those people with whom you are likely to have the most profitable conversations, prime them to ask the most useful questions, and leave a favourable impression both of you personally and of the work that you have done?

If you Google 'poster presentations' you will find a wealth of information on how to lay out posters for maximum impact. The essential messages are:

- You need to say who you are, where you come from and the topic covered by your poster – IN VERY LARGE WRITING.
- You need to have a clear 'path' through the poster so that people can follow the narrative easily.
- You cannot afford to waste a single word – 'Findings' or 'methodology' do not convey information by themselves. Something like '80% misunderstand age legislation' carries a message. Think newspaper headlines here. Write large, and with bar charts or other simple graphics to support them.
- You need a way of continuing the exchange when you have 'engaged' someone's interest. At the very least show your email address clearly on the poster. But it is even better to have a handout expanding on key points, with your email address on it. Safest of all, particularly if your key aim is to network, is to have people write *their* email address (or write it for them) and email a more substantial document – the text behind the headlines – a couple of days later, with a note saying how much you enjoyed talking to them.

Figure 10.1 shows two possible layouts for poster presentations for a standard research presentation. You may be able to be far more creative – but do remember the need for clarity from 2 metres distance. Messy and cluttered do not, on the whole, attract.

Controlling Your Nerves

It is natural to be nervous when standing up in front of a group of people, whether for a formal presentation or a poster display. The adrenaline it generates can give your performance an excitement that it would otherwise lack, so do not aim to become totally blasé about it. But excess nerves can be a liability, drying your throat and making you physically and verbally clumsy. If you think that you are worrying more than is reasonable, there are several things that can help considerably: get as much practice as you can; concentrate on exposing yourself to similar situations; practise deliberate relaxation and prepare for each specific presentation.

Figure 10.1 Possible layouts for poster presentations

> **Increase your confidence in presenting by:**
> * frequent practice
> * relaxation techniques
> * thorough preparation.

If you *are* over-nervous, you probably avoid situations where you need to talk in front of people. But the best way to reduce nervousness is to seek out such situations and force yourself to talk. Find the least threatening situations first – talking to a small group of students before addressing the whole class, getting used to the class before giving a paper at a conference would be good ways to start. But *do* it. Each time you will feel less nervous.

This is one form of practice which 'desensitises' you to the general trauma of the situation. Another form is to have one or more 'practice runs' of a specific presentation. This will mean that you are confident about the structure of the talk, have practised some of the phrases you will use, know where to use your OHTs or other visual aids and have checked how long it takes, so that you are not worried about having too much or too little material.

➤ **Ch 2** Relaxation techniques, discussed as part of stress management in Chapter 2, can help reduce this sort of stress too, though you need to be familiar with the techniques for best effect. If you have not yet practised them, a short period of deep breathing will help. And a *small* alcoholic drink can sometimes be useful.

But your best weapon against nerves is the knowledge that you have done everything possible to prepare for the event. If you have carefully researched your subject and audience, your talk (or poster) is well structured and your notes are well organised, your visual aids are well chosen and you have at your fingertips supporting evidence and examples, you have little to fear. Dry runs, described above, can be part of your preparation. Remember, a presentation is a challenge, but it can be exciting and rewarding, and can provoke interesting discussion on a subject dear to your heart. Preparation is so important that more detail is given below.

Even if you have prepared, you may well experience an initial onrush of nerves when you stand up to make a formal presentation. To get you over this, make sure that you have your introductory remarks written out in full, preferably learned by heart. Take a sip of water and a deep breath, go over your introduction and by then you will have calmed down enough to enjoy yourself.

Preparation

Preparation is the key to successful presentation and you cannot afford to cut corners if you want to do well. You need to have thought carefully about what to communicate, how to structure it and how to add impact to your arguments by examples and visual aids. For important presentations, you will want to rehearse your arguments several times. Much of this can be done piecemeal, for example while exercising or in a waiting room, *sotto voce*. But you will need one full-scale, real-time rehearsal to check timing, use of aids and flow of arguments – or responses to a poster and likely questions. Ideally, find colleagues or friends to act as an audience and ask them to give you feedback afterwards. If this is impossible, then, for a formal presentation, tape yourself and replay the tape after a decent interval, listening critically and noting points where you need to change something. For a poster, come back to it a few days later and try to pretend that you know nothing about the topic.

If you are giving a presentation at work, to clients or potential customers, or a paper at a conference, your preparation needs to extend to ensuring that the location is set up as you want it, temperature is appropriate and equipment working properly. You do not want to be struggling to get your laptop to talk to the data projection system in front of your audience! So arrive early and make all the necessary checks.

Preparation for your *next* presentation should be informed by feedback from the last, so it is important to capture as much feedback as possible. Make a note of your immediate reactions in the light of audience response. Do this as soon as possible after the event, noting in your learning journal your feelings and points for future action. If possible, have a friend in the audience charged with giving you their reactions and suggestions. You may even be able to design and distribute a short questionnaire for the audience to complete on leaving. If the presentation is one of a series, this can be extremely useful in helping you to adjust future events to meet audience needs more effectively. If you are likely to have the chance to participate in more than one poster display, feedback may have the same benefits. If you are preparing an exhibit on your presentation skills, it will

➤ **Ch 8**   be important to include all such feedback.

SUMMARY

This chapter has argued the following:

- Presentation skills are an important part of communication in the work context and may indeed be tested during selection procedures.

- During your studies you will have many opportunities to develop these skills and they may even influence some of your marks.

- Successful presentation depends on adequate preparation. You need to be clear on your objectives and those of your audience, and structure is even more important here than with written communications.

- Good visual aids help audience concentration, comprehension and retention. A range of presentation software is available, but it is important to use it to reinforce your message rather than to flaunt your technical skills.

- Audibility, visibility and ability to pace your delivery to suit your audience and your content are essential.

- Questions can be an asset or a disruption. Substantive ones are probably best taken at the end.

- Poster displays present major challenges of distilling the core message into words and graphics visible from 1.5 to 2 metres away.

- Extreme nervousness can be disabling but lower levels can help. Practice, relaxation and preparation will help you to reduce excessive nerves.

Further information

Bradbury, A. (2010) *Successful Presentation Skills*, 4th edn, Kogan Page.

Conradi, M. and Hall, R. (2001) *That Presentation Sensation*, Financial Times Prentice Hall.

Kermode, R. (2013) Speak So Your Audience Will Listen, Pendle Publishing.

Leech, T. (2013) *Say It Like Shakespeare*, 2nd edn, Presentations Press. This gives an interestingly different slant on presenting.
http://guides.nyu.edu/posters – there are many useful websites but try this one.

Customshow (2015) for a review of alternatives to PowerPoint at http://www.customshow.com /best-powerpoint-alternatives-presentation-programs/ for another 2015 comparison of alternatives to PowerPoint and explanation of how SlideDog works – but better still, look for a range of up-to-date alternatives to this (assuming you are reading the book a year or two after publication).
https://www.youtube.com/playlist?list=PL09A34EF19596B7BB for a series of tutorials on using Prezi.

PART 4
CONCEPTUAL SKILLS

Introduction to Part 4

This part of the book explores what is meant by the 'trained mind' that employers so often say they are looking for in graduates. The last part looked at the social and influencing skills which will make you a good leader. It looks at the other aspect of leadership – working out the direction in which to go. By now you should have become a more effective learner, and so better at absorbing the specialist skills and knowledge your course covers. You will also be developing your interpersonal skills, which are important for real-life problem solving. Most problems are better addressed in teams. The perspectives and information that other people bring to bear on the situation are vital for gaining a thorough understanding of the problem.

The third, and extremely important, aspect of effective problem solving – and of leadership – is working out what needs doing. This means using conceptual skills to explore different aspects of a problem, and test different sets of assumptions about it. You need to play mental games, experimenting with different ways of making sense of the complex situation that is problematic. This mental flexibility is essential if you are to avoid treating what is complex as if it were simple, and to cope with conflicting and/or inadequate 'information' about the situation. Most importantly, you need to be able to break out of the mindset that may be stopping you – and others – from seeing a solution.

Although this part of the book is about problem solving, much of it addresses those problems which you cannot 'solve' in the sense of logically working through to a solution that is unarguably correct. Such solutions are possible only if you know what you are trying to do, have all the information needed to decide between alternative solutions and can therefore, by a logical process, decide on the best. So committed do we tend to be to this kind of approach that it is adopted in situations where these conditions do not apply. The 'problem' is viewed from a narrow perspective that gives the illusion that it can be treated rationally. But remember Procrustes, the legendary Greek robber who stretched or shortened his captives to fit an iron bed. If you treat problems in this way, ignoring the parts which are cut off to make the problem easier to solve, you risk finding a 'solution' which makes things worse. The following chapters are designed to help you to avoid this trap and to accept that, for many situations, complexity is inevitable. There are, however, useful techniques that can help you to explore this complexity. And there are further techniques which can help you find creative approaches to resistant problems.

These skills will help you respond creatively and appropriately to any complex situations that you analyse during your courses or meet in real life. Case study analyses are obvious examples of this. So, too, are almost any significant management- or social-science-related projects. If you can develop your problem-solving skills before you graduate, you will have a significant advantage over work colleagues who lack them. You will quickly be noticed as someone with high-flier potential!

11

COMPLEXITY, CASES AND DIAGRAMS

Learning outcomes

By the end of this chapter you should:

- appreciate both the advantages and the limitations of a rational, systematic and logical approach

- be becoming more logical in your own thinking

- be able to locate this rational approach within a wider framework for exploring problem situations and making sense of them

- be using both hand drawn and computer drawn diagrams both as tools for problem exploration and interpretation, and to communicate your thinking to others

- be starting to use mental modelling and experimentation as part of an approach to problems

- have developed a systematic approach to case study analysis.

Introduction

Perhaps the most useful skill of all those you will learn during your studies is the ability to accept, and then to make some sort of sense of, the complexity inherent in problem situations. This is the purpose of most of the theories and frameworks that you will be taught. Yet all too many students find it extremely difficult to grasp that theory has a purpose, rather than simply being something they are required to learn. This chapter should help you see the point of much of what you are learning, and develop your ability to put it to good effect in analysing cases during your course, and making sense of situations in real life. This will make you a far more valuable employee in any managerial or problem-solving role.

Organisations are complex, and the problem situations that arise in them are equally complex. Graduates are attractive to employers in large part because they are believed to have the ability to think their way through such problems. Well developed 'cognitive skills' are perhaps the most important goal of higher education. Demonstrating these skills at interview and in your job will greatly help your career. Education tends to emphasise logic and rationality, and being logical is important. But real life often seems fairly chaotic and full of uncertainty, so you need additional skills to deal with complexity.

➤ Ch 1

Many problems *are* amenable to the application of a rational/logical approach: you can access all the information needed to work out the solution. But unfortunately this is not always the case. Key players may be unable to agree what the problem *is*, let alone what would constitute a solution. Even if they agree on the problem, it may seem to defy solution. I am not suggesting you should be *illogical*, but you may need to go beyond the strictly logical framework to find a totally new way through the situation. Playing mental games can help you find a *non-obvious* way of thinking about the situation. Once this shift of perspective has been achieved, logic can be more effectively used.

So you need to develop different, and rarer, conceptual skills with which to supplement your logical thinking. Combining a rational approach with the mental agility needed to go beyond the rational should enable you to deal with problems that have defeated lesser brains. This chapter looks at the more rational ways of approaching problems, with particular emphasis on how they can be applied to working with case studies. Ways of becoming more creative are discussed in the next chapter.

➤ Ch 12

Rational Approaches

In describing key *cognitive skills*, the Quality Assurance Agency (QAA, 2015, p 8) lists as second and third in its list of skills of particular relevance to business and management:

Problem solving and critical analysis: analysing facts and circumstances to determine the cause of a problem and identifying and selecting appropriate solutions', and 'Research: the ability to analyse and evaluate a range of business data, sources of information and appropriate methodologies . . . and to use that research for evidence-based decision-making

The ability to identify assumptions, to evaluate statements in terms of evidence, and to check the logic of an argument is crucial. Identifying assumptions, and questioning them, is central to the 'critical' approach described in Chapter 4: many of your assignments will be designed to test your ability to think critically.

Society quite reasonably places a high value on logic and rationality. Treating a faulty assumption as an unquestionable fact can prevent problems being solved, or generate 'solutions' that magnify the original problem. For example, a business school whose MBA applications were falling lowered its prices on the assumption that 'lower prices will increase demand', as the economists classical demand curve would suggest. While this assumption may be true in many cases, it is not a universal law. This particular MBA was already one of the cheapest available: indeed many people were applying elsewhere because they interpreted the already low price as meaning low quality. (An exclusive golf club might have encountered a similar effect if it lowered membership fees.)

Rationality is based on interpreting the world in terms of simple cause and effect – the underlying model is that the world runs as a well ordered machine. If rational thinking is widely valued, why do *irrational* approaches to problems abound? First, people are often less good at thinking rationally than they imagine. Second, the model itself may be faulty. This chapter is intended to make you better at being rational when this is appropriate, as well as more aware of the limitations of rationality, and of the benefits of not being rational all the time.

The classic approach to rational decision taking is straightforward:

- define the problem
- agree criteria for a solution
- generate possible solutions
- select best solution, according to the criteria decided
- implement solution.

Almost any manager would claim that this was how they operated. Yet, if you observe a group of people working on a problem you are likely to find a very different picture

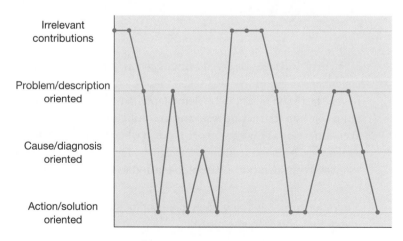

Figure 11.1 Kepner–Tregoe-type chart of discussion flow

emerging. In a classic work on the subject, Kepner and Tregoe (1965) graphically describe the irrational and unsystematic behaviour which they observed in discussions of organisational problems. The cost of some of the poor decisions which they observed as a consequence of this behaviour was enormous.

Managers tended not to follow an orderly sequence of steps such as that above. Instead, they jumped all over the place, leaping to solutions before establishing the nature of the problem. If they thought at all about reasons for the problem, they made *assumptions* about causes, rather than exploring them. As one fairly senior manager said recently: 'If only I could teach my managers that the correct sequence is "Ready, aim, fire". They shoot before they are even ready, never mind about taking aim.' Small wonder that many organisational decisions are the equivalent of shooting oneself in the foot. The following exercise should make you more aware of this point.

Activity 11.1

The next time you are discussing a case study or other complex quasi-problem, focus on the task contributions made by your colleagues and sort them into the following categories suggested by Kepner and Tregoe (1965):

- non-relevant information

- problem (what is wrong)

- cause (what made it wrong)

- action (what to do about it).

Plot the subject of discussion as time progresses using a chart similar to Figure 11.1. Even better, if you are in real problem-solving discussions and can afford to take a back seat for a while, observe the way the problem is addressed, using the same categories. If no such opportunities present themselves in the near future, get a group together to discuss a problem which all can relate to – anything from NHS underfunding to rowdy behaviour in the student union. The topic doesn't matter provided it is not too simple and is an issue of some concern to all members.

You may well have observed a discussion as 'jumpy' as that showing in Figure 11.1. I can remember a decision that was taken to sack a number of staff for non-performance, when the job they were meant to be doing (and had spent years learning to do) had been made impossible by a restructure resulting in conflicting objectives. Another time a decision was taken to develop a new version of a product when the problem with the old product was that demand had been reduced almost to zero by new technology. In each of these cases, lack of systematic consideration of the problem and its causes led to totally inappropriate action.

> **Iteration means looping back to an earlier stage in the problem-solving process as your thoughts become clearer.**

There is sometimes a good reason to 'iterate', that is, to make several loops through the stages of addressing a problem. (For example, as you start to understand aspects of the situation you may realise that your earlier diagnosis was faulty.) But many discussions are inadvertently unsystematic, rather than deliberately iterative. And you will almost certainly have observed inadequacies in understanding what the problem *is*, and subsequently, what caused it because of this unsystematic approach.

An analytical approach

➤ Ch 7

The rational approach to problem solving is supposed to be analytical as well as systematic. 'Analyse' is a term frequently used in assessment, and something you will frequently need to do as a manager. You will remember from the Chapter 7 helpfile that analysis was about examining something 'part by part'. In taking an analytical approach to problems you are trying to make sense of complexity by teasing out different elements in the situation. By looking at these separately and in combination you can advance your understanding of the problem.

Jumping straight to 'Action' is *not* an analytical approach. If you want to be analytical you need to put a lot of effort into exploring the problem in detail, looking for key elements and problem themes. Proper diagnosis is crucial. And you also need to separate out different causal strands. Few organisational problems have a clear and simple cause; it is much more common for a wide range of factors to be involved. Each of these factors may be fairly insignificant if taken alone, but in combination they produce something highly significant.

A good analysis will explore all these different factors and the different causal chains to which they contribute, drawing upon what you have learned about relevant concepts and relationships between them in your course. (A multiple cause diagram discussed later in the chapter is extremely useful for this.) This will normally be followed by a *synthesis*, which pulls this together into a coherent picture pointing the way forward. In the jumpy discussions described above, this analysis–synthesis sequence is clearly missing. When the essential first stage of understanding the problem situation is omitted, poor decisions and/or actions are almost inevitable.

Problem Definition: Description and Diagnosis

To become more effective at problem solving, then, you need to devote a large part of your energies to understanding the problem and its causes. You need somehow to resist the almost irresistible tendency to start suggesting solutions as soon as the first hint of a problem emerges. The more complicated the problem (and almost all problems involving people are complicated), the more important is the stage of problem definition. At the same time, the more difficult it will be. And all too often this difficulty will contribute to the tendency to skimp on problem definition.

> Unless you fully understand the problem, your 'solution' may make things worse.

Problem definition has two main constituents: description and diagnosis. You normally start with some unhappiness about a situation. Someone is 'hurting', or has judged that what *is* falls short of what *should be* (remember the control loop). Problem definition will depend on exploring both the 'is' and the 'should be' and the gap between them. This is the description stage. You then need to explore the reasons for this: this is the diagnostic stage. It is essential that these two parts of definition are addressed thoroughly before you go on to subsequent stages of deciding how to bridge the gap and actually taking the necessary action.

➤ Ch 2

Diagnosis, establishing the 'why', is important. If you do not understand why a problem has arisen and address only its symptoms, your 'solution' may well make things worse, not better. Medical examples make this clear. Taking aspirin because you have a headache may help, at least for a while. If you have a temperature, aspirin will bring it down. But both are possibly symptoms of something that is the real problem. Indeed, a raised temperature is probably part of your body's way of fighting an infection. To lower the temperature will make it harder to throw off the infection. Only if the temperature is high enough to be a problem in its own right does it make sense to take aspirin or paracetamol to reduce it. And if you think you have 'solved' a serious infection such as meningitis by taking aspirin and do not seek the urgent help that you need, the 'solution' has been downright dangerous. A doctor would look at other aspects of what is wrong with you. Do you have a stiff neck, hate looking at light and have a persistent rash? The doctor would also explore possible causes of the pattern of symptoms (hangover, contact with infected person, sunstroke, and so forth).

Description as a Basis for Diagnosis

There is clearly, therefore, a need to gather adequate information on which to base diagnosis during the prior stage of problem description. You should by now be aware of the importance of adequate description, but if you are working with a group of people who are less alert to this, you may need to 'educate' them. Ideally, discuss the importance of thorough diagnosis before you start to talk about the problem. If this is impossible, or if despite your efforts you think that discussion has moved on prematurely, say why you are uneasy and ask questions that will elicit more information.

In complex problem situations you are likely to need to include a great deal of 'soft' information. Facts and figures will be useful, but the feelings and beliefs that people have about a problem may be even more significant. Such problems are far better tackled by a group: discussion will allow these softer aspects to emerge. A carefully chosen group, representing a number of different perspectives on a problem and a range of expertise, can be a rich source of information about the nature of the problem. (If you are working alone, then you will probably need to arrange to talk to all these people individually, but this may be time consuming and it will be hard for you to elicit as much as would emerge in a good discussion.)

Descriptive diagrams

One way of checking that you have explored all the aspects of a problem is to try to represent these diagrammatically. For example, you might use mind maps (described in Chapter 4) as a tool. Suppose that customers are cancelling orders and complaining of both quality and delivery problems. The main branches of a diagram in this case might be cash, quality and delivery. You might then look for more detail to fill in twigs on each of these branches. What aspects of quality are they complaining about? Which stages in the manufacture–delivery chain are going wrong? Try also to explore what is *not* going wrong, as this information will be vital to you in ruling out some of the possible causes of the problem when you start your diagnosis.

Another useful way of exploring a problem is to use a technique called 'rich picturing', developed by Peter Checkland (1981). This is ideal for group exploration of a problem, as it allows you to build up a composite of the ideas of different group members about key aspects in the problem situation. A rich picture consists of all the elements that are seen as possible constituents of the *problématique* – the complex of factors which result in a problem for someone. To make it easier to grasp these at a glance, they are represented pictorially. Note that drawing skills are unimportant – the aim is to make the pictures 'talk', not to be artistic. As the relationships between factors are likely to be at least as important as the factors themselves, these relationships are shown too. Normally arrows or lines are used for this, with some symbol attached to show the nature of the relationship: £££ or $$$ signs are traditionally used for financial links, crossed swords for conflict, and so on. But it does not really matter what convention is adopted, as long as it is one that 'speaks' to all members of the group. Figure 11.2 shows an example of a rich picture exploring some of the pressures on academic staff. You might wish to draw a similar picture representing pressures on students.

Drawing such diagrams may seem eccentric at first, but if you try it a few times you will be surprised at how helpful it is and how it allows people to build a shared understanding of what is involved in the problem. If the cartoon aspect seems too bizarre, at least attempt a non-pictorial diagram showing key factors and the relationships between them. Such 'relationship diagrams', which use only words and lines rather than pictures, are less fun but they are still extremely useful at representing patterns of relationships which would be impossible to convey in mere prose. Figure 11.3 shows an example of a more restrained relationship diagram.

➤ Ch 4

Activity 11.2

Experiment with different ways of exploring a problem. This might be a problem presented in a case study or a real issue of concern to one or more of your group. (This exercise is best done in a group, but if this is impossible the exercise is still worth doing on your own.) First, simply use the list of diagnostic questions suggested in Box 11.1 as a basis for interrogating a situation. Add any other questions that seem to you to be appropriate. Then try writing down a problem summary using diagrams as an aid to representing the situation. Think about the effectiveness of each approach and, if possible, discuss this with others.

Box 11.1 Useful questions to ask about a problem situation

- What should be happening, when and where?
- What is happening (or not happening), when and where?
- Who thinks that this is a problem and why?
- What do other key people think about it?
- What related things are not problematic?
- What is the wider context within which all this is happening?
- Who or what can influence the problem situation?
- Who or what is influenced by it?
- What constraints are there in the situation that will restrict possible actions?

(A version of this is available on the website.)

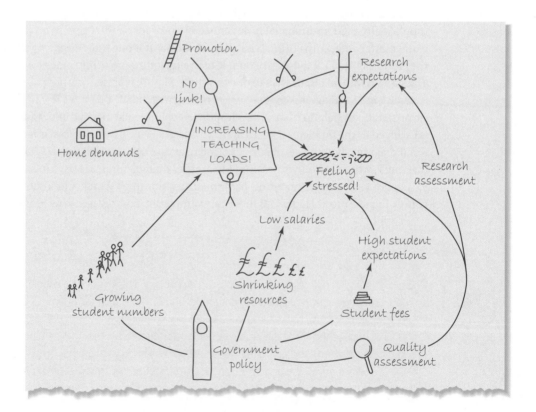

Figure 11.2 Rich picture exploring factors affecting pressure on teaching staff

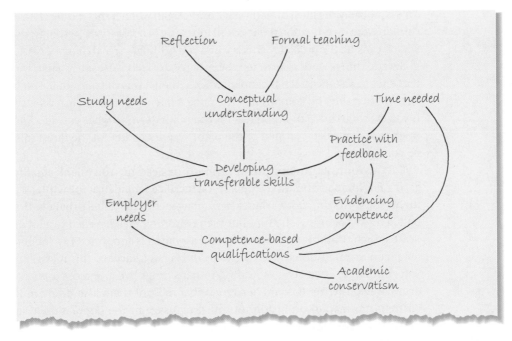

Figure 11.3 Relationship diagram showing factors relevant to developing transferable skills

It can be difficult to know when to stop exploring a problem and start thinking about the reasons underlying it. Clearly, it would be inappropriate to get locked into a never-ending search for perfect information. In real life, people seem to do what Simon (1960) called 'satisfice' – proceed on the basis of what is deemed 'enough' information rather than gather all the information it is possible to gather about all the complicated factors that might be of relevance, in pursuit of the optimal solution. What is enough will depend on the complexity of the situation, your understanding of the factors involved, the cost of obtaining further information and the cost of a poor decision. Expensive decisions are deserving of more investment in information gathering.

Sometimes you will discover that 'enough' is *not* enough. You initially thought that you had enough information and understood what was going on. But your work on a later stage, say exploration of causes, will raise questions that you cannot answer, perhaps because you are starting to look at the problem differently. This is when the iteration mentioned before becomes important and you attempt to seek what you now know you need, deliberately going back a stage and gathering more information about the situation.

Diagnosis – Exploring Causes

If you have managed to devote enough time to the first stage of problem solving to have explored all the relevant dimensions, and grasped the pattern of relationships and of 'symptoms' contained within it, you are in a position to start looking for possible causes.

This is probably the most difficult stage of all. Small wonder that, rather than doing the hard thinking and investigation required, all too many people assume, wrongly, that they 'know' what is causing the problem. This is when you get 'solutions' that make matters worse.

Several things work against us when we try to explore causality. First, we have a strong tendency to assume that if B happens *after* A, then A was the *cause* of B. *Post hoc ergo propter hoc* – presumably the Romans had the same tendency. It is often a good way of operating. If you eat something and then feel ill, you put it down to what you ate. And the shellfish might well have been tainted or the plant you discovered in the forest might have been poisonous.

But this form of thinking can be seriously misleading. You might, equally, have caught gastric flu from someone in the pub. If you sacrifice a maiden at the winter solstice, and the nights start growing shorter thereafter, it may seem reasonable to believe that the sacrifice halted the departure of the sun. But such reasoning may have led to a lot of unnecessary deaths. Such thinking is still common. If a woman is appointed to a job for the first time (or a man to a traditionally female role) and is not a success, this is attributed to gender. Soft drugs have been seen as leading to hard drugs because most users have taken soft drugs previously. Yet it could be argued that most of them also drank milk as children. Further information on history of soft drug usage in the population at large would be needed to make the case.

So while one important line of investigation will always be to explore what changes took place shortly before the problem started to emerge, this is not the only thing you need to know. Before assuming these changes were the cause, you need to understand the connection between the two. An argument can be made in the case of the drugs (assuming the difference is statistically significant – see Chapter 14). But if you really cannot see how the maiden's death influences the sun, you might be wary about this as a causal explanation.

➤ Ch 14

Another mistake we commonly make is to see *association* as proof of causation. If we are concerned about one thing and notice that another thing is always present at the same time, we may see the latter as the cause. Again, it may be. But again this is not necessarily the case, even if the relationship is statistically significant. Both might have a common cause (for example, a virus causing both spots and headache). Again, you need to work out what the cause really is.

A third fault is to assume that if you have found *a* possible cause you have found *the* cause. Students sometimes complain about a tutor and their tutorials or feedback on assignments. Clearly, a possible cause (and the one the students invariably cite) is incompetence on the part of the tutor. But it often turns out that the real cause for the student's dissatisfaction is that they are getting lower marks than they would like, or have unrealistic expectations about tutorials. You may find that the student has complained about every other tutor they have had.

Kepner and Tregoe (1965) describe another example of a likely cause not being *the* cause. This involved paper manufacturing, where softwood logs were chipped, chemically treated, boiled to a pulp then fed into a paper-making machine. One day, small pieces of wood started appearing in the finished paper. It was immediately assumed that the pulping machinery was defective and new equipment was bought at huge expense. Only one person questioned the 'obvious' explanation. He looked at the wood chips carefully, found that they were untreated hardwood, not softwood, and traced the problem to faults in a hardwood pipeline transporting the pulp.

In the above example, the experts were so sure that they 'knew' what could cause the problem that they did not trouble to look at the symptoms carefully. Once you are aware that *a* possible cause is not necessarily *the* cause you will put more effort into a thorough exploration of the problem situation, and resist accepting the 'obvious' view.

It is just as dangerous to assume that there is only *one* cause of a problem. All too often things go wrong only when a series of unlikely events come together. One part of a plant was shut down for maintenance, another had been badly repaired, the person who understood what needed to be done to adjust a regulator was off sick, someone less qualified adjusted it wrongly and suddenly there was an explosion. Even if we correctly identify one of the causes of a problem and do something about that, similar problems may occur if other contributory factors are not addressed.

Diagnostic diagrams

To overcome these tendencies to an overly narrow approach to diagnosis, diagrams are again useful. One form which is commonly used in quality analysis is the Ishikawa 'fishbone' diagram. This is closely related to a mind map, but tidier. Because the writing is aligned with the normal print on a page, it is easier to read. Because it looks neat, it can look impressive in a report, even if the audience is not very familiar with diagramming as a form of communication.

Fishbone diagrams aim to tease out all the possible sources of problems to enable you to identify those which are actually problematic. Again, you look for main areas and represent these as the main branches or 'bones', and, for each of these, try to identify possible sources of problems. Figure 11.4 gives an example.

Fishbone diagrams are a major tool in quality analysis, with 'bones' representing the stages in a process. They provide a systematic way of exploring all logically possible areas where things might be going wrong. In the manufacturing situations for which they were designed, or situations where the problem occurs within a clear process, they can be invaluable. Many of the situations you will encounter, however, whether in case studies or in real life, will be less obviously structured. The rich picture you drew as your first attempt at describing the situation may show a huge range of different sorts of potential factors and relationships between them.

In such cases, it can be helpful to focus on the *pattern* of causative factors: this is an instant antidote to over-simple views of causation. Fishbone diagrams look at what *might* go wrong. Multiple cause diagrams (similar to that used in Figure 7.1) look at all the relevant things that *actually happened*. They are quite difficult to draw because you start at the end, the problem situation that interests you. Most people have a tendency to start at the beginning so need to work to avoid this. Instead, the aim is to work back in time, looking at all the things that contributed to the situation. 'Multiple contributory factor diagram' might be a better title, if less catchy. In drawing them you need to fight against two temptations: to start at the beginning, and to exclude things that don't cause something, merely contribute to it. Succumbing to either of these will stop you from developing a clear understanding of the whole pattern.

➤ Ch 7

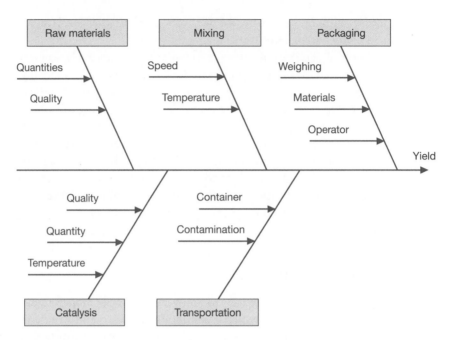

Figure 11.4 Ishikawa-type 'fishbone' diagram used in quality analysis

Suppose you wanted to work out why you were doing badly on a course. You would write this – 'Doing badly on X' – at the bottom of a piece of paper and put a ring about it. This is the 'event' whose causation you are exploring. You would then ask yourself: 'What is causing this?' Suppose you thought that it was because you hate the subject, fall asleep in lectures, haven't read the set book and haven't submitted the last two essays. At this stage you would add these to your diagram, so that it looked like Figure 11.5(a).

You would then ask *why* each of these contributory causes was happening. Perhaps the lectures are at 9 am, and the evening before you always go out to the pub until late. Furthermore, the lecturer is incredibly boring and you can't see what he is writing on the board. This is because you are sitting at the back. Why? Because you came in late. Eventually you might end up with a diagram like Figure 11.5(b). This is a fairly trivial example, chosen merely to show the process of working back in time, asking questions about why things happen. Even in this case, you can see that such a diagram could help you to think much more carefully about causes of a problem because it imposes a discipline on your thoughts and makes you ask questions that might be difficult to answer. Without such a discipline, difficult questions tend to remain unasked.

You may sometimes find that, rather than single, discrete 'chains' of causation, some factors may have several 'effects' which are causes in different chains. In this case you will find a diagram more like Figure 11.6 emerging. But note that you still have a single end point. Other 'effects' not on the causal chain for the end event are omitted in the interests of clarity. You may sometimes want to explore the likely effects of a proposed change and in this case a multiple *effect* diagram, starting with the change and looking *forwards*, can be useful. But do not mix the two – diagrams depend on simplicity and clarity for their usefulness, and mixing conventions and trying to do too much with one diagram will work against this.

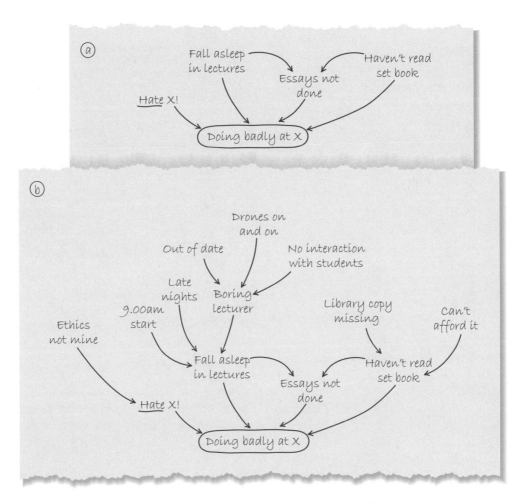

Figure 11.5 Construction of a multiple cause diagram (a) starting (b) later in the process

Activity 11.3

Think of a problem you are currently facing (or take the next one you encounter). Draw a multiple cause diagram and reflect on the extent to which it helps broaden your understanding. If the problem suits a fishbone approach, then do one of these *before* the multiple cause. Set the diagram aside for a day and then use the guidelines below to check it. If working in a group, have someone else 'read' the diagram back to you to see whether it communicates what you intended. Ask them to perform the checks too. They may be more alert to your shortcomings than you are and therefore a better source of feedback.

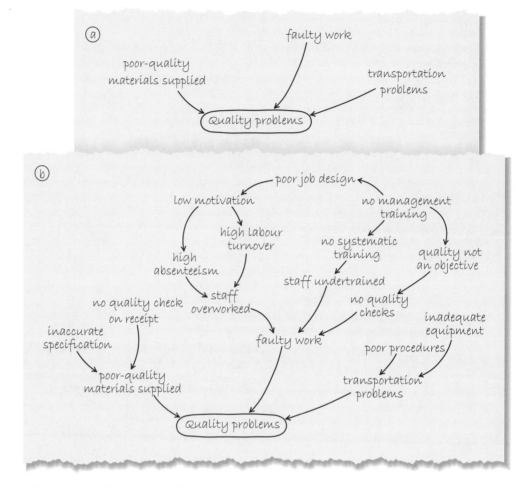

Figure 11.6 Multiple cause diagram showing factors leading to quality problems in an organisation

If you are working in a group, and each of you has a slightly different perspective on a problem and different information, working on a multiple cause diagram together can be useful in the same ways as a communal rich picture and can be a useful next step. But you will find it just as useful if you are working alone on any non-trivial problem where an understanding of causes is important.

Guidelines for drawing a multiple cause diagram

- Start at the end (a giveaway if you did not start here is that you will probably have a single causal chain rather than something that looks like a tangled tree with lots of things at the top of the page).

- Each of your arrows should read as 'a happening contributes to b happening' if you have shown a ➔ b. (Note that it is very easy to reverse arrows inadvertently so that you are showing causes at the arrowhead end, not effects. Beware of this!)
- Each set of arrows should represent all the contributory factors which together 'cause' the event to which they point.
- Your 'causes' should be events not things (machines don't cause problems, but changes in them may do).

(A web version is available for portability.)

There is a logical difference between multiple cause and fishbone diagrams. Fishbones were originally designed to explore *possible* causes of problems, whereas multiple cause diagrams were intended to explore *actual* causes. But this distinction is a fairly fine one, and because fishbone diagrams are much neater, there is a tendency now to draw multiple cause diagrams in the form of a fishbone. However, this 'tidiness' can make it harder to show where one factor is influencing several causal chains, and may limit your thinking.

Diagrams are intended as an aid to thinking, not a straitjacket. If you are drawing a hybrid 'multiple fish' do try to remember that the main conceptual benefit of a true multiple cause is that it pushes your thinking back through successive 'layers' of causality. Retain this thought process even if you alter the diagram form.

Models and causality

In drawing diagrams as suggested, you were producing models representing particular aspects of 'reality'. But in constructing these models you are using other models. In attributing causes, you will be drawing on a much wider range of frameworks of assumptions, many of them unconscious. Thus in the politically incorrect example of blaming poor performance on gender of employee, there was an underlying '(wo)men are no good at this' assumption. This was presumably part of a wider set of assumptions constituting a model, or internal representation, of how (wo)men behave.

McGregor (1957) identified one set of assumptions about employee motivation which seemed to be commonly held by managers. He called this 'Theory X'. It consists of the assumptions that people are basically lazy, passive, without ambition, disliking responsibility and resistant to change. Such a model would lead you to attribute causes of poor performance to failure of control and direction by the manager and to investigate whether rewards and punishments needed to be manipulated. Contrast this with the rather more complex expectancy theory introduced in Chapter 2 and the sorts of explanations which this would lead you to seek for a problem. (McGregor contrasted it with 'Theory Y' – the assumption that people will assume responsibility, and be motivated towards organisational goals, provided that management arranges the situation so that people can achieve their own goals best by directing their efforts towards organisational objectives – a theory directly congruent with expectancy theory.)

➤ **Ch 2**

Models are not reality

If your underlying models do not match key aspects of reality, they may be a barrier to understanding, or even create a situation you do not want. Managers with a 'Theory X' view of their staff will treat them in a way that will lead them to behave irresponsibly. On the other hand, theories that highlight important factors and relationships may be very helpful. A while back my car developed a rather frightening electrical fault. Unpredictably – and this might not happen for weeks at a time – using one electrical circuit would cause all the other electrics to fail. Switching on the radio, or even using the brake, would leave me without lights or gauges. After a while, things would function again, but for several days would cut out intermittently. Then for a while the problem would go away.

Three garages failed to diagnose the problem, despite hours spent (at my expense) trying to make it happen so they could 'see what was wrong', i.e. fiddle with the wiring until things came on again. They seemed to have a very simple mental model of my car's wiring as a lot of connections between parts, and all cases of electrical faults were because of a loose connection somewhere. They didn't want to listen to my description of what seemed a fairly bizarre but informative set of symptoms, or my suggestion that they focus on parts of the electrics which were common to all the things which went wrong. Fortunately, at the fourth garage there was a mechanic using a more complex underlying model, to which my description of symptoms was relevant. He quickly ruled out most of the wiring as a possible cause, looked at the earthing point (common to all circuits) and found that it was corroded.

Models that are a good *partial* fit can be really dangerous: their success leads you to equate the model with reality. You then expect the world to be like the model in *all* respects. When there is a mismatch your predictions may lead you to wrong decisions. One good way of making sure that you remember that a model is *not* reality is to work with several different models at any one time.

This helps if you are *consciously* using models. But many models are unconscious. The mechanics who wanted to twiddle my wires were not aware that they were using a mental model of my electrics. McGregor's managers were not aware of their Theory X or Y of motivation. The problem with unconscious models is that we never work at improving them. We do not use the Kolb cycle to refine them. Such unconscious models will act as hindrance rather than help in situations where they are inappropriate. It is important, therefore, to try to become more aware of the sets of assumptions that we are using. One excellent way is by exploring differences of opinion. Often something will be 'obvious' to you, yet 'obviously' something quite different to someone else because you are working with different sets of assumptions. Only by becoming aware of the difference do you become aware of your own assumptions. This is why groups which work well can achieve far more than individuals. It is why mixed groups can be better than homogeneous ones. And it is why it is so important to manage group process, and to ensure that conflict is explored rather than avoided or allowed to escalate to destructive emotional levels.

> **Discover your assumptions by:**
> - working with people who see things differently
> - exploring disagreements to identify reasons
> - looking at each other's diagrams.

➤ **Ch 3**

It is also one of the reasons why diagramming is important. It is possible, despite your talking and listening skills, to misinterpret what someone says because of the slightly different meanings you may attribute to things and the different importance you give them. Also, confusions are often quite hard to spot if you are talking about something complex. Diagrams are much less ambiguous, particularly if you follow a convention and use words and symbols in a particular and agreed way. The convention for multiple causes as described above requires you to use words for events or changes and arrows to point from contributory factors to the events which they help to bring about. If you draw such a diagram using this convention and then show it to someone else who is also familiar with the convention, you may be surprised at the sorts of questions that they ask you when they start to 'read' the diagram. Such questions can lead you into areas where your assumptions and underlying models differ, provided that you think carefully about what is prompting the question.

You will almost certainly work with case studies during your course (see next section). One reason for this is that case discussion will make you more aware of your unconscious models. Your capacity to understand the problem situations that you will encounter at work will be greatly improved if you reduce the extent to which unconscious models are limiting your thinking or leading you to make inappropriate assumptions about causality. Case work will encourage you consciously to use the models that you have been taught as part of your course. Using these models you will be able to suggest possible causes for the symptoms described in the case.

But beware of the limitations of pure rationality. Mitroff and Linstone (1993) similarly see a real danger in believing in your models – conscious or unconscious. They call this 'model myopia' and suggest a number of things you can do to reduce this tendency which you may find useful:

- Seek the obvious, but do everything you can to challenge and even ridicule it.

- Question all constraints, the greatest of which is likely to be the mindset of the problem solvers.

- Challenge every assumption – what seems self-evident to some may be less so to others.

- Question the problem scope – what is omitted from the problem statement may be more significant than what is included.

- Ask whether you need to 'solve', 'resolve' or 'dissolve' the problem – a solution is once and for all (and usually elusive); a resolution is good enough for now; and a dissolution is a realisation that the real problem is rather different.

- Question logic itself – it is possible to be logical and wrong. Logical solutions to complex problems should always be challenged.

Making Diagrams Work for You

To get full value from diagrams you first need to be clear about your purpose – drawing a diagram as a way of developing your own thoughts about a situation is somewhat different from drawing a group diagram as a way of developing shared understanding, and very different from drawing a diagram to communicate the results of that thinking to others. The one common factor is that symbols need to be used consistently and the 'code' used needs to be understood by the person or people looking at the diagram

Diagramming to help you think more clearly

While you are developing your thoughts, especially if you are doing this by yourself, it helps to be as 'free' with your drawing as possible. Scribbling on lots of (big) pieces of scrap paper is one good way, arranging smaller pieces of paper around the floor is another, Post-its stuck to a fridge will work, or if you have it, a whiteboard and dry wipe pens. Or you may prefer to use a drawing programme. This allows you to store the result electronically (though it is easy to use a phone camera for this) and can remove the (totally unnecessary) fears some have about their drawing ability. The downside is that screens are usually small, and your drawing software may constrain what you produce. (Presentation

➤ Ch 10

software can offer useful flexibility here).

Perhaps the most important point is to avoid seeing your diagram as a 'product' and worrying about what it looks like. When you are using diagrams as a thinking tool they are better seen as a temporary representation of your thoughts. This helps you work out what you *are* thinking, and see its strengths, weaknesses and confusions. This is why you need an agreed 'code' even for your own use. The effort of forcing your thoughts into the symbols you have decided to use – which might be as simple as the words and arrows of a multiple cause diagram – will help you be clearer about what you are thinking, as well as make it easy for you to 'read' the diagram and check whether the model you have created makes sense and fits the situation. A 'good' diagram for your own purpose is one which you almost instantly discard because it has made you realise there is a better way of seeing things.

Diagramming with others

When you are working in a group to explore a situation such as a case study similar considerations apply, only now everyone needs to be using the same 'code'. You will also need the interpersonal skills described earlier in order for the diagram drawing to help rather than hinder the process. Some people are really worried about their lack of artistic ability, for example, so may not join in freely. You need to encourage and appreciate such people just as you would shy members of a discussion group. Agreeing your objectives at the start is as important as with any task group – for the diagramming exercise this might be seen as being to explore everyone's view of the problem situation. Ensuring that you seek to understand rather than criticise others' contributions is equally important. The playfulness of rich pictures can be a real asset in fostering a creative approach. Again, the aim is to see each diagram not as a 'final product', but as a step on the way to producing a better diagram by causing you to ask questions about what the diagram means, and whether it hangs together, and what further questions it suggests you need to answer.

Diagramming *for* others

Once you have clarified your view of a situation a diagram can be a useful way of communicating this view to others. Here the requirements are rather different. You are aiming to produce something that will convey important points to your reader(s) that text alone could not convey as well.

Think back to the communication model discussed earlier. This suggested that it was important to think about the 'receiver' and how they would decode your message. If the message is in a diagram you need to think about how to cut out 'noise' that unnecessary features might introduce. You also need to communicate clearly what the diagram is about (in the title), and make clear the code you are using (partly by saying in the title what type of diagram it is and partly by including a key to any symbols used). You also need to spell out the key messages of the diagram in the surrounding text, rather than leaving the reader to work them out.

When communicating with others, whether in a report or a presentation, you may be seeking to do more than merely communicate your argument. It may also be important to create a good impression. This is where the advantages of more sophisticated diagramming processes may be particularly noticeable.

Guidelines for good diagrams

Although you have met diagrams earlier in the book, this chapter has introduced you to some new ones and to the most important uses you are likely to make of them: as a tool for clarifying thinking about problem situations, whether alone or in a group, and to communicate the results of such thoughts to others, often in a written report or an oral presentation. The following general diagramming guidelines apply to all three purposes, and to hand or computer drawn diagrams, though some will be more important in some contexts than others. They also serve as a useful summary of the points made.

General diagramming guidelines

- **Give yourself space.** Working diagrams should always be spaced out as much as possible. If hand drawing, take large sheets of paper and use the whole sheet. Space will allow easy addition and modification and will make your result much clearer. When using diagrams for communication, you should also avoid cramped diagrams. Adequate space will aid clarity and create a more professional impression.

- **Don't mix diagram types.** It may seem difficult to keep within a single diagramming convention when lots of different aspects of a situation seem important. But a convention helps your reader understand a diagram. And the structure of a convention helps you clarify your thoughts by focusing you on one aspect. So avoid showing 'things' on a dynamic diagram like a multiple cause – save these for a relationship diagram. If you want to show two different aspects, use two diagrams.

- **Seek clarity, not art.** Wanting your diagrams to be artistic rather than merely clear may inhibit you in your use of diagrams and distort your thinking – symmetry may be preferred to usefulness/congruence with features in the situation.

- **Keep diagrams simple.** For the majority of diagrams you are likely to use, it is the pattern that will be of interest and the ability to represent at least one aspect of a whole situation and communicate it. A diagram which is cluttered will hide any pattern and communicate very little. So get complex only if it is essential and, even then, start with a simple diagram and build up to a more complex one.

- **Give every diagram a title.** Always give a title to a diagram, saying what type of diagram it is and what it represents. If you are using symbols whose meaning is not clear from the convention, include a key to explain them.

- **Play with diagrams.** Be prepared to throw your diagrams away. Experiment with different versions of diagrams and different diagram types to develop your thinking about a situation. Remember, diagrams are models and their full value emerges only when you play with them. This will only work if you are prepared to see each model as a hypothesis and cheerfully discard those which are not helpful. This is another reason for not valuing art – if it is too beautiful it is harder to bin it.

(A web version is available for convenience.)

TECHSkills 11.1 Using diagramming software

If you have taken part in an online classroom session you may already have used a form of diagramming software to enable you to draw on a whiteboard. However, this may have merely enabled you to draw freehand and add text. Spreadsheets such as Excel allow you to create charts from numbers, another form of diagram, useful for conveying numerical information in a report or presentation. If you are working with Microsoft Office you will have a 'Paint' programme available. PowerPoint or other presentation software will also offer you a form of drawing programme. You may already be using one or other of these.

➤ Chs 5, 9

Basic drawing programmes such as these normally offer you a range of shapes and lines or arrows to join them, the ability to include text in the shapes, and the ability to arrange – and rearrange – the shapes and connectors on the page. You will be able to choose colours for text, shapes and backgrounds to improve the clarity and impact of your diagram.

If you have not used any form of diagramming software, then playing with what you already have is a good way to start.

If you want to use a wider range of templates than are offered by the software you already have (for example, to create fishbone diagrams) then explore the many free versions of diagramming software you can access online. Such programmes may have more intelligent ways of re-arranging connecting lines when you move items around so that they do not get tangled up,

Since anything written about software has a habit of dating quickly, you are advised to do some research for yourself to select what is best of what is currently available. Free software differs in both sophistication and ease of use. To begin with you will probably find ease of use a key consideration. A lot of software is designed to make a beautiful output – this may not suit your need for flexibility when using diagrams as a thinking tool, or clarity when using them for communication. Another variation is whether you download the software and draw on your own device, or use online software and save the resulting diagram to your laptop or a cloud.

If you want to draw diagrams with others, rather than merely showing them your diagram for comment, then you will either need to use a system provided by your university to achieve this, or choose an online system that allows collaborative drawing. (For example, Draw.io has a version that allows this.) Another thing to check before deciding is the quality of online tutorials available for the software.

Becoming proficient in producing diagrams for reports and presentations, and for shared exploration of a problem is a valuable skill. You might choose to use it as the basis of a portfolio exhibit in managing your own learning.

Activity 11.4

Decide on what you would like to be able to do using diagramming software, and what factors are important to you.

Search for diagramming software online, and spend half an hour or so selecting two or three products that look promising.

Look for any evaluations of your chosen products to check that they seem to meet your criteria.

Search for online tutorials on these products and look at one or two for each.

Choose one product, and devote an hour or two to learning how to create the sorts of diagrams you are most likely to need.

Reflect, if possible with others who have done the same activity, on your learning from the exercise, and plan any further learning activities that might develop your search, learning, or diagramming skills further, noting both reflection and plans in your learning journal.

Case Study Analysis

Case studies allow you to apply your problem-solving skills to a complex problem situation. They have been a popular teaching device since Harvard pioneered the method in its Law School in 1869 and went on to use it for its MBA teaching. They are particularly popular in business studies or other vocational courses. This is because they help to bridge the gap between course ideas and the work situations in which you will eventually apply them.

11

COMPLEXITY, CASES AND DIAGRAMS

A case normally consists of a written description of a situation faced by, or within, an organisation. It may be a brief outline of a scenario, or 100 or more pages of closely written description, supplemented by company accounts, sales figures and other information of possible relevance to the situation. Usually such cases are based on real-life situations encountered by the case author. In writing the case the author will, however, have simplified the situation or been selective in what was described. Sometimes shorter cases are fictional, but even so they will normally make valid points about organisations.

Advantages of using case studies

Working on a case, particularly in a small group, will exercise most of the skills you have developed thus far, and indeed some of those covered in chapters yet to come.

Case study work therefore presents a rich learning opportunity, where you learn from both the case itself and the process of working on it. Cases can:

> **Case studies:**
>
> - are interesting
> - introduce 'real' situations
> - allow application of concepts and techniques
> - give practice in handling complexity
> - help make you aware of your assumptions
> - develop team and communication skills.

- broaden your awareness of organisational situations – particularly valuable if you have little or no experience of organisational life – and give you a chance of looking at things from the perspective of the organisation as a whole
- give you something on which to practise using the concepts you have been taught as a basis for analysis in order to make sense of fairly complex situations (albeit less complex than those you will meet in real life)
- provide a useful basis for assessment – analysis of a case, although necessarily simplistic, will still be a more useful indication of your understanding of the way in which ideas can be used, and of your analytical skills in the face of complexity, than can many more conventional 'short question' types of assessment
- develop group-working skills – case study analysis is often done in small groups
- highlight tacit assumptions about organisations – in discussing cases with others you may find that you disagree: exploring this difficulty will often show that you have different underlying assumptions about people and the way they should (or do) think and behave.

Disadvantages of using cases

The benefits listed above are considerable. But if you are to learn effectively from case studies, you need to be aware that they have limitations. The first is that any case presents a partial picture. It has been 'filtered' by the author. Some things have been omitted. Others may have been given an emphasis that not all those concerned would agree with. Apart from any conscious selectivity by the author, the information on which the selection was based may have been inadequate or biased. Few interviewees, for example, will admit to their part in something which went wrong or volunteer information which shows them in a bad light. The slants and omissions may be particularly problematic if the author wrote the case for one purpose and you are being asked to use it for another.

You therefore need to remember all the time that case studies inevitably present a false impression of being 'real'. They are very much creations and as such should be treated with caution. Any conclusions which you draw about 'the world' based on such case studies should be regarded as provisional, to be confirmed by other sources before you trust them. (This caution does not, of course, apply to the analytical, interpersonal and presentational skills which you practise in the course of your work on the case.)

It is worth pointing out that similar cautions apply to computer-based 'business games', which are a sort of interactive case study. Here the outcomes of any decisions you might take will reflect the particular model of organisational functioning espoused by the game's author and built into the computer model. Although many of these authors are experienced managers, and familiar with the theories you are being taught, this is not always the case. Thus although what you learn from the process of taking part will be valid, what you learn from the results of your decisions may not be.

Approaching case study analysis

Many students find being given a case to work on a daunting experience, sometimes so daunting that they fail to learn as much from the process as they might. Difficulties include deciding what exactly you are meant to be doing, getting the group to work together effectively, coping with time pressures, sorting out a mass of information and structuring it in some way that makes sense. It may also be difficult to draw conclusions from the information and to communicate these via a written report or oral presentation. Coping with, and learning from, the experience of realising that other groups have done better than you is a further challenge. Practically all the skills covered thus far will help you work on cases, and group work on case studies will itself develop those skills further. What has already been covered implies a sensible way of approaching case studies. You need to go through the following stages.

> **For effective case analysis:**
>
> - clarify and agree objectives
> - manage the process to:
>   – encourage contributions
>   – sustain motivation
> - use course concepts to aid analysis
> - manage the task by:
>   – apportioning work
>   – coordinating effort
>   – monitoring progress.

Clarifying objectives

Case studies are often presented on a 'here it is – get on with it' basis. The first time you encounter a case presented in this way you may feel totally bemused by the increased responsibility for your own learning. If your tutor has told you little about why you are studying the case, or what you are meant to achieve, you may not know where to start.

When this happens, groups often talk for a long time without really feeling they are getting anywhere. To avoid lengthy and unfocused discussion, you need to be sure that everyone in the group agrees on the objective of the exercise. If it becomes clear that you cannot agree, or that you are all similarly confused, seek help from your tutor. Without clear and agreed objectives you are likely to learn nothing (except the impossibility of getting anywhere without clear and agreed objectives). You need to know what sort of output is required, and when it is required. If you are acting in the role of consultants, you need to know who (within the case study) is your notional client.

Working as a group

➤ Ch 9

If the group is newly formed for the purpose of the case, you can expect to go through the stages of group formation described in Chapter 9. Groups working on case studies under pressure will experience many aspects of group behaviour, so it would help to re-read that chapter before you first tackle group-based case work. If the group is to be effective, you will need to ensure that the group *process* is managed so that everyone feels they can contribute and they remain fully committed to the task. In particular, disagreements need to be treated as valuable and their roots explored as a potential source of useful insights into the scenario. If treated otherwise, this potential benefit will be lost, and disagreements may seriously detract from the motivation of group members. At worst, the group will disintegrate.

The group *task* will also need to be managed so that members make a maximal contribution. Some of the information searching and sorting may need to be split between subgroups to save time. The efforts of such subgroups will need to be coordinated. Time management will be a constant problem and there will probably be a need for frequent reviews of progress and adjusting ways of working in the light of this. Where different group members have different skills, the group may want to split responsibilities in a way that exploits their strengths.

Analysing a complex situation

Case studies typically provide you with an overabundance of 'information'. Not all of this will be relevant or capable of reducing your uncertainty about what you want to know. Thus case studies give you a chance to practise turning data into information. (You will

➤ Chs 13, 14

therefore need the skills addressed in Chapters 13 and 14 if the case is at all complex.)

First, however, you will want to use the approach described earlier in this chapter to impose some sort of structure on the complexity, so that you can determine what constitutes relevance. The guidelines below will help.

Communicating results

➤ Ch 10

You may well be asked to make a presentation on the results of your analysis. Re-read Chapter 10 for guidelines on this. Remember to think about your audience's perspective and starting point, to clarify what it is necessary to communicate and then do this in as straightforward a way as possible, using visual aids to reinforce your message. Remember the time you are allowed for presentation and keep within this to allow for questions. It is very easy to overestimate what you can say in a particular time.

If results are to be communicated in the form of a written report, then re-read Chapter 6. Exactly the same communication principles apply as in a spoken presentation. You need to have clear in your own mind what you aim to communicate and the perspective of those with whom you are communicating. You need clarity in the way in which you write and to use diagrams and tables to support your writing. This is easy to say but far from easy to do until you have had a lot of practice.

➤ Ch 6

Guidelines for case analysis

- Explore the problem situation, using diagrams such as multiple cause and rich pictures to make sure that the whole group agrees on the 'symptoms' of a problem and on the possible features of the situation relevant to this.

- Based on your understanding of the problem situation, define the problem facing the organisation or protagonist in the case study, probably using course ideas as a framework for diagnosing the underlying causes of the symptoms presented in the case.

- Decide on criteria for a 'solution', or at least for action to improve the situation. Here you will need to relate back to the client or protagonist, and their objectives and constraints as described in the case or provided by your tutor.

➤ Ch 12

- Generate alternatives for action. Here you will often find it useful to try some of the creativity techniques you will meet in Chapter 12, although sometimes, once you have diagnosed the underlying problem correctly, the type of action needed will become fairly obvious.

- Evaluate options by exploring what it would take to implement them, the effects they would be likely to have, and checking how well they score against your criteria for a solution.

- Design an implementation strategy (if this is part of your brief) which will meet the needs of the client/protagonist, which will be feasible in cost and other terms and which will be acceptable to other stakeholders in the situation.

(A case is available on the website for practice.)

Exploiting learning opportunities

You can see from the above that you will need to use almost all your transferable skills to do a good group analysis of a case study. Similarly, the situation allows you a chance to develop these skills, provided that the necessary conditions for learning, namely feedback and reflection, are present. It is worth gaining your group's agreement to a secondary set of objectives, those concerning learning, and to a way of progressing these. You will also need to be open to receiving feedback from others in the group or the class as a whole and from your tutor. And you need to think about how you can give feedback to others in a way that will help them to learn.

11

COMPLEXITY, CASES AND DIAGRAMS

For group skills, you will find it helpful to supplement your personal reflection on the effectiveness of the way you and others are working with periods of group reflection and discussion.

➤ **Ch 9**   Use the list of group behaviours in Chapter 9 and the questions in Box 11.2 to aid your reflection.

Box 11.2 Questions to aid group reflection on process

- How well do people feel the group process is working?
- What behaviours are contributing to aspects that are going well?
- Does anyone feel they are not contributing as much as they would like?
- If yes, what is making contribution difficult for them?
- Is anyone beginning to feel reduced commitment to the task?
- If yes, can they pinpoint the start of this feeling, and the reasons?
- What is sustaining this feeling?
- Has there been any conflict?
- If yes, what was the source of this (e.g. different values or assumptions)?
- How has any conflict been handled?
- Is anyone talking more than their fair share?
- If yes, why do they think they are doing this?
- How do others feel about this?
- What things could the group do differently to improve process in future?

(A web version is available to allow use after each session.)

These process-reflection periods can also be used to take stock of how the task is progressing. Are you managing time effectively? Is everyone happy with the way work is allocated and the methods you are adopting? If things are not going well, *why* are they not going well? Your tutor may be able to help here if you cannot work out the answers within the group. Ask for assistance on this if you need it.

It is important to take advantage of feedback opportunities such as the above *during* your work on the case. It is easier to learn from the experience while the process and management issues are live than when the detail has been forgotten. It is equally important to take advantage of feedback when you present your results. All too often the competitive nature of presentations by a group to the class as a whole means that 'winning' or justifying 'losing' takes precedence over learning.

If you feel that your group has done well in some way – perhaps because those presenting on behalf of the group are good at this – there is a strong tendency to sit back and congratulate yourselves on your success. You may talk about the shortcomings of less successful groups. While it is great to celebrate when things have gone well, you still need to identify the particular aspects that contributed – *why* were you successful? And harder, you still need to think about those aspects where there was room for improvement, and why. Maybe it was a brilliant presentation, but actually your analysis failed to identify one or two key points that other groups addressed. Why was your analysis not so rigorous? It is much easier to feel smug than to admit to areas of improvement, yet you will learn far less if you do not explore these slightly less comfortable aspects.

If you feel that you have done really badly, there is an even stronger tendency to avoid constructive reflection on your performance. You may scapegoat a group member for having done a bad job presenting or having been disruptive in the group. You may blame the tutor for not having briefed you well enough or helped you out when you were having problems. Or you may cling on to the belief that your work was excellent even if others did not recognise this. But unless you accept that things could have been done better, you will fail to learn anything from the experience. Nor will you be developing the transferable skills that will serve you well when you start to work.

➤ **Ch 9**

> **Failure is a great learning opportunity.**

It is important therefore to see failure as the richest learning opportunity of all. Mine it for all the lessons it offers with respect to both group processes and the task on which the group was engaged. Learning from doing badly is one of the most useful skills you can develop. Most organisations will tolerate your making a mistake – provided you make it only once! Indeed, they may feel if you never make mistakes you are not trying hard enough.

Absolutely the worst sort of colleague is someone who never admits to being wrong. I once had someone working for me who made many mistakes. He put a huge amount of effort into covering them up – far more effort than it would have taken either to put them right or to learn to do things properly. Worse, because he was always telling me that things were going well and even fabricating evidence to that effect, I could not take action to avert disaster. He was never going to learn because he was not open to recognising that there needed to be a change. And as his manager, responsible for the overall job, I was close to a nervous breakdown by the time he was replaced.

Activity 11.5

Start a section of your file for case study learning and develop the habit of writing a 'lessons learned' entry for your file after every case you work on. Even if the group does not want to evaluate what happened, you should reflect carefully on your own experience to make sure that you gain what you can from it. Link this to your initial SWOT and any action plans you have made for improving your team-working skills. If preparing an exhibit of your team skills then your reflections and the output of your work – written report, presentation notes or other supporting evidence – can be used to help show that you have the skills in question.

Case-based assignments

➤ Ch 8

Although a major use of cases is for group discussion, you may also find cases used as the basis for individual written assignments. If so, you need to draw on both the assessment guidelines in Chapter 8 and the suggestions for group case discussion given earlier. The guidelines below are suggested for cases where there is evidence of a problem and you are asked to analyse the situation and make recommendations.

Guidelines for case-based assignments

- Read the question carefully, identifying all the elements in what it is you are being asked to do.
- Scan the case with the question in mind, highlighting relevant issues or information.
- Note down as many potentially relevant course concepts as you can – aim for as long a list as possible at this stage.
- Read the case again more carefully, concepts in mind, trying to identify the evidence for a problem.
- Draft a brief description of key features in the problem situation – it may help to include a relationship diagram or rich picture. Aim to make clear the evidence for the problem and its significance (cost, potential for future disaster, and so on). Use course ideas in the description where appropriate (e.g. declining market share, high labour turnover).
- Clarify key contextual factors – the relevant factors within and outside the organisation that may contribute to or constrain the situation.
- Diagnose causes of problems using course concepts and diagrams to help you understand how the problem situation arose and what is sustaining it. Be alert to interrelationships between factors – how policy relates to strategy (e.g. How does reward structure relate to required behaviour? How does the marketing mix relate to changing factors in the competitive environment?).
- Draft your analysis of the situation.
- Go back to the brief and contextual factors to work out criteria and constraints for a solution (e.g. time, cost).
- Draw on course concepts to compile a range of options for improving the situation (e.g. redesigning the reward structure, moving to using distributors for your product).
- Evaluate the options against your criteria.
- Draft recommendations.
- Draft introduction.
- Redraft whole assignment in appropriate format, checking for logic, and clear arguments from evidence through diagnosis/analysis to recommendations. Check, too, that you have answered all parts of the question.
- List references used.
- Use spell check and grammar check.

SUMMARY

This chapter has argued the following:

- A systematic approach is needed for complex problems.
- Before solutions can be considered, you need to give due attention to understanding the problem and then exploring causes.
- Diagrams, particularly relationship diagrams and rich pictures, can help you to explore important factors in a problem situation and the relationships between them.
- Complicated problems tend to have complex patterns of causation.
- In attributing causes you will be using both conscious and unconscious models – it may help to become more aware of those which are unconscious, and you need to question these **and** models used consciously
- Diagrams can help you to think more clearly about a situation and make any confusion or assumptions more clearly apparent to others, provided that you adopt good diagramming practice.
- Rough hand drawn diagrams work best as a 'thinking tool' but releant software can help you produce clear and professional looking diagrams for reports or presentations.
- Case studies are a vehicle for practising the analysis of complex problem situations (as well as for practising most of the transferable skills which are the subject of this book).
- Cases require you to apply knowledge and techniques learned in your course to quasi-real situations.
- Cases increase your awareness of the business (or other) context in which you may eventually find yourself working.
- Difficulties with case studies stem from the need to manage your own learning to a greater extent than with traditional lectures, from possible lack of clarity over objectives, from the overall complexity of the situation described and because much of the case 'information' may be over-detailed or irrelevant, while information you need may be lacking.
- Cases tackled in groups exercise both task- and process-management skills.
- Case study analysis needs to be structured by the use of relevant course concepts. A useful sequence is to explore the situation and symptoms presented, define the problem, diagnose its causes, decide on criteria, generate options, evaluate them with respect to objectives and criteria, choose one, design an implementation strategy (if required), and communicate your findings or recommendations clearly.

Further information

Cameron, S. and Pearce, S. (1997) *Against the Grain*, Butterworth-Heinemann. This is a fairly gentle introduction to conceptual tools for complexity, particularly relevant to both this chapter and Chapter 15 on creativity, but touching on many of the other topics in the book.

Easton, G. (1992) *Learning from Case Studies*, 2nd edn, Prentice Hall. This gives much more detailed guidance on case study analysis than is possible here.

Mitroff, I.I. and Linstone, H.A. (1993) *The Unbounded Mind*, Oxford University Press. This is a rigorous approach to changing the way you think about complex situations, again relevant both to this chapter and to Chapter 15.

Pidd, M. (2009) *Tools for Thinking: Modelling in Management Science*, 3rd edn, Wiley.

Senge, P.M. (1990) *The Fifth Discipline*, 2nd edn, Random House.

Senior, B. and Swailes, S. (2010) *Organisational Change*, 4th edn, Pearson.

12
BECOMING MORE CREATIVE

Learning outcomes

By the end of this chapter you should:

- understand the place of creativity in problem solving

- be aware of some of the ways in which creativity is restricted

- be able to use a range of techniques to increase individual and group creativity.

Introduction

Organisations face such rapid and dramatic changes at present that the ability to think creatively, as well as rationally, is highly valued. New situations may need totally new responses. The ability to think creatively, to break out of the 'box' of existing assumptions, will therefore make you much more attractive to many employers. People vary in the ease with which they can think in creative ways, but there are techniques that can help them become more creative, whatever their starting point. This chapter will introduce you to some of these techniques.

Creativity is the ability to think in new ways, to see new patterns and come up with new ideas. The techniques introduced in this chapter will help you become a little better at identifying, and then overcoming, the limitations of your existing mindset and assumptions. If you continue to develop your mental flexibility during your career, and locate your rationality within a wider, less limiting approach, you will be a great asset to any project group you join, whether as a student or in employment.

The Need for Creativity

Since the 1970s organisations have faced not only the continuous, 'more-of-the-same' change of the past, but also major discontinuities. Consider, for example, the impact of IT and of 'streaming' on the music business. Handy (1989) expressed this well when he said that 'change is not what it used to be'. Continuing development of the Internet, and the globalisation it has enabled, are among the drivers for such change.

In coping with discontinuous change, and preparing for futures that are hard to guess at, we need to go *beyond* what is known. Handy says that we are entering the 'age of unreason', drawing on George Bernard Shaw's observation that all progress depends on the unreasonable man. (Note that this is not the same as irrational!) In such an age, he says, we need *discontinuous thinking*. Others refer to lateral (rather than vertical) thinking, divergent (rather than convergent) thinking, unbounded thinking or, more generally, creativity. All are talking about ways of breaking away from the limitations of traditional mindsets, traditional sets of assumptions, and traditional rational approaches to problems.

The terms 'right brain' and 'left brain' are still often used to refer to creativity and pattern perception in the first instance, and logical, linear thinking in the second. Current developments in neurocognitive science suggest that this is something of an oversimplification: both sides of the brain are involved in most forms of activity. And although language does tend, in right-handed males, to be more laterally represented (located in the left brain for 95 per cent), for left-handers the laterality is far less pronounced (60 per cent). Findings for women are also less clearcut than for men.

Regardless of whether, and if so where, 'thinking' is located in the brain, it is still worth making a distinction between these two different *types* of thinking. People vary in their preferences for these types, and there is a suggestion that this may influence their creativity. For example, Hughes *et al.* (2013) demonstrated that the 'Big Five' personality factor 'openness to experience' (these five factors are often tested during recruitment) was a strong predictor of self-estimated creativity, and also predicted self-rated cognitive ability. Since both forms of thinking have an important part to play in dealing with complex situations, it is worth becoming comfortable with *both* forms. This may require actively practising your non-preferred style of thinking, perhaps by using the techniques described later in the chapter.

While definitions vary, 'creativity' is generally taken to mean originality, new ways of seeing, new ideas, the thought processes associated with imagination, insight, intuition, ingenuity, inspiration. The adjective 'creative' can be applied to people, their mental processes and the ideas or other things that they produce. (Innovation often refers to the ability to put such ideas to profitable use in terms of products or processes.)

➤ Ch 11

One way of seeing how the two types of thinking can complement each other is to look at the need for creativity at each stage in the rational problem-solving model introduced earlier, particularly when 'the problem' is different from problems previously encountered.

Problem definition

Defining a problem with a fixed mindset can be incredibly limiting in terms of what you can 'see' in a situation, and therefore how you subsequently think about it. For example, if poor performance is seen as a 'control problem', only control solutions will be generated. (It might be this sort of thinking that created the situation in the first place!) A more creative approach to the initial situation might generate a far broader definition of the problem, indeed even to see it as an opportunity.

Removing constraints to thinking at the outset is therefore essential if the situation is to be fully understood and exploited. Henry (1991) emphasises the need to reframe the problem from a number of different angles before settling on a problem statement that encapsulates what appear to be the crucial factors. She says that she finds that some 70 per cent of people will end up exploring a *different* problem from that with which they started.

➤ Ch 11

The rich pictures which were suggested as a way of mapping possible elements in a problem situation are part of a whole methodology (Checkland, 1981) for approaching 'soft' problems, those where people and their perceptions are important, not everything can be measured, and objectives may be less than clear. The next stage in this methodology is to tease out a number of 'problem themes'. Following a methodology such as this, with its specified stages aimed at creating a wider understanding of the situation, helps resist the temptation to a narrow and premature diagnosis of problem causes. (The pictorial stage also involves the right brain.)

➤ Chs 1, 2

Success in a changing world demands more than merely maintaining the status quo. Goals need to be reformulated continually to take account of the changing environment (it is essential to 'move the goalposts'). Forecasting significant changes in this environment (remember Fayol?) will be important. In a situation of discontinuous change, it takes real creativity to conceive of a radically different future, or even to see the implications of changes already happening. Many organisations were slow to grasp the full implications of the ICT revolution. Indeed, it is likely that much of its impact has yet to be dreamed of.

Deciding criteria for a solution

Creativity may seem irrelevant to criteria for a solution, but consider the 'it's a control problem' example earlier. A narrow definition of the problem will lead to equally narrow – and perhaps inappropriate – criteria for a solution. So creativity at the earlier stage is relevant here.

Generating possible solutions

Your choice of solution is limited by the options you have thought of. Again, an open-minded view of the situation, freed from open-preconceptions and accepted limits, can in itself go far towards creating a wider set of options. Idea-generation techniques may create even more. The wider the range of options the greater your chance of finding one or more which will allow you to improve a situation which has previously seemed insoluble.

Idea generation will often involve successive *divergent* and *convergent* stages. For example, in looking for a project topic you might generate a range of broad subject areas (divergent activity) before selecting the area which seemed most promising (convergent). You might then focus on this area, generating a range of ways of approaching it before selecting one, and then go through further stages of divergence and convergence before formulating the exact area to be researched. Figure 12.1 shows this diagrammatically.

Implementation

Figure 12.1 makes the point that having chosen your broad option you often have scope for creativity in implementing it. There may be many ways of taking action to bring about a particular change. For example, the decision to introduce more self-directed work teams might require decisions about how to form such groups, how best to involve group

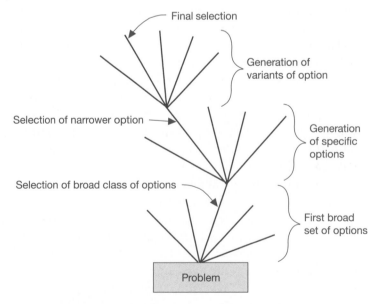

Figure 12.1 Option selected by successive choice and divergence

members in that formation and what control mechanisms to use to allow coordination without loss of autonomy. If the earlier stages of your attack on the problem adopted a broad perspective, then it is likely that your chosen approach has already broken away from preconceptions and limited frameworks. But this may be further helped by use of the divergent/convergent/divergent sequence described above when planning ways of implementing the changes that have been agreed.

Mintzberg (1976) makes the interesting suggestion that while planning is essentially a 'left-brain' activity (it is, after all, important that a plan does follow a sequence that enables things to be done in a logical order), the implementation of plans, that is, the *managing* that comes after, is essentially a 'right-brain' activity. He bases this claim on his observations of very senior managers at work. The good managers looked at the situation as a whole, seeing patterns therein, and relied heavily on intuition.

These observations led Mintzberg to argue that truly effective managers can harness *both* halves of their brain effectively. Note the earlier caution regarding actual location in the brain. But the point about harnessing both types of thinking is still valid. If you are planning a career which includes management, this is yet another reason to experiment with the creativity techniques which follow and to use diagramming wherever possible. Both should develop your ability to use your right brain.

Creating a Creative Environment

➤ Chs 2, 5

Individuals may vary in their preferences for lateral or linear thinking, but the creativity they show may also depend on their knowledge and experience, and importantly, an organisational context which supports creativity. From this perspective, creativity is seen as an emergent property of a system involving individuals and organisational structure and climate. Indeed, Csikszentmihalyi (1996) who has long explored the related ideas of creativity, motivation and flow, suggests that it may be easier to enhance creativity by working on the environment than the individual.

Nevertheless, Csikszentmihalyi (2013) does attempt to describe the 'creative personality', suggesting that creative individuals are notable for their ability to adapt to situations and make use of whatever is available in pursuit of their goals. He describes the creative personality in terms of its 'complexity', showing contradictory extremes. For example, creative people show movement between periods of high energy and rest, and tend to be both wise and childishly naïve, humble and proud, aggressive and cooperative, extrovert and introvert. While immersed in tradition they are also iconoclastic, and can combine fantasy with a strong sense of reality. They can think in both a convergent and divergent fashion. He also suggests that creative individuals have escaped at least some of the gender-typing of their culture, with artistic women being more aggressive than the female norm, and creative men showing more 'feminine' sensitivity.

So what sort of context will allow creativity to be expressed? Perhaps the most important conditions are:

- a clear goal (both Csikszentmihaly (1996) and Peralta *et al.* (2015) draw attention to this)
- time (there needs to be a freedom from pressure)

12

BECOMING MORE CREATIVE

- for people to think together (working with others leads to more creative solutions)
- about difficult things (an element of challenge is necessary for creative people to experience
- 'flow' – the loss of all sense of time, or even of the distinction between themselves and the task (and creativity is most needed when problems are 'difficult')
- valuing – rather than frowning upon – playfulness and 'crazy' ideas (see brainstorming below).

Barriers to Creativity

If you are to develop your creativity, you need to understand the pressures *against* you. One of the main barriers to creative thought is the belief that a rational/logical/scientific way of thinking is the *only* way to think. This is because most education is directed towards this view and because most of the time it is an extremely useful and productive way of thinking. The inability to be rational and logical is a serious shortcoming. Even the greatest creativity enthusiasts suggest that creative or divergent thinking constitutes no more than 5 per cent of all the thinking that is needed (though I am not sure how such a figure is arrived at).

➤ Ch 11

> Being creative for 5 minutes can transform 95 minutes of rational thought.

But the quality of the 95 per cent of logical thought will depend on its direction. This will depend on the extent to which a creative interpretation of the original situation was found. The amount of time devoted to creative thought may be small, but in any situation where 'soft' problems are addressed, the quality of your output will depend equally on the two types of thought process.

Setting logic aside

To overcome the 'logic habit' you need to practise deliberately setting aside your ingrained logic, *even though you still need to use it most of the time*. Spend some time indulging in a way of thinking that is in many ways its antithesis. The list of contrasts in Table 12.1, derived mainly from De Bono (1971), shows dimensions in which the two ways of thinking differ.

If you are good at vertical or rational thinking, gain praise for it, and are making progress because you are more rational than other people, it will be particularly difficult for you to move to a more lateral approach. The 'vertical' habit will have been strongly reinforced. Out of this, and out of some of the other differences, come more emotional barriers to lateral thinking.

Feeling happier with creativity

It is usually uncomfortable to move away from your 'comfort zone' of established habit, especially when the habits are familiar ways of thinking and of approaching problems. People are afraid of failing or looking silly. Many are uncomfortable with ambiguity, and like things to be clearly 'right' or 'wrong'. Many have a compulsion to judge ideas,

Table 12.1 Creative (lateral) vs logical (vertical) thinking

Lateral	Vertical
Seeks questions	Seeks answers
Diverges	Converges
Explores different views, seeking insight	Asserts best/right view
Restructures	Uses existing structure
Seeks ways an idea might help	Says why an idea won't work
Welcomes discontinuous leaps	Uses logical steps
Welcomes chance intrusions	Concentrates on what is relevant
Open-ended	Closed

Barriers to creativity:

- existing thought habits
- fear of failure or ridicule
- ambiguity avoidance
- pressure/lack of time
- inability to play.

To become more creative:

- value playfulness
- draw
- deliberately break mindsets
- practise creativity techniques.

whether their own or others'. They cannot relax enough to play mental games with ideas. This seems so 'unserious' as to be inappropriate. All these feelings get in the way of creativity.

Most education discourages lateral thinking while encouraging rational, convergent, 'left-brain' thought.

Creativity techniques are broadly directed at breaking convergent habits by deliberately specifying steps in problem solving when you do things that have the effect of broadening your thinking. They aim to overcome emotional resistance to this by creating a situation in which 'play' is in some way made respectable and/or by encouraging use of the right brain. For example, drawing a rich picture, when you put down everything you can think of as potentially relevant, acts *against* the convergent habit. Involving a group in drawing fairly juvenile cartoon representations makes play respectable and, being non-linear, encourages right-brain involvement. (Indeed, most diagrams will aid creativity.) Practising such techniques should help you to develop the skills you need if you are to be creative and overcome any emotional resistance to this sort of approach. Indeed, you should become equally happy with using either type of thinking.

Techniques for Improving Creativity

There are many, many techniques for encouraging lateral thinking. These can help you come up with new ways of looking at a situation and new approaches to making it less problematic. A small selection is described below. If you want to try a wider range, read some of the books suggested at the end of the chapter.

➤ Ch 11 The first way of overcoming limitations is to try to ensure that nothing is left out. Techniques already introduced in the problem-solving chapter serve this purpose. These include rich pictures, the use of fishbone diagrams and systematic 'questioning', trying to answer the 'who', 'what', 'when', 'where' and 'why' questions about the problem situation. Aiming for this breadth of understanding of the scenario is equally important for rational and arational or lateral approaches, so it should not be forgotten when aiming for a creative approach. The other techniques given here are more clearly aimed at going beyond rationality.

Brainstorming

You will almost certainly be familiar with this term, but may have used the technique in a watered-down form which did not allow for much creativity. The intention of brainstorming is to create a situation where people feel free to play. The idea is to disable the judgemental censors within ourselves. These sensors normally kill many ideas before they surface into consciousness. Because brainstorming is done in a group, it provides social rewards for this way of operating. It also offers scope for chance associations and discontinuities: one person's ideas will interact with those surfacing in another person. This can lead to a completely new train of thought. The following classic technique is designed to make this easier.

> **Brainstorming 'rules':**
> - warm up first
> - ban criticism
> - capture everything
> - the sillier the better
> - have fun
> - sort ideas afterwards.

Preparation

You need a *lot* of writing surface – a room with boards all round or flipchart paper stuck to several walls. Also appropriate pens and someone prepared to act as scribe and write fast. Although you can brainstorm alone, ideally you need to assemble a group of people to take part. You also need to think about the question you wish to address. Aim for an open, 'ways to . . .' question. If you are looking for a topic to practise on, you could always brainstorm ways of selling more copies of this book, or better titles for it, and let the publisher know! There might be a reward for any adopted.

Rules

Next, you all need to agree to abide by the only 'rules' in brainstorming: that *all* suggestions are treated as valid and written down, and *nobody* voices criticism of any kind, whatever the idea. Silliness is to be welcomed as one person's silly idea may spark off a productive train of thought in someone else. After all, you are brainstorming because the sensible ideas have failed to resolve the problem. (This is why the unreasonable person may make progress where reasonable ones have failed.)

Warm-up

Once you have agreed to the rules, you start to brainstorm a silly problem. You use this to warm-up and get into the mood before moving on to the serious issue with which you are concerned. Silly ideas could be anything: uses for a dead cat or for the discarded plastic cups by the drinks machine; stopping a flatmate from breeding snakes; persuading your tutor to give everyone in the class 100 per cent. The more frivolous the topic the more likely you are to loosen up. You might even try thinking up silly topics for warm-ups at brainstorming. Everyone starts to shout out ideas and the scribe writes them large enough that people can read them easily. Reading back over past ideas while others are shouting can prompt further ideas. It doesn't matter if an idea is voiced twice – better risk this than get into judgemental mode. Five minutes should be enough for a warm-up.

Brainstorming the real question – idea generation

Put up fresh paper and start on the real thing. You may want to spend a few minutes in 'private brainstorming' with group members writing down their initial thoughts, or prefer to work in a group from the outset. If you do list privately first you may find it interesting to compare the number of ideas generated by individuals (duplications removed) with those generated by the group. Continue brainstorming until you run out of steam.

Convergence – organising the results

The final stage of brainstorming is the convergent one. A smaller group takes away all the ideas and selects the most promising ones. They may look for themes, grouping related ideas together and then looking for solutions to the problem theme that the solutions suggest. Or they may simply select the best of the original suggestions. If they wish to go through a further creative stage, they can choose the two or three most impossible or the craziest ideas and see if they can think of ways in which they could actually be made to contribute to a solution.

One interesting variant on this approach is negative brainstorming – a good example of upside-down thinking. Instead of brainstorming ways of *doing* something, you brainstorm ways of *not doing* it. This may throw up a whole new set of ideas about a problem situation, highlighting contributory factors to a problem or things that will militate against a solution.

Brainwriting

Brainwriting is a variant of brainstorming which can be used face to face, or in a virtual group. You sit down alone to write down all your ideas. You then share these with others, which is likely to prompt further ideas. You can then share these, and so on. You can even use this alone, coming back to your list at intervals and adding to it. Things that have happened to you in the interval may prompt new reactions to items on the original list. Try sticking it to the wall near the stove, or in the loo. Leave a pen nearby. As you are likely to be more creative when using diagrams, supplement your list by a cumulative rich picture.

Activity 12.1

In a group, use the brainstorming technique several times, as described above, until you are comfortable with it. When using it as part of solving a real problem (for example, for identifying possible key words for a literature search or for suggesting project topics), document it as an exhibit to demonstrate your competence in applying the tool.

Forced associations

One idea sparks another. Brainstorming works partly by throwing up ideas which may fortuitously associate themselves for some people – Chris shouts out 'Dig a sandpit' and Jo suddenly thinks something like, 'We could sandpaper the rough edges'. Other approaches are specifically designed to *force* such associations as a way of breaking out of a particular mindset. These can be useful alone or for a group.

Random words can be used to force associations. Simply stick a pin in a dictionary or newspaper and see what word is selected. Then see what associations you can make between the word and the problem. Suppose your pin penetrated 'plant'. This grows, needs attention, soil, cross-fertilisation, may grow better in some places than others, and so on. What thoughts do each of these characteristics of 'plant' prompt about your original topic?

Superheroes can be used in the same way. Each group member nominates a favourite superhero (see the link with fun again?) and these are listed on a board. Or list a few yourself if working alone. Any sort of hero is acceptable: Homer Simpson, Judge Dredd, Barak Obama and Mother Theresa are all equally valid. The hero's sponsor is asked to give their characteristics – special powers, weaknesses, idiosyncrasies. Then the group tries to answer the question (again, fairly frivolously): 'How would X approach the problem?'

Greetings cards provide a more pictorial basis for association. Get a group of helpers, ideally people unconnected with the problem, to cut two or three pictures that take their fancy from a magazine or similar and paste them on to a card, writing 'Get well', 'Happy Anniversary' or other greeting. The cards are then given to those working on the problem and used in the same way as random words. Without helpers, it would be possible to use your pin to select a random illustration rather than a word.

Activity 12.2

In a small group, experiment with each of these idea-generation techniques, writing a brief description of your experiences and thoughts about contexts in which each might be appropriate, storing this in your file.

Cartoon by Neill Cameron, www.neillcameron.com

Metaphors and analogies

The use of metaphor – talking of something as if it *is* something which it merely resembles – is deeply rooted in our speech and thought. Whether we are saying a politician is a demon, dove or pussy cat, or speaking of light waves, or of 'the machine' when we speak of an organisation, we are using metaphors. This helps us to feel we understand something with which we may not be very familiar because we are describing it in terms of something with which we are more familiar, ascribing properties of the second to the first. In so far as the two are similar in their properties, this can be very helpful. But when only *some* of the properties are common, a metaphor may be limiting or misleading. You would not expect a pussy cat politician to lap milk from a saucer, or a dove MP to take wing. Many people, however, *do* unconsciously expect organisations to behave exactly like machines. And this can seriously limit understanding of what is really going on in them. If you take this view and want to introduce a change, you will merely decree that the change should happen. It will be a great surprise to you when it does not, or when what happens is very different from what was intended. Metaphors are often not explicit – you are unlikely to hear someone say, 'this organisation is a machine' – but you may hear words like cog, oil, lever, breakdown that give you a strong clue that this metaphor is unconsciously underlying thinking about what is going on.

➤ **Ch 4**

Unconscious use of metaphor can be particularly dangerous as you will be unaware of many of the assumptions you are making and cannot check their reality. (When you are argument mapping, and seeking hidden assumptions, look carefully at any use of metaphor.) But conscious use of a range of metaphors can work in a similar way to forced associations. The potential is richer, as the metaphor will often carry a wider range of implications. This is discussed in more detail in Cameron and Pearce (1997).

Activity 12.3

Listen carefully to people talking about a problem and try to identify unconscious use of metaphor from the language they are using. Machine metaphors of organisation are

➤

indicated by such words as 'cog', 'clockwork', 'tool', 'spanner in the works'. Military metaphors are indicated by 'attack', 'strategy', 'guns', 'heavy armoury', 'captain', 'breach', 'bombshell'. When you have identified the underlying metaphor, try to think what such a metaphor will lead the speaker to consider and what to ignore. Look out for more organic words, too, and think about *their* implications. Note your reflections in your file.

The organic metaphor and systems thinking

The commonest alternative to the machine as a metaphor for organisations is that of the organisation as organism. The systems approach uses an analogy with a living organism as the basis for analysis. Organisms have goals and purposes to which their behaviour is directed. They exist in an environment which has a profound influence upon them, but which they can influence in only limited ways. This environment changes, so they need ways of maintaining a steady state in the face of this change. Systems are separated from their environment by some sort of 'boundary'. Although they are entities, they are made up of many components which interrelate. Some of these components (for example, the respiratory system, and the digestive system) can be seen as systems in their own right. The organism is much more than just the sum of its parts. It needs to be looked at as a whole, with all its parts and their interactions, if it is to be understood. Some of its properties only emerge at the level of the whole organism. This approach has been highly influential in management thought, where the need to look at things as a whole, to consider how their parts are related, and to see how they interact with their environment is now widely recognised. For example, 'systems thinking' is at the heart of Senge's 'fifth discipline' (Senge, 1990). It also underpins much of this book. Mitroff and Linstone (1993) describe 'unbounded systems thinking: the fifth way of knowing' (the other ways they identify are agreement, logic, multiple realities and conflict.)

➤ **Ch 15**
Ideas of control and multiple causality are central to systems thinking. So too is the emphasis on problem definition and diagnosis. The rich pictures introduced earlier are art of Checkland's 'soft system methodology'.

Box 12.1 Systems thinking

A systems approach explores:

- the *goal* of the system and how it is measured
- the *components and subsystems* that must be part of the system if it is to achieve this goal
- the *relationships* between these
- any *wider system* of which the system of interest is itself a subsystem

➤

> - the external *environment* of the system and its components
> - the influences exerted by this environment – for example, via resources and constraints
> - the *control loops* that maintain internal stability in the face of change.

The deliberate use of a systems metaphor can be useful in any problem analysis that involves human activity. If you are working with problems in organisations, it can be another way of ensuring that all aspects of a problem situation are looked at, in much the same way as the fishbone diagram can be used for exploring all aspects of production that might be contributing to quality problems.

➤ Ch 11

Seeking non-obvious systems

Such uses of the systems metaphor may not seem particularly creative, but drawing rich pictures can introduce an element of fun and free up thinking about a problem situation, allowing you to escape from the narrow definitions that may be preventing you from thinking of whole classes of possible ways forward. Going beyond the 'obvious' system can, however, aid creativity greatly. If you choose a variety of non-obvious but relevant systems, and describe them in systems terms, this can markedly broaden your perspective and help you to escape from conventional limitations in thinking. The Checkland (1981) methodology starts with rich picturing and then goes on to extract problem themes. It moves from that into identifying *relevant systems* for each theme. These are not intended as blueprints for a solution: they are not systems which, if introduced, would solve the problem. Instead, they are ways of looking at the situation which prompt constructive thought about it. By *mapping* such systems, you can obtain a very simple picture. Yet if you draw such a map you may be surprised at the number of useful questions it can cause you to consider and the amount of debate which it can prompt among group members.

This is particularly the case if you choose non-obvious systems, having no generally accepted counterpart in reality. Thus a university might obviously be seen as a system to teach young people academic subjects. Less obviously, it might be viewed as a system to allow academics to do research and travel a lot, to keep young people out of the employment market, to allow employers easily to select people with certain skills, or to indoctrinate all the reasonably intelligent people in the country in a particular approach to 'knowledge'. The potential list is endless and each title would generate a different map of the system.

Activity 12.4

Listen to your own language when you are discussing organisational problems. Is it mainly mechanistic or do organic metaphors (or, indeed, political or other metaphors) predominate? Consider whether this is helping or limiting your thinking.

Activity 12.5

For one of the problems you worked with earlier, perhaps the one for which you already have a rich picture and problem themes, try to describe some relevant systems. Find titles in the form 'A system to . . .' which reflect the purpose of the system and what it does. Then try to draw a picture of the system showing components, subsystems and key environmental factors. Draw a boundary separating the system and environment. Figure 12.2 shows examples of simple maps of different systems.

Morgan (1986), in a fascinating development of the idea of metaphor as an aid to understanding organisations in new and creative ways, suggests additional metaphors. In addition to the conventional machine and organism metaphors, we can consider the organisation as brain, culture, and psychic prison, product of flux and transformation, and instrument of domination. Each of these metaphors suggests a different set of properties which pose new questions about organisations and from these suggest new insights.

Although most of the problems you will analyse as a business student, and most of the problems you will encounter during employment, will have organisational contexts, metaphors can be useful in any context to help you escape from an existing set of assumptions.

Visual metaphors

Just as diagrams are useful, *drawing* a metaphor can be surprisingly powerful, tapping into emotions that you were not aware of and highlighting aspects of a situation that you were not aware had any significance for you. This technique is particularly useful for finding out what you would like a future to be, but it has a wide range of applications generally.

Personal vision

Pictorial storyboarding can be extremely useful in working out how to progress your life in the way that you want it to develop. Gaining a clear picture in your mind of your desired end point is called 'visioning': it is a popular technique in coaching.

Activity 12.6

Think of a metaphor for your future life. This could be a journey, a home, a country, a piece of art, whatever suits you. Now *draw it*. Artistic ability is irrelevant. If it worries you that you were bad at drawing at school, draw it as a caveman might, or as a 5-year-old child might. You may find that you become surprisingly involved in this endeavour. When you have finished, show your drawing to a friend and ask what it tells them about your hopes and/ or fears and/or predictions. Then look at it again yourself and ask *yourself* what it is saying.

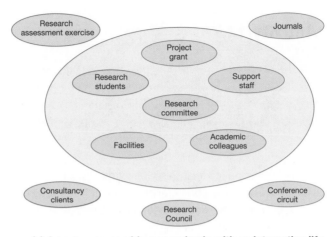

(a) A system to provide an academic with an interesting life

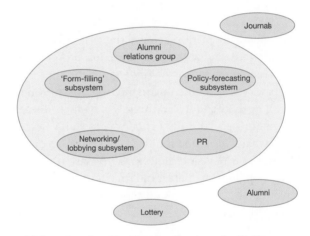

(b) A system for attracting funding to an institution

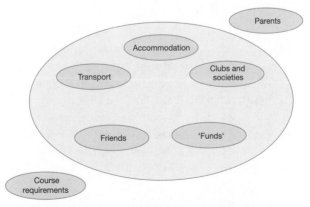

(c) A system for providing an enjoyable time at college

Figure 12.2 Three simple maps reflecting different systems relevant to higher education

12

BECOMING MORE CREATIVE

Activity 12.7

Now draw your present life. And then draw a series of intermediate pictures, as if it were a cartoon story of how to get from 'present' to 'future'. (This is called 'storyboarding'.) With your friend, or alone, see what ideas this suggests for action. List these and file the 'story'. It may be useful to you when you work through the final chapter.

Many writers on leadership see developing and communicating a vision for the organisation as the defining characteristic of great leaders. 'Shared vision' was one of the other four disciplines which Senge (1990) considered essential for a learning organisation, and he saw the ability of key people to build their personal visions as crucial to this. Organisational visions, he says, are rooted in personal visions. Personal vision is frequently seen as a key component in leadership, as well.

Visions can be surprisingly powerful in creating change in your life, even if you do not deliberately plan to achieve them. It is as if you have set up an instruction to your subconscious, and without further effort on your part it will gradually move you towards your vision. Research on US undergraduates showed that those who had visions as undergraduates were far more successful twenty years on than those who did not. (If you want to explore more about how this might happen, doing some reading about neurolinguistic programming – NLP – is a good way to start). Because of their power, it is important to ensure that your vision is indeed your personal one, not what other people want for you. Also that you 're-vision', building a new vision at regular intervals – as your understanding of what might be available, and what is important to you, develops. The following activity can be done alone, or with a listener (it is a good exercise for practising attentive and some-
➤ Ch 8   times active listening).

Activity 12.8

Imagine that it is some time into the future and you have just come to the end of the best day you can imagine. Indeed, it has been the best week, the best month, the best six months. 'See' where you are, what sort of room you are in, where you are living, who you are with, what work you have been doing, and how you have spent your leisure time during this period. Try to make this 'vision' as vivid as possible. Add colours, sounds, smells. A listener can be helpful in noting down what you see and in prompting you with questions such as: Where is the house? What sort of people are you working with? What did you do last night?

When the vision is as clear as you can get it, use your listener's notes or your own memory to write/draw/perhaps even collage the picture. Put it somewhere safe and make a diary note for a set date each month to look at your vision, remind yourself of its contents, and make any changes necessary.

Morning pages

A somewhat different approach to creativity in a work context is suggested by Bryon *et al.* (1998). These authors posit not only that we are all creative, but that we can become yet more creative, becoming happier, healthier and more successful in the process. They offer a range of tools to help this 'creative emergence' which you might like to explore. The first is remarkably simple, and can be surprisingly powerful.

All you need do is wake a little earlier each day, and write (longhand) three A4 pages continuously. Just keep writing, putting down anything that occurs to you. It doesn't matter what. Thoughts about study, work, or anything else, brain dump, to-do lists or whatever. It is *intended* to be messy, disorganised and chaotic. Do not stop to think. Do not re-read. Do not show to anyone else. When you have finished, simply put it away.

It is claimed (and it works for me) that the act of writing creates a safe psychological space, and starts a process of reordering: the 'rubbish' gets cleared, goals and aspirations emerge from the chaos, you will find that you get more done, are more focused, and although it takes time (20–40 minutes at first, though you will speed up with practice) it also *creates* time at work, and frees up a great deal of energy. The result is not instant, but should be felt within a matter of weeks. If you have time before your course starts, this is something well worth experimenting with. (It has the added bonus of giving writing practice, so that you will answer any exam questions much more fluently!)

➤ Ch 7

Dangers of creativity

After such a discussion of the value of creativity, it may seem strange to talk about its dangers. But these stem from the point at which we started: the need for rational as well as creative thinking.

The danger of creativity is that it can become so exciting that the rational world, with its all too real constraints, is devalued or ignored while play and fantasy rule supreme. While this may feel wonderful, the results of such 'unanchored' creativity may be disappointing or non-existent. It is from the *combination* of the two forms of thinking, and out of the tension between them, that progress and innovation will come.

By nesting creative thinking within a wider rational approach and by exploiting the strengths of each form of approach, you will become the flexible, innovative thinker that organisations say they want. But you will still be able to bring your thoughts to fruition and plan carefully for their successful implementation.

Finding Opportunities to Be Creative

At first sight your degree course may appear to offer you few opportunities for creativity. Indeed, there may be many occasions where being creative would be seriously discouraged. This will, of course, depend on your subject and on how it is taught. You may not need creativity to apply a specific equation, for example. However, there may be more scope than you think. If you can find new ways of approaching essay topics your originality may lead to high marks.

Of course, your interpretation would have to be valid (and you might need to justify its validity), and your logic within this original approach would need to be sound. Remember, to be effective creativity needs to be combined with rationality. There will always be a slight risk of a spectacularly low mark if your tutor is not impressed by your creativity – it is up to you to assess this risk and to decide whether you want to take it.

➤ **Ch 11** If you are working on case studies, then in the early stages you can experiment with creative approaches such as the sequence of rich picturing → problem theme → relevant systems, or using a range of non-system metaphors. These may well lead you to a better approach to a problem than you would otherwise have chosen. If you have to do a dissertation or research project as part of your course, you should find

➤ **Ch 15** idea-generation techniques helpful in producing a topic and may then be able to use systems ideas or other metaphors as an aid to finding ways of addressing your chosen problem.

Practising creativity will not be limited to your course work. During your time as a student you will encounter many problems apart from those posed by your lecturers. If you take these as opportunities for experimenting with the sorts of techniques described above, you will be developing skills that will be immensely useful to you in employment, as well as finding better solutions to your immediate problems.

Indeed, you may already find it useful to start thinking creatively about possible careers, and about ways of increasing your chances of achieving your career goals.

Activity 12.9

Each time that you hit a problem, try to use at least two of the techniques suggested in this chapter as part of your attempt at solving it. Document your efforts and write down your reflections on the strengths and weaknesses of the approach in that context, together with thoughts about difficulties and how you might have done better. Review this growing 'creative problem solving' part of your file at intervals.

SUMMARY

This chapter has argued the following:

- Creative thinking is in many ways the antithesis of rational thinking and because of this may be difficult for those who have been trained in the latter. While you may need to spend much less time being creative than being rational, they are equally important. It may be helpful to think of it in terms of an essential complement to rational thinking.

- Creativity depends on becoming comfortable with ambiguity, mental experiment and play, while suspending judgement. Holism rather than linearity, pattern rather than sequence, 'right-brain' rather than 'left-brain' activities, are all important.

- Forced associations and conscious use of metaphor can add to ideas already generated by chance associations.
- Visual representations can be hugely powerful aids to creativity, as in addition to their other advantages they engage the right brain.
- Developing a personal vision can be a key element in leadership and important for commitment to an organisational vision for change.
- Success will depend on keeping a balance between convergent and divergent thinking and using both halves of the brain effectively.

Further information

Bryan, M., Cameron, J., and Allen, C. (1998) *The Artist's Way at Work*, Pan Books. Provides a range of techniques to make you more creative generally.

Cameron, J. (1992) *The Artist's Way*, Tarcher. This is the source of the ideas in Bryon *et al*., above, and addresses creativity in the more general sense. Either is well worth looking at.

Cameron, S. and Pearce, S. (1997) *Against the Grain*, Butterworth-Heinemann.

Checkland, P. (1981) *Systems Thinking, Systems Practice*, Wiley. This gives a clear description of how to use a particular methodology.

De Bono, E. (1971) *Lateral Thinking for Management*, Pelican. This is a classic.

Handy, C. (1989) *The Age of Unreason*, Business Books.

Henry, J. (1991) *Creative Management*, Sage.

Mitroff, I.I. and Linstone, H.A. (1993) *The Unbounded Mind*, Oxford University Press. This is not an easy read, but is well worth the effort.

Morgan, G. (1986) *Images of Organization*, Sage. This is a fascinating and stimulating development of the use of metaphor.

Senge, P.M. (2006) *The Fifth Discipline*, 2nd edn, Random House.

Senior, B. (2010) *Organisational Change*, 4th edn, Pearson.

Kolar, T. (2012) 'Using metaphors as a tool for creative strategic sense-making', *Economic and Business Review,* 14, 4, 275–297, available at http://www.ebrjournal.net/ojs/index.php/ebr/article/viewFile/171/pdf (accessed 15/7/15).

12

BECOMING MORE CREATIVE

13
DATA, INFORMATION AND DECISIONS

Learning outcomes

This chapter looks at the idea of information itself and some common ways of obtaining it. By the end you should:

- have a clearer idea of what constitutes information

- be aware of the different sorts of data you are likely to need

- have developed further skills for searching existing literature and other information

- know the requirements that data must meet if they are to be of use

- have an appreciation of how to go about conducting a survey

- appreciate the requirements for effective interviewing.

Introduction

Good decisions are based on sound evidence. Many organisations take decisions that are dangerously bad, sometimes threatening the organisation's survival. Small wonder that skills relating to finding, judging and using evidence are one of the most important things a business degree can develop. Haigh and Clifford (2010) quote QAA Scotland findings showing that a key skill for graduate employability is to '... identify, retrieve, evaluate and apply relevant information and current technologies to advance understanding, solve problems and complete work tasks creatively'. The 'creatively' in this quote will depend on an initial exploration of the problem situation which is not constrained by assumptions and past ways of thinking. But there is also scope for creativity in finding and using data.

This chapter looks at common methods of obtaining data, how to evaluate that data, and at how to turn data into information and use it as evidence. It will help you to use existing information to good effect, to know when further data are needed, and to obtain those data in an appropriate way. This will be invaluable for any project work as a student, but equally important to you as a manager or consultant. Whenever you need to make sense of information provided by others, or to seek information yourself in order to take a decision or determine ► Ch 14   a way out of a problem situation, the ability to make appropriate use of data will be essential.

When faced with a complex problem at work you usually need to understand it better, its history, how it relates to other situations, what is available and so on. For this you usually need to seek further information by talking to people, looking through records and/or searching online. Who thinks it is a problem? Why? What is it costing? What technology is available? What are competitors doing? Your course will provide you with many opportunities to develop your skills in identifying information requirements, and obtaining and using information, probably culminating in ► Ch 15   a substantial dissertation or investigative report (addressed in Chapter 15). But long before this you will need to be able to find and use information for essays and other assignments. In this case the topic will usually be specified. But eventually you will need to identify key research on the subject, decide on a useful question to address, and seek the information needed to answer it. For a dissertation, the bulk of your effort will be directed towards identifying the information that you need, the best ways of generating or finding it elsewhere and evaluating it.

Some information will already exist and can be gathered from your library, and/or online sources. Some you may need to gather for yourself – surveys and interviews are common approaches. But the value of your conclusions will depend on the adequacy and validity of your information. The ability to judge the value of data and information is really important. For this, you need to understand the nature of information, and how to collect information that is both valid and reliable. Obtaining information costs time and/or money. So you need to decide what is important and then collect it efficiently. Computers can handle huge volumes of data, and the Internet provides an overwhelming amount. Unless you understand the difference between data and information you may put a vast amount of effort into collecting and presenting data, without achieving anything of informational value.

Information versus Data

The first important distinction to grasp is that between information and data. The words are often used interchangeably, but there is a crucial difference.

- **Data** (literal translation, 'things given') is used to refer to 'facts' or signals collected from the environment in some way and usually expressed in numbers.
- **Information** refers to data that have been organised in a way relevant to your needs, so that they help you to answer a question that concerns you.

Suppose you had access to all the exam marks for all courses in every university in the country. This would be a (large) set of data. But if you wanted to choose a course for next year with a high pass rate, you would find it much more *informative* to be given only the pass rates for the courses you are considering.

> Information is data selected and organised to tell you something you need to know.

➤ Ch 14
This simple example shows that 'more' is not always 'better'. Selecting relevant data and then summarising (more on this in the next chapter) and organising them makes them more useful. Clearly, what you select and how you summarise it will depend on the question you want to answer. A funding council might want to compare mark distributions in particular faculties in every university it funds, so would select differently and would not summarise in terms of pass rates.

As with all other purposeful activity, when seeking information the most important thing is to establish your objectives. You must be clear just what question you are trying to answer. *Why* do you need the data? The easiest data to obtain may not provide you with information relevant to what you need to know. (Remember the joke about the drunk looking under the lamp post for keys he dropped elsewhere 'because the light is better here'.) Data become information only when they are organised to help you understand the particular thing you are interested in. So *what* you organise and *how* you do this inevitably depends on what it is that concerns you.

'Facts' was in quotes in the definition of data above because data can be more or less 'factual'. Before getting into arguments about what you can and cannot do to data to

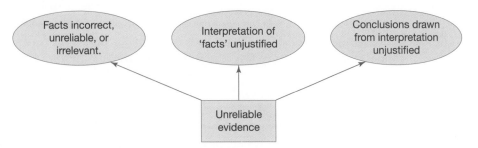

Figure 13.1 Possible causes of unreliable evidence

➤ Ch 14
create information, you need to be aware of the ways in which the data themselves may be unreliable. (The reliability of the conclusions you draw from data will be discussed in the next chapter.) Reliability will depend to some extent on the type of data concerned, so it is worth considering these types first.

Types of data

One important distinction is that between *primary* and *secondary* data. Primary data you collect yourself, by direct observation, measurement, interview, questionnaire or other means. Such data can be tailored to your own requirements (within resource constraints). They can be designed to give you answers to precisely the question which concerns you, using an appropriate sample. You will know the conditions under which data were collected and should have a clear idea of the ways in which inaccuracies or unreliability may have crept in. But there is a price to pay for this. Collecting your own valid data is usually costly. It is much cheaper to exploit data which have already been collected, perhaps for other purposes.

Secondary data are other people's 'facts and figures'. They include the results of surveys carried out by other people, sets of government statistics, company reports or records, reports of research in academic journals, sets of figures available on the Internet, and so on. Secondary data can usually be obtained far more quickly and cheaply than primary data, but again there are drawbacks. You may not know how much reliance to place on secondary data, particularly if they were collected for purposes other than your own. Even seemingly straightforward figures may be not be valid, in that they do not measure what they purport to measure.

I once came across a set of production figures for a coal mine which were remarkably consistent. It turned out that the 'purpose' for which they were being collected, was – in the eyes of those collecting them – to keep senior management happy. Any drop in production figures brought a visitation from head office! So in good weeks some of the coal was stockpiled and not recorded, and in bad weeks some of this stockpile was sent off and included in the production figures. 'Weekly' production figures were more an average of quarterly production than a measure of output in any single week. If you had been trying to explore influences of different factors (in my case, employee absence) on output, the figures would have been useless to you.

Secondary data may also relate to a different situation from the one which interests you, so *relevance* is an issue. Suppose the most recent survey you could find of employer views on recruiting computing graduates was five years old. You might reasonably wonder about the extent to which you could draw conclusions about attitudes now. If the survey was recent but had covered only very large manufacturing organisations, whereas you were interested in small service organisations, you might again be worried.

➤ Ch 11
The other important distinction to make is that between *quantitative* and *qualitative* data. Most people think in terms only of quantitative data, sets of numbers derived from relatively unarguable measures. But Chapter 11 showed that there may be many important 'soft' aspects to a problem situation. Such factors are difficult or impossible to quantify.

Attitudes and feelings may be important. Differences in how various groups perceive a particular situation may be crucial. Because techniques for structuring and dealing with such qualitative information are less well known than the techniques of basic parametric statistics used for quantitative data, such factors may be omitted altogether.

Even if qualitative factors are included, numbers may be attributed to them in various ways. These numbers are often treated, unjustifiably, as if they were normal measures. This can lead to totally false conclusions about the meaning of the data. Fortunately, software exists that can help you with various forms of qualitative analysis. Even without this, provided you are aware of the type of data with which you are dealing and how any numbers have been attributed, you can still make considerable use of qualitative data.

> **Data can be:**
> - primary or secondary
> - quantitative or qualitative
> - textual, nominal, ordinal, interval or ratio.

This may become clearer if you consider the classifications usually applied to research data. '*Textual* data' refers to verbal description, for example quotations from an article or interview. Such data can be a splendid source of ideas. Carefully selected quotations can create a vivid picture for the person reading a report. At the start of the book I quoted a couple of friends who recruit graduates in the hope of giving you a feel for how an employer might see things. But you have no idea how much reliance to place on their opinions. My friends may be such unusual people that few other employers share their views. (Note that there *are* occasions when text itself can be the basis of a more quantitative analysis. You could count the number of times advertisements required particular qualifications, or analyse transcripts of wage negotiations to identify the commonest sequences of 'moves' made by negotiators. But this requires fairly specialist techniques and you should seek further advice if contemplating something as complex as this.)

Nominal or *categorical* data are those where some sort of categorisation or classification has been made. You might be able to group your data by country, by income or profession, by star sign, by degree subject or whatever. You could count the number in each category, for example finding out how many chemistry graduates, how many physicists, how many economists, etc. were recruited by a large multinational. For convenience you might number the categories, calling chemists category 1, physicists 2, and so on. But it would be nonsense to try to relate the categories mathematically. In no sense does one physicist equal two chemists.

Ordinal or *ranked* data are those where it *is* possible to tell something about the relationship between categories from their number, but not everything. For example, a graduate recruiter might have four requirements in looking for new staff. When interviewing an applicant, the recruiter might choose to use a 5-point scale, from 5 (excellent) to 1 (unacceptable), and rate each interviewee on each criterion using this. You could tell from this that on any of the scales someone ranked 5 was thought to be better than someone ranked 4. But you could not say that the difference between a 5 and a 4 was the same as between a 2 and a 1, or that a 4 was twice as good as a 2. And it would be wrong to do any arithmetic or use any statistical techniques on the scores which assumed that the numbers meant more than a ranking.

Interval data are those where the intervals *are* the same. On the centigrade scale, it would take the same heat to raise a given volume of water from 5° to 10° as from 50° to 55°. But there is no real zero on this scale. It was mere convenience that dictated the freezing point of water as zero. So although you can add or subtract meaningfully on such a scale, you cannot multiply or divide. It does not make sense to say that 40° is twice as hot as 20°. Most questionnaire scores are best treated as either interval or ordinal data.

Ratio data are those where intervals are meaningful, and there is also a real zero, so that you can multiply, divide and describe things in terms of ratios. If you make 40 people redundant this is twice as many as if you had got rid of 20. An inflation rate of 12 per cent is three times a rate of 4 per cent. Such statements are meaningful. Ratio data are the only ones on which you can use any mathematical technique you wish. But even then you have to choose your statistical techniques carefully, as some of these depend on the way in which the data are likely to be distributed. If values clump in different ways, some techniques may give misleading 'answers'.

Data deficiencies

Why is it that 'facts' may be less reliable than you think? Data purport to represent reality, but reality rarely presents itself in the form of numbers. Someone has to measure something, or classify something, or record and count something. And they have to decide what to count or measure in the first place. There are all sorts of ways in which the decisions and processes which resulted in a particular set of data can seriously influence that data.

Accuracy and *reliability* of data are obviously vital. If my petrol gauge is totally erratic, data it provides about the state of my tank is worth very little. If my eyesight is poor, I may misread the gauge and introduce further errors. If there is scope for judgement and I want one result more than another I may unconsciously influence my measures in the direction I want. This will lead to a biased result. You need to ask, or if possible check, whether measures are *reliable*. This means that another observer gets the same result. Or that the same observer gets the same result if the measure is taken again.

> **Data need to be:**
> - accurate
> - reliable
> - valid
> - consistent
> - representative.

If there *are* differences, they may be random or biased. Slight random variation is common and, with luck, errors will cancel each other out. But often inaccuracies are all in one direction. For example, accidents at work are often under-reported. And although there is a system for doctors to notify any adverse reactions to drugs, these too seem to be very seriously under-reported. If there are omissions in data, you do need to check whether they are random or tend to occur in one particular direction. (In the example of 'adverse effect' reporting, this systematic bias has led to considerable delays in identifying drugs with dangerous side effects.)

Validity is also important. Do the data actually measure what they purport to measure? Can you take in-company data at face value, given the various purposes for which it might be collected? Consider the 'measure' of test performance in schools. This might be a measure of teaching effectiveness. But it might be that it reflects the intelligence or social background of the children attending that school. To take an extreme example, if children at a school for those with learning difficulties scored poorly, this would not suggest that the school was unsatisfactory. And lesser variations in ability between intakes in normal schools in different locations could still have a significant influence on test scores. If you were sufficiently unprincipled as to include work done by someone else in your portfolio, would this be valid data on *your* competence?

This issue is important in a number of situations. In surveys and interviews it is possible to get very different answers depending on how you ask the question. Piaget's classic research offered pre-schoolers two lines of counters and asked which had 'more'. He found that, if four counters were spread out to take more space than a line of five, the children indicated that the line with four had 'more'. It was only many years later that the validity of this test as an indicator of children's concept of number was questioned. Using a line of sweets, rather than counters, and asking them to 'Choose one line' led to the infants taking the line of five every time, no matter how it was arranged.

Indicators or measures?

► Ch 2

In fact, it is worth noting that many 'measures' are in fact 'indicators' rather than direct measures, and the issue of validity is crucial. Remember the example of 'measuring' paperwork rather than the resulting bank loans which was given in the discussion of measures for control. (Note that control is still the reason for much of the information collected in organisations.) This demonstrated how easy it can be to manipulate an indicator. A direct measure of loans awarded would have been less susceptible to manipulation.

Consistency in measures is also important if you wish to make comparisons. Sometimes data are consciously altered so that the same situation would generate different data when 'measured' again. I think it was during the 1970s/1980s that the government changed the way of calculating the unemployment figures something like nineteen times in many fewer years. Although good reasons were always given, each change in the way unemployment was measured resulted in a lower unemployment rate than the previous formula would have generated. Each of the measures was a good indicator of unemployment – in that sense it was valid. Each would have been reliable – a second civil servant working out a given year's figures with the prevailing formula would have come up with the same answer. But the changes in method meant that it was impossible to make meaningful comparisons between different years. This is why 'consistency' is such an important accounting principle. There may be different approaches to, say, costing or depreciation, but whichever is adopted it should be used consistently. Otherwise it is impossible for investors to compare financial results from year to year.

Representativeness is also vital. There is always a temptation to use data which are readily available, even if they are not exactly what you would want if you had endless resources. Thus I might ask friends what they think of graduate recruits. It is easy for me to do this. But my few friends are not representative of all employers, and drawing sweeping conclusions from what they say would be highly dangerous. Similarly, you would not wish to predict election results from a survey of home owners in two rather exclusive neighbourhoods. It might be easy to ask them because they live near you and are likely to be at home when you knock on their doors. But their voting intentions would be a poor indication of how the population at large was likely to vote.

➤ Ch 14

This may seem obvious, yet I have examined far too many student projects where conclusions about hundreds or even thousands of people the world over were drawn from perhaps as few as six interviews conducted in a single branch of one organisation. How you interpret your data will depend heavily upon the sample from which it is drawn. This topic is dealt with in the next chapter.

From data to information

Much of the next chapter is devoted to how you turn data into information using graphical techniques and statistics. Indeed, you might prefer to move directly to that and read it before reading the rest of this chapter, which addresses the main ways in which you are likely to obtain data. Either order will work. I have covered topics in the order you would be likely to proceed if doing a research project within an organisation: literature search, interview and questionnaire here and, in the next chapter, analysis and presentation of data. But, equally, you do need to understand how to turn data into information before you plan the data you need. Otherwise you risk collecting data that are incapable of giving you a clear answer to the question which interests you. So you really need to read both chapters before doing anything beyond the very basic. And for anything other than a small project, you probably need to find out much more about statistics and research methodologies than it is possible for this book to cover. Better still find a good statistician to ask.

Looking for Information – Academic Literature and Other Sources

➤ Ch 4

Throughout your course you are likely to be searching the literature for additional references to supplement or replace those suggested by your lecturer for an essay topic. The basics of how to search were introduced in Chapter 4; this section starts from the assumption that you read that some time ago, and have been carrying out basic literature searches since then, using your library's facilities. (If this is not the case, go back and read it now, before continuing with this chapter.)

This section looks at the more detailed search for resources that you will be expected to carry out for a dissertation or project, or when faced with making decisions at work that need an evidence base. Early in this process you will probably be looking to the academic and professional literature to deepen your understanding of concepts that might help you explore a scenario in more depth and make sense of what you find. This will help you to frame the questions that you would like to be able to use data to answer. You might then look for government, industry or other statistics, and academic research to find relevant secondary data.

Refining your question

In early assignments you will probably be seeking fairly general information on a given topic. Your tutor may be looking for basic search skills, an understanding of two or three significant theories related to the topic, and the ability to summarise and connect these. As you progress you will be expected to be increasingly critical of the theory – how recent is it, what assumptions underpin it, what does it add to other theories on the topic, and how well does it relate to the case or problem which concerns you?

Similar questions are equally essential in any search for information to inform decision or action. But once you have some freedom in defining your topic there will be a prior question that is even harder to answer – 'What would it be helpful to find out'?

For most topics in business and management there is so much now available that looking for 'everything about' something like motivation or staff turnover or consumer behaviour would take the rest of your life. Remember, information has a cost, and you are looking for a question you can 'afford' to answer in terms of the time and other resources available to you. Until you have some experience in using data to answer questions it is very hard to judge this. The discussion which follows will help you understand some of the requirements you need to consider. Experience will give you a better idea of how much effort it will take to meet these requirements! To begin with, you can safely assume that everything will take at least twice as long as you think, and to scale back your ambitions accordingly!

Getting started can be the most difficult. Suppose you already have a topic you are interested in, and an area of theory that concerns you. The first step is to do some very rapid reading around the broad topic in the light of the problem presented. Finding out what has already been done in the area which interests you will first help clarify your research question, second help you work out how to approach your own research. You will also be able to use this initial reading to provide context for your subsequent more detailed search when writing the part of your report on literature search.

In the case of the Welsh coal mines mentioned above, absence levels were running at something like 20 per cent and management wanted to know how to minimise its impact, and how it could be reduced. I had some part-time research assistants, but nowhere near the resources to tell them. I focused on looking in the literature for factors shown to affect decisions to attend work in physically demanding industries. I also spoke to as many miners as possible about what influenced their decisions to come to work, and what they thought caused others to be off 'sick'. An initial rapid search of the literature on absenteeism had established that much 'sick absence' has nothing to do with actual illness. For an academic project you will start with the academic literature. If writing a report at work for your manager you will again need to search, though perhaps with a different type of literature and with fewer search tools to help you. In all these searches you will need to act critically, to question assumptions, and to evaluate and analyse the sources you find. Otherwise you may be seriously misled by the data and ideas your search reveals.

As Chapter 4 suggested, once you have some idea of what you are looking for, a good first step is to get to know your university library and the resources it offers. You may be surprised at how much is available, and how easy it is to search the resources. Librarians are a source of great expertise in what is available and how best to find what you want. If you have not already done so, check what tutorials and other support your library offers, and take advantage of these as much as possible. If you need more, there are also excellent online tutorials – often developed by universities. Look for those with .ac or .edu in the address, as they are likely to be designed for academic use. What follows is a brief general outline of some of the ideas and distinctions that may help you search more effectively.

While most universities have excellent libraries, not all allow full access from off-campus. If this is so, and you need library access during the vacation, explore your local university and public library facilities. You can normally obtain reader privileges in any university library if you are a student elsewhere. (This may also be helpful if a nearby university has a better library than your own institution.)

Different 'layers' of literature

As with numerical data, it is possible to classify literature. Here the categories are:

- **primary sources** – the first time something appears, possibly for restricted circulation, e.g. theses, company reports, unpublished manuscripts
- **secondary sources** – subsequent publication of primary literature, aimed at a wider audience, e.g. books, journals, some government publications
- **tertiary sources** – designed to help you find the relevant primary and secondary literature, or to provide an introduction to a topic, e.g. abstracts, bibliographies, citation indexes.

If you are starting with only a very general idea of what you are looking for tertiary sources are a good starting point. They can give you a 'feel' for the topic, and of concepts which are emerging as potentially useful. So look for a recent review article in a reputable journal, and see if your library holds any recent dissertations on closely related subjects. You may even get some ideas from Wikipedia, provided you use these only as a starting point. Once you have found some potentially useful ideas, you can use them as the basis for asking questions about the situation, or searching the literature for relevant research and further ideas.

Parameters and key words

Once you have at least a rough idea of the question you are investigating and concepts which may be helpful you can translate this into search parameters to help to define the search area. (You may still change or refine your parameter further as you read more.) For a business studies project you would want to know:

- the subject area, e.g. marketing, impact of legislation, or motivation
- the language of your search. Note that American and English are different languages! Many words you might wish to use to search indexes are either completely different (car/automobile) or spelt differently (behaviour/behavior, skilful/skillful). This can be important in electronic searching, though search engines are quite good now at guessing what you mean
- the business sector, e.g. manufacturing, not-for-profit, defence
- how far back you want to search, e.g. five years
- the type of literature, e.g. refereed journals only

The last point is important. Even when you are searching the literature for an assignment early in your studies your tutors will normally expect you to look in refereed journals

➤ Ch 4

rather than relying solely on the sort of online digests discussed in Chapter 4. More on this shortly.

Then you need to generate a list of *key words* to drive your search. Think about the sorts of words that authors might have used in the title of the kind of article you want to read. Suppose you were interested in career paths for women in the oil industry. You might search not only on women, but on female and gender, as an author might have described their research in any of these terms. You might use brainstorming

➤ Ch 12

(see Chapter 12) either individually or in a group to generate possible key words and phrases.

Once you have something to start with, you can use that to generate other possible terms. Suppose you have used a key word and found a useful-sounding article. If you then display the full entry, it will normally show you 'subject headings' or 'descriptors', or some other term relating to the index terms used. Among these there may well be other potentially useful key words.

Another useful approach is to construct a relevance tree – a close relative of a mind map. At the top you write the question or subject you are investigating. Branching down from this you write areas which seem important, then move successively downwards, teasing each apart into sub-areas. Figure 13.2 gives an example of a relevance tree. Having spread out the various topics, you can identify those which you need to search immediately and those which you think may be the main focus of your research. Highlight each category in a different colour, or underline or asterisk – as long as you can see at a glance which are the 'urgents' and which the 'importants', it doesn't matter how you distinguish them.

As it is inevitable that you will refine your thinking when you start to read more about a subject, you may like to regard your relevance tree as a working document. Update it if you realise that there are different ways of looking at the subject, or when new issues emerge as important.

13

DATA, INFORMATION AND DECISIONS

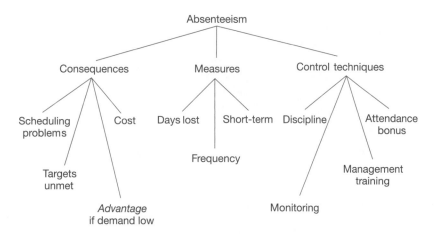

Figure 13.2 Relevance tree for the early stages of a research project

TECHSkills 13.1 Combining search terms – using link words.

Sometimes you may want only papers that have both your search terms in them, sometimes either will do. For example, if you were to be offered everything there was about women, you would be swamped. If you limited your search to resources referring to women *and* career *and* oil industry this would narrow it down considerably. Sometimes you might want to exclude a subset – thus perhaps you were interested only in non-graduate or non-ethnic minority women. Link terms derived from Boolean logic, allow you to do such things. You need to understand the basic ideas and then find out how to communicate them to the particular system you are using. The terms AND, OR and NOT are the usual term to use, though your system might use some other way of representing these meanings. Figure 13.3 shows how these relate pictorially. Thus you could ask for 'pay AND appraisal' and the link term 'AND' (or '+' or whatever) would ensure that only references containing both keywords were offered to you. This would be a much shorter list than that generated by either 'pay' or 'appraisal' alone. Asking for 'appraisal NOT financial' would spare you hundreds of references on financial appraisal but give you all other sorts of appraisal, whereas 'downsizing OR redundancy' would bring you articles on either topic. (Because there is not yet uniform acceptance of 'AND', 'NOT' and 'OR' for this purpose, you do have to check on the symbols in each index you use.) You can even look for part of a word, thus 'motiv*' might generate references on motivation, motivators, and so forth.

If you do not use link terms, your search engine may use a weak idea of 'and', offering you mainly terms with the combination of words you typed in, but then moving on to a wider search. If you feel you need more help with online search, there are many tutorials available online (a few of which are suggested in online resources).

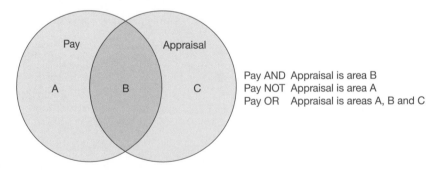

Pay AND Appraisal is area B
Pay NOT Appraisal is area A
Pay OR Appraisal is areas A, B and C

Figure 13.3 The Boolean logic of searches

Deciding where to look

Once you have at least a rough idea of what you are looking for, you need to decide where to look. Your library is one obvious place. It is likely to have an extensive database of journals, e-books, government reports and other sources of information relevant to business and management, and it will cost you nothing to look at these. It will also have a means of searching these databases in order to find things relevant to your search terms. Once you have identified potentially relevant papers, reports or books, you will normally be able to look at an abstract, and download a full copy if the abstract looks promising.

TECHSkills 13.2 Using google scholar

A popular alternative is Google Scholar. While it is usually easy to find a book or article in a university library if you know the journal or author you are looking for they can be less easy than Google to search for a particular topic. My own students often find it easier to search for likely articles on Google Scholar, read the abstract (which is free) and then go to the university library for free access to full article if the summary suggests it is worth reading in full. You may be able to set your preferences in Google to link through seamlessly. (If you access sources direct from Google there will often be a charge.)

Google Scholar has its own way of deciding which sources to put at the top of the list it offers, based not only on how closely it matches your search terms, but factors such as an assessment of the author, and how often the work has been cited subsequently (beneath each suggestion it tells you how many such citations). Google Scholar is not infallible – although its database is massive there are sources such as individual researchers' web pages that its crawlers do not reach. But it is pretty good, and a more likely limitation is your choice of keywords to search on.

The number of citations will give you an indication of how useful other researchers have found this source. Of course older publications have had time to be cited more often, and papers in very specialised areas are likely to have been cited by fewer people. So if you are looking at a narrow topic that has only recently attracted the attention of researchers, do not worry if the citation number is fairly small – this is inevitable. When you start to publish papers yourself you can use this feature to see how often others cite your work!)

Another useful feature of Google Scholar is the ability to limit your search to papers published this year, in the last year, or in the last five years, and to set up alerts in order to be notified of further relevant publications.

If you are not sure that you are using the best keywords as search terms, looking at the references cited by some of the papers you find that look relevant may suggest other possible search terms. Looking at the papers that have subsequently cited the paper you are considering can suggest further terms. (Click on the suggestion, and then on 'Citations' at the bottom to bring up a list of these.)

Storing what you find

➤ Ch 4 You will remember from Chapter 4 how important it was to organise what you find for future reference. You may already be using EndNote or similar bibliographic software to help with this. Another facility which Google Scholar offers is easy construction of your own library – at the click of a button you can save things found to 'My Library' – which you can organise into folders for different topics to make it easier to retrieve.

Since this is stored on a cloud, your work is protected from theft or breakdown of your computer. You can also choose to share your library with others working with you. However, if you are accessing the full text of papers through your library rather than via Google you might also want to create the equivalent of 'my library' within your university's system. (Remember if you do this – as with a portfolio – you will probably need to migrate any references you want to keep to another system at some point after graduation. Most university systems withdraw access to their own systems once students' graduate, or fairly soon after.)

Because of this, and because of the ease of the Google system, it may be worth keeping both sorts of library – Google for things you might want to read eventually, and another system for those you have read and found useful enough to want to refer to in detail in future.

Reading and evaluating literature

The ease of creating your own library of relevant resources may fool you into thinking that once you have done this, the bulk of your work is done, and you can relax. Alas, there is still no substitute for actually reading what you find, and thinking critically about it, and extracting key points in the form of notes you can use in essay or literature search report. As you become more independent as a learner, and take more responsibility for defining the scope of your reading, the ability to read critically becomes even more crucial.

Chapter 4 suggested some ways of evaluating what you read:

- author's perspective and any potential for bias
- recency/currency
- soundness of methodology
- clarity/logic of arguments
- adequacy of data
- relevance to your particular research question.

You may also want to consider where something was published and citation information when you are deciding whether a concept or research data deserve inclusion in your research. Peer-reviewed journals used to be the 'gold standard' for quality. But journal publishing has undergone major change in recent years. All respectable journals used to exploit 'free' academic time to write and peer-review articles, and serve on editorial boards, while printing costs (and profit) were generated from journal subscriptions, mainly from university libraries. Such journals still exist, but the Internet combined with shrinking university journal budgets has led to a massive growth in 'open access' journals.

These are freely available to users. Instead of subscription income, academics (or their departments) pay for their work to be published. This has had two negative consequences. Instead of anonymous peer-reviewers deciding whether a paper is worth publishing, the decision is effectively taken by faculties, as they decide how to spend their 'publication budget' – such decisions may favour more established researchers making it difficult for junior research staff to publish their research. Worse, a large number of dubious journals have sprung up, often with impressive names, but more interested in getting the money for publication rather than ensuring the quality of what is published (Nelson, 2013). You cannot therefore place the same reliance on the journal for ensuring the quality of articles it publishes.

The librarian who first noticed that this was happening maintains a list of such 'predatory' journals (Beall, 2015) which you may find interesting. While it may do an injustice to some *bona fide* journals which are just starting up, many librarians find it a useful resource.

Even in top quality refereed journals, you may find data that offer little potential as evidence in the arguments you are developing. Evaluating what you read depends very much on the purpose for which you are reading it. Are you looking for general information on how people think about an issue at present, or issues which are of particular concern in an area, or how a classic idea has been applied to similar scenarios, or what new ideas have been helpful in understanding similar scenarios? Or something completely different? The range of possible types of 'uncertainty' that you might want to reduce is huge, and will be different depending on whether you are at a convergent of divergent stage of thinking about an issue. There is more on this in the chapter on projects. But whenever you are seeking data or information you can save yourself lots of time, and improve the effectiveness of your search, but spending much more time than you probably feel inclined to in thinking about just what it is it would be helpful to find out!

Finding Relevant Secondary Data

Some of your reading will provide ideas some may provide data resulting from research. You may also be able to access data from government statistics, industry reports and other sets of statistics. In the UK the Office for National Statistics offers a wealth of free statistical information and the main (.gov.uk) website has a many free reports – again often including useful information. Other countries have equivalent government resources. Your university library is also likely to subscribe to a range of commercial databases providing industry and other useful data.

If you are doing a project on a particular company you may find they have a wealth of past reports relevant to your topic that may provide useful data.

Activity 13.1

....

Choose a topic that interests you (e.g. use of zero hours contracts in the UK between 2012 and the present, retail sales of ready-meals in three different countries during the last year, childhood obesity rates in different parts of the world, or average adult carbon consumption since 2010 in a country of your choice) and see how many different sources of relevant information you can find using Google or a similar search engine, or searching directly in your university library's resources.

Interviews

➤ Ch 8

One of the most popular ways of generating primary data for student projects is to conduct a series of interviews. This requires you to use the talking and listening skills developed earlier, but you need additionally to know a little about the potential hazards of collecting data in this way.

Interviewing sounds wonderfully simple. You merely ask some questions, either standard ones or, even better, anything that on the spur of the moment you are inspired to ask. Provided these fall under a set of fairly broad headings this can be called a 'semi-structured' interview. You record the results, analyse them and you have the answer to your research question. Alas, it is rather more difficult. Although you can learn a great deal from merely talking to people, provided you listen carefully, it is difficult to put together what each person tells you and make collective sense of it. There is also a possibility that they will misunderstand your questions or you will misunderstand their answers. They may even tell you, or at least you may hear, only what you want to hear.

➤ Ch 8

Skilful interviewing therefore requires that you add to your talking and listening skills certain other abilities. You need to be able to:

- formulate unambiguous questions which do not indicate, even subtly, the 'right' answer
- avoid giving any other hints as to what you want
- use a style which encourages a person to answer questions freely and to the best of their ability
- probe and clarify if the answer is not sufficiently full or clear
- record interviewees' answers accurately for subsequent analysis.

Of course, as with everything else, you also need to be absolutely clear about what it is that you want to know. And you need to have thought about the number of people to ask and how to choose them, given the question that your project is trying to answer.

Interview types

Before you can do this, you need to think about the type of interview which best suits your purpose:

- **Structured interviews** are those where you work out a set of questions before you start, and ask each interviewee exactly the same questions, in the same order, and even in the same tone of voice, so as not to inadvertently bias your results.
- **Semi-structured interviews** are those where you 'know what you want to know', that is, you have a set of themes, issues or topics which you want to explore. But you 'go with the flow' to some extent, approaching these issues in an order that seems appropriate given the way the conversation is going, dropping issues which seem inappropriate with a particular respondent and adding others which the conversation suggests may be important.

- **Unstructured** (or **in-depth**) **interviews** are even more informal and non-standardised. The interviewee is given free rein to talk about a topic in depth.

Different types of interviews will depend both on what you are trying to find out and on where you are in your investigation. At an early stage, while your thoughts are developing, unstructured interviews are likely to be most useful in suggesting issues that seem to be important to the people that you talk to and relationships that seem to exist between these issues. Having this information could help you to formulate a set of questions for a structured interview. While you can gain strong impressions from such interviews, and they may uncover whole areas you had not seen as relevant, they are very difficult to analyse in any systematic way.

If you want to be able to describe tendencies or patterns in a group of responses, then you are likely to need a structured interview. Then you can compare the responses of different groups to the same questions and explore whether responses to one set of questions are related to responses to others. Analysis is usually easy: there is normally only a limited range of answers to any of these questions. You may be able to code answers while the person is talking. Several people can do the interviewing and their sets of answers are easily amalgamated. A structured interview is really a questionnaire which is administered by someone else. It has all the advantages of a questionnaire (see next sub-section, where question design for either is discussed), but if you use an interview you are more likely to get answers to *all* the questions and a higher response rate – all too often questionnaires go into the bin. Many people, for example senior managers, will agree to be interviewed but would never complete a questionnaire.

Despite the rather cynical comment earlier, semi-structured interviews can be extremely useful. For example, if you are trying to find out *why* a structured interview gives you certain patterns, you are likely to need a semi-structured interview. Suppose you had used a questionnaire to find out how satisfied people were with their jobs and whether they had applied for jobs elsewhere. You might have found that, in most departments, people were satisfied, but in two they were not. In one of these unhappy departments everyone was applying for jobs elsewhere; in the other they were not. To find out both why they were unhappy and why they were behaving differently with respect to other jobs, a semi-structured interview would be useful.

Types of questions

The exact way in which you phrase your question can have a significant effect on the answers you are given by the interviewee. For semi-structured and unstructured interviews you will need to rely on three main types of question: open, probing and closed.

Open

Open questions allow the interviewee to decide what is important to include in an answer. Questions which are *too* open can produce long and sometimes irrelevant answers. 'What do you think about the recent redundancies?' might produce anything.

'What methods have your organisation used to make people redundant?' would produce a more focused answer (assuming that it was methods that interested you). 'What', 'who', 'when', 'where', 'why' and 'how' are among the words useful for open questions.

Closed

Closed questions are those which tend to generate a yes or no answer, for example: 'Were recent redundancies handled well?' This type of question might be useful either as a starting point, or as a follow-up to clarify your understanding. 'So, on balance, do you think that the methods chosen were appropriate?', could be useful as a check on your understanding of part of an answer to a more open question. Use such questions sparingly, though. If you use closed questions too early you risk closing a topic before you have found out what you want. If you use them too often your interviewee will tend to give shorter and shorter answers.

> **For effective interviewing:**
>
> - use active listening
> - set the scene carefully
> - ask simple, neutral questions
> - probe if necessary
> - minimise closed questions
> - close the interview carefully
> - record data immediately.

Probing

Probing questions are used to explore answers in more depth. If you want to know more than the interviewee has given in an answer, you can say something like: 'That's interesting. Could you tell me more about the reasons for . . .?' or '. . . why the relationship between . . .?' or whatever it is that you wish to be expanded. Probes are very useful if you realise that you have inadvertently asked a closed question.

Interviewing skills

Once you have selected your respondents, gained their agreement, know what you want to find out, and the sorts of questions you need to ask, there are some basic guidelines to note. These will help you to generate valid data.

Guidelines for interviewing

- Practise active listening and observe body language.
- Manage the start of the interview very carefully – it is crucial to its success. You need to make the person feel comfortable. Thank them for their help and explain again the purpose of the interview and how long it is likely to take. You need to stress confidentiality, making clear whether anyone else will have access to the results of the interview. It usually helps to make clear that the interviewee will not be identifiable in the final report (unless of course they have agreed to be identified). You need to indicate what will happen to the results of your investigation. It is helpful, too, to give an idea of the sort of responses you want (e.g. brief or more discursive, immediate or

considered). And you need to explain how you are recording answers (normally notes or tape recorder) and make sure that the person is happy with this.

- Keep questions as short and as simple as possible. If you roll three complex questions into one, it will be hard for your interviewee to make sense of what is required. It will also be hard for you to make sense of what they say. Also, if your question is rambling, your respondents will tend to follow your lead and speak at great length without saying very much. This makes both recording and analysis difficult.

- Use language that your interviewee will understand. It is pointless to use jargon or over-intellectual language with people who are not used to such words.

- Ask neutral questions. It is extremely easy to bias answers by using negatively or positively loaded words in describing some of the options.

- Use closed questions sparingly, only when you mean to.

- Start with questions that the interviewee will find easy, interesting and non-threatening. This will allow them to settle and feel comfortable with you. Later in the interview you can ask more challenging questions, or touch on sensitive issues, with a good chance of getting a valid response. The same questions early in an interview might elicit very little.

- Conclude by thanking the interviewee and giving them the chance to raise any concerns they may have as a result of the interview.

- Record your data as soon as possible after the interview. If you have made notes, sort them out and do any necessary classifying of responses while the interview is still fresh. If you are tape recording, do not let the tapes accumulate. Transcribing takes ages and is best done as you go along in most cases. You may wish to modify later interviews in the light of early responses, so thinking immediately after you finish about how the interview has gone and any problems and new thoughts that it prompted is important, particularly at the start of your interviewing.

(This is available on the website.)

Focus Groups

Thus far the discussion has covered interviews with individuals. Focus groups, a technique widely used in market research, provide a way of exploring the views of a small group, (usually 6–10 people) whose opinions are relevant to your research. The group is asked to discuss your chosen topic. The aim is to allow group members to develop their own ideas through unstructured interaction. This can throw up ideas that research has not considered, and show that other issues are more or less important than anticipated.

As the researcher, you facilitate the group. This should be a fairly passive role once the topic has been introduced. You are trying merely to encourage interaction within the group, not to steer it. If the discussion flags, you can ask supplementary questions such as 'What about ...?' If one person dominates, you may need to gently subdue them. If some people do not contribute, you may need to encourage them. If the discussion veers totally off the point, you may need to gently redirect it, but you need to be careful not to steer the discussion too firmly. Such steering would reduce your chances of finding out anything that you do not already know. In the industry, focus groups are often run by trained psychologists, but the group skills you developed in Chapter 9 should help you to make a reasonable job of it.

➤ Ch 9

You will need to keep a careful record of the discussion. This can be video- or audio-taped for later analysis. Alternatively, or additionally, notes are taken. If at all possible, find someone to help you with this. It is very hard to take adequate notes while doing a good job of facilitation.

Focus groups can be extremely useful at the start of a project when you are trying to identify important issues or research questions. But they have the same drawback as informal interviews. The sample is likely to be too small for reliable conclusions. The process of making sense of what was said is also highly subjective, with the researcher struggling to extract meaning from a fairly free-ranging discussion. You will normally need to supplement focus group findings with a more systematic investigation.

Questionnaires

Surveys requiring respondents to complete a questionnaire are a popular way of collecting information for all sorts of purposes. You may have received various 'market research' questionnaires through the post or been sent a questionnaire after you bought something or made use of a service. Although you can include open-ended questions on a questionnaire, the fact that you cannot probe or clarify responses can make analysis of responses to these quite difficult. The main strength of questionnaires is that they allow you to identify and describe the extent of variation in answers on particular topics and to look for relationships between positions on one set of questions and positions on another. Thus you could use a survey to establish factual things like the educational qualifications of users of a particular sports facility, or frequency of usage, or attitudinal aspects such as their satisfaction with the various sports on offer. You could also look for relationships, such as between level of education and preferred sport and/or satisfaction levels.

Questionnaire design is crucial, particularly if the respondents are supposed to fill in the questionnaire themselves. (Sometimes questionnaires are administered over the telephone or face to face in a structured interview.) You need to have a very clear idea of what you need to know, to ask it in a totally unambiguous way and to make clear how the respondent is to reply.

Activity 13.2

Imagine that you work in a medical centre and you want to collect information from patients on their alcohol usage. Think about the way in which you and people you know might respond to the following questions and how much information this is likely to give the practice. If possible, ask a few people, using only one of the questions below, followed by informal discussion to check what it means, then ask others all three, in the order shown.

A Does alcohol play a part in your life? ——

B Would you describe yourself as a light, moderate or heavy drinker? ——

C How many drinks do you have a week on average? (Count a half pint of beer, one glass of wine or a single shot of spirits as '1'.) ——

    0–1 ❑   2–3 ❑   4–7 ❑   8–14 ❑   15–21 ❑   22–35 ❑   36–42 ❑   43+ ❑

You need to be very careful in interpreting answers, as your follow-up discussion may have shown. Question A (taken from a real questionnaire) presumably elicited both yes and no from people with very similar levels of drinking. Question B may well have elicited some 'light' responses from people who consume rather more than those who see themselves as 'moderate' drinkers. The range of possible drinking levels given in question C may make it easier for people to admit to drinking, say, 22 units than if the scale had stopped at 22+, as it makes them appear well within the range on offer, rather than at the extreme. For areas that are often under-reported, such as drinking and smoking levels, this may be an important consideration.

You can perhaps see from this why it is important to pilot a questionnaire with a small number of people – try it out and then look at the answers that are given. Do some questions produce the same answer from everybody? If so, those questions may not be generating much information. Do some questions get omitted? This may be because people do not realise that they must turn the page, or because the question looks like part of the instruction, or because it is not clear what the question means or how to answer it. Talk to those who filled out the questionnaire about whether they had difficulty with any of the questions and probe the meaning of their answers to check that you will be interpreting them correctly. Check too that your layout and the way the questions are to be answered make it as easy as possible to analyse the results.

Response rates

It is extremely important to get a reasonable response rate. What constitutes reasonable will depend on the size of your sample, the complexity of the analysis you want to do and the randomness or otherwise of the 'sample within a sample', that is, those people who *do* fill in the questionnaire.

Activity 13.3

Suppose that you send a questionnaire to 100 people. You write a pleasant covering letter explaining what you are doing and why, as well as why their participation is important and that responses will be treated confidentially, but you receive only 10 replies.

Think of reasons for people not replying, what this means about the usefulness of the 10 you get back and how you might be able to increase the response rate. If possible, discuss this in a group, drawing on your own responses to questionnaires you have received.

You probably came up with reasons such as 'questionnaire looked too long and time consuming', 'first few questions were difficult/intrusive/boring/incomprehensible so didn't go further', 'why should I pay for a stamp to give them information?', 'meant to but somehow didn't get around to it' and so on. Increasing response rate will depend on the reasons: a well-designed, appealing questionnaire will address the first two, use of email or a stamped addressed envelope, the third. Small incentives such as a prize for the lucky reply and a better prize if the questionnaire is returned within seven days will address two reasons, and reminders are also helpful.

It is vital that you *do* ensure a better response rate than this. If you send out 100 questionnaires and get 10 back, you will have very little data to analyse. Worse, you will not know if the 10 were reasonably typical of the 100, or the only 10 who were different in some significant way. For example, it might be that the only people who reply to a questionnaire about the quality of nursing care during a recent hospital stay are the tiny minority who had a bad experience and are still angry enough to want to tell someone about this when the questionnaire arrives. If you assumed they were typical, you could be seriously misled about the quality of care that most patients at the hospital receive.

If you use questionnaires, you are facing a minefield. Plan to spend some time reading about questionnaire design and sampling, or consult an expert, before designing your questionnaire, and never use a questionnaire without first piloting it. Try it out on several people and afterwards ask them to interpret their questions and to comment on any uncertainties or difficulties they had in answering.

Developing Your Information-Gathering Skills

Although you will probably not need to do a major research project until well into your degree programme, you can be starting to develop the necessary skills long before then. Not only will the information you gather be useful in its own right but it will mean that, when you do face the challenge of a project, you will approach the information gathering in a more effective way than might otherwise have been the case.

There are two main approaches and you might wish to adopt both. The first requires you to treat information gathering as a series of discrete skills to be developed. Thus, you might consider your familiarity with the resources in your university library and how to access them, and seek help in mastering any aspects in which you do not yet feel confident. You could practise searching for information online. You could set up a series of practice interviews and work with others to design a questionnaire, pilot and refine it and administer it. All these are extremely worthwhile activities. Any or all could constitute exhibits demonstrating 'managing learning' for your portfolio.

The second approach involves adopting the 'reflective practitioner' approach outlined in Chapter 3 and making use of the learning cycle model. This means that first you need to be alert to information and its uses – by now you should be a little more so. You then need to think about situations in which you will need actively to seek and use information. Obviously, any project in your degree course is likely to fall into this category. But before this, essays and other coursework offer opportunities. And courses may have other, smaller-scale investigations which you are required to carry out. Your life will also offer occasions when, by seeking information, you can take a better decision or action. Your work on specific skills could therefore be supplemented by seeing all such situations in informational terms and using at least some of the ideas here as a framework for finding that information. In all cases pay particular attention in the beginning to considering the areas of uncertainty you face, and what data and information would be most helpful in reducing that uncertainty.

Activity 13.4

Use the following prompts to assess your information-gathering skills. Score 5 if an item is completely true, 4 if it is more true than untrue, 3 if it is somewhere in the middle, 2 if more or less untrue, 1 if totally untrue.

I have explored the library and know what resources it has available.   ___

I can easily locate sources that might be relevant using Google Scholar
and/or the university's search facility sources in the library's catalogue
and appropriate link terms and key words.   ___

I am comfortable using abstracts and citation indices to assess
the likely usefulness of articles I find.   ___

I know how to access particular electronic journals and to find specific
papers within them.   ___

I know how to use citations and references to extend my use of search terms.   ___

I am comfortable in searching for government and other statistics.   ___

I routinely record and organise all potentially useful references and can easily
locate references, the original article or my notes on something I have read.   ___

➤

I would never use a questionnaire without piloting it to make sure that my intended recipients understood the questions and I understood the meaning of their answers   ___

I would always decide on what the minimum acceptable response rate was before sending out a questionnaire, and do all I could to get maximum returns   ___

I am careful never to draw conclusions beyond those justified by the data   ___

Total   ___

On most of the previous skills assessments a perfect score would suggest optimism or bending the truth. Here you really should be aiming for a perfect 50 by the end of your degree. Start to plan now to reach that point. Re-score yourself at intervals to check progress.

SUMMARY

This chapter has argued the following:

- Data are measures or indicators of some kind derived from a situation. They may be more or less selective, accurate, reliable and valid.

- Data may be primary or secondary, quantitative or qualitative, textual, nominal, ordinal or ratio. In interpreting data it is important to understand their characteristics.

- When data are organised in a way that is relevant to a question that concerns you, they become information. In order to obtain useful information, you need to be clear about your objectives and the questions which you are trying to answer.

- Many quests for information will start with a literature search, using key words. Citations and references can help you extend your list of relevant key words.

- It is essential to organise your references using bibliographic software of some kind.

- In generating your own primary data, you may need to use focus groups, questionnaires and interviews. Whichever you use, clear communication is crucial, question formulation is critical and it is important to avoid bias.

- Further reading will be necessary if you wish to rely heavily on either questionnaires or interviews for a major project.

Further information

Cameron, S. and Price, D. (2009) *Business Research Methods: A Practical Approach*, CIPD.

Gill, J. and Johnson, P. (2010) *Research Methods for Managers*, 4th edn, Sage.

Saunders, M., Lewis, P. and Thornhill, A. (2012) *Research Methods for Business Students*, 6th edn, Pearson. This contains considerably more detail on the topics covered here.

www.zoo.com – useful meta-search engine.

www.scholar.google.com – for access to scholarly publications.

www.ukonline.gov.uk – searches UK government and related websites.

http://www.uic.edu/depts/lib/reference/services/tutorials/Tutorial--Final%20Version.swf for an online tutorial on search terms.

14
MAKING SENSE OF DATA

Learning outcomes

By the end of this chapter you should:

- be able to show sets of figures graphically, interpret graphs and use them to estimate future values

- see how graphs can help you to answer questions

- understand how calculus can help you to solve problems

- be able to summarise sets of figures in terms of central tendency and range

- understand what is meant by probability and significance levels

- appreciate how significance will be linked to the size and distribution of your sample of observations.

Introduction

Raw data are seldom informative. They need interpretation. The interpretation needs to be communicated. This chapter looks at ways of summarising and communicating data, and drawing valid conclusions from them. It is all too easy to draw invalid conclusions from seemingly clear sets of figures. A vast range of statistical techniques exists to prevent this, and statistical software packages exist to help you to use these. While this chapter can do no more than introduce the basics of statistics, it should help you understand some of the key concepts, and make you less likely to misinterpret statistics that you read or produce. Such misunderstandings could cause you to fail your dissertation. In an organisation they could prove very expensive indeed.

Transforming data into information is a delicate art. It is not easy to interpret data and communicate their meaning to others. You may need to reorganise data so that patterns become clear. You need to be able to interpret the implications of these patterns and judge how much reliance to place on any conclusions you draw. You therefore need an understanding of statistical techniques and of the ideas about probability on which they are based. Sadly, such understanding is fairly rare. And its absence leads to flawed decisions. A single chapter cannot turn you into a statistician, but it can give you an appreciation of what statistical techniques can achieve. This should help you with planning any student projects. Perhaps more importantly, it will help you to exploit the 'information' with which you are likely to be deluged in any job, and save you from being led astray by it.

Before introducing you to the basics of statistics the chapter introduces a further area of mathematics: the calculus. You may already know this, or may not need it – in either case, skip it. But I have known not a few students come to grief because a calculus course was taught assuming far more than they knew, making it impossible for them to pass this compulsory subject. In case this is your situation, or you are simply interested in how differential equations can be an aid to answering questions involving numbers and equations, then work through this part of the chapter. In the process you will be able to revise
➤ Ch 5   some of the techniques introduced in Chapter 5.

'Lies, Damned Lies and Statistics'

Statistics is all about making data informative. The quotation in the section heading (attributed to Disraeli) reflects an ignorance of statistics that appears to be as widespread today as it was a century ago. For example, the *Western Daily Press* once claimed that motorists were much less likely to have a car stolen in Bristol than elsewhere because 'New figures from the AA show that, nationally, one car is stolen every 79 seconds, while the figure for Bristol is one car every 35 minutes.' Similar ignorance allowed a national paper to claim that 20 per cent of the population died each year from smoking-related diseases.

This ignorance is often dangerous rather than amusing. Consider the high-profile case some years ago of a man accused of murdering his wife. It emerged that the accused had regularly beaten his wife. His defence team presented the jury with the 'statistic' that only 1 in 1000 wife beaters go on to kill their wives. The jury presumably drew the obvious conclusion – that the evidence of wife beating was not really relevant. Yet, what was not relevant was that particular 'statistic' – or at least it was relevant only if combined with information about the chance of the wife being murdered at all, and the chances that in any given year a husband will kill his wife. If you use these to work out the chance of a wife beater being the culprit if his wife is murdered, you find that it is roughly 50:50, significantly higher than the probability of a non-violent husband being responsible.

Juries are not the only people interpreting – or misinterpreting – evidence. You will need to assess all sorts of evidence throughout your life. Whether you have done a lab experiment, conducted a series of structured interviews or are reading a report done for your company by a consultant, you need to know what conclusions you can safely draw from the data. The ability to make sense of numbers and to draw valid conclusions from them is vital in all areas of research and in virtually all organisations. In particular, many organisations are now involved in risk management, for which an understanding of probability is essential.

Because we are amazingly bad at making such judgements without help, a basic understanding of how statistical techniques can be used for assessing significance is invaluable. Such understanding needs to encompass the ideas of sampling, distributions and probability which underlie the techniques, as well as more basic ideas about how to represent numbers in a way that is more accessible than the figures themselves. And while we are looking at graphical representations, we can usefully take a detour into using graphs of equations to solve problems.

Drawing and Using Graphs

Turning numbers into pictures can make them much easier to grasp. A few people can look at a page covered with rows and rows of figures and instantly grasp what these numbers mean. Most people find it far easier to extract the sense from numbers if they are represented in the form of pictures. But it is easy to extract the wrong sense if you do not understand the basics of how the graphical representation was produced. Because spreadsheets can translate figures into pictures at the press of a button, it is much easier to use graphs and charts without understanding them than it was when you had to draw them yourself. If you are not familiar with turning figures on a spreadsheet into graphs or charts, do spend a little time finding and working through an online tutorial for the spreadsheet software you are using. These will explain things far better than I can do in text alone, as you will be able to see relevant screen shots throughout the tutorial.

➤ Ch 5

Different sorts of graphical representation are appropriate for different sorts of figures. Bar or column charts, scatter graphs and pie charts all have their value. As does one you will probably remember from school, called a graph.

Plotting graphs

The graphs you remember were probably those that showed the relationship between two variables, typically *x* and *y*. You drew two axes at right angles. The vertical line you called the *y*-axis, the horizontal *x* (*x* is a/cross). Both had numbers along them. The value of *y* depended on the value of *x*. You probably had an equation of the form $y = $ (something)

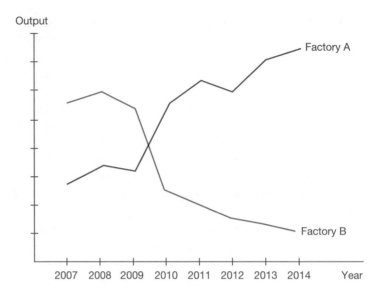

Figure 14.1 Graph showing annual production from two factories 1997–2004

$x +$ (something). Perhaps there was a (something)x^2 term as well. For each of the numbers along the x scale you worked out the value of y and put a dot at that height above the x. When you had all the dots, you joined them to form your graph.

Of course, you do not have to have an equation. In most business research you are more likely to be observing values of y and plotting them against the appropriate x. Figure 14.1 shows such an example, where production is plotted year on year for two factories. You can see that it is easy to spot trends and to make comparisons, whereas if you had been presented with, say, quarterly figures for each factory, each reflecting a degree of seasonal variations from quarter to quarter it might have been much more difficult.

The graph also allows you to make tentative predictions. Where you have a clear trend, as in both these lines, it is a fair bet that the line will continue, so you could guess at, say, the next two years' output from each factory and use these to inform recruitment strategy or marketing plans. Of course, your estimates would be on an 'other things being equal' basis, and other things are not always equal. Clearly, they were not in 2010. But in the absence of any other information, these estimates might be a better basis for planning than assuming that production will stabilise at present values.

Estimating will be easier if the trend is fairly clear. If the line is jumping around somewhat it will be difficult to say exactly where it will go next. But if there is an underlying trend, then you may still be able to use the graph to get an idea of the area within which future points are likely to lie.

In the above exercise you should have realised that it is not always necessary to have your axes meet at the zero point on each scale. If the variation is all within a certain band, then you will not see it very clearly if that band takes up only a tiny fraction of your scale. The line will look almost flat. Sometimes this could be the best way of showing it. Any variations might be insignificant, perhaps the result of measurement errors. It would

Test Exercise 14.1

Plot graphs of the following sets of figures, leaving room for two more points on the *x*-axis.

(a)

Year	1995	1996	1997	1998	1999	2000	2001	2002	2003	2004
Applicants accepted on to business and management degrees	4800	5000	6000	7500	9000	11 000	11 500	12 500	14 000	15 500

(b)

Year	1990	1991	1992	1993	1994
Rabies cases (Germany)	5500	3800	1500	800	1400

Add your estimated next two points on the graphs you have drawn. (Before looking at the answer you might like to practise using Excel to generate the two graphs.)

be wrong to make them look important by stretching the scale. But in other cases the variations might be important. If you were measuring plant growth, small variations in temperature might be crucial and to use a scale starting from zero might be totally inappropriate. You need to think carefully about your axes, about where they cross and where they end in terms of the scale with which you label them, if the meaning of the figures which the graph represents is to be clear. In both cases above there is no data before a certain point, so no need to go back to the year zero, whenever you deem that to be.

Using graphs to answer questions

There are many things you can do with graphs apart from just looking at them for patterns. For example, you can work out from a graph of observations the equation which best represents the relationship between the two variables observed. And you can use graphs of three or more sets of relationships to work out the best values of each

Cartoon by Neill Cameron, www.neillcameron.com

of the variables used, if you want to solve a problem such as the best mix of products for a factory where each product has different labour and materials demands, say, and the resources are finite.

One common example of the use of graphs is to find the 'breakeven' point for production. Suppose that you have information about a planned product. First, you know what it will cost to produce. In the simplest case, there will be some costs which you will incur regardless of the number you produce – the fixed costs. These might be buying the machine to do it and hiring an operator for it. Other costs, such as those for materials, will depend on the volume you produce – the variable costs. What you get back will depend on how many products you sell and the price. Assume that you know what you can charge. What will vary is the volume of sales. Managers like to know how many units they need to produce before they will start to make a profit. This is called the breakeven point.

If you plot the costs on one graph, with money on the *y*-axis and number of units on the *x*-axis, and draw another line showing the income to be derived, assuming that you sell this number of products, you should find that (provided the price you plan to charge is greater than the variable cost) the two lines will cross at some point. Figure 14.2 gives an example of a simple breakeven chart, with fixed costs of *F*. The number of units where the two lines cross (*B*) is the breakeven point. If you sell less than this you will lose money. Every sale beyond this will result in profit. You are likely to make a number of dubious assumptions in drawing the graph, not least about the nature of costs – for example, once you go into overtime, variable costs are likely to increase – so what the graph appears to tell you needs to be treated with caution. And it will not tell you anything about what price you should charge to maximise returns. Too high a price and very few people may

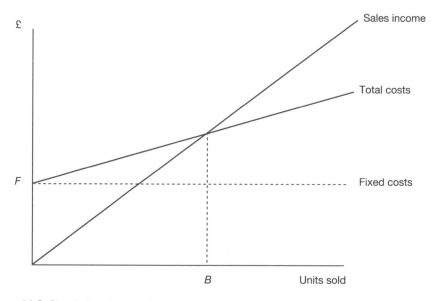

Figure 14.2 Simple breakeven chart

buy your product. Indeed, it will not tell you how many you can sell at *any* price. But it provides a simple example of how you can find answers to questions by drawing graphs, and of how you can use graphs to make a point. Explaining the idea of breakeven to someone is much easier if you show them the graph.

Test Exercise 14.2

Fixed costs are £500. Variable costs are £1 per unit. Price intended is £2 per unit. Find the breakeven point by drawing a graph. Repeat the exercise for a price of £4 per unit.

In Test Exercise 14.2 you could have expressed the costs and income as equations. Call the total cost C, the fixed cost F and the variable cost V per unit. Call the income I and the price P per unit. Then for x units:

$$C = F + Vx \quad \text{and} \quad I = Px$$

Test Exercise 14.3

As revision, express the value of x at which the lines cross, B on your graph, in terms of F, V and P.

The lines in Figure 14.2 are straight because neither equation has powers of x in it (apart from the power 1). If the equation had x^2, or a higher power, the line would be curved. For example, the materials cost of producing a flat, square product would depend on the square of the length of one side. Draw a graph of this, for practice. Sometimes a curve can rise very steeply indeed – the average waiting time in a simple queue will rise dramatically with increases in the rate at which people are joining. (You will have experienced this sort of effect on motorways when there is a reduction in the number of lanes.) Figure 14.3 shows such a situation.

Other relationships will show an increase then a decrease. One typical example is the relationship between stress levels and performance. At first, an increase in stress helps you to perform better. But eventually stress levels are such that you start to perform less well with every increase until you become totally useless. Figure 14.4 shows an example.

Calculus

There is one further area of mathematics you are likely to need: calculus. If you are seriously unhappy about dealing with numbers and equations, and do not need it, skip it. If you are only slightly uneasy, it may be worth proceeding with it because it is useful in

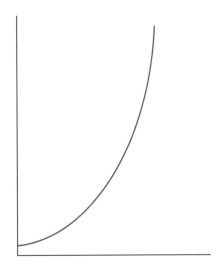

Figure 14.3 A rapidly increasing curve

its own right and because it offers useful revision of some of your earlier number work. It isn't an easy area, but it is the only difficult part of this chapter. The remaining sections are much easier.

If you can plot observed values of variables and then see the shape of the curve which emerges, you can work out the equation of a line which is close to that observed.

Sometimes you will know the equation without needing to draw the curve. Then the *equation,* rather than the plotted curve, can be used to answer certain questions. Two important questions you are likely to ask are:

● What is the rate at which a value is changing at a certain point?

● At what point on the curve is a value highest (or lowest)?

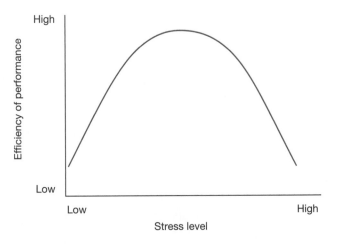

Figure 14.4 Relationship between stress levels and performance

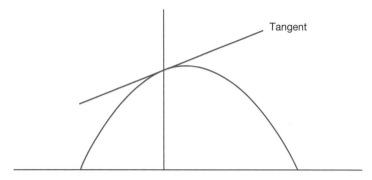

Figure 14.5 A tangent to a curve

For straight lines, the rate of change is constant – for each unit across, the line will go up by the same amount. For curved lines, the rate will be changing all the time. Note, though, that if you look at shorter and shorter parts of the curve, you will get closer and closer to a straight line. When the part is infinitely small, you will have the rate of change at that point. If you extend this line you can see what that is. This line is the *tangent* of the curve, the line which touches the curve at only one point. Figure 14.5 shows such a tangent.

At the optimal point on the stress curve, where performance is highest, the tangent is flat – it has a slope of zero. This would also be the case for a tangent to a U-shaped curve at its *lowest* point. This suggests that, by looking for points at which the rate of change is zero, we can find the answer to the second question.

Doing all this by eye is somewhat imprecise. Calculus, which you may have encountered at school, gives you some rules for working out exact values. You may well be spared the calculus – you can survive as a manager in most situations without it. But if you *are* required to learn it, and find it horrific, or are expected to know it already and have forgotten, just remember that one of its main components, *differentiation*, is about finding rates of change to curves as described above. Use the 'idiot's guide' below to work things out and you should not find it too bad.

Box 14.1 Idiot's guide to differentiation

1. The slope of the line showing values of some variable y against known values of x (think of that infinitesimally small triangle you could draw which has the same slope as the tangent) is called (usually) 'D Y by D X' and written (usually) dy/dx. The operation of working it out is called 'differentiation of y with respect to x'.
2. If y is some function of a power of x, then dy/dx will be a function of one power lower of x. Thus if y is a function of x squared, dy/dx is a function of x. If y is a function of x cubed, dy/dx will be a function of x squared.

▶

3. This function includes the *number* of the power of the x in the original equation. (My apologies to the 'theorists' among you – there is no room for an explanation. The pragmatists may be satisfied by the next exercise, which suggests ways of experimenting to check that this works in practice.) Thus if $y = x^2$, $dy/dx = 2x$. If $y = x^7$, $dy/dx = 7x^6$.

4. If you have several different powers of x in one equation, you apply the same rule to each term. Thus if $y = x^4 + 2x^3$, $dy/dx = 4x^3 + 6x^2$ (remember that there was a 2 in there already).

5. Remember that x is actually x to the power 1, so if $y = x$, $dy/dx = 1$. And if $y = 7x$, $dy/dx = 7$.

6. Remember too that x to the power 0 is 1. Thus any constant terms in your equation, i.e. terms which do not depend on x, can be thought of as an 'x to the nought' term and will be multiplied by zero when you differentiate. They therefore vanish. The fixed costs on your breakeven chart were constant, regardless of x. And, indeed, it is clear that the slope of your total cost line was unaffected by the value of the fixed costs.

7. To find the maximum or minimum of a curve, you work out dy/dx and then find the value of x for which this is zero.

8. Although it is traditional to use y and x, you can differentiate an equation whatever the letters it uses, as long as one letter is used for the value of an equation expressed in terms of the other letter. If the terms are mixed up, with both letters on the same side of the equals sign, you will need to sort out the equation before differentiating.

9. dy/dx is known as a 'first-order derivative'. You can work out a second-order derivative by differentiating a second time, i.e. by differentiating dy/dx. This would give you the rate at which the rate of change was changing. It is (usually) called d^2y/dx^2. And third- or higher-order derivatives are possible too, by successive differentiation.

(This is also available on the website.)

Test Exercise 14.4

Plot the graph showing y against x in the following cases:

(a) $y = x^2$

(b) $y = 3x + 1$

(c) $y = x^3 + 2x + 2$

You will need to work out a few values in each case: five points should be enough. So use values of x from 1 to 5. Choose a scale for your y, or vertical, axis that allows you to include all the values of y that you get.

Calculate dy/dx in each case.

Now draw the tangents and see how close the slope is to the result of your differentiation.

Test Exercise 14.5

Differentiate the following equations:

   (a) $t = 3d^2 + d + 4$

   (b) $y = 2x^4 + x^2 + 5x$

   (c) $r = y^2 + 10y - 21$

   (d) $y = x^7 - 3x^5 + \sqrt{x}$

Integration

Think about the opposite operation to differentiation. It is called *integration* and allows you to find something out about y if you know dy/dx. Try for a minute to think about why you can find out only 'something', not the whole equation for y. The complication lies in the constant which was present in the original, but not in the derivative. Remember that dy/dx for $y = x^2 + 1$, $x^2 + 100$ or $x^2 + 1000$ is $2x$. You have no way of guessing what that constant might be. You therefore need to put something into your answer to remind you of this. Suppose you use K to represent this constant. Then the integral of some function of x, say $2x^2$ (written $\int 2x^2\, dx$), will be $2/3x^3 + K$. (You can see that to calculate the integral you must go through the reverse of the procedure for differentiation, i.e. you must add 1 to the power of x and divide the number in front of x by that new power.)

One important use of integration is to tell you the area under a curve. If you know the rate of change of a quantity, the integral is the total of that quantity accumulated. Figure 14.6 shows the number of males of different heights in a particular population. The area under the curve to the left of a particular height value, shaded on the diagram, will be the number of people of that height or less. In case you want to practise integration, Test Exercise 14.6 gives you some examples. The idea of area under a curve will be clearer in the simpler examples of distributions shown as histograms, which follow shortly. You will be relieved to know that they require no mathematics beyond the ability to count.

Test Exercise 14.6

Find the integrals with respect to x of the following expressions:

   (a) $3x^2$

   (b) $8x^3 - 12x^2 + 1$

   (c) $\frac{1}{x} + 3$

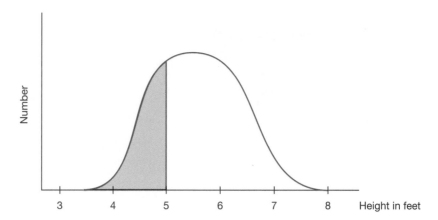

Figure 14.6 Graph showing height distribution of males in a particular population (shaded area represents those less than 5 ft tall)

If you need to know more about the calculus than this primer can offer, and there is no basic maths course available at your institution, then you will need to buy a book on the subject. But this brief introduction should mean that you feel brave enough to fight your way through such a book if necessary. If you need only a *little* more explanation and practice than it was possible to provide here, Morris and Thanassoulis (1994) is fairly user friendly.

Even if you do not need calculus, being able to plot things in a simple graph will add greatly to your ability to show a pattern from figures and to communicate patterns. If you are writing a report arguing for a need to take action before a situation becomes critical, then including graphs at relevant points to strengthen your argument can be a great help in convincing your reader that you do have a point. And extrapolating from graphs which show a clear trend can be a useful aid to forecasting and therefore planning.

Frequencies and Histograms

Quite often, I find it helpful to chart how frequently various events occur. At our residential schools we use a questionnaire to assess how successful the school and its various components have been in the students' eyes. This questionnaire also asks students to rate tutors on various dimensions using a 5-point scale (an extract is shown in Figure 14.7). One easy way to see how each tutor has been viewed by students is to log the distribution of scores awarded on key variables. An example of a tally showing this for one item on the questionnaire and a tutor with 12 students in the group is shown beneath the question. When doing this by hand, it is clearest to tally by drawing four verticals and a fifth diagonal. Adding up groups of five afterwards is then a simple operation.

Such a tally can equally be represented as a *histogram*, where the categories are on the *x*-axis and above each is a bar, its height showing the frequency of observations in that category. In the questionnaire example above each score is a category. But if you have a wide range of possible scores, say from 1 to 100, you might wish to group scores into bands and

---

Q13
Please rate your core group tutor on the following items:

	Excellent				Poor
Presentation skills	5	4	3	2	1
Knowledge of course content	5	4	3	2	1
Facilitation skills	5	4	3	2	1

Presentation skills		Course knowledge		Facilitation skills	
5	|	5	||||	5	
4	|	4	⌴⌴⌴	4	
3	||	3	||	3	|||
2	⌴⌴⌴ |	2		2	⌴⌴⌴
1	||	1	|	1	||||

Figure 14.7 Extract from a student feedback questionnaire, with tally

draw a bar for each band of scores. As the bands are 'continuous', i.e. there are no gaps in the scale of scores, you can draw bars touching each other (though of course if one band had no scores, there would be a bar of zero height, which would look like a gap). If you choose the width of band carefully, it will show you the pattern of how the scores are distributed far more clearly than if you tried to show the frequency of each possible score – after all, no single score might have more than two 'scorers' and many might have none at all.

Suppose that two tutors had taught the same course and marked their students on an exam paper common to both groups, and that the results were as follows:

Tutor A: 20, 70, 80, 83, 50, 55, 75, 60, 61, 30, 95, 55, 54, 51, 40, 57, 69, 70, 75, 81

Tutor B: 40, 43, 47, 60, 49, 55, 51, 60, 63, 49, 42, 70, 75, 50, 46, 41, 49, 67, 60, 42

These are a classic example of figures from which it is hard to extract meaning without some sort of organisation. But by representing the figures graphically, in the form of a histogram, it is possible to see clear differences, which might prompt a number of questions.

In Test Exercise 14.7, each category was of equal size – each represented a band of 10 marks. It is possible to use categories of different sizes – sometimes you might wish to use some categories that cover a wider range than others. Perhaps you could not measure with equal accuracy over the full range of the scale. If you do this, you must remember that the *area* of a bar must correspond to the number of instances. Thus if the first category in the above had been 0–40, then its height would need to be 1quarter that of a bar for a 10-mark band with the same number of occurrences. Otherwise a false impression of frequency would be created. For example, suppose there had been 1, 2, 2 and 3 examples in each of the four 10-mark bands, thus 8 scores in the amalgamated 0–40 band. Whichever way you choose to group the categories, the overall shape should be approximately the same, allowing for the inevitable flattening caused by the broader category. A broad band 8 units high would give a very different picture from that using each separate category, whereas one 2 units high would look fairly similar.

Note that, just as using broader categories will lead to flattening of parts of the histogram, increasing the 'stepped' effect, so using narrower bands, will lead to a smoothing of the steps, until you approximate to a graph. Thus if instead of two tutor groups' scores you

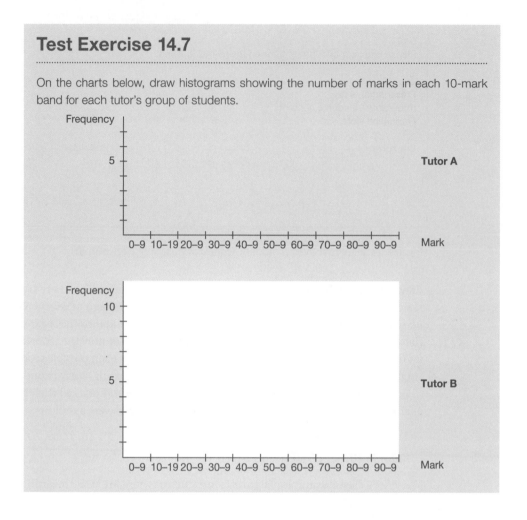

Test Exercise 14.7

On the charts below, draw histograms showing the number of marks in each 10-mark band for each tutor's group of students.

had all the GCSE scores for the country, you could use 1-mark categories and end up with something like a graph of frequency of each score.

Bar and Column Charts

When plotting a graph you are plotting two 'variables' – things which can take different values on the scales you show on your axes. The scales need to be ordinal scales so that you know how to draw and interpret them. A histogram also uses two ordered scales, though one is frequency. But if you could not order the categories you were counting, you could not use a graph or histogram to make sense of a distribution of values.

It is possible to draw bars horizontally, like the histogram tallies in Figure 14.7, or vertically, as in Figure 14.8. Historically both were called bar charts. But Excel usefully distinguishes between horizontal *bars* and vertical *columns* and you might find it less confusing to follow the same distinction.

Sometimes you may have one variable that is *not* measurable on an ordinal scale. Suppose you had annual rainfall and average temperature data for a series of different countries. Countries are categories, so this is categorical data. You could order them in many different ways – by size, by alphabet or by geographical position, for example. Therefore, plotting rainfall by country, or temperature by country, would not make a lot of sense. You will sometimes see graphs where one axis is actually a set of categories, but this is not good practice: if read as a graph it can be misleading.

Where you have one genuine variable and one set of categories, you should use a bar chart instead. This still gives you a picture of figures and allows you to spot, for example, high and low values very easily, but does not imply that you might be able to find an equation which related the two sets of figures. If you have measured two or three things for each category, you may be able to get a feel for any strong relationships between these by plotting them side by side (see Figure 14.8).

Test Exercise 14.8

Represent the following information on a bar chart.

	Percentage of recruits who are:	
Organisation	Graduates	Female
Anglewide Windows	30	20
Biobreed Technology	60	50
Countrywide Clerical	15	90
Downtown Designers	25	35
Everyman Eateries	10	60

In bar charts as with graphs, you do not need to have your *y*-axis start at zero (as the *x*-axis is a set of categories, the question of where it starts does not apply). This can help you to make differences clear, as you probably found in Test Exercise 14.8. But if you do this, you will need to remember that a bar that is, say, twice as high as another does not represent a value twice as great. There is probably a stronger tendency to assume that it *does* than there is with a graph, so beware.

Sometimes it is necessary to use each interval on the scale to represent an increase in size gained not by adding but by multiplying. This is known as a *logarithmic* or *exponential* scale. (You can use logarithmic scales for plotting graphs as well.) It allows you to represent a much wider range of values on a single scale than would be possible with an interval scale, yet still to see how things at the small end of the scale relate to each other.

You will see an example of such a scale in Figure 14.9.

Because the meaning of a chart (or indeed a graph) depends so much on the scales on the axes, you must always take care to make the scale clear when drawing a chart or graph, and to note carefully the scales used when you are reading them. If you are using

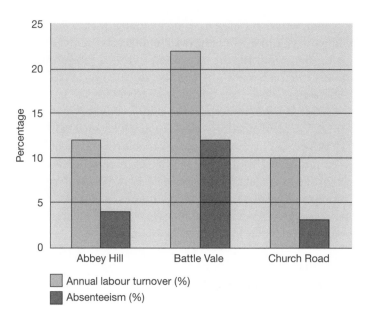

Figure 14.8 Column chart showing absence and labour turnover rates at three sites

anything other than a normal interval scale starting at zero, you may wish to alert readers to this in your text, in addition to labelling axes clearly in your diagram. The scope for giving a wrong impression is huge. Look, for example, at the chart in Figure 14.9, which is similar to one which appeared in a reputable scientific periodical. What would you say, at a glance, is most likely to kill you?

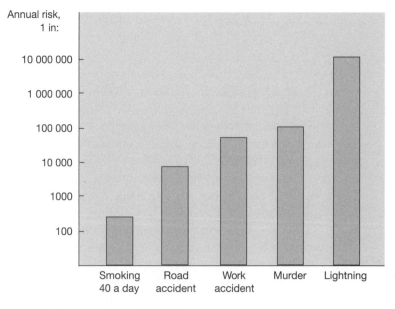

Figure 14.9 Risk of some causes of death

It is only when you stop to think that surely lightning *can't* be so much more dangerous than smoking that you realise that the scale is dealing in risks, expressed in such a way that bars for *unlikely* things are taller than bars for *likely* things, which is completely counterintuitive. A 1 in 10 chance is much bigger than a 1 in 100 chance, yet is lower on the scale. Note this is not because it is a logarithmic scale – it would be the same with a normal one. (In fact, a set of figures seen recently suggested that of 1000 regular smokers aged 20, 250 will die of smoking-related diseases in middle age and a further 250 in old age, compared with 1 by murder and 6 by road accidents – assuming that their smoking habits and crime and road accident rates continue as at present.)

Although here vertical columns have been shown, you could just as well draw them as horizontal bars. Indeed, this has the advantage of allowing you to write the bar label in the same direction as the bar itself, which may make both constructing the chart and reading it somewhat easier. Bars also tend to make differences more obvious (experiment to see the effect). The choice is up to you, as long as you make clear what your axes are and thus what the bars represent.

Sometimes bars/columns are used to show proportions. If this is the case, the height of all the bars will be the same, representing 100 per cent. But within the bars there will be different colours or shadings showing the different proportions of the various quantities making up that whole. For example, a survey of a small village over a number of years might show the proportion of owner occupation rising. This could be represented as in Figure 14.10.

Note that it is not possible to tell from this sort of column chart how *many* of any type of dwelling existed in any year. This is a difference from the other bar charts described. The village may well have been growing significantly over the period shown, but there is no way of telling this from Figure 14.10. All you can tell from that chart is how the

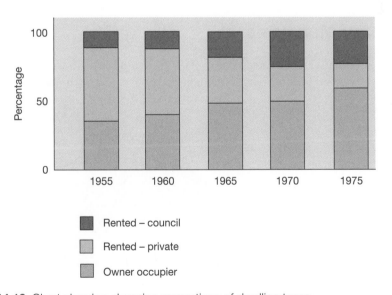

Figure 14.10 Chart showing changing proportions of dwelling types

total housing available in any one of the years surveyed was divided between the three categories. The chart is a rectangular version of a pie chart (above). You would need to be extremely careful not to draw conclusions about whether actual *numbers* of dwelling in any category are increasing or decreasing.

Pie Charts

A popular way of representing this sort of proportional data is a pie chart. This has the advantage over a bar chart that it is clear that the whole pie represents unity. Again, the ease of producing computer-generated pie charts has led to their proliferation in reports, often in glorious colours, sometimes in mock 3D (avoid this feature at all costs – keep to a 'flat pie' for clarity). Such charts have obvious attractions. They look good, far prettier than simple bar or column charts, especially if bright colours are used. They are easy to understand, even for those who have difficulty with fractions. Such people might have some difficulty in working out how ⅙, ⅓ and ½ relate to each other, but they could see this immediately from a pie chart such as Figure 14.11 – though note how the 'mock 3D' in this and 14.12 actually makes it harder to 'see' the relationships between slices because tilting the circle produces distortion.

While pie charts are great when they have only a few 'slices', they become difficult both to label and to interpret once they contain a larger number of categories. We are not good at judging fine differences between angles at a glance and it can be quite difficult to see whether one slice is marginally greater than another. This problem is made worse by the 3D effect, if used, and by the different colours and shadings used to differentiate slices (see Figure 14.12). If you have more than four or five categories it is better to use a bar chart, as lengths are easier to judge, although even then it can be difficult.

Summary Measures

Graphs are not the only way of giving a summary of a set of numbers. Numerical summaries are possible too. You will be all too familiar with one, the *average*. Whether you are

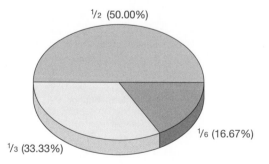

Figure 14.11 A very simple pie chart

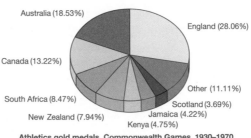

Athletics gold medals, Commonwealth Games, 1930–1970

Figure 14.12 A pie chart with too many slices

talking about average marks, average rainfall or average wages, you mean the figure you would get if you added all the scores (rainfalls or whatever) together and divided by the number of exam papers, or years for which rainfall measures had been taken. More generally, you add together all the values you have and divide by the number of values (again this is easy with Excel or similar).

Test Exercise 14.9

Estimate the average mark for tutor A's student group and for tutor B's student group in Test Exercise 14.7, then see how close your estimate was by working it out using a calculator.

When I am doing my rough analysis of questionnaire data, I calculate the average rating tutors have received, as well as obtaining a histogram of distribution of rating. Rather than adding up all the scores on my calculator, which is a fairly error-prone operation as you may have found in the exercise above, I work from the histogram. The formula for doing this can be written using the vocabulary or code introduced in Chapter 5. If you use *x* to refer to the scores the tutor had, or whatever the measures obtained happen to be, and ➤ Ch 5 *f* for the frequency with which each measure occurred, the formula is:

$$\text{mean} = \Sigma fx / \Sigma f$$

Thus you work out the total value of scores in each category – 5 ratings of 5 would give you 25, while 5 ratings of 1 would give you only 5. You add all these together and divide by the number of ratings. Grouping scores into bands makes the calculation easier, though slightly less accurate.

If you are using bands, as in the tutor A/tutor B example, then your *x* will be the mid-point of the band. Thus the mid-point of a 1–5 band would be 3. And the mid-point of a 0–9 band such as we used would be 4.5. It is perfectly acceptable to work with fractional values of *x* such as 4.5, but it makes the arithmetic slightly more difficult. If you are planning to use this method and want to calculate in your head, you might want to choose a band size and location that will make the calculation easy.

Test Exercise 14.10

Work out the average value of tutor A's and tutor B's groups working from the histogram you drew. You will need to construct for each set of scores a table with columns:

Band value	Number of scores (f)	Band mid-point (x)	fx
0–9	----	----	----
10–19	----	----	----
etc.	----	----	----

See if you take fewer attempts to get it right using this method!

Sometimes an average, or arithmetic mean, gives a misleading picture of the centre of a distribution. Suppose the numbers were distributed in an odd way. There might, for example, be one or two huge numbers which made the mean come out as higher than any of the other numbers in the group. Say you were working out the average income of inhabitants of a medieval village and included the lord's income alongside those of the peasants. Then an average calculated from the total sum of income would be fairly useless. There are many situations today where you might get a better picture of the middle of a group using some other measure.

Median

There are two other commonly used indicators of central tendency. The first is the *median*. To obtain this you order your numbers by size and count along to the value which is in the middle of the line. This is the *median*. Thus suppose you had the values 4, 1, 11, 10, 5, 10, 7, 10, 1. You would rearrange these in order to give 1, 1, 4, 5, 7, 10, 10, 10, 11. There are 9 measurements, so the middle will be the fifth one. Counting from either end, as it is immaterial which, you reach 7. This is the median of that set of values.

Test Exercise 14.11

Write down the general formula for knowing which term in an ordered series of *n* terms will be the median.

Your answer to the Test Exercise 14.11 will be a whole number when n is odd – after all, in any series with an odd number of terms, as in the example above, 1 is in the middle. But what if there had been only 8 measurements? If n is 8 then $(n + 1)/2$ (the answer to the exercise above) is 4.5. Where this happens, it is normal to take a point midway between the two middle numbers as the median. Suppose the 11 in the above example had not been there. Then the fourth term would be 5 and the fifth term 7, so the median in this case would be 6. (For very large distributions, you can ignore this and use either. If you had 100 observations, it would usually be sufficiently accurate to take either the fiftieth or the fifty-first observation as the median.)

Mode

The other indicator of the middle of a distribution is the mode. This is the most commonly occurring value. For small sets of numbers it is easy to see what the mode is – in the example above it was 10. For larger sets you will need to tally the values occurring, or draw a histogram. On a histogram you can see it easily because it is the value of the score or band with the highest bar.

Test Exercise 14.12

Locate the modal mark for tutor A and tutor B from your histograms in Test Exercise 14.7.

Test Exercise 14.13

Find the mean, median and mode for each of the following sets of values:

		Mean	**Median**	**Mode**
(a)	5, 5, 3, 2, 6, 7, 9, 11, 1	___	___	___
(b)	3, 3, 7, 2, 1, 4, 3, 3, 13, 10	___	___	___
(c)	Now experiment with writing lists where mean, median and mode all have different values (no answer given for this part).			

Measures of Dispersion

The way in which the values you have obtained are spread out is important for a number of reasons. You may simply need to know the range you can expect in order to plan for all possible situations. But more often, you will want to know how *important* differences between groups are, and the importance of differences in means will depend on the variation in the data. Suppose 1 group you observed had an average value of some measure of 5, and another group had an average of 6, and you wanted to know if this was a significant difference or just happened to have come out that way on the day you measured. If all the values in the first group were between 4.5 and 5.5 and all the values in the second group were between 5.5 and 6.5, you might be surer about the difference than if numbers in each case were scattered about between 1 and 10. You therefore need some measure of this scatter or dispersion.

The bell-shaped curve shown in Figure 14.6 is frequently found in nature. It occurs when you have a large population and you are measuring a continuous variable. The curve may be taller and thinner, or flatter (this will depend upon the scale you are using in any case), but is basically the same shape. So common is it that it is called the 'normal distribution'. Examples of normal distributions range from children's IQ scores to actual dimensions of parts produced on a machine. Many statistical tests assume that a sample is drawn from a population with this distribution. If you have a sample drawn from a population with a different distribution, you may need to use other tests.

Range

There are several measures of dispersion. The simplest is the *range*, the distance from the smallest to the largest measure observed. Thus in Test Exercise 14.13, the range in (a) is 1–11 and in (b) is 1–13. It is the most obvious indicator of the dispersion of the set of figures and the easiest to ascertain. But it has fairly obvious drawbacks. Even more than the mean, it is susceptible to being distorted by one or two maverick figures. This may not be a distortion if you genuinely need to know the *possible* range. But if you are trying to get a quick picture of the distribution, then it may be misleading. Also, you may not *know* the end of a distribution because you used an 'open' category; for example, the question on alcohol consumption in Activity 13.2 in the previous chapter had a '43+' category. You would have no idea of the

➤ Ch 13   highest alcohol consumption in your survey if you had some respondents in this category.

Interquartile range

One indicator of spread that avoids these problems is derived by developing the idea of the median. Just as the median tells you the position of the middle observation, so you can find the middle of observations to each side of the median, by treating each as a distribution and finding *its* median. These values will represent the positions one-quarter and three-quarters along the distribution and are called the *quartiles*. The distance between the upper and lower quartile is called the *interquartile range* and tells you the range within which half your values are likely to lie. It is not distorted by the odd deviant value and is almost as easy to work out as a median.

The idea of quartiles can be extended still further, to deciles and percentiles. For example, you might be designing a car seat and need to know the range of adjustments to build in. It would not be much good to use the interquartile range. If you did, the seat would be uncomfortable for half your potential customers. Equally, you would probably not want to design a seat that would suit every adult on the planet. It would be expensive and the small number of potential purchasers who are over 8 ft or under 4 ft do not justify this expense. For many such design situations, percentiles are used, dividing the distribution into hundredths. And traditionally the lower five percentiles and the upper five percentiles are disregarded. If you are at the outlying end of a distribution, say one of the five per cent shortest or five per cent tallest people, you will have problems finding chairs, cars, kitchen units or whatever to suit.

Standard deviations

If you have done any statistics at all, you will have heard of standard deviations. They are widely used in a variety of situations as a measure of dispersion. If you want to know how representative your mean is, you might reasonably ask: 'How closely do the values observed cluster about this mean?' One way of answering the question would be to work out the difference between each value and the mean, add these values together, and average them. There is a snag to this, which you have probably spotted. By definition the answer will be zero. Some of the numbers will be negative and will cancel out the positives. You could get around this by ignoring the negative signs. But statistics of this kind were developed by mathematicians, who do not feel comfortable with such ideas! So instead, they chose to get rid of the negatives by squaring each deviation. Negative numbers multiplied by negative numbers are positive. The average of these squares will be a positive number. And if you take a square root of this, you will have something close to the average deviation worked out by the obvious 'ignoring signs' method. If $\bar{x}$ is the mean value of x, and n is the number of values, we can write this as a formula:

$$\text{standard deviation} = \sqrt{\frac{\Sigma(x - \bar{x})^2}{n}}$$

or, by working out the bracket and cancelling the ns that result

$$= \sqrt{\frac{\Sigma x^2}{n} - \bar{x}^2}$$

The second way of writing this is much easier to work out when you want to insert your values of x and n.

This gives you the standard deviation of a whole population if you have measured every member of that population. If you have only a smallish sample, the calculation will give you values that are smaller than you would expect from the population sampled. A better estimate of the standard deviation of this 'parent' population when you have a smallish sample is given if you divide by $n - 1$, rather than n. For a large sample, the difference will be insignificant, as $n - 1$ will be virtually the same as n. Dividing by 8 rather than 9 may make a noticeable difference. Dividing by 81 rather than 80 will not.

If you have a *normal distribution* (see Figure 14.6 for an example) of values, 68 per cent of scores/values/measures will lie within 1 standard deviation of the mean and 95 per cent within 2 standard deviations of this.

Drawing Conclusions from Figures

In talking about both graphical representations of data and the numerical descriptors such as means, medians or indicators of dispersion, we are organising data in a way that makes patterns or aspects clearer. But although some things may look 'obvious' from histograms, or from differences between means for different sets of figures, they need to be treated with caution. This is because the world has a habit of producing what we interpret as 'obviously' weird results when there is nothing weird going on at all.

How likely do you think it is, for example, that in a class of 32 students at least 2 will share a birthday? The chances are about 3 to 1. Or guess the probability that if you toss a coin just six times you will get either six heads or six tails. Most people would assume that this was extremely unlikely, unless the coin was weighted in some way. In fact, the chance is as high as 1 in 32. So if each of the students in the class above tosses six coins, you can expect one of them to get six of a kind and should not be surprised if they do. Few people choose consecutive numbers in the lottery, yet it is as likely that there *will* be two consecutive numbers as it is that there will not. Your chance of winning will still be minuscule, but if you choose consecutive numbers and *do* win, your prize will probably be bigger, since there will be fewer other winners.

In collecting data to inform a decision or test some hypothesis, we can usually afford to look only at a *sample* of the population in which we are interested. If we wanted to know how people were likely to vote, we would not survey every voter. If we wanted to know whether one form of testing predicted later performance better than another form of testing, we would try each out on a reasonable-sized group of people, not on the entire world. If we wanted to know whether a new drug was effective, we would try it on a sample of people with the disease it was supposed to help, rather than on everyone.

In drawing conclusions, as was clear from the previous chapter, the nature and size of sample are important. If we did not choose our sample carefully, the data could be unrepresentative. If you tried the drug only with those who were sickest, this would not tell you how well it compared with a drug normally used on people who are not very sick. If you tried it on a tiny number of people, you would also find it hard to be sure what your results implied for the world at large.

Note that in each of these examples the 'data' might also be imperfect. People might say they will vote one way and then either not bother to vote at all, or change their mind at the last minute and vote for some other candidate. Some might hate surveys so much that they deliberately mislead the surveyor.

As we are so prone to go wrong even when assessing the likelihood of simple things like birthday coincidences and results of coin tosses, considerable caution is needed in making inferences from a sample of imperfect data relating to more complex situations. And yet this is the sort of data that we are normally using to provide information. Because this area is so important, a considerable battery of statistical techniques has been developed to help with drawing conclusions about the meaning of sets of numbers. Unfortunately such techniques are often ignored and faulty conclusions are drawn as a result.

Levels of Significance

To know whether to be surprised at coinciding birthdays or tossed coins, you need to know how likely they were to happen 'by chance'. In knowing whether apparent differences in recovery rates on the old and new drugs mean that the new drug is actually better, you need to know the same thing. How likely is it, given all the other factors that influence recovery that the difference you observe might have just happened by chance? Statistical tests of significance give you an idea of this. They will indicate how often a result as extreme as yours could happen if there were in fact no difference in the populations from which your samples were drawn, that is, how often you could expect to get this result 'by chance'. You will often see at the end of a table of results in a research paper '$p < 0.05$'. This means that only one time in twenty would you get such a difference if the populations sampled were the same or so strong a relationship if the two things you were measuring were in fact unrelated in the population from which your sample was drawn.

This can also be expressed as 'a confidence level of 95 per cent' or 'with 95 per cent confidence'. Normally journals are prepared to publish results which are as significant as this, but not results with a lower probability. But beware of two ways in which the meaning of such confidence levels can be affected by how they were derived. The first factor is the prediction or hypothesis you are testing. You might test either '*this drug is better*' or '*these two drugs are different in their effect*'. When you are predicting the *direction* of the difference, rather than merely hypothesising that there would be a difference of some kind, a smaller actual difference is sufficient to give you a 95 per cent confidence level in your result. Think about the bell curve. The area under both extremes is obviously twice the area under one end only. So it is twice as likely that you will get a result that is 'extreme' as that you will get one that is 'at this extreme'. Because you are talking about 'tails' of distributions, significance tests are referred to as 'one-tailed' or 'two-tailed' to differentiate these two cases. It is important to decide *beforehand* whether you are predicting a result at one end or at both ends, and therefore whether you need a one-tailed or two-tailed test. Otherwise you can rationalise your result – 'well, of course, if you think about it, it had to come out that way' – and end up accepting as significant something which could happen 1 in 10 times, say.

The other slight caution about significance testing is that, while a single very extreme result would be worth taking seriously, if 1 of 20 results came out this way, by definition this is what you would expect. So it is misleading to work out lots of relationships or differences and throw away all the non-significant results, including in your paper or report only those that came out as significant. And it is equally dubious to draw conclusions from a matrix of results of which something like 1 in 10 or 1 in 20 reaches a significance level of 0.05. (Watch out for this in journals – it is still fairly common.)

Activity 14.1

If you are studying a course that has suggested readings including research papers in journals, look carefully at the significance levels reported, the number of such results tested and, if appropriate, whether one- or two-tailed testing was done. See if you can find examples of papers where conclusions seem to be rather stronger than the numbers warrant.

Developing Your Inference Skills

The coverage of statistical inference given here has been an American-style, whistle-stop, 'if it's Tuesday this must be Rome' tour. But it should have introduced you to some very important issues in drawing conclusions from data, alerted you to the ease with which you can draw unwarranted conclusions and made you appreciate that there is a wealth of knowledge about this area on which you can draw and techniques which you can use.

The actual use is fairly easy now, as you can use spreadsheets or statistical packages to calculate the relevant statistics. But you do need to know which statistics are appropriate for the sorts of measures you have obtained, and the size of your sample, and the likely distribution of values in the parent population. You also need to know how to design your data collection to get usable data from which, using appropriate techniques, you can draw conclusions with confidence.

Do take advantage of any basic statistics courses your university offers, and the many online tutorials freely available. This is an area where a little understanding can pay off handsomely. It will be a great help in planning any research you do, either during your degree, as a postgraduate or in employment. (Even more helpful will be to find a statistician and consult with him/her about your plans at an early stage. This can save you a great deal of wasted effort in gathering data that are unlikely to tell you anything at all.) Even the small amount of understanding of probability and statistics that you now have should make you suitably cynical about many of the conclusions you will find being drawn from data, both in research and when data are used in organisations to inform decision making.

SUMMARY

This chapter has argued the following:

- Graphs and charts are a useful way of making it easy to see patterns and discontinuities in sets of numbers. They can usefully be included in reports to illustrate a point or strengthen an argument.

- Graphs can also be useful for estimating future values, by extending them in the direction in which they are moving.

- Numbers can also usefully be summarised in terms of their central tendency and dispersion, using means, medians and modes for the first, and range, interquartile range and standard deviation for the second.

- In drawing conclusions from numbers it is easy to overestimate the significance of seemingly striking differences and relationships. Statistical tests of significance will provide an antidote to this by indicating the level of confidence you can have in predictions or conclusions.

- It is worth studying at least some basic statistics and, for research design or interpreting figures to inform an important decision, seeking the advice of an expert.

Further information

There are many good books on statistics available. The following are merely suggestions.

Huff, D. (1991) *How to Lie with Statistics*, Penguin.

Morris, C. (2011) *Quantitative Approaches in Business Studies*, 8th edn, Pearson.

Stutely, R. (2006) *The Definitive Guide to Business Finance*, 2nd edn, Pearson. Very good on spreadsheets (and finance).

Taylor, S. (2007) *Business Statistics for Non-mathematicians*, 2nd edn, Palgrave Macmillan.

https://www.youtube.com/watch?v=-btUxQi76qI for an example of an overview tutorial on different charting functions in Excel 2010 (but find one appropriate for your own software) (accessed 9/1/15).

14

MAKING SENSE OF DATA

PART 5
INTEGRATING YOUR SKILLS

Introduction to Part 5

Thus far, the skills you will need for successful study (and frequently for success in employment as well) have been addressed independently, although it was often clear that they needed to be used together. This final part of the book looks at how to integrate them so that you become effective as a manager, both of your own future and of projects for which you are given responsibility at work. It also shows how some refinements of the skills already developed can help you meet the specific demands of both these areas.

This final part therefore looks first at project management – a term with multiple meanings. Projects can be tiny, massive, or anywhere in between. The project or dissertation you are likely to be asked to do towards the end of your degree course is a small-scale induction to the art of project management. Yet it is likely to share many features with the more substantial 'internal consultancy' projects often given to recent graduates, or to managers assessed as having 'high-flier' potential, and the same skills will eventually be relevant to far larger projects involving major investments over a long timescale. (One of the still young managers quoted in the book has just been given a £3billion project to manage.)

Projects require the same skills as effective self-management but with a strong emphasis on communication, and present a variety of other challenges. It may be difficult to establish clear, and agreed, objectives for the project team. You will need to plan and coordinate work on a wide range of tasks over a longer timescale – setting meaningful interim deadlines will be essential, as well as ensuring that final deadlines are achievable. Projects demand a high level of discipline and advanced time-management skills. If you are doing a group project interpersonal skills will be crucial, as is the case when you are part of an organisational task force – an increasingly common way of organising work.

For a project on your course, you will need to write a coherent and persuasive report of 10 000 words or so, incorporating the analysis of a considerable body of data. This will probably tax you more than anything you have so far written, but again the skills required will be hugely valuable during your career. For any project directed towards bringing about change, senior management will need to be convinced of the need to implement any recommendations you make. A well written report may play a key part in persuading them. A dissertation may require fewer interactive skills, but will make similar demands on research and personal management skills.

The final chapter looks at the specific 'project' of getting the sort of job you want once you graduate. You will need to revisit and redefine your objectives, and to research job opportunities. You will need to apply your written communication skills to making an application and use your 'talking and listening' skills to good effect in interviews. These final two chapters therefore further develop skills particularly relevant to your career success post-graduation.

You will probably find you need to work intensively on Chapter 15 when you are starting to think about how to approach your project, and then again while you are planning and doing the research. However, since in one sense all your work is building up to the ability to carry out projects, it is worth reading the chapter now and re-reading it at intervals – to ensure that you are making full use of earlier modules to develop project-related skills. Similarly, it is worth thinking about your career plans, at least from time to time, from the start of your studies. So a quick read of the final chapter will be helpful, even during your first year.

Find a way of reminding yourself to revisit them later on, when their significance may be even more readily grasped. For example, some of the project-management skills will be best practiced when you are actually planning a project – though you may do smaller projects earlier in your course. Some of the job-seeking skills will similarly depend on your being ready to apply for jobs (though they can be addressed in the context of seeking vacation work, or industrial placements). Look at these chapters now, to familiarise yourself with their contents, and think about how soon you can start to develop the skills covered. As Chapter 1 pointed out, to increase your chances of getting a really good job you *need* to take action in advance. So you should draw up your action plan now.

15
MANAGING PROJECTS AND DISSERTATIONS

Learning outcomes

By the end of this chapter you should:

- understand the specific demands of project work and how they relate to skills already covered

- be able to choose a suitable topic for a project or dissertation to meet your course and personal objectives

- be aware of the steps needed to gain access or commitment to a project within an organisation

- be able to draw critically on relevant literature

- know how to draw up an initial research plan

- understand some of the specific requirements of project reports or dissertations.

Introduction

Task forces and project teams are a common form of work organisation today, and you may find yourself working on specific time-defined projects to design, develop and/or install some major equipment or system either for customers or internally, or a project team to manage some other change initiative. Indeed, large parts of your working life may be spent in leading or working in task forces and project teams. Understanding what is required for successful project management will therefore be helpful throughout your studies, will increase your employability, and will contribute to career success. Most of the skills needed to manage projects have already been covered. They include diagnosis, self- and time-management, interpersonal skills, research skills and the ability to learn from feedback and adjust to changing conditions. A student project will give you the opportunity to practise all these skills in a single piece of work, and develop them further. Potential employers are likely to be impressed by a coherent account of how you have managed a non-trivial project. Most courses therefore include a substantial project or dissertation. This chapter will help you to do well in course projects and to contribute effectively to a range of projects at work.

'Project' can be used in many different ways, but normally includes the idea of some specific task that is non-routine, somewhat complex and discrete. Unlike much traditional management, which is fairly continuous, there is a clear goal to *complete* the project by a specified time, and with specified resources. This greater clarity brings into sharp focus the managerial roles described earlier. Because they relate to something specific, they are easily identified. Control, in particular, is highly visible. The chapter looks at each stage of project management from the viewpoint both of a course project and of the sort of project you may well encounter at work.

Project Teams

A project is a distinct and defined piece of work, with clear resource allocations and a final deadline. A project-based form of organisation has many advantages. It allows for devolution of authority – a task force with a clearly defined remit can be left to get on with it, subject to fairly simple controls. When the project is complete, the team can be reassigned to other projects. The project leader or the team as a whole can adapt rapidly to changes in the environment in order to remain on target. It is thus a more flexible structure, with the same benefits as autonomous working groups, but the additional benefits of a clear time-line. People organised in this way are more motivated: a clearly defined and manageable task – as expectancy theory suggests allows for closer links between performance and both intrinsic and extrinsic outcomes. In addition to the autonomy already mentioned, the job is high on task identity, so feedback is more immediate. Objectives can more easily be specified in CSMART terms.

➤ Ch 2   Such project teams require their members to have virtually all the skills covered in this book:

- self-management skills to perform their part of the collaborative task effectively
- planning skills to help them contribute to designing the project and the way in which the team will share the work

- interpersonal skills for communication with any project sponsor and with other team members

- problem-solving skills both to address the task and to deal with the inevitable snags that will arise

- creativity skills both to generate a wide range of options from which to choose, and to enable the unforeseen to be envisaged and difficulties which defy resolution by a merely rational approach to be overcome.

These skills will be equally relevant to any project you do as part of your coursework.

Group Projects

➤ Ch 9

You may well be required as part of your course to do a group project. This is excellent preparation for being part of a project team at work, and will allow you to reinforce the team-working skills addressed in Chapter 9. (Revisit this to check on your skills levels.)

Although team working offers many advantages as outlined above, there is one very real potential hazard when doing a group project on a course. The success of the project, and hence your grade, will *not* be totally under your control. It will depend upon the efforts of others, as well as your own, so it matters who you are working with. Aim to be in a group with others who are prepared to exert the same level of effort as you are, and have a similar level of concern for success. There is nothing worse than being part of a group where you feel you are the only one who actually cares about getting the work done well. It can be fairly difficult, too, if you take a relatively relaxed approach and the others in the group want to work every hour there is in pursuit of perfection.

> **Group project work will be more satisfying if:**
>
> - members are equally committed
> - there is a good mix of strengths
> - objectives are clarified and agreed
> - meetings are frequent
> - attention is paid to process
> - efforts are coordinated
> - progress is monitored regularly.

Managing the group process is equally important. When forming a group it is a good idea to aim for a mix of academic strengths and of preferred team roles. You will do better if at least one in the group is good at analysis, one is good at organising people's contributions one is good at drafting and so on. Most of the rest of this chapter is written primarily from the perspective of work on an individual project. If you are working as part of a team, you need to remember all the time that, as well as all the aspects which concern individual

➤ Ch 9

project work, a lot of attention needs to be paid to managing the team process. You will probably need to refer to Chapter 9. It will be essential that every team member has a clear and agreed view about what you are trying to do and how. At each stage you need to have a clear and *shared* understanding of the group's overall objectives, of how responsibilities have been allocated and of how progress will be monitored. You will need frequent meetings to share progress so that you continue to move in the same direction, and to build on each other's work.

Coordination will be crucial throughout, and thus good communication is essential. Any conflicts need to be addressed as soon as they surface. You will not have time to repair damage later. In particular, you need to be firm about setting, and *meeting*, interim targets. While you may feel sorry for a friend who has troubles, whatever those troubles are, and feel it is mean to insist that he or she keeps on schedule regardless, sympathy without planning for the difficulties that a member's problems are causing the team can be dangerous. And so is optimism. You cannot afford to *hope* that a colleague will sort things out in time to catch up with their part of the work. You need as a group to address any such problems and work out ways of handling any slippage as soon as it occurs.

➤ **Chs 6, 8, 9**

A related key element is making group members feel valued within the team and thus wanting to continue to contribute to its success. So there is room for the sympathy and caring described above – indeed, they are important. So, too, is showing your appreciation of tasks well done, and of help offered in cases of difficulty. This aspect of team building requires a high level of interpersonal skill: developing these skills will significantly increase your 'leadership potential'.

If, despite your best efforts, not all members play a full role, this needs to be discussed with your tutors. Your report can often usefully indicate the roles played by different group members. If you end up having to do more than your fair share, it is worth documenting this fact, together with the unsuccessful efforts you made to avoid the situation occurring.

Whether you are doing it individually or as part of a team, working on a project which appears to be under control can be highly motivating and the experience deeply satisfying. You will be aware of using a wide range of skills to achieve a challenging objective and your success or otherwise will be clearly apparent. Conversely, a project which goes less well, whether because you lack the necessary skills, or because you fail to exercise them as well as you might, can be a nightmare.

Figure 15.1 maps some of the necessary skills on to the stages you are likely to go through in such a project, indicating the chapter numbers where these are covered. This shows clearly the function of project work in integrating a wide range of skills. The discussion which follows looks at the different stages of such a project, expanding on the way in which the skills shown on the diagram are needed. This should help you to manage any project more successfully, whether it is academic or work related.

Finding a Topic

Some students know from an early stage what topic they want to investigate. Perhaps there is something they have been burning to pursue in more depth ever since they encountered the topic in their first year. Or maybe they are studying part time and there is an organisational problem which they are longing for the excuse to address. Some universities have a limited range of projects 'on offer', which again makes choice relatively easy. For other students the choice is terrifying: indeed they don't know where to start. Yet topic choice is perhaps the most important stage in any course project or dissertation, so start thinking about project topics, and your learning objectives as soon as you can.

A good starting point is to consider the stakeholders in your project, and think about their objectives. Figure 15.2 shows likely stakeholders.

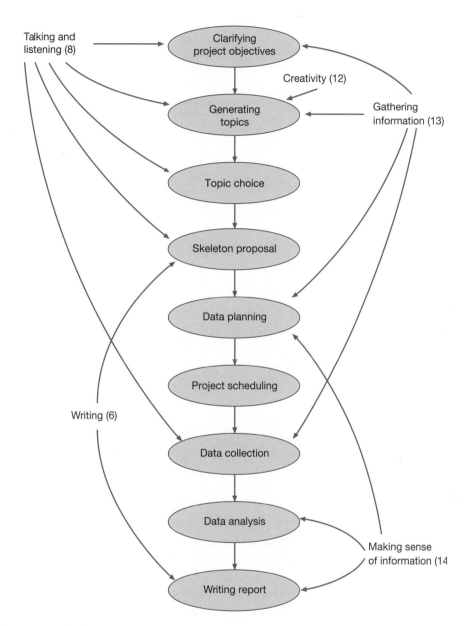

Figure 15.1 Skills needed for project management

(NB: for clarity, project and self-management skills, which are needed at every stage, are not shown, or are the group skills needed at every stage of a group project.)

Clarifying objectives

Organisational projects typically have objectives in relation to:

- performance
- cost (and any other resources)
- time.

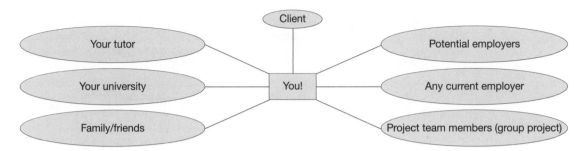

Figure 15.2 Potential stakeholders in a project

For example, a project might have the objective of designing a new IT system to a particular specification, within a specified cost, for implementation in eighteen months' time. You may need to modify these slightly when considering a student project, but should still consider all three.

You are the central stakeholder, and the first and obvious step is to clarify your own objective. Is there something you particularly want to learn more about? Are you seeking to use your project to develop skills or expertise to increase your attractiveness for a particular type of job or an anticipated promotion opportunity? Are there particular constraints you need to consider as well as objectives? It is worth thinking about resources available (and needed) and costs when considering 'performance' or what you want to achieve.

Your university is another key stakeholder as there will be rules for what is acceptable in a project or dissertation. Are you expected to do an academic dissertation or a more applied project? You need to be very clear about what is required, and to read this chapter in the light of your university's particular emphasis. The university will also want students to show the basic graduate skills an employer (or postgraduate course) would reasonably expect in order to protect their own reputation.

➤ **Ch 1**

Your tutor/research supervisor is also important. They will translate general university requirements into requirements specific to your programme, and will probably be one of the people marking your work against these standards. Far more importantly, your supervisor can offer invaluable help, guidance and feedback, provided you are open to this. Do not underestimate their knowledge, judgement and willingness to help, and take all their comments very seriously.

Your organisational client, if you are doing a work-based project, is also a crucial stakeholder. They can help you with a suitable topic, and provide excellent advice and resources, or they can be a source of huge problems because they are very powerful and may not understand your objectives, or may not be clear about (or even change) their own. Because they are so crucial, a separate section is devoted to managing organisational clients later in the chapter.

Current and/or future employers are another key stakeholder group. A current employer may also be your organisational client. If so, you need to consider them in both roles. An employer – whether current or future – is likely to have strong objectives about work-related skills and competences they seek in potential and/or promotable employees. There is therefore a strong link between their objectives and your own learning and evidence-of-learning objectives.

Activity 15.1

Considering your own stakeholders.
Draw a map of your own project or dissertation stakeholders, highlighting those you feel are most important in your case. For those who are highlighted, consider the objectives they are likely to have for your project.

Types of management research

Before choosing a topic you need a broad understanding of the main types of management research. Management research can take a number of different forms. It may aim to do one or even most of the following:

- resolve theoretical questions
- explore a topic of general interest to managers
- evaluate some aspect of an organisation's performance
- address a practical organisational problem, culminating in a set of recommendations for action
- implement changes, perhaps based on recommendations as above
- evaluate changes, either made as part of the project or some time earlier.

Where your project will lie on this theory–action scale will depend on the practical bias of your course and whether or not you have an organisation willing to host a project. Potential learning opportunities will depend on the nature or your project, but may include the ability to practise a selection of the following:

- liaison with 'clients', developing negotiation, communication and other interpersonal skills
- diagnostic work on complex situations, using concepts, diagramming and other techniques and talking and listening skills
- problem-formulation and data-planning skills
- evaluation of different methods and choice and use of an appropriate approach
- techniques for planning and scheduling your work
- information-gathering skills (both primary and secondary data)
- data analysis
- evaluation of information and its limitations

- research skills expected of a graduate
- written communication skills needed to integrate data and descriptions into a compelling argument.

If you are doing a dissertation, you will not practice the more interpersonal skills, but the reading you do will also deepen your knowledge of a particular aspect of organisations or management. For a project you may spend more time finding and analysing information, but will still need to deepen your knowledge of issues and approaches relevant to your topic.

Creative topic generation

Once you are clear about the range of possible types of research you are in a better position to devote the necessary time and energy to a suitable topic to pursue for your own dissertation or project. Even if you are burning to investigate something in particular it is wise to think of as wide a range of topics as possible from which to select. As Chapter 12 pointed out, your choice will never be better than the best option you come up with, so thinking creatively to generate a wide range of possibilities is important.

➤ **Chs 11, 12, 13**

Some of the techniques discussed in Chapters 11, 12 and 13 can help you to look at a situation from a broad perspective in order to identify possible problem themes. An initial literature search can show you what related research has already been done, and may suggest interesting questions seeking an answer.

Once you start to think about how to find further useful information, an understanding of data and its interpretation will be invaluable. Without this understanding you will not be able to judge whether a project is feasible. You will also need talking and

➤ **Ch 8**

listening skills as covered in Chapter 8, and the ability to listen to and use feedback since discussion with tutors and others will be extremely valuable at this stage.

If you are finding it hard to think of even a single topic, there will be a strong temptation to put off even *thinking* of the project until dangerously late. If you wait long enough inspiration *may* miraculously strike, but, all too often it does not. And if so, you will be faced with the same difficult issue when you should be well into your planning stage. There is then a risk that you will grasp at *any* suggested topic, regardless of its interest, and a further risk that this will turn out to be both difficult and tedious. So avoid procrastination at all costs.

Look for ideas for projects from:

- tutors
- the literature
- existing interests
- past projects
- discussions
- brainstorming.

Ideally you should start to think seriously about your project at least six months before work is scheduled to begin. If this is not possible, then worry away at the issue of project choice as soon as you can and don't stop thinking about it until you have a topic that you are happy with. Use creativity techniques. Work with others who are similarly uncertain. Look at past projects to find topics that are potentially interesting and which you might explore in a slightly different way or with a different sample. Talk to people in any organisation to which you have access about issues which are of current concern to them.

Activity 15.2

List all the subjects or topics that have particularly interested you during your studies and any questions they have raised in your mind. If you are working, list any potential work issues that you would love to sort out.

Activity 15.3

List titles of past projects or dissertations that interest you in some way, noting beside each the aspects of the topic which particularly strike you and why.

Activity 15.4

For one or more broad areas of potential interest, draw mind maps showing all possible questions concerning the area which might be part of, or lead to, a project topic. (Figure 15.3 gives an example of such a diagram.)

Make a project section in your file, and start to file all your project-directed activities and thoughts there.

Dealing with organisational clients

For any company-based project your organisational client will be a key stakeholder: Their objectives will be as important as your tutor's, but may be less compatible with your university's requirements. A key skill, particularly if you spend part of your career as a change agent or consultant, is to be able to build rapport and trust with clients. Communication – talking, listening and body language – will be crucial. Equally important will be ensuring that understanding is shared at the outset, and trust sustained throughout, by behaving professionally, ethically and with the client's interest to the fore.

It is just as vital to admit any difficulties or slippages to your client as it is to face up to these within a group. Your interpersonal (and leadership) skills will be essential. There are several potential conflicts of interest between you and your client. One may be that their pet project does not actually allow you to satisfy course requirements (more of this later). Another is that you are being used to serve a hidden agenda. Another is that they are not prepared, for whatever reason, to give you access to essential resources.

The best approach in almost any of these circumstances is to express your concerns as soon as they start to be felt. Talk them through within the team, with your tutor, and then where appropriate with the client. It may be possible to modify the brief in a way

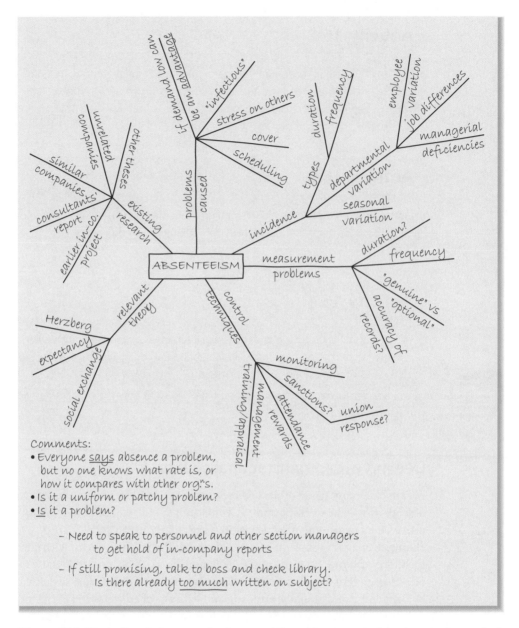

Figure 15.3 Student's mind map and subsequent thoughts on a possible absenteeism project

that will enable you to meet your objectives while still doing something of value for the client. Many such concerns may be prevented if you discuss course requirements with the client, and come up with several possibilities before finalising your choice of topic. It is essential that the 'client's' objectives for the work are consistent with those of your tutors. You cannot firm up your choice of project until this has been established. If you are doing project work for real, it is equally important to check that client objectives are appropriate. They need to be capable of being met within the resources likely to be available, and to raise no ethical concerns. Furthermore, meeting these objectives should be likely to improve the situation.

Choosing between options

➤ Ch 12

Once you have a range of possible areas, the process of clarifying objectives and choosing and refining a topic will be crucial. You may well need to go through an iterative process of broadening and narrowing, generating a range of possible areas and narrowing them down on one. Tease apart a range of ways of approaching this or sub-topics within the wider area. Choose one and again pull this apart. Figure 12.1 showed this sequence diagrammatically.

➤ Ch 12

Yet again there will be a need for communication – with your tutor to check that your shortlist of proposed topics meets course requirements, with those in any organisations which are hosting the project or allowing you access for research purposes, and with your tutor again (and again) as your ideas progress. You will need to use skills from Chapter 12 to generate key words, search the literature (including projects by previous students) and refine your research question. The following factors should influence your choice.

Interest

It is important that the topic you choose interests you (and interests your organisation if you are doing a work-based project). You are likely to be investing considerable effort in your project. If you need organisational facilities for observation or interviewing or access to other data, the organisation will be investing too. If neither you nor the organisation care much about the outcomes, the labour can be soul destroying. But if your client organisation does care about the topic, you may gain considerable support and help in your work and find that your final report is used to inform policy. If you are really concerned about the topic too, you will find project work engrossing.

> **Project topics need to:**
> - be interesting
> - offer suitable scope
> - have symmetrical outcomes
> - be feasible
> - be low risk.

If you are doing a literature-based rather than an organisation-based project, then you may be able to make it more interesting by thinking of it as a potential publication. This could perhaps be in a non-academic periodical. By thinking of a potential outlet for something derived from your research, and perhaps making sure that you collect additional titbits that would make the derived article more interesting to readers, you might add to the interest value of the project for yourself.

Scope

It is important that your chosen topic is potentially broad enough and deep enough for you to exhibit the range of skills that your tutors expect. Such expectations will vary somewhat depending on where you are studying, but usually a project or dissertation will be expected to develop generalizable investigative skills, and you will be expected to evaluate possible research methods or approaches as part of your project and to select an appropriate one and to justify this choice in your final report.

A narrowly defined topic is unlikely to allow you to demonstrate either methodological awareness or strategic thinking. If you are working with an outside organisation and it offers you a very narrow operational topic, check with your tutor that this will allow you to meet the university's requirements. If not, you may need to practise your talking and listening skills in order to increase the organisation's understanding of what the university means by a project. Once it understands, you may be able to explore other topics of equal interest to the organisation but better suited to your course needs.

Too broad a scope can be as problematic as too narrow. If you take on too much you will either be driven to superficiality or fail to make much progress at all – see the discussion of feasibility below.

The breadth issue is slightly different for a dissertation based on secondary sources.

Symmetry of research outcomes

The idea of symmetry of research outcomes may be less familiar to you, but it is an important criterion for choice. What it means is that your research results should be of interest however they turn out. Research to 'prove a point' should therefore be avoided. If it fails to prove the point it may not be of interest. Worse, you may be so keen for your results to come out in one particular direction that bias creeps in.

To take an unlikely example, suppose you were convinced that, contrary to popular opinion (and most research) a degree does not improve job prospects. You might carefully design some research to demonstrate this. Certainly, there would be a stir if you were right. But if you were wrong, and your research came out in line with what people think they 'know' already, the general reaction to your findings might be, 'So what?'

This does not mean that you should never question received wisdom, but do it in a way that generates interesting outcomes even if the basic principle is supported. Look at whether class of degree influences prospects when A level grades are controlled for, or effects of other aspects of students and their courses. Such supplementary information could produce an interesting result even if the obvious view *is* supported by the main finding. Normally, though, it is a safer bet to pick a research question which is characterised by equal interest in all possible outcomes.

Feasibility

Feasibility is obviously crucial. No project manager in industry would want to take on responsibility for a project doomed at the outset to failure. Yet, I see far too many student projects that were so ambitious they had a near zero chance of achieving what they set out to do. It is therefore essential to make sure that your proposed topic is feasible given the time and resources at your disposal. To attempt the impossible shows a distinct lack of judgement. Until you have experience of project work, judging feasibility may be difficult. Accept your tutor's guidance on what is a realistic aim. If you have to decide for yourself, you may like to note the following.

> Most student projects take considerably longer than expected.

All projects have a way of expanding to use at least twice the time and energy expected at all stages from planning to writing up. To allow for this, be cautious in your aims, talk to your tutor if at all possible, and act on their advice.

Be wary of any project which will incur significant costs, or need access to data that may be commercially sensitive or require significant investment of time by others over whom you do not have control. In general, the world is not sitting there waiting to help students with projects unless very clear advantages are apparent as a result of such cooperation.

Potential risks

Scope for catastrophe – particularly in organisation-based projects – is closely related to feasibility and is just as important. Feasibility is based on various assumptions – for example, that the person sponsoring you will continue to support the work, that people will be available for interview and willing to take part, and so on. It is important that your assumptions are justified, in that they are consistent with information you have at the time. But even if they are, things can change in ways you do not expect. Risk assessment looks at the potential for things to go wrong, and the impact this might have.

For example, redundancies might suddenly be announced for the group of staff you were planning to interview: if so, you may find that you are suddenly denied access. A topic may become highly sensitive because of other changes happening. Your sole champion in the organisation may leave and be replaced by someone who is unhappy about your project, or not replaced at all, so that you no longer have access to key resources. Real-time projects are particularly high risk. Organisations are prone to reschedule things for a variety of reasons. For example, your project might be to evaluate the impact of a new training programme. It would therefore depend on the programme's introduction. If this is delayed until after your report has to be written, this would be a 'catastrophe'. It is worth 'hazard spotting' for all suggested organisational topics in order to assess the scope for catastrophe associated with each, and the extent to which risks can be managed. You may find a table such as 15.1 helpful.

Table 15.1 Example of possible format for risk assessment of project

Risk	Likelihood	Impact on Project	Potential for Minimising Risk or Impact
1.			
2.			
3. [etc.]			

Obligations and Responsibilities

Whenever you do something that can affect others, ethical issues arise. Your own set of values about what is right and wrong will be relevant, as well as the values of those around you. When you are in a position of unequal power for some reason, these issues become more obvious – the greater the power imbalance, the greater the capacity to do harm. (If you saw two children tussling on the school playground you might not be too concerned. If one was twice the size of the other, you would probably feel it was very wrong.) You may not think that you have much influence when doing a project, but you usually have. This section is intended to sharpen your awareness of your obligations and responsibilities.

One way of thinking about your obligations and responsibilities is to classify them. For example, you might think in terms of the following types of obligation:

- **Legal** – a society's laws apply when you are doing research as much as at any other time.
- **Professional** – professional institutions, including those relating to both management and consultancy provide ethical guidelines which members are expected to follow.
- **Your university's research ethics policy** – you will normally need to demonstrate that you comply with this by filling in the relevant ethics approval form, so it is worth familiarising yourself with the policy at an early stage.
- **Cultural** – while legal obligations are explicit, cultural norms set implicit rules, a particular problem if you are working within more than one culture.
- **Personal** – your own internalised set of values and ideas of right and wrong – the sorts of values which are important and relevant to research in a Western culture include honesty (to yourself and others), respect, loyalty, trust and doing no harm to others.

When doing projects it is worth making sure that not only that you are acting legally and complying with all relevant policies and codes, but that you have thought about how your values translate into good research practice.

A useful approach here is to identify your stakeholders and think your potential influence on them, and therefore your capacity for doing harm. A stakeholder is anyone who can influence or be influenced by an organisation – or in this case, a project. Stakeholders who can influence your project will need particular consideration when you are doing your risk analysis. When thinking about your responsibilities, you need to consider both categories.

You may have found it difficult to see yourself as having power, but the mere association with a university, and the use of the word 'research' may cause some people to be in awe of your education, and to believe anything you say. (Consultants, especially those charging high fees, have similar 'expert' power.) You will also be in possession of 'privileged' information, given in confidence. It is surprisingly easy to pass on something interesting without thinking, or realising that your listener might be able to identify an employee even if you have been careful not to mention their name. There is therefore potential for damage:

- to your tutor's reputation if you hand in incompetent work
- to the reputation of your university if you are not seen to be acting responsibly and professionally

- to interviewees if you pass on something they said in confidence
- to your organisational client if you make recommendations that go beyond what your evidence supports, and they follow them in good faith.

If you do research which has implications for theory, consider the harm to fellow researchers if you misreport or over-interpret your results, or neglect to mention sources of bias. You also need to give credit for research which has influenced your work.

Activity 15.5

Consider *all* the stakeholders in the project(s) you are considering, not just those you considered earlier to be important. Consider what responsibilities you might have to each, and any potential for doing harm, and write these down. If you are doing a group project, compare your list with those of team members. You may also like to compare your list with Table 15.2. Don't look at this until after you have thought seriously about your own project. Every project is different, so your list may justifiably bear little relation to the table. However, if this is the case, think carefully about any differences in case they suggest additions or alterations to your own view. Many of the stakeholders shown are relevant to a significant proportion of projects.

You may have thought about responsibilities to clients and those providing information for their research, but Table 15.2 includes stakeholders you may not have thought of – fellow group members, your family and friends, and most importantly, yourself! The table makes general points. Once you have a project in mind you can usefully consider specific stakeholders in that project, their stake in the project, potential risks, and actions you need to take to minimise risk.

Having considered all the aspects relating to choice discussed above, you are in a position to make your selection. Although you will need to use different techniques at different stages (brainstorming, literature search, discussion at the start, for example), the general approach for project choice is fairly standard, and can be summarised by the algorithm shown in Figure 15.4.

Activity 15.6

When you have settled on one or more likely topics use the choice algorithm in Figure 15.4 to help with your decision. Note your likely topic, and your initial thoughts about it, in your file.

Initial literature search

You should by now be familiar with searching the literature for assignments, but your approach may be slightly different for a project. For a start, since your reading has different purposes at different stages, you will need to shift focus. Once you have a likely topic, you

Table 15.2 General ethical issues relating to stakeholders in a project

Potential Stakeholder	Responsibilities	Implications
You!	To do no harm to your health, state of mind, reputation or your future.	Avoid anything likely to be highly stressful, conflict with your values, require every waking minute to complete.
Family and friends	To spare some time/energy for their needs. If a family firm is your client, client issue need to be considered too.	As above! Plus remember that they do have needs, and maintain communication with them even if you are stressed out etc.
Fellow group members	To contribute fully to the shared work, and support the team as a whole.	Be on time for meetings, do work as promised, and to schedule, support other group members if they encounter difficulties, show your appreciation of their contributions.
Tutor	To do a worthwhile project to a competent standard.	Meet and submit work as agreed. Consider and act on feedback and suggestions. Put in the time and effort to do the best work of which you are capable.
Wider university	To bring credit rather than disrepute to the university.	Consider the potential for bad publicity from anything you do (or say) and act carefully in the light of this.
Client	To act professionally, do nothing to damage their reputation, treat them with respect and deliver something of value.	Be careful to make your own – and the projects' – limitations clear, do not agree to anything about which you have misgivings, let them know as soon as anything goes adrift so that you can agree corrective action together.
Subjects	To use their time to good effect, cause them no harm, honour any promises.	Ensure that subjects know what they are agreeing to, be punctual and use no more time than you have said for interviews etc., observe total confidentiality over anything said in interview, give copy of results if promised.
Other researchers	To use their work in full understanding. To make sure that anything you publish makes only justified claims.	

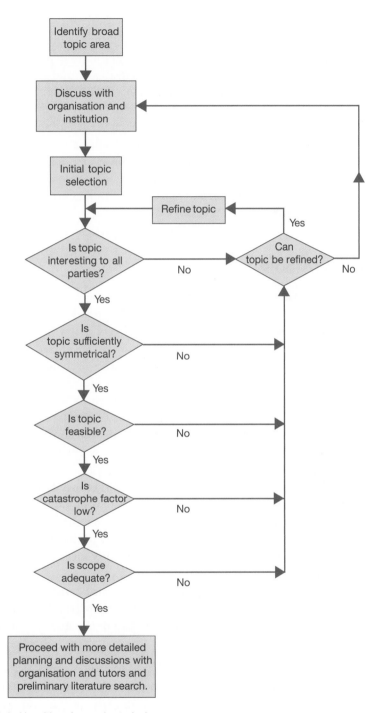

Figure 15.4 Algorithm for project choice

15

MANAGING PROJECTS AND DISSERTATIONS

will probably need to do a rough literature search to check what already exists in terms of investigation of this or similar topics and the methods which have been used in such investigations. It is also useful to start thinking about potentially useful areas of theory. Course projects will need to be informed by theory, and a dissertation will need to address theory even more explicitly and directly. An initial search should help you to refine your topic still further. Critical reading skills will be important here.

Projects at work may require less explicit theory – though your organisation may use an established project management approach such as Six Sigma project management. This is highly evidence based, and uses ideas first developed in the context of process design and improvement. Theory learned on your course will still enable you to understand a problem situation and manage a project, but you may make it less visible in your project reports.

➤ Ch 4

Project Proposals

Having made your initial choice, write as clear and detailed a draft project proposal as you can. This will assist you in planning the project and will help your tutor to know just what you have in mind. Your final project proposal will need to be completed at the end of your planning stage when your thinking has developed. But a skeleton is invaluable at this earlier stage. If anything looks unrealistic, or inappropriate, your tutor will be able to point this out and there will be time for you to rethink. If your organisational client has reservations about the way your thoughts are developing, again the sooner you know the better. At this stage your thoughts will not be fully clear, so for the first draft of your proposal simply outline your intentions under the headings which follow, leaving spaces if you are unsure of anything. And then discuss this skeleton proposal with tutor and (if appropriate) organisational client.

Pay close attention to any reservations either may have. Your objective is to identify and understand these rather than try to 'sell' your proposal as it stands. If differences of perspective emerge, it will be relatively easy to redirect the project at this early stage in order better to meet both sets of objectives. Later it will become more difficult. If there is a substantive difficulty it is important to find this out as soon as possible, while there is still time to choose another topic.

Receiving feedback is an important skill. As an external examiner I see many projects that have been complete disasters and were doomed to be this almost from the outset. When I ask the tutors involved why they did not guide the student into something more realistic or less risky they usually say that they tried their hardest, but the student would not listen.

➤ Ch 4, 8

The areas your skeleton proposal needs to cover are:

- **Problem or topic description** – background to the project, its context and significance.
- **Value of investigation** – why would the client organisation or other reader want to know what the project aims to establish, why would they want the answer to the question it is addressing?

- **Relevant theory** – something which you might downplay with an organisational client.

- **Likely project design** – possible methodology, timescale and the skills likely to be employed.

- **Data requirements** – the information needed and how data will be obtained and analysed.

For organisational projects intended to address a problem situation, one area on which you may need more detail at this draft stage is the nature of the diagnosis which you will need to go through before you can firm up on your project proposal. This means you will need some initial information about the situation before you can plan in any detail and firm up your proposal. So the draft proposal you agree with your client should be more than draft with respect to this preliminary information gathering.

Once the skeleton has been agreed, and you have gone through the stages outlined in the following sections, it is useful to develop a full and clear project brief that you and your client, sponsor and/or supervisor can use as a reference document. Although you will not be drawing up the final proposal yet, knowing what this will look like helps to focus your thinking as you go through the interim stages. Possible headings for a final project brief include:

- project title
- client and researcher names
- date brief agreed
- project start and finish dates
- significant milestones
- key project objectives
- success criteria
- scope of project (including constraints)
- resources needed
- communication arrangements during project
- form of final report (this may be specified in module requirements).

As with the skeleton proposal, the fuller brief needs to be agreed with key stakeholders.

Activity 15.7

File your agreed draft project brief, together with any comments such as areas of continuing concern, or things still to be resolved. Make a plan for progressing these and for gaining agreement with key stakeholders. File subsequent developments of the brief and other plans, with comments on reasons for changes.

Objectives Clarification

Your work towards a draft proposal should have established a set of objectives which will reflect the course and learning requirements, any client requirements and the topic-specific objectives as currently envisaged. It is important to distinguish these different types of objectives. 'Define objectives' is easily said but less easily done. Clients may be unclear about what they want. Or they may express their objectives clearly, but you may feel that these reflect a faulty diagnosis of the situation or no real diagnosis at all. You may feel that further investigation is necessary before you can be sure that the specified objectives are appropriate. In the early stages of a project you may need several iterations – quick circling through the loop. You may move from discussion to tentative objectives to an element of diagnosis to a draft proposal to discussion of this to refined objectives, more diagnosis, and so on. The initial objectives proposed by you or your client may be a long way from those you finally agree.

Suppose that your client is demanding a new IT system. You have a strong suspicion that the existing one could more than meet the required specification if staff could use it properly. If you are in the market for supplying such systems and the existing system was provided by a competitor, you might be tempted to go along with this (although this raises interesting ethical questions). If you are an 'internal supplier' you may do your company better service by questioning the stated objectives, showing what could be achieved by

➤ Chs 8, 11

➤ Ch 11, 13

training and perhaps saving hundreds of thousands of pounds. This is just one example of the need to question given objectives. It is for this reason that the diagnostic and investigative skills covered in Chapters 11 and 13 are so important.

Diagnosis is crucial. In any complex situation, diagnosis is essential to ensure that objectives are clear, appropriate and understood by both you and your client. Talking to those likely to be affected by the project can give you valuable information. And implementation of any proposed changes is likely to be more successful, and less problematic because of this communication. The plans themselves are likely to be far better because of the information you gained at this stage. Furthermore, people are more likely to cooperate if they feel that they have contributed to planning a change. Changes seen as imposed

➤ Ch 11

from above are likely to be strongly resisted.

In work contexts you are likely to be given a project with specified objectives, but that does not (usually) mean that you have to accept these without question. When you start to explore the context which generated the idea for the project and perhaps try to clarify what the client really wants, you may find that a slight shift in focus will make you feel far more confident of being able to deliver what is wanted. The client may even realise that the problem needs to be redefined. Such early shifts in the light of discussion and diagnosis can greatly increase the likelihood of a satisfactory outcome both for the internal or external client and for you as project manager. If your student project is one which is done in-company, and perhaps suggested by the company, your position is very similar to that of undertaking a project as part of your job. If you are doing a literature-based dissertation you will have more scope, but ensuring that the objectives are appropriate is perhaps even more of a challenge.

Literature Search

➤ Chs 4,
13

While you are working on objectives you will also need to be continuing with, and deepening, your literature search. The two stages can sometimes usefully be done in parallel, as developments in one area can impact upon thinking about the other. You will find information relevant to a project literature search in Chapters 4 and 13. Here I want to concentrate less on *finding* material than on *using* it to inform your project work.

Digitisation has made it is easy to find thousands of books, scholarly papers, less scholarly papers, newspapers, and consultant promotional 'pieces' on almost any topic. It is easy, too, to feel overwhelmed by this abundance. Often students try to read everything they can find on a topic, and then to summarise all of this in their final project report. Usually there is a word limit that renders this task impossible. Also, while such summaries of theory are fine if you are writing a text book, they add little to a project report. For that, you need to be far more focused, and concentrate on ideas and information and research that have influenced your project.

It is important, therefore, to read selectively, and report even more selectively. Rather than trying to give a general overview of a topic, you are trying to show that you know enough about the current state of thinking in that area to select key pieces of literature and draw upon them to help you to answer whatever question your project addresses. This casts the literature search in a very different light. Remember, too, the need for a critical approach to what is written: you need to understand the context in which something was produced, and the assumptions which underpin it, as well as the content *per se*. Your search should help you:

- understand the problem scenario
- refine your project question
- find a framework or methodology to shape the way you approach answering that question
- possibly find relevant research data
- provide a theoretical basis upon which you can develop improved theory (though normally this would not happen until you are a research student).

Thus when you are writing up your literature search, you will need to provide not just a series of summaries 'X found this, Y found that', but something tailored to your particular project. What did you read that establishes the importance of your topic, and how does it do this? What questions are left unanswered by what you have read that you are going to try to answer in your own work? What is assumed or claimed in what you have read that you are going to test? What theory is likely to cast light on your particular topic, and why? (This will usually be a theory or framework that addresses relationships between factors that seem important to you in the situation which you are looking at.) Where is there conflict between key authors that you might hope to resolve? How does what you read contribute?

If your report on your literature search is cast in a way that raises, and answers, such questions, then it is likely to play a key role in your final report. It will explain to your reader why you explored the topic you chose, and the particular questions you sought to answer. It may also explain why you chose the approach you did. Furthermore, your reading will have led you to do a far better project than could have been done in the absence of knowledge of the relevant literature.

Box 15.1 Some key questions in literature searching

- What concepts are important?
- Who are the key *current* writers on these concepts?
- Who are the classic writers on the idea?
- What do they say?
- Where do they differ?
- What methodologies do they use?
- What assumptions do they seem to be making?

Data Planning

Detailed and realistic project planning is essential and should begin as soon as you are happy with your project choice, certainly well before you are due to commence any data collection. The bulk of the work on many projects consists of data collection and analysis, so data planning is an important early stage in the planning process. You cannot fully assess the feasibility of your proposal until you have a detailed plan of what will be involved. This will depend on the data that you decide you need and the approach you decide on for collecting them.

No matter how carefully you have thought about possible topics and used the algorithm to test/refine them, detailed planning may highlight difficulties you had not envisaged. You need to allow time to go through further cycles of topic choice and development should such iteration be necessary. So data planning should commence as early as possible – for most projects, the bulk of your work will consist of data collection and analysis. The adequacy of any report you write and of the conclusions you present therein will depend on the evidence on which these are based. If your information is biased or inaccurate, your conclusions will be worthless.

➤ Chs 13, 14

Obviously, the type of data sought will depend on your particular project. If you read Chapters 13 and 14 some time before starting your detailed project planning, re-read them with your particular topic firmly in mind. When you have done this, map out the data you will need to address your chosen problem or answer your research question.

Activity 15.8

When you have decided on the data you will need to collect, and the approach you will take to collecting them, ask yourself the following questions:
- How accurate and reliable will the data be?
- Is the proposed sample large enough to warrant the conclusions you are likely to draw?

➤

- Is your sample sufficiently representative of the population in which you are interested?
- Will any measures actually measure what they purport to measure?
- If they are indicators rather than direct measures, will they be the best available indicators?

Once you are satisfied that the data you propose to collect will be adequate for your purpose and the way in which you propose to collect them is an appropriate one, you are in a position to start detailed scheduling.

Gaining Client Agreement

It is at this point that you are in a position to firm up your proposal with your client, if you have one. As was suggested earlier, in real-life consultancy the key skill is maintaining good relationships with the client. A clearly written and *agreed* research proposal is a great help in maintaining such a relationship as it acts as a reference point for both parties. You should, if at all possible, obtain written agreement to your more detailed proposal and to any necessary access to information or other resources. This may seem unnecessarily legalistic, but it can provide an essential protection if your contact in the organisation moves on and is replaced by someone less committed to the project. A written agreement will not prevent all the problems such a change can cause, but it can strengthen your case for continued facilities. It is also a useful protection against claims from some quarters that your research has in some way failed to meet the client's objectives. By the time the disagreement arises your client's view of the objectives that you have 'failed to meet' may be very different from the agreed project objectives. Reference to your written agreement may help to establish this, and may make it easier to resolve the problem.

> A clear proposal, agreed in writing with your client, is essential.

Project Scheduling

Once a project manager has clarified the performance, cost and time objectives for an organisational project, careful planning is needed to ensure that necessary resources are acquired, tasks identified and scheduled, and control systems set in place. Normally, completion on time will be crucial, with cost overruns and other financial penalties if the project is not finished. For a student project or dissertation, the penalties of overrun may be at least as severe – your degree is probably at stake.

➤ Ch 2   Chapter 2 introduced the ideas of charts and networks, and you might find it helpful to revise these briefly before tackling the more detailed treatment which follows. You need to be clear about the use of Gantt or planning bar charts as planning and scheduling aids. For simple projects, these can simply be hand drawn. Or you can use a spreadsheet's charting facility to produce a better looking version. (For more complex projects there is a wide choice of project management software.)

If you have many interdependent activities, it would be difficult to work out how to arrange things so that everything gets done in the right order, in the minimum time and without overstraining resources at any point. Networks and critical paths were introduced in Chapter 2 as a logical approach to optimal sequencing. Your project may well be the first time that you need to construct a network 'in anger'. The following more detailed description may help.

➤ **Ch 2**

Critical path analysis

When you were considering charts and networks as an aid to the relatively straightforward case of managing your study, you probably did not need to draw network diagrams. However, for project management, where planning is crucial and often complex, constructing a network will help greatly. It is possible to construct networks by hand. Figure 15.5 is an example of such a diagram. But software is readily available for constructing network diagrams and identifying critical paths, and scheduling activities efficiently as a result of these. It is worth using this as a planning aid in any moderately complex situation. (You will be developing another IT-related skill in the process, which could add to your portfolio in this area.)

In either case, you construct the network by looking at each activity, at how long it will take and at what needs to be completed before it can start. You can see that the

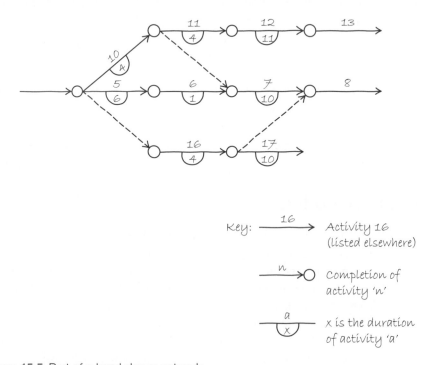

Figure 15.5 Part of a hand-drawn network

diagram does indeed look a bit like a net. The diagram is drawn, and read, from left to right. No activity can be started until those on paths leading to it are complete. There are different ways of drawing networks. (A common minor variant is to write the name of the activity on an arrow, rather than the numbers shown in the diagram.) The example described is merely one common approach. Whichever convention you choose, as with other diagrams, it is important to use it consistently. If you combine aspects of different conventions in a single diagram, you are likely to end up with a muddle. As the whole point of the exercise is clarity, avoid this!

In the diagram shown, activities are identified by a number on the arrow, (there will be a key explaining these elsewhere). Duration of the activity is indicated not by the length of the arrow but by a number in a semicircle beneath the arrow, and 'events', that is, the completion of activities, are indicated by circles. The dotted lines on the chart represent so-called dummy activities, normally of zero duration. Such dummies are necessary to show constraints between activities – something cannot be started until several other activities have been completed. Rather than superimposing these events at the start of the next arrow, which would be hopelessly confusing and impossible to read, the dummy device is used.

Estimating how long it will take to complete various activities can be difficult. Ask advice and then allow some extra. Remember that there will be 'dead' time to be included, time when you are waiting for people to return telephone calls, for surveys to be posted back or for someone else (if you are lucky) to process your data. (Examples in employment might include time for an advertisement you have designed to appear in a specialist journal, or for a training course to be available for staff, or for machinery or materials that you have ordered to be delivered.) 'Dead time' means that you can schedule activities in parallel, as was shown on the bar chart in Chapter 2, as you can work on one activity when waiting for something that will allow you to progress another.

➤ Ch 2

In order to do this juggling and make full use of your time despite such waits, you need the ideas (see Chapter 2 again) of critical paths and floats. To work out the minimum time a project can take, you need to look for the path of longest duration through the network. You get this by adding together the estimated activity times on the arrows forming each pathway through the net. This longest time tells you the earliest at which the end event can be reached. Any delay to any activity on this path will delay completion. Activities on this path are therefore critical, hence critical path analysis. Activities on non-critical paths *can* be delayed without affecting the completion time. This scope for delaying or slack is called 'float'.

To calculate float you work in the reverse direction, from right to left, subtracting activity durations from the time of the last event. This gives you the *latest* permissible start time for achieving each event. The difference between this and the *earliest* possible time for starting the activity is the float. In a bar chart, this can be shown by a shaded area. On a network, you could use, say, a big circle above an event enclosing the earliest event time and a square above events enclosing the latest time. (Remember, for critical events these times coincide.)

Your network gives you the information that will enable you to draw a schedule, or Gantt chart. Figure 15.6 shows part of a hand drawn schedule for a project where there is some float. Drawing a chart by hand gives some people more of a 'feel' for what they are

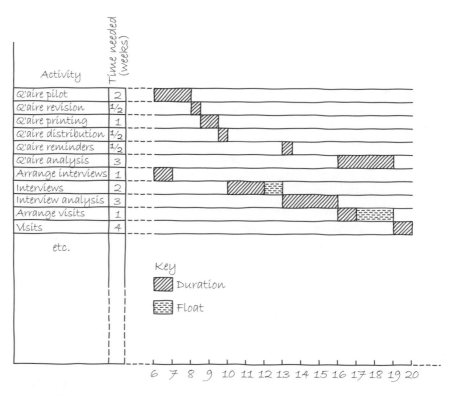

Figure 15.6 Part of a hand-drawn schedule for project planning

up against. Of course, doing it on the computer allows for better presentation to a client, and easier modification if schedules need to be altered. A wide range of planning software is available, or you can use a spreadsheet's charting facility.

➤ Ch 2

Milestones

You will remember that control needs to be exercised while there is still time to take remedial action if necessary. In planning a project it is necessary to plan for control, and the idea used most frequently is that of milestones. In a complex project, with subgroups working on sets of tasks, project managers cannot monitor every activity and all the inevitable adjustments that their subordinates will make to cope with varying circumstances. It is therefore helpful for them to identify points on the critical path at which agreed and recognisable criteria need to have been met. Normally, these criteria would relate to the three sets of objectives distinguished earlier: those to do with task progress and the cost and time taken to achieve this. Your task may be somewhat simpler, but the idea can still be a useful review mechanism and help you sustain motivation.

Some milestones may be set for you. You may be required to submit a project proposal by a given date, a progress report by another and a draft report chapter by a third. But it is worth looking at your critical path and selecting other milestones that relate to completion of significant sub-tasks and highlighting these on your schedule.

You will probably find that each time you approach one of these milestones you will need to put in some extra effort in order to prevent slippage. If you do this, you will find the achievement of your deadline deeply satisfying and reassuring, and your motivation to do well in the project is likely to be strengthened. If no amount of effort enables you to hit the milestone on target, you know you have a problem! But provided the milestones are sufficiently frequent (say, approximately every 20 per cent of the time allotted for completion, perhaps more often on a really long project) the problem will become apparent while there is still time to do something about it.

Activity 15.9

Draw up a network for your project, including all the tasks necessary for completion. Identify the critical path and milestones on it. Then convert this into a schedule, drawing a bar chart to represent it and highlighting the milestones. Remember to schedule the final draft of your project proposal and gaining approval to this as either your first or a very early task.

Negotiating Access

If you need to gain access to organisations in order to gather the data you need, or require the cooperation of people within an organisation who are not obliged to help you, then you need to give careful thought to how you will do this and allow considerable time for it in your plans. Some of the reasons for difficulty have already been indicated. Common reasons include:

- lack of interest in your project or failure to understand its relevance
- reluctance to commit organisational resources to anything other than normal work
- nervousness about what may be found (whether political, commercial or personal sensitivity)
- concerns about confidentiality
- knowledge (which is still secret) about imminent change that makes research invalid or undesirable
- doubts about your competence as a researcher
- worry that research, whatever its findings, may be disruptive or generate expectations which cannot be met.

In order to gain access, you need to slant your approach in a way that best addresses whichever of these reasons are important to your potential 'client'. It will be easiest to do this if you can identify your best contact person and find their views about the topic you propose before you make your request, though this is not always possible. If you cannot, then think about their likely concerns and aim to address these. You will normally find it helpful to do the following:

- *Use existing contacts.* Here your networking skills are important. Whom can you contact through members of your current network? If existing contacts are inadequate, then develop new ones. Initial informal contact by telephone or email can be useful.

- *Be very clear about what you want, why and what it will involve.* Few organisations will be willing to agree to something open-ended or unclear. For example, if you want to interview some staff, you will need to say how many of which kind(s) of people you want to interview, how long the interview will take, where and when it would need to be conducted and what will happen to the results. (Confidentiality will usually be a major worry.)

- *Make equally clear the benefits of collaboration to the organisation.* If there are none, you might want to think again about the project.

- *Make a formal request in a way that reinforces your credibility.* A neatly laid out, word-processed letter, on headed (your college or department) notepaper, giving your tutor as a reference, will help greatly. Even if you have gained informal agreement by other means, you need to confirm this via such a letter.

- *Make replying easy.* A proforma and stamped addressed envelope may seem trivial, but they could increase the number of positive replies considerably. A suggestion that you will phone to discuss this after a stated period (if it may be difficult for them to phone you) may also help.

- *Keep to agreements.* If you go outside what was agreed, you may lose access. So if you have sworn not to reveal what individuals say and then tell someone's boss the views they express, you can expect (deservedly) to be denied further access. In the interests of those who may request access for future projects, you should also keep to any agreements about what you will do subsequently. If you promise someone a copy of the report, for example, make sure that they get one.

Monitoring and Managing Progress

One of the greatest hazards with any project is failing to keep to schedule. Personal time-management skills are crucial here. It is very easy to feel relaxed at the start of a project, as final deadlines are so far in the future, and there may be few interim deadlines imposed by your tutor or university. You may therefore 'steal' project time for more immediate crises. This is likely to leave you with an impossible amount of work to do towards the end. It is therefore essential that you manage your time to give full weight to project work throughout the period, and to check that the time you are allowing is adequate. For this, you need interim deadlines or milestones, against which you can check progress. Your planning chart is therefore an essential tool throughout your project. Display it prominently, refer to it frequently and modify it if this proves necessary. Although you should be monitoring progress all the time, find some way of ensuring a more formal progress check at each milestone. Perhaps you could schedule meetings with your tutor at

➤ Ch 2   these points, or at least agree to send in progress reports.

Any slippage should be treated extremely seriously. Resist the (strong) temptation to attribute it to 'one-off' factors which will not happen again. Excusing yourself in this way, and adjusting subsequent schedules to allow for the delay that has already occurred, is likely to mean you merely have worse 'slippage' when you reach the next milestone. Instead, you should look carefully at the possible reasons for the delay and address these causes. Above all, resist the near-universal tendency to see the final deadline as so far away that project work is not urgent. If you are to do a good project, it is urgent from the start. Time will not expand as you approach the deadline.

Unless you are absolutely sure that you *can* get back on track and avoid any similar slippage in future (and this doesn't mean that you *hope* all will magically go more smoothly), you should discuss the situation with your tutor and adjust your plans accordingly. You may need to reduce the scope of your project in some way.

If you are working on a group project, it is important that the group sets individual as well as group milestones and that the group as a whole meets regularly to review progress against these. If one group member encounters problems, ways of adjusting workloads may need to be found and of supporting the member in difficulty, if the project is to be completed successfully.

Writing a project log

As well as your planning chart, you should keep a detailed record of progress in the form of a project log. In this you should record all project activity, reasons for decisions, times taken, details of what happened, snags encountered and insights gained. This can be enormously helpful when you come to write up your report. It is surprising how things which seemed burned into your memory at the time can fade into oblivion before you come to describe them. Your log can be a source of observations made at the time and will be eminently quotable at appropriate points in your dissertation.

Project work offers rich learning potential, and many institutions require students to include in, or with, their report a series of reflections on lessons learned and points where with hindsight it is realised that the project could have been approached better. This is intended to demonstrate that you have indeed learned something about the process of this kind of research, are aware of any limitations in your work, and can learn from critical reflection. (As an examiner, I find such reflections a valuable source of necessary marks for the student whose project has gone wrong for some reason.) Such a reflections section can draw heavily on your log. If you are keeping a learning journal, you will also find it useful to reflect for your own benefit on the more general learning from the project.

 Because a project draws on almost every skill covered in this book (and many more), your final report is a potential exhibit for almost any key skill or management competence you are likely to want to demonstrate. It can therefore be a valuable component of your portfolio. You would need to include a covering document with it which made explicit to your assessor the competences demonstrated and how. Again, a detailed project log would be a useful part of the 'story'.

Keeping track of references

The importance of noting full references was mentioned earlier, but cannot be stressed too often. If you are not already using bibliographic software of some kind, as suggested in Chapter 4, now is the time to start! You can waste a huge amount of time hunting for references if your notes are incomplete. And you will probably be doing it just before the project is due while you are struggling to write a substantial report to a tight deadline. The last thing you need at this point is to be distracted by a search for complete references. Avoid this by getting into good habits now.

Remember too to keep full Uniform Resource Locators (URLs) for material accessed online, together with the date accessed, as well as more conventional references (in whatever form your institution requires). It really is worth using a bibliographic software package if you can.

➤ Chs 4, 13

Activity 15.10

Look at the references you collected while doing your initial literature search at the topic choice stage. If they are not complete (i.e. with full title, author and publication names, publishers and/or page numbers) fill in any gaps now.

Writing a Project Report

If you spend some of your career as a consultant, report writing skills will be invaluable. Consultancy is a service, and largely intangible. When people are purchasing a service, they tend to be disproportionately impressed by the few tangible aspects there are, and a report is one of these. A consultant friend of mine freely admits that clients normally read only the first few pages. Yet he sees it as absolutely crucial that the report is fat, glossy and full of colour. It is the 'thwack' factor (when you thwack it down on the table) that gets him future business, he says.

You may not want to go to these lengths (though presentation will still be important). But after data collection and analysis, the most substantial task is likely to be writing your report. This activity can usefully be started much earlier than most people think. It may seem absurd to start drafting when you have scarcely started to collect your data and have little idea of what your eventual conclusions will be. But actually it can be most enlightening to write a skeleton draft based on guesses as to what the results might show. Often this will uncover a need for additional data: you may realise that, even if your results turn out as you expect, they will support only a weak argument. If you find this out at the data-collection stage, you have time to amend your plans accordingly.

➤ Ch 13

Topic choice is therefore not the only time when iteration can be helpful. As with any complex problem-solving activity, a constant process of thought, experiment and refining of thoughts is necessary. This point is made explicit in many of the systems methodologies which you may be taught during your course. It also reflects the Kolb learning cycle introduced in Chapter 3. It is difficult to make sense of complexity all at once. But

➤ Ch 3

we can make a little sense of it, see ways in which our ideas might be improved, try these new ideas, refine them further in the light of experience and so on. Thus step by step we improve our understanding.

The other advantage of starting drafting early is that it is much less frightening to draft what you *know* is only a dummy draft. Sitting at the keyboard towards the end of your project knowing that you have to write 10 000 words or so at a single bite can, in contrast, be a prospect too awful to contemplate. If, in consequence, you postpone the exercise, the task becomes quite impossible. You have no time left for revisions, no time even for proper thought. The resulting dissertation, despite much burning of midnight oil, is a disappointment to you, to your tutors and to any client organisation.

➤ Ch 6

If you have written a skeleton draft at an early stage and are reasonably competent at wordprocessing, writing your report can be relatively stress free. You can flesh out parts of the skeleton as you go along, revise these longer versions, incorporate your references and start analysing your data, all in parallel. Your final draft will gradually and relatively painlessly emerge from this process. Revisit Chapter 6 on clear writing at about the time you start to draft. There is more detail on report writing there. And most important, keep back-up copies of your work somewhere absolutely safe and update these back-ups regularly. This is work you *cannot* afford to lose.

Style and format

You may be given a specified format, but if not, the following is one which is widely accepted:

- Title page
- One- or two-page summary – you may be required to submit this separately, rather than binding it with your report
- Preface and acknowledgements
- List of contents – numbering should usually reflect major and minor sections, e.g. 4, 4.1, 4.2 (see Figure 6.4 for an example)
- List of tables, figures, etc.
- Numbered sections – these should include an initial statement of project aims, a short statement of major findings and recommendations and then detailed descriptions of relevant literature, chosen methodology with justification, data collected, analysis, conclusions and probably reflections
- List of references
- Additional bibliography, if expected – or a wider bibliography may include your specific references rather than these being separately listed – check your university's requirements
- Appendices.

Style should be clear. You will normally be expected to use academic concepts wherever appropriate, but avoid any unnecessary jargon. Equally, you need to avoid sounding over-colloquial and 'chatty'. A report should be 'considered and careful' in its expression.

In particular, do not make unsupported assertions. It should always be clear how your results are derived, or upon what evidence you are basing your statements. (Where there are shortcomings in your evidence and you need to make assumptions, you should say so clearly and discuss any resulting limitations to your conclusions.)

It will be much easier for your reader to absorb your developing argument if you give a short introduction to each section. This should clarify the structure of what you are about to write, and make it easier to grasp your arguments as they are reached.

Large chunks of text can be hard to read, so it helps to include relevant diagrams and tables at appropriate points. This breaks up the text, and is easier for the reader than having to turn repeatedly between text and appendices. (Very detailed or complex diagrams, tables or other information should be included as an appendix – it would interrupt your argument if included in the main text, and only a few of your readers may want to have that level of detail.)

Errors in spelling and grammar can make your meaning unclear, and, additionally, will make people less likely to believe you know what you are writing about. It is important to check what you have written – if your wordprocessor highlights possible spelling or grammar issues, do not ignore them. If you need further help, ask a competent friend to check your work. Double-check that you have entered figures in tables correctly. It is very easy to make errors that can alter the whole meaning of the table.

You can further improve the impression created by your report by thinking about fonts, graphics, and use of colour. Marking projects has a substantial subjective element. While content is crucial, presentation can have a strong influence on the mark you receive. If you are asked to submit work in hard copy, use good paper and submit work for binding in good time. Follow any university specifications for binding. If there are none, think carefully about the best way of presenting your report.

If you allow yourself sufficient time (twice as long as you imagine you can possibly need) for drafting, and present your work well, your finished dissertation/report can be one of the most satisfying things you have done. It will have uses as an exhibit of your competence in a number of areas when you are seeking employment or a competence-based professional qualification and it may be a source of articles should you wish to start writing for a wider audience. The process of producing it will have developed skills that will be vital in many of the jobs for which you are likely to apply. May I wish you success in your endeavour!

SUMMARY

This chapter has argued the following:

- Work in organisations is increasingly carried out in task or project groups.
- Project management, whether in employment or for projects you are required to do as a student, draws on almost all the skills covered in this book.
- Group projects need to be very carefully managed.

- Clarity of objectives is essential and topic choice should be approached as soon as feasible.

- It is important to be familiar with key relevant items in the literature and to use these to inform your thinking about your topic and how to approach it.

- Through iteration you should aim to select a topic that meets course requirements, is interesting and, if you have a client organisation, meets client needs.

- Detailed project planning is essential and cannot be undertaken until you have a clear idea of how you will proceed and the data that will be required.

- Networks, critical paths, milestones and bar charts are invaluable aids.

- Negotiating access is time consuming and needs to be done with care, making clear what you want and why and what benefit there will be for the organisation. You need to do this in a way which reinforces your credibility.

- Progress should be monitored carefully and corrective steps taken as soon as any delay occurs – optimism is not enough.

- Drafting should start early, allowing time for insights from drafting to influence data collection. Ongoing redrafting will reduce the pressures of producing a final report.

- The final report should be clear, well presented and in appropriate style, format and binding.

- Project work presents major challenges, but can be a source of substantial learning and satisfaction.

Further information

Bryman, A. (2012) *Social Research Methods, 4th edn*, Oxford University Press.

Cameron, S. and Price, D., (2009) *Business Research Methods: A Practical Approach, Chartered Institute of Personnel and Development.* This provides a much more detailed coverage of the subject than is possible in a single chapter.

Collis, J. and Hussey, R. (2009) *Business Research: A Practical Guide for Undergraduate and Postgraduate Students*, 3rd edn, Palgrove Macmillan.

Cook, C.R. (2005*) Just Enough Project Management*, McGraw-Hill. Although designed for those managing work projects you may find the planning content particularly useful.

Saunders, M., Lewis, P., and Thornhill, A. (2012) *Research Methods for Business Students*, 6th edn, Pearson. This provides more detailed treatment particularly of data-collection methods and analysing both quantitative and qualitative data. It also includes a number of case studies.

For more on critical path analysis see http://www.mindtools.com/critpath.html (accessed 10/1/15) or http://www.project-management-skills.com/critical-path-method.html for more information on critical path analysis (accessed 10/1/15).

16
MANAGING YOUR CAREER

Learning outcomes

By the end of this chapter you should have:

- reassessed your work objectives

- identified sources of information on ways of meeting these

- drawn up a plan of action to take between now and graduation

- compiled a basic CV

- learned how to write a letter of application

- become more confident about being interviewed

- considered how to seek opportunities to use developing skills

- be starting to think about how to plan subsequent career moves

- considered how networking and other skills in this book can help you develop your career.

Introduction

You may be studying business or management prior to starting work, or already be in a management role and wanting to understand it better. In the first instance, the most important and challenging project you face is probably obtaining a job after graduation. If you are studying while working, you may be looking for a role which reflects your graduate status, and face similar challenges. Sooner or later, depending on whether you are already in that sort of role, you may want to use what you have learned during your studies to progress more quickly in your career. This can work in two ways. One way is to apply the knowledge and skills you have developed to the work you are doing in order to become more effective, the other is to apply those same skills to actively managing your career. The skills you have developed thus far will serve both purposes, In this chapter they are integrated, so that they can have a major impact on your employability and career.

You can expect to change jobs several times in a career, so your first job need not be 'perfect'. But ideally it will be a good starting point for the sort of career you want – one that will allow you to develop skills that will be useful in the future, or learn more that will help you decide in more detail where you want to go. It should also be a job you would like to stay in for a while. There are costs involved in changing jobs too quickly. The emotional and financial costs will be immediate. The longer-term cost is that potential employers will start to doubt your reliability or perseverance if you change too often. Whether you are looking for your first or subsequent job, your aim is therefore to find a job that will suit you for several years, and will give you the experience and learning opportunities you need to prepare you to move further along a path that appeals to you. Continuing professional development and active career management will be needed throughout your career if you are to reach your full potential.

Looking Forward

You are more likely to get where you want to go if you know where that is. The power of having a vision was discussed earlier, and you could usefully revisit and refine your own vision at this point.

Activity 16.1

As orientation to this chapter it may be helpful to revisit the 'vision' that you developed in Chapter 12, and develop the 'work' part of that vision, aiming to make it as vivid as possible. Try to imagine yourself five years from now in the 'perfect' job situation. Then look at what it is about that situation that makes it so good for you. Having a clear picture of this may in itself help to move you towards a job that will make your vision a reality before too long.

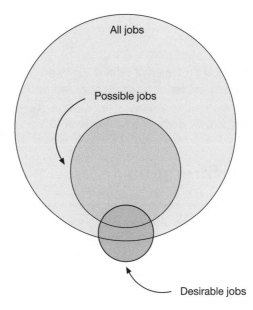

All jobs

Possible jobs

Desirable jobs

Figure 16.1 Circles of employment

It may take considerable research, and perhaps some creativity, to identify the sort of work that will meet your objectives and to find the kind of organisation offering it. You need communication and search skills to find out about job opportunities. You need to manage your learning in order to make yourself a stronger candidate for your target job/ organisation by doing things before you graduate. Your written communication skills will be taxed by preparing a compelling letter of application and professional-looking curriculum vitae (CV). You need both talking and listening skills for an interview. If other assessment methods are used to supplement the interview, 'being assessed' skills will also be relevant.

There can be fifty or more applicants for a good job. You need to put considerable effort into job search, building contacts, developing your skills and making a good application if you are to be at the head of the queue.

One way of orienting your work to this chapter is to think in terms of three circles, the largest representing all jobs, the second jobs you would like and the third jobs you could reasonably be offered. Your aim in working through this chapter is to find out more information about the first two circles, so that you can map them and their boundary more clearly. You then need to work on enlarging the third circle, or at least on maximising its overlap with the second. This you can do by developing skills, gaining relevant experience and making contact with target organisations in a positive way. Your career future lies within the third circle. Figure 16.1 illustrates this view. Note that this diagram suggests the category 'jobs you would like but which do not exist'. This will upset logicians, but the point is important. What do the other overlaps (or failures to overlap) suggest?

Activity 16.2

In order to gain more practice in diagramming, experiment to see whether any of the other techniques described in the book will help you to visualise your task in ways that suggest new lines of attack, or raise useful questions other than that of whether what you want actually exists. Start a 'job seeking' section in your file, and log your thoughts.

Reviewing Your Strengths

If you are to target realistic jobs, those in the intersection between possible and desirable, you need a clear and realistic view of your strengths so that you do not set your objectives too low – or fail to work on developing strengths you need. If you are working through this chapter during the second or third year of your degree, your skills will have developed considerably. Try to resist temptations towards either modesty or overestimating your strengths. If you have some way to go to graduation you may find it useful to pull together development needs you have identified while working through the book and construct a unified action plan for improving your employability.

Any decision about what you want to do for the next few years can influence the rest of your life. As with any complex problem you may need to work on several strands simultaneously. Here, objectives and strengths and weaknesses need to be worked on in parallel.

Activity 16.3

You started to consider your strengths and weaknesses in Chapter 1. Go back to that now. Use the list of key skills outlined there to update your lists of strengths and weaknesses. These skills include:

- number

- communication

- information skills

- leading and working with others

- learning

- problem solving.

You may now be able to identify specific relevant skills under these broad headings; for example, presentation or report writing under communication skills, networking under working with others, or facility with particular software packages under information skills. Looking at advertisements for appealing jobs can highlight other areas of strength and weakness. Remember to add experience as well as skills to your list. Again, your trawl of websites and advertisements should give you an idea of the kinds of experience which you need to be able to offer. This might be, for example, to have worked in a particular sector, or a particular function such as sales, or a particular context such as a 'lively creative team, or have demonstrated particular skills such as leadership.

➤ **Ch 1**

You also need to be prepared to modify your assumptions and thinking in the light of insights gained. As strengths and weaknesses will be of different significance for different jobs, you may need to do several analyses, one for each possible area of work, and to iterate several times, working through this section, then the next, then returning to this and so on as your ideas become clearer.

Once you have your updated list of strengths and weaknesses and have thought about how important they might be for the sort of jobs you might wish to take, you are in a position to think seriously about the actions you need to take. Some will be short term, some longer, but all will be aimed at increasing relevant strengths and reducing relevant weaknesses so that you will be well positioned to gain a 'desirable' job at the end of your planning period. These plans will need to be revisited and amended at intervals, and the planning horizon extended. This planning process can help you to develop your career throughout your working life.

16

MANAGING YOUR CAREER

Activity 16.4

Develop a draft series of action plans for making yourself more employable by targeting key strengths and weaknesses. Follow them! Monitor progress at regular intervals and update plans regularly.

Reassessing Your Objectives

Both your life objectives and your career objectives are likely to have altered markedly since you started your studies. Your perspectives will have broadened, you will have made new contacts, and you will be aware of a wider set of options. So in parallel with thinking about your strengths and weaknesses you need to reassess your objectives.

Again, you should have already started this process at the start of the book, when you began to think about what you might want from a job and to question people about their experience of work, and will have been developing your thoughts about this ever since. Developing your 'vision' will have helped the process. If you have not yet worked on these aspects, start by making a list of the things that are important to you in life as a whole.

What makes you feel satisfied? What would you like to achieve? Once you have answered these overarching questions, narrow down to the area of employment and consider how this might help you achieve your wider objectives. Draw upon any work experience you have had and conversations with people about their jobs. Think about which of the skills you listed you really *enjoy* using. Use the careers resources your university has available.

Activity 16.5

➤ Ch 1

You can also 'interrogate' the vision you developed in Activity 16.1. What was it that felt good about the job you visualised? What does this tell you about yourself? Revisit the 'hopes and fears' exercise in Chapter 1 (Activity 1.4) and see how they have altered since then. If they have not altered much, or if you found your imagination didn't come

➤

up with much, spend some time talking to family, friends, mature students and those who have had vacation jobs in order to find out what they see as the elements of a 'good' job, and use this to refine your thinking.

Activity 16.6

Develop a hierarchy of objectives related to employment, highlighting those branches which are particularly important to you. Space this out on a large piece of paper and annotate it with thoughts about experiences and jobs which might help you achieve these objectives. (If you hate this degree of freedom, a tabular format is available as a web resource.) File your objectives.

Activity 16.7

Think about the implications of your objectives and then redraft your SWOT to reflect these, adding in opportunities and threats that the employment market offers, given your particular objectives. (You should revisit this SWOT throughout your work on this chapter, as part of the iterative process, aiming to have it fairly fully worked out by the time you have finished the book. Then revisit it at intervals throughout your career.)

Work experience is possibly the most powerful tool of all for making you aware of what you like and do not like, are good at and not good at, want and do not want of a job. Vacation jobs, a placement year, or work before starting your degree will make exploration of the 'circles of work' much easier. If you are still in your first year, think seriously about a placement if you have not already committed yourself to one. If you *are* committed, but have not yet decided what to do with your year in industry, then the work in this chapter, including discussions with your careers service if at all possible, will help. You need to choose a placement likely to contribute to your development of relevant skills. This will enlarge your 'possible' circle.

Activity 16.8

Construct a series of objectives trees for your goals for the next five years (longer if you can think that far ahead). Focus your hierarchy on broad life objectives, with the job objectives that will serve these slotted in. Spend some time on this, talking through your diagrams with others if possible – they may ask you questions which prompt further thought. You should by now need no persuading that clarity of objectives is all-important. File the results when you are satisfied with them.

Finding Out about Opportunities

Once you have a clearer idea of your objectives, you can better focus your exploration of the circle representing 'all jobs'. You are only really interested in the part of that circle that is relevant to your objectives, therefore, potentially in the 'desirable jobs' area, you can probably safely ignore things such as road sweeping, telephone sanitising, or assembly line operating (these attract few graduates). Focus on jobs relevant to your career ambitions. But because it is important to avoid an uncreative, over-narrow approach, avoid drawing too firm a boundary yet.

You will remember that for an investigative project you need first to formulate your 'research question' and then to identify information sources. At some stage the question is likely to be of the form: 'What sorts of job in which sorts of organisation will offer me' [X] and avoid [Y]?' But you may need to ask more global questions first or start with something more specific. Use whatever questions seem best to fit your own situation. You

➤ Ch 13   may find relevance trees (Chapter 13) useful here. Certainly, if you can identify some key words this may help you in your later investigations.

16

MANAGING YOUR CAREER

Activity 16.9

Formulate a question or series of questions about theoretical (there is no need yet to be limited by what is *possible*) employment opportunities that will enable you to identify areas for more detailed investigation.

You now need to explore sources of information. Everyone who has ever worked is a potential primary source, as are all employers, so you may need to use secondary or tertiary sources. Probably the best starting point will be your university careers service. Make an appointment with them now, even if you are not yet near the end of your degree. The sooner you can use their expertise to focus your thinking the better, and the sooner you establish the information resources which they have, the longer you will have to take advantage of them. Identify resources that could help you to refine your search, or perhaps to enlarge it to interesting areas which you had not previously considered.

Another source of information is job advertisements. Collect ones that interest you, even if you are not yet in a position to apply for the jobs they concern. Try to see whether patterns emerge from this. Are there some aspects which many of these advertisements have in common? Does this make you aware of new objectives you could add to your tree? If possible, obtain further particulars for some of the jobs that interest you. Even if you will not be in a position to apply for the job for a year or two, the information will be invaluable in helping you to see what employers think they offer and what they require. Look at graduate recruitment pages of newspapers. Go to the websites of organisations you might like to work for and find their job opportunities pages. Look at some of the main recruitment agency pages (you will be able to find these from their advertisements in recruitment pages, or your careers service may provide you with lists of useful URLs). Explore **www.prospects.ac.uk**. This is the official UK graduate recruitment website; it offers a wide range of useful material, from how to maximise your vacation work potential to writing a good CV.

Activity 16.10

Find ten websites that you think will be really useful in your job search, making a note of the main advantages of each. If possible, compare lists within a group, and add any interesting ones which you had missed.

Start to assemble a file on job opportunities which can act as a reference point for future considerations. Guard against premature narrowing by collecting information on a few jobs which do *not* look interesting, as a check on your selection criteria and the boundaries these imply.

Employers who are *not* advertising jobs may still be a source of information. Your search of currently available jobs may help you to identify an area where you would like to work, but where there are no current vacancies. If so, see what you can easily find out about organisations from their websites or other sources. Contact the HR department to find out whether they anticipate openings for which you would be eligible, with your degree, to apply, and if so, see what you can find out about these.

Does the organisation have any sort of 'open day'? Do they take on students for vacation work? When vacancies arise, where are they advertised? Could you go for an information interview, just to explore possibilities? This is an application of the networking approach suggested in Chapter 8. You could extend it by exploring your existing network of contacts (family, friends, past employers, and so on) to see whether you have any links to this organisation or similar ones. In making contact with someone in an organisation whom you do not yet know, you are likely to get furthest if you make telephone contact first. You will need to draw on your talking and listening skills. As you will be moving into the area of 'extending the possible' here, do not make any such contacts until you have finished this chapter.

➤ Ch 8

If you have yet to do a placement, or if you still have time to arrange relevant vacation jobs, you will have another way of finding out about one organisation in particular (more if you have several vacations still to go) and perhaps working with or for people with experience of similar organisations and jobs. All this will help to increase your understanding of the sector, of jobs within it, their satisfactions and demands and their likely potential for meeting your own needs and desires. Some students are offered jobs as a result of making a good impression during a temporary job.

Activity 16.11

Start to work seriously on the employment section of your file in which you organise all your information relevant to jobs and their characteristics, their attractions, their requirements and criteria for selection if advertised.

Becoming More Attractive to Employers

As you develop a clearer idea of how much more you need to do to become an attractive applicant for the sort of job that interests you, and of how much more you need to find out about this, you can start to plan your strategy for becoming a more attractive applicant. Start by listing the tasks which you still need to dot in order to clarify your objectives, and to map the most relevant part of the 'employment circle' in more detail. Then seek further information about the sorts of job which you most want, and the skills and experience you will need to be an attractive applicant

Once you have listed these tasks, you can think about their duration and the order in which they need to be done. Either draw a planning chart directly, or if this is difficult, construct a network, and identify a critical path to help you draw up your schedule. Remember to set some milestones to allow you to monitor your progress.

16

Activity 16.12

Draw up a schedule for all the tasks still needed to become an attractive applicant for the sort of job you want, and for making contact with potential employers. (Note: talk to careers guidance people about when best to do this is – it may be sooner than you think.) Monitor your progress against this plan.

Four aspects are particularly important for your project of getting a job consistent with the sort of career you seek:

- identifying skills and competences important to your target jobs and developing these where necessary
- making contact with potential employers
- preparing a good CV and letters of application
- thinking about how you can perform well in selection.

Check that your schedule includes all these – add any which are missing. Then start to put your plan into action.

Contacting potential employers

In addition to developing the general skills which will help you to become a successful candidate, you need to add in activities that will increase your chance of gaining a specific job – you can schedule these only once you have identified the job. As the following discussion of written applications, CVs and interviews points out, all need to be viewed as attempts to communicate the extent to which you will meet a potential employer's needs. To do this, you have to put some effort into identifying those needs in each case and finding out as much as you can about a job for which you are preparing an application.

Potential job applicants are normally sent some information about the company and further particulars of the job. Study such information carefully, trying to work out the sort of person, and the sorts of skills, that will best fit the job requirements. Indeed, go further. Seek out other sources of information, from libraries, people you know, the Internet, products or services, shops or branch offices of the organisation in question. If a contact name or telephone number is given for further information, use that as a starting point for finding out as much as possible about the job and competences which would contribute to success in that job. Try to get the names of other people to talk to and arrange a visit if possible.

Organisations are likely to be impressed by the fact that you have clearly gone to considerable lengths to understand their needs and have worked out a good case that you will meet these. If you go further, and find out more about the sector or industry and about customers and their likely needs, and can use this information to good effect in an interview, they will be even more impressed. Remember to be courteous and professional in your contacts, but not boring. If you can form relationships with people prior to an interview, they may well give you invaluable information and they could even be involved in the selection process. The nature of your contact with them is therefore important.

Activity 16.13

Pick a job for which you plan to apply. (If you are some way short of graduating, pick one which you might apply for if you were ready.) Find out as much as you can about the job, the organisation and the organisation's competitive environment (customers and competitors). Then think about the ways in which you can use this information to identify the strengths which you would want to offer and any weaknesses you might have. See whether you can complete a SWOT on yourself as a product for this *particular* customer, looking at opportunities and threats which the organisation might offer you too.

Preparing a Good CV

Most recruiters will ask you to include a curriculum vitae (translated roughly, the course of your life), or CV. This is really a personal data sheet, laid out for ease of reference so that a potential employer can easily tell your age (though age discrimination legislation in the UK means that you cannot be required to give this information), qualifications, employment history and relevant skills. Once you have a long employment history, you may need to 'version' the CV to emphasise points relevant to each application. If your experience is limited, it should be easy to fit into any word limit set for the CV without needing to be too selective. Even if no limit is specified, be as concise as you can, and aim to keep your CV to a maximum of two sides of A4, focusing most on what is relevant to the particular job.

Remember that this is a written communication aimed at impressing as well as informing the reader. Ensuring that your CV is focused, up to date and immaculately presented is essential. If you are asked for hard copy, do ensure that you print it on good paper, and make it look as professional as possible. One of your goals is to stand out from other applicants, so without getting too fancy it may be worth departing from the standard word-processor format. The order may be helpful, but make yours look slightly better than the standard which many applicants will probably use.

Layout preferences vary. If you are given a format by your careers service, or one is suggested in further particulars, then use that. Otherwise, take the following format as a starting point for an application for a first job. (Later in your career you may want to focus more on your career history, and give less detail on your education.) You may like to think about centreing the basic information in the first section, using a larger font for your name so it stands out, and generally making this part look attractive.

YOUR NAME (in full)

Address (in full, but can put on a single line to save space)
Term address (if different)
Phone number
Email (if you have a 'joke' email address consider setting up a more professional-sounding one
Nationality, and work permit status if applying to a country other than your own.

CAREER OBJECTIVES
This section is optional – only include it if you feel you can strengthen the impression you make with no more than four to five lines of information specifically tailored to this job – waffle or generalities are unlikely to impress.

EDUCATION AND QUALIFICATIONS
Give both qualification and awarding body.
Start with the most recent.
If you do not yet have your degree, say what you hope to have, including your expected class of degree if known.
List any relevant professional qualifications.
Give the recognised UK equivalent for any foreign qualifications you list.

EMPLOYMENT HISTORY [or WORK EXPERIENCE]
Again, give most recent first.
Give dates you held the job, and if not obvious from job title, what it involved.
Remember to include unpaid as well as paid work.
If you have worked for some time, and the list is very long, you can afford to mention less relevant jobs only briefly, but avoid leaving unexplained gaps – a recruiter may draw the wrong conclusion!

SKILLS
Here you can highlight skills particularly relevant to the post. Avoid simply making claims like 'I am an excellent communicator.' Instead say how you have developed and shown your communications skills. If you have been building a portfolio of evidence you can draw on this here.

Remember to include any useful skills gained outside work and education, such as fluency in other languages, or IT or graphics skills.

ACTIVITIES AND ACHIEVEMENTS

This section gives you the opportunity mention non-work activities that show you as an interesting person well suited to the role. Remember to include any positions of responsibility, or showing leadership, for example chairman or treasurer of a society, or captain of a sports team. Focus particularly on things relevant to the particular job or organisation, and aim to sound as impressive as the facts allow. (If your first draft suggests that your interests are rather restricted and you still have time, develop some fast!)

REFEREES

You should normally include the names and contact details of two people who have agreed to act as referees.

Referees should be people who have some position that will make their opinion of you believable – tutors, past employers or, at a pinch, family friends who have an impressive-sounding job title. These will be contacted by an interested employer and asked about such things as your character and skills. You need to gain your chosen referees' permission before giving their names and addresses, as you are asking them a fairly substantial favour. You must be sure that they are happy to be quoted and will actually respond to requests for references. This means that you need to alert them each time you apply for a job, to check their continued availability and willingness. If they are about to go off to some far-flung research site just at the time you are applying for jobs, find someone else. If you are asked to include referees on an application form which you are sending with the CV, they can obviously be omitted from the latter. If you have yet to ask your potential referees, and if you are not specifically asked to provide them, it is usually acceptable to say 'referee details supplied on request'. (This is also an option if you are limited to a two-side-CV and run out of space.)

Because impression is so important, pay careful attention to your layout. Even CVs submitted electronically need to look good on paper as they may be printed off for panel members. So try your design out for both paper and screen reading. Think about use of colour and how this will appear if printed out in black and white. Email the CV to a friend and ask them to comment on how well it communicates to them using their (preferably different) machine.

Activity 16.14

Prepare your CV now, aiming for the best possible layout and a maximum of two sides of A4. Aim to emphasise the strengths which you have with respect to employment in general. You can version this basic document to suit specific vacancies when you get

> to the stage of applying. Compare yours with those of friends and/or others on your course to see whether you can, between you, find ways of improving the different CVs. Your university's careers office may well have further guidance and examples. If not, you can easily find both online. File the 'core' version of your CV for reference, together with any versions you produce.

Completing Application Forms

Note the closing date for applications and ensure that you submit yours in good time. Applications received after this will usually be deleted/binned. (If hospital or accident prevents you meeting the deadline for your dream job it might just be worth telephoning, explaining your predicament, stressing your interest and pleading for a late application to be accepted.).

Think carefully about the application form and how to complete it. The form you submit has to create a good impression and therefore has to be well-presented and error free, as well as making maximum use of available questions and space to show you as a candidate worthy of shortlisting. You may be in competition with hundreds of other applicants. If this is the case, most applications will be discarded after a cursory inspection of the form alone so the first impression has to be impressive. Think about how you can emphasise your strengths in relation to this particular job. Refer to your SWOT. And remember that you are selling yourself and need to do this professionally.

To reach the shortlist:

- research both job and organisation
- version your CV to fit job requirements
- pay attention to presentation
- make form and letter error free
- highlight strengths for the job
- if unsuccessful, seek feedback.

You should normally supplement your CV and any application form with a letter. This, free from the formal constraints of form or CV, is your main chance to convey an impression of what you are like as a person. Use it to emphasise your key strengths, cross-referring where appropriate to the relevant parts of accompanying documents. The letter needs to be properly laid out (look back at Chapter 6), error free, and to show that you have identified what is important to the person recruiting, thought about how you meet these needs and can communicate this clearly. If you can justify your motivation in applying, this will also strengthen your case. 'I am looking for a job which will enable me to use the skills I have already developed in the area of ..., while offering opportunities to learn/do/gain experience of . . . with a view to moving eventually into . . .' will make your application sound more serious than one from someone who has not mentioned motivation, or mentioned only what they want out of a job. This is a fairly tall order for a short letter, but again is a vital part of standing out from perhaps hundreds of other applicants as a candidate who is worth seeing. (A job application checklist is available as a web resource.)

➤ Ch 6

If you do not get shortlisted for a job for which you seemed well qualified, it is worth seeking feedback as to why not. This is not an accusatory 'I want to know why I wasn't shortlisted since I am obviously perfect for the job' letter, but a polite request for information. Say that you were very interested in the job and would like to know what you should do to increase your chances of being shortlisted for a similar job in future. You would therefore be extremely grateful if they could find time to give you any relevant information that would help. They are under no obligation to reply, but you may be lucky and receive some helpful advice, or even luckier and get shortlisted if for some reason they do not like the first set of people they interview and decide to see some more.

Interviews and Assessment Centres

Despite considerable research suggesting that interviews are not a very good way of choosing new staff, they are the selection device you are most likely to encounter. They test your talking and listening skills and your ability to think through a question and answer clearly and to the point. From this, interviewers will probably infer a whole raft of other intellectual skills. In an interview a potential employer can also see what you look like and what you sound like, and will guess from this how well you are likely to get on with other employees and any customers with whom you may come into contact. (They will also be able to see your ethnic background, judge social class from accent, and access information on a number of things which should not influence a fair selection process.)

There is a strong tendency for people, particularly if they are untrained as interviewers, to decide on your suitability within the first minute or so of your entering the room. First impressions are therefore crucial. Part of your research prior to the interview should be into the sorts of people already working for the organisation and what they wear. You should then aim for a slightly smarter version of this, given that the interview is a formal situation. If you cannot find out, aim to look smart, tidy and professional – if taking anything into the interview think about the impression it will create. Interviewers have been shown to rate candidates carrying a briefcase much more highly than those (actually the same candidates) with a rucksack (though the nature of the vacancy was not reported and might affect this). Whatever you have chosen to wear, aim to arrive early enough to spend time in the cloakroom repairing the ravages of travel and ensuring that you look calm and tidy by the time you are interviewed.

Perhaps the most important part of your interview preparation is to think very clearly about what the interviewer(s) are likely to be looking for, and how you can answer their questions so as to demonstrate that you are offering precisely these qualities. What qualities did the advert and further particulars specify? Are they looking for leadership abilities? For the ability to pay attention to detail? For creativity? For each of the qualities mentioned try to think of occasions when you have demonstrated that you have this quality. What was the situation? How and why did you show the quality? What was the outcome? You can draw on examples

For interview success:

- prepare carefully
- dress appropriately
- arrive slightly before due
- behave professionally
- listen carefully
- check understanding
- answer clearly and succinctly
- observe body language
- think before speaking
- seek feedback if unsuccessful.

from your course, or your leisure activities, as well as on any jobs you have had. Many interviewers are now trained to ask questions in the form 'Can you tell us about a time when. . ?' This is likely to generate far more informative answers than 'Would you say you are a good leader?' But unless you have thought about possible answers to such questions, you may find the interview quite difficult.

Activity 16.15

List a range of such questions, drawing on the job specifications you have so far received. (Alternatively, look in one of the many books on interviews that are available for ideas.) Review your portfolio. Look at your list of strengths. Talk to your friends about what they think you might say. Then work out a list of examples of 'times when . . .' you have demonstrated the qualities in question.

This mental preparation should have the additional benefit of increasing your confidence in your abilities, which will have a positive impact upon your interview performance. But you should also be aware of, though not apologetic about, any weaknesses, and think about how they could be overcome. Would you need particular support in one part of the job, or training in a specific skill? It is better to admit to fairly obvious shortcomings in your skills and experience than to pretend that they are not there. If you can at the same time propose feasible ways of overcoming these it will demonstrate your commitment to doing well in the job, and may impress your interviewers.

The other almost inevitable question for which you should be prepared is the final: 'And have you any questions you would like to ask us?' Obviously, if concerns have surfaced during the interview you would wish to raise these at this point. You would not wish to accept a job that was not going to make you happy and it is better for all concerned if you raise any concerns at the interview stage rather than later. An interview is a two-way selection process. You are selecting the organisation just as much as it is selecting you. But if no such concerns surface, it is as well to be armed with an intelligent question or two. Such questions do *not* include 'What pay will I get?', 'When will I hear?' or 'How many holidays are there?' Such questions will not impress panel anywhere near as much as an intelligent question about future strategic developments in the light of what you have found out about the organisation, or something else which suggests you have researched, and thought about, the organisation and its context. This or similar questions allow you to show that (a) you have found out a lot about the organisation, (b) you have thought about what this means for the job in question, and (c) you are interested in further development.

During the interview it is important to listen very carefully to the questions asked and to think before answering. If you are not sure what the interviewer wants, ask for clarification. Try not to get bogged down in minutiae. If you are asked for an example of when you showed leadership, give an outline of key demands in the situation and how you rose to them, rather than the whole story of the walking holiday in which you all got lost, and

Jim broke his ankle, and you ran ahead and met these really nice people who were able to help you get him off the mountain.

Body language is crucial. One very successful interviewee of my acquaintance swears that his success is due solely to his way of looking at the panel and smiling at them. He claims that, if he can make them feel good about themselves in the interview, they will feel good about him. Certainly, it is important to *look* interested. Thus you need to lean slightly forward, maintain a fairly high level of eye contact with whoever is speaking, or with all members of the panel if you are speaking to them, and to smile a reasonable amount (too much can be rather offputting as it seems false). And you need to avoid defensive postures such as crossing arms, fidgeting or leaning back.

Activity 16.16

If you are nervous about interviews, and have not experienced many, find someone who will help you to practise beforehand. Think up a range of likely questions with your helper, then role play the interview several times, using the sort of furniture layout you might expect. Ask them to give you feedback on your answers and on your behaviour and the impressions they created, and to suggest different ways of approaching answers. Try out the interview again, incorporating their suggestions. If possible, tape record or video one of your trial interviews and listen to it carefully; looking for ways of improving the impression you give.

Because of the limitations of interviews as a selection device, employers now often use other means of selection as well. Psychometric testing, basic numeracy and literacy tests and group activities carried out under observation are now widely used. Increasingly, testing is done online, and scoring may be automated as well. Where a mix of tests and activities is carried out at a particular location, this is often referred to as an assessment centre. This approach is common in big organisations seeking to recruit a number of graduates with senior management potential.

Your course, and your work on this book, should have prepared you fairly well for an assessment centre, but you may want to think about whether further preparation would be useful. Basic skills tests such as basic arithmetic and English usage *are* susceptible to improvement through practice. Bryon (2000) suggests that 12 hours' practice can achieve a 15 per cent improvement in score, the improvement levelling off at around 20 per cent after 20 hours' practice. Your work on Chapters 5 and 6 should have given you some of

➤ Chs 5, 6, 9

this improvement already. Similarly, Chapter 9 and your subsequent work on skills development should have prepared you to do well in any group activity exercise. (Employers will often be looking for the ability to take the lead on occasion, though not to dominate, and to cooperate effectively with fellow group members.)

Verbal reasoning and reading comprehension tests are fairly common. Neither has been seriously addressed in this book. If you suspect weaknesses here you might want to buy a book of practice tests and work through them.

There is probably little you can do to prepare for 'personality' type tests. You will not know the score profile that recruiters have decided they are looking for. There will also be checks built into the test. Inconsistencies in answers, or over-idealised ones, will usually be taken as an indication of dishonest answers. It is best therefore to answer as honestly as you can, though without going out of your way to emphasise any extreme aspects of your personality.

The more selection processes you go through, the better you are likely to get and the more relaxed you are likely to be. Role playing and test practice can act as a partial substitute for real interviews. But you might additionally like to apply for one or two jobs which only slightly interest you in order to get some practice at real selection processes before applying for the job which you are desperate to get. If this is not possible, practise stress-reduction exercises before the interview, and remind yourself that the interviewers and assessors are decent people, merely looking for someone who will be competent to do a good job, motivated to perform well, reliable but still fun to work with. And remind yourself that you are a decent person, competent to do a good job, motivated and reliable, and therefore there is no reason why you should not enjoy convincing them of this during the selection process.

As in cases where you are not shortlisted, it can be helpful to ask for feedback if you take part in a selection process but are unsuccessful. Again, this may point up areas where you need to make changes in order to increase your chances of success.

16

MANAGING YOUR CAREER

TECHSkills 16.1 Your online presence and LinkedIn

Alongside portfolios, employers almost always check online presence before inviting someone for an interview. That includes checking social media accounts like Facebook, Vine, Tumblr, Instagram and Twitter (so make sure that the public facing profile does not contain compromising photos or comments that betray lack of professionalism or 'bad' character).

More importantly, employers expect you to have a LinkedIn profile. These are free, and you can set them up at *linkedin.com*. You can upload your CV and portfolio, but first of all update your education and any experience you have – that includes work experience and volunteering. You can also list awards, any professional bodies you belong to or honours received.

Make sure you start building your network by joining LinkedIn groups and connecting with interesting people. LinkedIn, at the time of writing, introduced many ways in which you can share useful or insightful updates – whether that's sharing articles, motivational pictures, quotes, graphs, etc. If you share 'quality' updates regularly (and by quality I mean – professional, useful, practical and applicable in a work setting) that should help you grow your network.

LinkedIn allows you also to share Recommendations of others. This should be particularly useful for you if you can ask a lecturer or the employer from your work experience to write a paragraph about you. Others' references always speak more than a standard CV.

➤

Good tip: When you are sending an invitation to connect to someone, make sure to personalise the message. The standard template provided by LinkedIn does not allow you to introduce yourself, and makes it difficult for someone to understand why they would benefit from connecting with you. Invest some time in writing a good, short introduction.

(Written by Natalia Jaszczuk)

Activity 16.17

Go to *linkedin.com* and set up your profile (or update it, if you've got one already). Make sure it looks professional (including a work-appropriate photo), and start building your network by connecting with 10 suggested people (these suggestions will come from LinkedIn) as well as joining 2 or more professional groups.

Keep checking your profile and updating it as and when you have something new and significant to share.

Developing Your Career

Your first 'career job' is only the start. Organisations are faced with constant, often radical change, restructurings and downsizings are common, and keeping your job may be even more of a competition than getting it. Progressing in your organisation or career is also highly competitive.

To compete successfully you need to pay constant attention to positioning yourself in the job market. This means considering both the internal organisational context, and the wider employment market – repeating the SWOT on yourself in relation to both layers of

➤ Ch 1   the environment can be extremely helpful.

Your ability to manage your learning and to learn not only from formal study but through personal reflection on experience and collaborative reflective dialogue should be a considerable strength in relation to most jobs. For example, if you see an emerging opportunity for which you are not yet quite an ideal candidate, you can take steps to develop the necessary skills or experience in good time. (I studied for a coaching qualification in order to become a stronger candidate for a forthcoming job I knew I wanted – it was a bonus that I found I loved coaching!) If you see an opportunity to become involved in a new project at work that will really stretch you, again this can help develop your potential. And if things do not go wholly as intended, you can also learn a great deal by reflecting on the experience. Working through this book should have sensitised you to the learning potential in a wide range of situations, and given you the skills to exploit it.

Social and networking skills are important, and again the book should have given you these. The classic Luthans (1988) study found that networking was particularly important for career success (as opposed to task success). Managers who are noticed (in a favourable sense) by seniors in their own organisation and/or other organisations to which they might apply may well be more successful in interviews for jobs at a higher level. If they further raise their profile thorough active participation in professional organisations and perhaps writing in relevant publications, they may also be noticed by headhunters.

➤ Chs 1, 8

When networking you would want to convey yourself in a particular light - and this would depend on being clear about what your 'brand values' are (if you have not encountered these yet, you will have done before you graduate. Brand values are the qualities that differentiate one brand from another, and influence a customer to purchase. Thus for the Co-operative grocery stores, an ethical approach to farming might be something that differentiates it from some competitors. For Marks and Spencer it might be reliably high quality combined with mid-range prices. For an individual such values might include integrity, reliability, good fun to be with, or whatever.

Activity 16.18

Think of the brand values that you would like to convey, and the behaviours that would be needed to support these values.

1. Try to come up with 4–6 words or phrases that encapsulate how you would like to be seen by a potential employer.
2. Write a paragraph of description which says in more detail what each of these key 'values' means.
3. Think about how you would need to behave at work in order to convey these values.
4. Think about any changes you can make in order to strengthen your desired message.

It is dangerous to focus on the next job, and forget the importance of this one, even if it is not quite what you wanted. From the outset of your career, your overall aim should be to do the job you are doing as well as you possibly can. At the same time, take advantage of every development opportunity offered. (Such offers are more likely to be presented to those who are doing their job well.) These opportunities should enable you to improve your current performance and become a better candidate for a more demanding and still more developmental job, whether in the same organisation or elsewhere. While changing jobs too frequently looks bad on a CV, many successful people have changed jobs every two years or so during their early careers to maximise learning and experience. If a job turns out to be completely wrong for you, perhaps because it was wrongly described during selection, then you might see whether an internal transfer is possible. If not, seek another job elsewhere. One or two such 'mistakes' are allowable on a CV, and staying in a job which makes you unhappy, or which you cannot do well or which uses none of your skills is not good for your soul or your development.

It is clear from the above that the skills developed during your degree will continue to be crucial to managing your career. The following guidelines may help.

Guidelines for successful career management

- Review your career objectives at regular intervals (visioning may help).
- Regularly seek information on job opportunities and changing patterns of employment.
- Construct action plans for positioning yourself for future jobs.
- Monitor your progress at regular intervals.
- Seek every opportunity to develop yourself.
- Reflect daily on the effectiveness of your performance and on any learning.
- Keep a learning journal and assemble exhibits of competence.
- Use informal feedback from your superior and more formal feedback from performance appraisal to revise your self-assessment of strengths and weakness.
- Network to develop useful contacts and gain information.
- Be a supportive team member at all times – you may on occasion need support yourself.
- Manage your time and stress levels so as to sustain effective performance.
- Use your creativity and skills in handling complexity to turn problems into learning opportunities.
- Accept that setbacks will occur and take each as a new starting point.
- Find discreet ways of ensuring that your successes are recognised as such.

If you can continue to question both your career objectives and your life objectives, act according to your personal values and follow the guidelines above, you should continue learning all your life. You should also enjoy a career that is interesting and rewarding and supports rather than interferes with other aspects of your life. May it prove better than you can possibly imagine!

SUMMARY

This chapter has argued the following:

- You cannot start too soon to think about what you want from a job and the sorts of job which might meet your needs. You should develop an action plan now which includes activities needed to clarify objectives with regard to employment, identify suitable jobs and increase your chances of getting one of them.
- When a suitable opportunity is identified, you need to research the organisation and job and think carefully about how to demonstrate your suitability via application form, CV and covering letter. Each should be specifically tailored to the job in question.

- Your application needs to look professional and be error free.
- Practise for selection tests if you think you need to.
- Prepare for interviews carefully, thinking about the qualities you wish to demonstrate and experience which you can quote in support of these.
- Listen carefully to questions and ask for clarification if you are unsure. Answer clearly and without straying into irrelevant detail. Try to express confidence and interest through your own body language and be sensitive to the body language of others.
- Ask for feedback when you are unsuccessful.
- Once in employment, aim to continue to learn and question, thus increasing your chance of success in future applications.

Further information

Boldt, L.C. (2009) *Zen and the Art of Making a Living: A Practical Guide to Creative Career Design*, Penguin Arkana. This is very American, but has a wealth of useful activities, and includes self-assessment and interview preparation.

Bryon, M. (2013) *How to Pass Graduate Psychometric Tests*, 4th edn, Kogan Page.

Hopson, B. and Scally, M. (2014) *Build Your Own Rainbow: A Workbook for Career and Life Management*, 5th edn, Management Books 2000. This is deservedly becoming a classic.

Hornby, M. (2012) *How to Get That Job: The Complete Guide to Getting Hired,* 4th edn, Pearson.

Robinson, J. and McConnell, C. (2003) *Careers Un-ltd*, Pearson.

Rooke, S. (2013) *The Graduate Career Handbook*. Palgrave Macmillan.

16

MANAGING YOUR CAREER

ANSWERS TO TEST EXERCISES

Exercise 4.1

1. False. Poor readers fixate more than once on some words. This backtracking is a major cause of slowness and you should have remembered this.

2. True, provided it is specially designed practice.

3. False. According to the text which claimed three to six fixations per line, although it may well be true as later text will show. You may have *known* that the statement was really true, but it is often necessary to note what is actually *in* a piece of writing, even if it conflicts with what you believe to be true.

4. False. You would still need to practise the techniques at intervals to maintain high speeds.

5. False. Rapid reading may increase comprehension. This was another very important point.

6. True.

Exercise 5.1

(a) 258.8

(b) 1215

(c) 1502

(d) 55

(e) 1234.57

(f) 1230

(g) 150

(h) 52%

(i) 1:7

(j) $1\frac{5}{27}$ or $\frac{32}{27}$

(k) $\dfrac{3a + 3b}{a + b}$

(l) 600

(m) 1509 (if you got 2085, see p. 87)

Exercise 5.2

(a) 0.75, 3.0, 1.3333333, 2.1428571, 0.8181818, 0.75

(b) 200%, 75%, 133%, 91%, 25%, 67% (taking the nearest whole percentage as the answer)

(c) 8, 196, 81, 81, 1728, 1, 1

(d) 2^7, 3^6, 10^0, 17^9, 21^{18}, $x^{(y-2)}$, x^5, $z^{2(x+y)}$

(e) 4, 12, 6, 6.16, 1.41, 3.16 (giving answers to two decimal places)

(f) 2^8, 10^2, $3^{3/5}$, xy, z^2

(g) 6

(h) (ii) and (iii)

(i) $2x + 2y$, $3x - 3y$, 0, y

(j) 13, 17, $x^1 x^2/y$, 3.8832787 (3.88 to two places of decimals)

Exercise 5.3

(a) My rough guess was 8600, actual figure 8689.

(b) My rough guess was 4100, actual figure 4507.7.

(c) My rough guess was 10 000 000, actual figure 9 850 028.3.

(d) My guess was 110, actual figure 111.95.

Perhaps your guesses were better!

Exercise 5.4

(a) 1.27 **(b)** 12.98 **(c)** 129.76 **(d)** 129 763.56

Exercise 5.5

(a) 137 **(b)** 0.000786 **(c)** 3980 **(d)** 1.00

Exercise 5.6

£38. It doesn't matter which order the discounts are calculated: $0.95 \times 0.8 \times 50$ is the same as $0.8 \times 0.95 \times 50$. Or work out the price after subtracting first a fifth, second a twentieth, or vice versa if you prefer.

Exercise 5.7

(a) ⅔ **(b)** ¾ **(c)** ⅔ **(d)** 2 **(e)** ⁴⁄₃ or 1⅓ **(f)** ¾ **(g)** ½

Exercise 5.8

(a) ⅕ **(b)** ⅓ **(c)** $\dfrac{1}{y(1 + y)}$ **(d)** ¹⁄₄₀ **(e)** $\dfrac{1}{x}$ **(f)** $\dfrac{(y + 1)}{10}$ **(g)** $\dfrac{xy}{2}$

Exercise 5.9

(a) ⅛ **(b)** ⅑

Exercise 5.10

(a) ²⁄₉ **(b)** $\dfrac{3y}{2x}$ **(c)** $\dfrac{3(x + 4)}{(x + 1)(x + 2)}$ **(d)** $\dfrac{5(y + 1)}{4x(x + 1)}$ **(e)** $\dfrac{9x}{8y}$

Exercise 5.11

(a) ¹³⁄₈ or 1⅝ **(b)** $\dfrac{(2y + 4x)}{xy}$ **(c)** $\dfrac{(3x - 1)}{y}$ **(d)** $\dfrac{(9x + 10)}{15}$ **(e)** ⅜ **(f)** $\dfrac{y(5x + 1)^2 + x^2 y}{x(5x + 1)}$

(g) $\dfrac{5(x - 2) - 3(x - 1)}{(x - 1)(x - 2)}$ or $\dfrac{(2x - 7)}{(x - 1)(x - 2)}$

Exercise 5.12

(a) 32% (b) 32:100 or 8:25 (c) 128:272 or 8:17

Exercise 5.13

(a) 12.5% (b) 198% (c) 33% (d) −4%, i.e. a negative return

Exercise 5.14

After two years debt will be £1322.50, after three years £1520.87.

Exercise 5.15

(a) £2260 (b) £2343.75 (c) £20 113.57

Exercise 5.16

(a) $x = 2y - 5$ (i) −1 (ii) −11 (iii) −5

(b) $x = \dfrac{(y + 3)}{3}$, or $\frac{1}{3} + 1$ (i) $\frac{5}{3}$ (ii) 0 (iii) 1

(c) $x = 4$ (i) 4 (ii) 4 (iii) 4

(d) $x = \dfrac{y}{2} - 6$ (i) −5 (ii) −7½ (iii) −6

(e) $x = \dfrac{3}{y}$ (i) 3/2 (ii) −1 (iii) infinity (or undefined)

(f) $x = y^2 + \frac{1}{2}$ (i) 5 (ii) 7½ (iii) 0

(g) $x = \dfrac{y}{4} - 3$ (i) −2½ (ii) −3¾ (iii) −3

(h) $x = (y + 4)(3y + 1)$ (i) 42 (ii) −8 (iii) 4

Exercise 5.17

(a) $6ab + 4ac$

(b) $3xy - 2xz$

(c) $3rs + 6rt + 6rs + 3st$, or $9rs + 6rt + 3st$

(d) $2xy + 4x + y^2 + 2y$

(e) $\dfrac{3z + 4y}{4a + 4b}$ Note it was possible to divide top and bottom by $(2y + z)$

Exercise 6.1

Correct versions are:

1 The father's going to take his children **there**. The mother is away on holiday. (Even better, The father is going . . .)

2 The dog is **completely uninterested** in **its** ball.

3 Studying English is very different **from** studying engineering.

4 When I **received** them the data surprised me.

5 The essay **comprised four** separate parts. (Or The essay **consisted** of . . .)

6 He **was unique** in having a choice between a career as a rock singer in a leading band **and** as a brain surgeon. (Well, maybe he wasn't unique, who knows, but you are or you aren't.)

7 A range of statistics was available from **their** search of the literature. (Still not very nice, but technically, I think, correct.)

8 I will probably come to see you and **him** tomorrow.

9 There were many mistakes in your letter, **including your** spelling and **your unskilful** choice of words.

10 One can easily improve **one's** writing by redrafting after an interval has **elapsed**. (Or **You** can easily improve your . . .)

Exercise 6.2

The main clause (I think) is 'the overall effect of complexity is usually far from satisfactory' – all the other clauses qualify or explain this. I think I counted nine subordinate clauses.

Exercise 6.3

The number of words is 122. It is a single sentence therefore this is the 'average' sentence length. The number of words of three or more syllables is 21. This is 17% of the total – not bad. 122+17 is 139. Multiplying by 0.4 gives 55.6. No wonder you had difficulty following it. This is seriously in excess of 12.

Exercise 7.1

Note there is no 'right' answer to this. Many forms of map and outline could produce a good answer. What follows is merely an example.

Initial notes in form of mind map

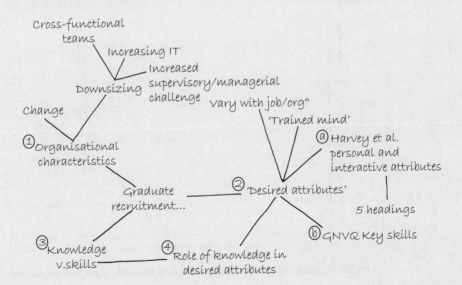

Subsequent plan

1 Introduction
   Brief overview of approach: required attributes depend on job and organisational situation; evidence drawn from employer statements and GNVQ key skills specification; conclusion that true for some jobs, for many more, transferable skills more important.

2 Relevant characteristics of organisations
   Outline: IT revolution, downsizing, restructuring, emphasising continuing change, cross-functional teams, management responsibilities at lower levels, near-universal IT use.

   Draw out implications: need for flexibility, continuous learning and range of relevant skills.

3 Graduate recruiters' perspective
   Note variability depending on job and specialism (and sophistication)

   Outline Harvey *et al*. personal and interactive attributes and derived headings, cross-linking these to GNVQ skills.

   Note that even for specialist jobs these skills also likely to be necessary.

4 Knowledge/skills relationship
   Discuss role of knowledge within skills outlined – more important for some (e.g. IT) than others (e.g. 'fitting in'/working with others) Comment on extent to which this 'knowledge' likely to be gained during degree studies or merely during time as a student.

5 Conclusions
   Suggest (referring back) that while true for a minority of jobs, unlikely to be true for majority of graduate recruitment, reiterating important skills and suggesting even where statement strictly true, these would still be important.

Exercise 8.1

(1) aggression; (2) avoidance; (3) aggression; (4) assertion; (5) avoidance; (6) assertion; (7) avoidance; (8) assertion; (9) avoidance; (10) avoidance; (11) assertion (probably); (12) aggression; (13) avoidance.

Exercise 14.1

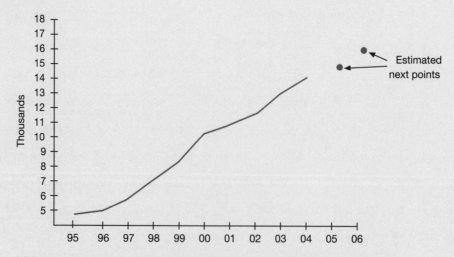

(a) Applicants accepted onto selected business and management degrees (UK)

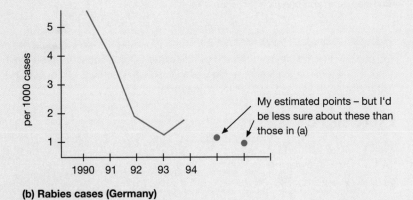

(b) Rabies cases (Germany)

Exercise 14.2

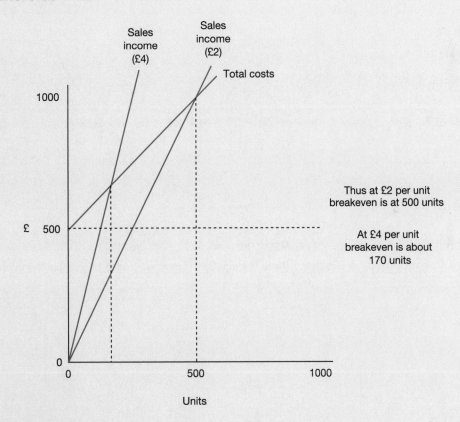

Exercise 14.3

$C = F + Vx$

$I = Px$

At breakeven $C = I$ so $F + Vx = Px$

Arrange x terms on one side: $F = Px - Vx$

or
$$x(P - V) = F$$

Divide both sides by $(P - V)$: $x = F/(P-V)$

You can use this to test your answers to Test exercise 14.2, substituting 500 for F, 1 for V and either 2 or 4 for P. In the first case breakeven is 500 divided by $2 - 1$, or 500. In the second it is 500 divided by $4 - 1$, i.e. by 3, which is approximately 167.

Exercise 14.4

(a) If $y = x^2$, $dy/dx = 2x$

(b) If $y = 3x + 1$, $dy/dx = 3$

(c) If $y = x^3 + 2x + 2$, $dy/dx = 3x^2 + 2$

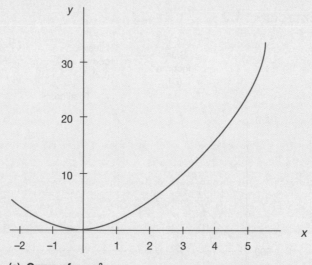

(a) Curve of $y = x^2$

(Note that additional points are added to give the 'feel' of the curve)

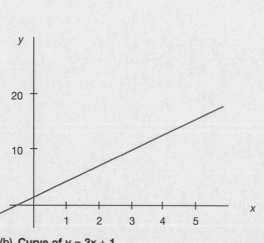

(b) Curve of $y = 3x + 1$

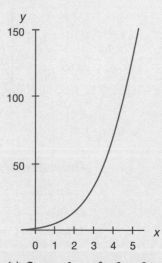

(c) Curve of $y = x^3 + 2x + 2$

Exercise 14.5

(a) $dt/dd = 6d + 1$

(b) $dy/dx = 8x^3 + 2x + 5$

(c) $dr/dy = 2y + 10$

(d) $dy/dx = 7x^6 - 15x^4 + \frac{1}{2}x^{-\frac{1}{2}}$

   or $7x^6 - 15x^4 + \dfrac{1}{2\sqrt{x}}$

Exercise 14.6

(a) $\int 3x^2\, dx = x^3 + K$

(b) $\int (8x^2 - 12x^2 + 1)\, dx = 2x^4 - 4x^3 + x + K$

(c) $\int (1/x + 3) = \log x + 3x + K$

(Sorry, this was unfair. The only place the rule does not work is for $1/x$. After all, when you differentiate a constant it disappears: it doesn't turn into $1/x$.)

Exercise 14.7

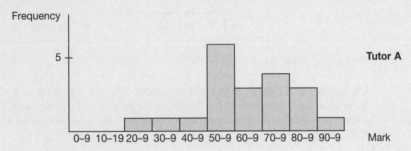

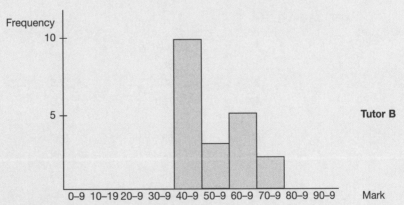

Exercise 14.8

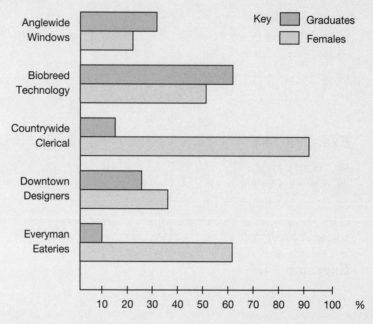

Exercise 14.9

My estimate of A was upper 60s and of B upper 50s. The calculator gave 61.55 and 52.95. Both were lower than expected. When I looked at the figures for an explanation, I realised that both tutors were marking in 'round tens' quite often, so within each band a lot of figures were right at the bottom.

Exercise 14.10

	f	mid-point (x)	fx
Tutor A	1	95	95
	3	85	255
	4	75	300
	3	65	195
	6	55	330
	1	45	45
	1	35	35
	1	25	25
			Total 1280 mean 64
Tutor B	2	75	150
	5	65	325
	3	55	165
	10	45	450
			Total 1090 mean 54.5

(Like my estimates, these are higher than the actual means, for the same reason. This is an example of the inaccuracy that working in bands can introduce.)

Exercise 14.11

½ (*n* + 1)

Exercise 14.12

Modal mark: Tutor A   50–59 (take the midpoint as best estimate, so 55)

Tutor B   40–49 (take the midpoint as best estimate, so 45)

Exercise 14.13

	Mean	Median	Mode
(a)	5.4	5	5
(b)	4.9	3	3

BIBLIOGRAPHY

Adair, J. and Allen, M. (2003) *The Concise Time Management and Personal Development*, Thorogood.

Andreas, S. and Faulkner, C. (1996) *NLP: The New Technology of Achievement*, Nicholas Brealey.

Back, K. and Back, K. (1999) *Assertiveness at Work*, 3rd edn, McGraw-Hill.

Baguley, P. (1992) *Teams and Team-working*, Teach Yourself Books/Hodder & Stoughton.

Barker, A. (2002) *How to Manage Meetings*, Sunday Times/Kogan Page.

Beall, J. (2015) 'Beall's List of Predatory Open Access Publishers 2015', available from http://scholarlyoa.com/2015/01/02/bealls-list-of-predatory-publishers-2015/

Belbin, R.M. (1981) *Management Teams*, Heinemann.

Belbin, R.M. (1993) *Team Roles at Work*, Butterworth-Heinemann.

Bell, J. (1999) *Doing your Research Project*, 3rd edn, Open University Press.

Bentley, T.J. (1978) *Report Writing in Business*, Kogan Page.

Bird, P. (1998) *Teach Yourself Time Management*, Hodder Arnold Teach Yourself.

Blamires, H. (2000) *The Penguin Guide to Plain English*, Penguin.

Bloch, S. and Bates, T. (1995) *Employability*, Kogan Page.

Bolt, L.C. (1999) *Zen and the Art of Making a Living*, Penguin Arkana.

Bowden, J. (2004) *Writing a Report*, 7th edn, Howtobooks.

Bradley, A. (2006) *Successful Presentation Skills*, 3rd edn, Sunday Times/Kogan Page.

Bryon, M. (2000) *How to Pass Graduate Recruitment Tests*, 2nd edn, Kogan Page.

Bryon, M. (2007) *How to Pass Graduate Psychometric Tests*, 3rd edn, Kogan Page

Bryon, M., Cameron, J. and Allen, C. (1998) *An Artist's Way at Work: Twelve Weeks to Creative Freedom*, Pan.

Bryman, A. (2001) *Social Research Methods*, Oxford University Press.

Burchfield, R.W. (ed.) (1996) *The New Fowler's Modern English Usage*, 3rd edn, Oxford University Press.

Burley-Allen, M. (1995) *Managing Assertively - A Self teaching Guide*, 3rd edn, Wiley.

Butler, D. (2013) 'Investigating journals: The dark side of publishing', *Nature*, 495: 433–435, available from http://www.nature.com/news/investigating-journals-the-dark-side-of-publishing-1.12666

Buzan, T. (2003a) *Use Your Head*, BBC Publications.

Buzan, T. (2003b) *The Speed Reading Book*, BBC Publications.

Buzan, T. and Buzan B. (2003) *The Mind Map Book: Radiant Thinking - Major Evolution in Human Thought*, BBC Publications.

Cameron, J. (1992) *The Artist's Way*, Tarcher.

Cameron, S. and Pearce, S. (1997) *Against the Grain*, Butterworth-Heinemann.

Caunt, J. (2000) *Organise Yourself*, Kogan Page.

Caunt, J. (2001) *Stay Confident*, Sunday Times/Kogan Page.

Checkland, P. (1981) *Systems Thinking, Systems Practice*, Wiley.

Clegg, B. (1999) *Instant Time Management*, Kogan Page.

Collins, J./Video Arts (1998) *Perfect Presentations*, Marshall Publishing.

Conradi, M. and Hall, R. (2001) *That Presentation Sensation*, Financial Times Prentice Hall.

Cook, C.R. (2005) *Just Enough Project Management,* McGraw-Hill.

Crosby, A.W. (1997) *The Measure of Reality,* Cambridge University Press.

Csikszentmihalyi, M. (1996) Chapter 5, Harper/Collins, available from http://isites.harvard. edu/fs/docs/icb.topic868772.files/1018CsikszentmihalyiChapter.pdf

Csikszentmihalyi, M. (2013) *Creativity: The Psychology of Discovery and Invention,* Harper Collins.

De Bono, E. (1971) *Lateral Thinking for Management,* Penguin.

Dobson, A. (2002) *Touch Typing in 10 hours,* Howtobooks.

Drucker, P.F. (1999) *Management Challenges for the 21st Century,* HarperCollins.

Easton, G. (1992) *Learning from Case Studies,* 2nd edn, Prentice Hall.

Eggert, M. (2000) *The Best Job Hunt Book in the World,* Random House Business Books.

Entwhistle, N. (1996) 'Recent research on student learning and the learning environment', in J. Tait and P. Knight (eds) *The Management of Independent Learning,* SEDA/Kogan Page.

Fayol, H. (1916) *Administration Industrielle et Générale, published in English in 1949 as General and Industrial Management,* Pitman Publishing.

Fineman, S. and Gabriel, Y. (1996) *Experiencing Organisations,* Sage.

Forbes (2014) 'The 10 skills employers most want in 2015 graduates', available from http://www.forbes.com/sites/susanadams/2014/11/12/the-10-skills-employers-most-want-in-2015-graduates, accessed 14/07/15

Forster, M. (2006) *Do it Tomorrow: And Other Secrets of Time Management,* Hodder & Stoughton.

Frost, P.J., Mitchell, V.F. and Nord, W.R. (eds) (1997) *Organisational Reality: Reports from the Firing Line,* 4th edn, Addison Wesley Longman.

Giles, K. and Hedge, N. (1994) *The Manager's Good Study Guide,* The Open University.

Gill, J. and Johnson, P. (1997) *Research Methods for Managers,* 2nd edn, Paul Chapman Publishing.

Goleman, D. (1998) *Working with Emotional Intelligence,* Bloomsbury.

Golzen, G. and Garner, A. (1992) *Smart Moves,* Penguin.

Gowers, E. (1954) *The Complete Plain Words,* HMSO, now available from Penguin.

Graham, L. and Sargent, D. (1981) *Countdown to Mathematics,* Addison-Wesley.

Gravett, S. (1998) *The Right Way to Write Reports,* Elliot Right Way Books.

Graduate Management Admission Council (2005) *GMAT Quantitative Review,* Blackwell.

Hackman, J.R. and Lawler, E.E., III (1971) 'Employee reactions to job characteristics', *Journal of Applied Psychology,* 55: 259–65.

Haigh, M. and Clifford, V. (2010) 'Widening the graduate attribute debate: a higher education for global citizenship', Brookes eJournal of Learning and Teaching, 2, 5, available from http://bejlt.brookes.ac.uk/paper/widening_the_graduate_attribute_debate_a_higher_education_for_global_citize-2/

Handy, C. (1989) *The Age of Unreason,* Business Books.

Hardingham, A. (1995) *Working in Teams,* Institute of Personnel Development.

Harris, T.A. (1973) *I'm OK - You're OK,* Pan Books.

Hart, R. (1996) *Effective Networking for Professional Success,* Kogan Page.

Harvey, L., Moon, S. and Geall, V. (1997) *Graduates' Work: Organisational Change and Students' Attributes,* Centre for Research into Quality, University of Central England in Birmingham.

Health and Safety Executive (2015) 'Work related stress, anxiety and depression statistics in Great Britain 2014/15', available from http://www.hse.gov.uk/statistics/causdis/stress/, accessed 01/01/16

HECSU (2015) 'What do graduates do?', available from http://www.hecsu.ac.uk/current_projects_what_do_graduates_do.htm, accessed 31/12/2015

Henry, J. (ed.) (1991) *Creative Management,* Sage, in association with the Open University.

Herzberg, F. (1966) *Work and the Nature of Man,* World Publishing Co.

High Fliers Research Ltd (2014) 'The graduate market in 2015', available from http://www. highfliers.co.uk/download/2015/graduate_market/GMReport15.pdf, accessed 31/12/2015

Honey, P. and Mumford, A. (1986) *The Manual of Learning Styles,* Peter Honey.

Hopson, B. and Scally, M. (1999) *Build your own Rainbow: A Workbook for Career and Life Management,* 3rd edn, Management Books 2000.

Hornby, M. (2000) *3 Easy Steps to the Job You Want,* Pearson Education.

Hourd, S. (1999) *Creating a Successful CV,* Dorling Kindersley.

Howard, K. and Sharp, J.A. (2002) *The Management of a Student Research Project,* 3rd edn, Gower.

http://www.belbin.com/resources/faqs, for access to the Belbin questionnaire on preferred roles.

http://www.colorado.edu/conflict/peace/example/fish7513.htm, for a summary of Fisher and Ury's (1983) classic on negotiation, accessed 06/01/15

http://www.open.edu/openlearn/money-management/management/leadership-and-management/managing/systems-explained-diagramming, for a series of excellent resources on using systems thinking and systems diagrams in analysis, accessed 13/07/15

http://www.pon.harvard.edu/freemium/negotiation-skills-negotiation-strategies-and-negotiation-techniques-to-help-you-become-a-better-negotiator, for Harvard Negotiation report, accessed 05/01/15

http://www.ted.com/talks/julian_treasure_5_ways_to_listen_better?language=en, for how to listen better, in a more general sense, accessed 06/01/15

http://www.williammury.com/books/getting-to-yes, for an entertaining short video communicating the key points in Fisher and Ury's book, accessed 06/01/15

https://www.youtube.com/watch?v=8L1OVkw2ZQ8, for good introduction to Excel spreadsheets (the first in a series).

https://www.youtube.com/watch?v=J4zq3R8b5dQ, for an alternative series of tutorials.

https://www.youtube.com/watch?v=rxO7wjl4Vbo, for Debra Fox on Assertive Communication Skills, accessed 06/01/15

Huff, D. (1991) *How to Lie with Statistics,* Penguin.

Hughes, D.J., Furnham, A. and Batey, M. (2013) 'The structure and personality predictors of self-rated creativity', *Thinking Skills and Creativity,* 9: 76–84

Jankovicz, A.D. (2005) *Business Research Projects,* 4th edn, Thomson.

Kepner, C.H. and Tregoe, B.B. (1965) *The Rational Manager,* McGraw-Hill.

Kline, N. (1999) *Time to Think,* Cassell Illustrated.

Kneeland, S. (1999) *Thinking Straight,* Pathways.

Kolb, D.A., Rubin, I.M. and Mackintyre, J.M. (1984) *Organisational Psychology,* 4th edn, Prentice Hall.

Krishnamurti, J. (1995) *The Book of Life,* HarperCollins.

Lawler, E.E., III and Porter, L. (1967) 'Antecedent attitudes of effective managerial performance', *Organizational Behavior and Human Performance,* 2: 122–42.

Leech, T. (2001) *Say it like Shakespeare,* McGraw-Hill.

Lifeskills International (1999) *Staying Healthy at Work,* Gower.

Luthans, F., Hodgetts, R.M. and Rosenkrantz, S. (1988) *Real Managers,* Ballinger.

Manchester Open Learning (1993) *Making Effective Presentations,* Kogan Page.

Maslow, A.H. (1943) 'A theory of human motivation', *Psychological Review,* 50: 370–96.

McGregor, D.M. (1957) 'The human side of enterprise', reprinted in Vroom, V.H. and Deci, E.L. (1970) *Management and Motivation,* Penguin.

Mintzberg, H. (1976) 'Planning on the left side and managing on the right', *Harvard Business Review,* 54: 49–58.

Mitroff, I.I. and Linstone, H.A. (1993) *The Unbounded Mind,* Oxford University Press.

Moon, J.A. (1999) *Reflection in Learning and Professional Development,* RoutledgeFalmer.

Morgan, G. (1986) *Images of Organization,* Sage.

Moroney, M.J. (1951) *Facts from Figures,* Penguin.

Morris, C. (2000) *Quantitative Approaches in Business Studies,* 5th edn, Financial Times Prentice Hall.

Morris, C. and Thanassoulis, E. (1994) *Essential Mathematics: A Refresher Course for Business and Social Studies,* Macmillan.

Morris, S. and Smith, J. (1998) *Understanding Mind Maps in a Week,* Institute of Management.

Naughton, J. (2003) 'How PowerPoint can fatally weaken your argument', *The Observer,* 21 December.

Peralta, C.F., Lopes, P.N., Gilson, L.L., Lourenço, P.R. and Pais, L. (2015) 'Innovation processes and team effectiveness: The role of goal clarity and commitment, and team affective tone', *Journal of Occupational and Organizational Psychology,* 88: 80–107.

Pidd, M. (2003) *Tools for Thinking: Modeling in Management Science,* 2nd edn, Wiley.

Powell, J. (1991) *Quantitative Decision Making,* Longman.

QAA (2015) 'Subject Benchmark Statement: Business and Management', available from http://www.qaa.ac.uk/en/Publications/Documents/SBS-business-management-15.pdf, accessed 22/05/15.

QAA (2015) 'Subject Benchmark statement Business and Management', available from http://www.qaa.ac.uk/en/Publications/Documents/SBS-business-management-15.pdf, accessed 28/05/15.

Race, P. (1999) *How to get a Good Degree,* Open University Press.

Robinson, J. and McConnell, C. (2003) *Careers Un-ltd,* Pearson.

Rose, C. and Nicholl, M.J. (1997) *Accelerated Learning for the 21st Century,* Piatkus.

Rowntree, D. (1987) *Statistics without Tears: A Primer for Non-mathematicians,* Penguin.

Russell, L. (1999) *The Accelerated Learning Field Book,* Jossey-Bass/Pfeiffer.

Sandberg, A. (ed.) (2007) *Enriching production: Perspectives on Volvo's Uddevalla plant as an alternative to lean production,* Avebury, available from http://mpra.ub.uni-muenchen.de/10785/1/MPRA_paper_10785.pdf

Saunders, M., Lewis, P. and Thornhill, A. (2007) *Research Methods for Business Students,* 4th edn, Financial Times Press.

Seeley, J. (2002) *Writing Reports,* Oxford University Press.

Senior, B. (2006) *Organisational Change,* 3rd edition, Pearson.

Senge, P.M. (1990) *The Fifth Discipline,* Century Business.

Simon, H. (1960) *The New Science of Management Decision,* Harper & Row.

Smith, N. (2012) 'Employees report how stress affects their jobs', *Business News Daily,* 28 March, available from http://www.businessnewsdaily.com/2267-workplace-stress-health-epidemic-perventable-employee-assistance-programs.html

Stewart, M.A. and O'Toole, F.J. (1998) *30 Days to the GMAT CAT,* Arco.

Stutely, R. (2003) *The Definitive Guide to Managing the Numbers,* Pearson.

Targett, D. (1983) *Coping with Numbers,* Blackwell.

Thompson, G. (2005) *Stress Buster,* Summersdale.

Truss, L. (2003) *Eats, Shoots and Leaves: The Zero Tolerance Approach to Punctuation,* Profile Books.

Tuckman, B.W. (1965) 'Developmental sequences In small groups', *Psychological Bulletin,* 63: 384–99.

Vroom, V.H. (1964) *Work and Motivation,* Wiley.

White, B. (2000) *Dissertation Skills for Businesss Students,* Continuum.

Williams, J.S. (1995) *The Right Way to Make Effective Presentations,* Elliot Right Way Books.

INDEX